Mendelssohn, Goethe, and the Walpurgis Night

Eastman Studies in Music

Ralph P. Locke, Senior Editor
Eastman School of Music

Additional Titles in Nineteenth-Century Music

Analyzing Wagner's Operas: Alfred Lorenz and German Nationalist Ideology
Stephen McClatchie

Berlioz: Past, Present, Future
Edited by Peter Bloom

Berlioz's Semi-Operas: Roméo et Juliette *and* La damnation de Faust
Daniel Albright

European Music and Musicians in New York City, 1840–1900
Edited by John Graziano

Debussy's Letters to Inghelbrecht: The Story of a Musical Friendship
Annotated by Margaret G. Cobb

Explaining Tonality: Schenkerian Theory and Beyond
Matthew Brown

French Organ Music from the Revolution to Franck and Widor
Edited by Lawrence Archbold and William J. Peterson

Historical Musicology: Sources, Methods, Interpretations
Edited by Stephen A. Crist and Roberta Montemorra Marvin

Musical Encounters at the 1889 Paris World's Fair
Annegret Fauser

The Musical Madhouse (Les Grotesques de la musique)
Hector Berlioz
Translated and edited by Alastair Bruce
Introduction by Hugh Macdonald

The Poetic Debussy: A Collection of His Song Texts and Selected Letters
(Revised Second Edition)
Edited by Margaret G. Cobb

Schubert in the European Imagination Volume 1: The Romatic and Victorian Eras
Scott Messing

Schubert in the European Imagination Volume 2: Fin-de-Siècle Vienna
Scott Messing

Schumann's Piano Cycles and the Novels of Jean Paul
Erika Reiman

Substance of Things Heard: Writings about Music
Paul Griffiths

Wagner and Wagnerism in Nineteenth-Century Sweden, Finland, and the Baltic Provinces: Reception, Enthusiasm, Cult
Hannu Salmi

A complete list of titles in the Eastman Studies in Music Series, in order of publication, may be found at the end of this book.

Mendelssohn, Goethe, and the Walpurgis Night

The Heathen Muse in European Culture, 1700–1850

JOHN MICHAEL COOPER

UNIVERSITY OF ROCHESTER PRESS

First published 2007
Reprinted in paperback and transferred to digital printing 2010

University of Rochester Press
668 Mt. Hope Avenue, Rochester, NY 14620, USA
www.urpress.com
and Boydell & Brewer Limited
PO Box 9, Woodbridge, Suffolk IP12 3DF, UK
www.boydellandbrewer.com

ISSN: 1071-9989
Cloth ISBN-13: 978-1-58046-252-5
Cloth ISBN-10: 1-58046-252-9
Paperback ISBN-13: 978-1-58046-368-3

Library of Congress Cataloging-in-Publication Data
Cooper, John Michael.
Mendelssohn, Goethe, and the Walpurgis night : the heathen muse in European culture, 1700-1850 / John Michael Cooper.
p. cm. — (Eastman studies in music, ISSN 1071-9989 ; v. 43.)
Includes bibliographical references (p.) and index.
ISBN-13: 978-1-58046-252-5 (hardcover)
ISBN-10: 1-58046-252-9
1. Mendelssohn-Bartholdy, Felix, 1809-1847. Erste Walpurgisnacht. 2. Goethe, Johann Wolfgang von, 1749-1832. Faust. 3. Europe—Religious life and customs. 4. Other (Philosophy) I. Title.
ML410.M5C66 2007
700.94'09034—dc22

2006034692

A catalogue record for this title is available from the British Library.

This publication is printed on acid-free paper.

For Stephanie, Christie, Allen, and Jackson

Contents

Illustrations

Figures

Tables

Music Examples

Preface

> In the last days of paganism in Germany, the druids' sacrifices were subject to punishment by death at the hands of the Christians. Nevertheless, at the beginning of springtime the druids and the populace sought to regain the peaks of the mountains so that they could make their sacrifices there, and to intimidate and chase off the Christians (usually through the latter's fear of the devil). The legend of the first Walpurgis Night is supposed to be based on such attempts.[1]

This book is founded on convergences of contradictory elements. At its center is the Walpurgis Night, a supposed celebration of evil that is named after a British saint whose good deeds took place deep inside what is now Germany. That fabled convergence of good and evil was treated in literature in a short ballad and two topically related scenes of the *Faust* tragedy by Johann Wolfgang von Goethe (1749–1832), a pantheistic scientist, draftsman, and poet. The earliest of Goethe's literary treatments is the one that most overtly sympathizes with the participants of the Walpurgis Night revelries, but it is also the one that became the basis of a complex cantata by Felix Mendelssohn Bartholdy (1809–47), a devoutly Lutheran composer of Jewish descent and grandson of the Enlightenment's most influential philosophical advocate for the assimilation of Europe's Jewish and Christian citizenry. Goethe's ballad and Mendelssohn's cantata both center on the struggle for religious freedom and the nature of historical processes by mediating between the legend of the Walpurgis Night and a conjectural reconstruction of its historical basis, the conflict between Christianity and paganism a millennium before they took it up. Finally, in ballad and cantata alike the supposedly evil protagonists are courageous and pure, while their supposedly good antagonists are cowardly and superstitious: the characters with whom readers and audiences would not expect to identify represent values generally accepted in modern society, while those characters' antagonists personify values generally rejected. Other and Self thus become mirror images. The nexus of those reflections provided the inspiration for Goethe's and Mendelssohn's handlings of the Walpurgis Night as a cultural, historical, and social topos. As a result, their handlings of that topos invoke significant social issues that are no less crucial to latter-day discourse than they were in the eighteenth and nineteenth centuries—not only conceptually slippery but ideologically potent issues such as the nature of the differences between ignorance and fear, superstition and faith, belief and knowledge, but also (especially) the broader themes of cultural, religious, and social tolerance and acceptance.

In order to explore these complex historical and artistic convergences of ideologically charged issues, this book moves gradually from context to text, and then on to reception. Chapters 1 and 2 establish the general historical, religious, and biographical contexts for the creation of Goethe's and Mendelssohn's treatments of the Walpurgis Night as a subject for artistic discourse. Chapters 3, 4, and 5 discuss those treatments themselves, reviewing the essentials of their genesis and interpreting their salient features as individual and interrelated artworks. The book closes with a discussion of the critical receptions of Goethe, Mendelssohn, and their Walpurgis Night essays (chapter 6) and the issues involved in the performative reception of Mendelssohn's cantata in the nineteenth century and today (chapter 7).

As a footnote, I should add that the potency of the political and social connotations of the Walpurgis Night extend well beyond the specific parameters of this book. To discuss the legion manifestations of this influence would require an entire volume in itself; for purposes of these prefatory remarks two examples must suffice. First, the Night's acquired symbolic purport as a chaotic and surrealistic social conflict celebrating the temporary reign of evil led the brilliant and intrepid Jewish-Austrian journalist, critic, playwright, and poet Karl Kraus (1874–1936) to invoke it in his *Die dritte Walpurgisnacht* (The Third Walpurgis Night), a prophetic critical essay on the so-called Third Reich of Adolf Hitler and the Nazi Party written shortly after Hitler became chancellor of Germany in 1933.

Second, the profound social and ideological dimensions of the Night's symbolic import also played out in geographical terms. Many of the legends of the Walpurgis Night center on the Brocken, the highest peak of the Harz Mountains, which straddle the divide between the former German Democratic Republic and Federal Republic of Germany. Because of the militarized border between the two German states, much of the Harz was zoned off until reunification in 1990—a situation that had both positive and negative consequences. On the one hand, the Harz and the Brocken were shielded from the Western world's ritual sacrificing of natural beauty to the gods of commerce, industry, and tourism, so that they still retain more of their historical rugged beauty than do their counterparts in other sectors that were not spared the fates of progress. On the other hand, the fact that Germany's most celebrated peak was off-limits to most of the populace of both states (as well as the rest of the world) renewed its symbolic power. For most of the late twentieth century it stood as a symbol of the division of the German state and the compulsory political division of German-speakers' cultural heritage, articulating the line between Self and Other for millions of individuals on either side of the German borders. And the newly regained accessibility that attended the German states' unification rendered it an important symbol of German unity itself, more localized than (for example) Berlin but nevertheless potent because of the vast body of literature and art that centered on it. Even today, with the lore of the Walpurgis Night largely relegated to popular culture and superstition, the Brocken and its fabled Witches' Sabbath retain something of the serious social and political connotations that made them such attractive prospects for artistic treatment in the seventeenth, eighteenth, and nineteenth centuries.

A Word on Terminology, Nomenclature, and Editorial Method

As a rule, this book does not regularize the orthographies of names and places used in historical documents. The exceptions to this rule are names that have entered the standard vocabularies of this book's presumed readership in a regular form. Thus, I use "Walpurgis," "Wuotan," "Freia," and "Valkyries" instead of their variants. "Heathen" is used to denote persons, places, and ideas that are neither Christian, Jewish, nor Muslim; "pagan," the specific Saxon heathens who figure in the conjectural historical lore of the Walpurgis Night. "Die erste Walpurgisnacht" (in quotation marks) refers to Goethe's 1799 ballad on the subject; *Die erste Walpurgisnacht* (italicized), to either of Mendelssohn's two settings of that ballad. The earlier of those two settings comprises only two designated movements, headed "Einleitung" and "No. 2" and comprising the beginning through No. 4 and Nos. 5–9 of the published version; to avoid confusion with the designated movements in the later setting, this text refers to those in the early setting as Part I and Part II. "Introduction" (upper-case *i*) refers to the instrumental overture in both versions of Mendelssohn's setting; "introduction" (lower-case *i*) to any other introduction. Except where otherwise noted, translations are my own. When original texts are taken from manuscripts, out-of-print items, or other rare materials, the text in original language is provided either in the endnotes for that chapter (for brief quotations) or in appendix A (for lengthy quotations). Finally, for considerations of space the music examples are given as piano reductions. When these are taken directly from Mendelssohn's own piano arrangement, this is noted in the example caption. Editorial slurs are perforated, editorial dynamics and expressive indications are enclosed in brackets, and editorial accidentals are notated as *ficta*.

Acknowledgments

This book has been made possible through the assistance of numerous institutions and individuals. For his splendid 2003 image of the *Irrlicht*, photographed on Mt. Etna (Sicily), thanks are due to astronomer Arne Danielsen (Vestby, Norway). For permission to consult and reproduce manuscripts and other archival materials, and for assistance in dealing with these sources, I wish to thank Brigitte Geyer of the Bibliothek der Stadt Leipzig, Agnieszka Mietelska-Ciepierska of the Biblioteka Jagiellońska, Krakow; Catherine Massip of the Bibliothèque Nationale de France; Peter Ward Jones of the Bodleian Library, Oxford; Yoshiaki Obara and Imai Yoshiko of the Museum of Educational Heritage at Tamagawa University, Tokyo; Hellmut Hell, Hans-Günter Klein, and Roland Schmidt-Hensel of the Musikabteilung mit Mendelssohn-Archiv in the Staatsbibliothek zu Berlin—Preußischer Kulturbesitz; and Naoko Ideno of Yushodo Press (Tokyo). For supporting this project through two Faculty Research Grants and several smaller grants I thank the University of North Texas, and for equally generous support supplied during the push to complete the book I thank the Margarett Root Brown fund and Southwestern University.

The book also owes its completion to numerous other individuals for various sorts of assistance. Special thanks are due to Hiromi Hoshino (Rikkyo University, Tokyo) for her invaluable assistance in gaining access to the little-known autograph piano/vocal reduction of Mendelssohn's second setting of Goethe's poem; and to Jackie Cooper (Mableton, Georgia) for her comments on the illustrations by Retzsch and Delacroix discussed in chapter 2. To Lynne Wright and the entire staff of the Interlibrary Loan Department of Willis Library at the University of North Texas (UNT) I am especially thankful not only for their thorough and extensive assistance but also for considerable patience; the same goes to Morris Martin and the staff of the UNT Music Library. For help in dealing with ideas, queries, and points of information large and small I thank Ralf Wehner, Christoph Hellmundt, Armin Koch, and Salome Reiser of the Mendelssohn-Forschungsstelle of the Sächsische Akademie der Wissenschaften, Leipzig; Julie D. Prandi (Illinois Wesleyan University), Siegwart Reichwald (Converse College), Lothar Schmidt, Juliette Appold, and Regina Back (Mendelssohn-Briefausgabe, Universität Leipzig), Douglass Seaton (Florida State University), R. Larry Todd (Duke University), Jeffrey Sposato (University of Pittsburgh at Greensburg), Pietro Zappalà (Università di Pavia, Cremona), and Bennett Zon (University of Durham, U.K.). For her fine work in proofreading I wish to thank Stevie Garza (Southwestern University), and for likewise excellent work in proofreading and indexing I thank Randy Kinnett (University of North Texas). At the University of Rochester Press I wish to thank Ralph Locke, Suzanne Guiod, and Sue Smith for their patience and assistance along the way, and I owe a special debt of gratitude to Katie Hurley, whose meticulous ingenuity was invaluable in bringing the book to fruition.

Finally, I wish to thank my wife, Cindy, for her help at every turn along the way. Without her patience, prodding, and inspiration this book would have been impossible.

John Michael Cooper
Georgetown, Texas
May 30, 2006

Abbreviations

Bibliographic Abbreviations

GA	Beutler, Ernst, ed. *Johann Wolfgang Goethe: Gedenkausgabe der Werke, Briefe und Gespräche, 28. August 1949.* 27 vols. Zurich: Artemis, 1950–71.
HA	Trunz, Erich, Lieselotte Blumenthal, et al., eds. *Johann Wolfgang von Goethe: Hamburger Ausgabe in 14 Bänden.* Neubearbeitung. Munich: C. H. Beck, 1981.
LMA	Schmidt, Christian Martin, ed. *Leipziger Ausgabe der Werke von Felix Mendelssohn Bartholdy.* 80 vols. Leipzig: Breitkopf & Härtel, 1960–.
MA	Richter, Karl, ed., with Herbert G. Göpfert, Norbert Miller, and Gerhard Sauder. *Johann Wolfgang Goethe: Sämtliche Werke nach Epochen seines Schaffens, Münchner Ausgabe.* 21 vols. Munich: Carl Hanser, 1985–.
NZfM	*Neue Zeitschrift für Musik.*
WA	Loeper, Johann Ludwig Gustav von, Erich Schmidt, et al., eds. *Goethes Werke, herausgegeben im Auftrage der Großherzogin Sophie von Sachsen.* 143 vols. Weimar: Hermann Böhlau, 1887–1919.

Library Sigla and Other Abbreviations

D-B	Staatsbibliothek zu Berlin—Preußischer Kulturbesitz.
D-B MA	Staatsbibliothek zu Berlin—Preußischer Kulturbesitz, Mendelssohn-Archiv.
GB-Ob	Bodleian Library, Oxford.
GB-Ob GB	Bodleian Library, Oxford, "Green Books" collection of correspondence and other papers of Felix Mendelssohn Bartholdy. (Items are cited according to volume number and the item number assigned within each volume. Thus, "GB 19: 54" denotes item 54 within volume 19 of the Green Books collection.)
GB-Ob MS MDM	Bodleian Library, Oxford, M. Deneke Mendelssohn collection.
PL-Kj	Krakow, Biblioteka Jagiellońska.

Chapter One

The Cultural and Religious Prehistories

Nature can have little unity for savages. It is a Walpurgis-nacht procession, a checkered play of light and shadow, a medley of impish and elfish friendly and inimical powers.

William James, *A Pluralistic Universe*

Kind or species: A novel? No, certainly not: a witches' Sabbath of the spirit, a gigantic "Capriccio," a phenomenal cerebral *Walpurgisnacht.*

Stefan Zweig, "Anmerkung zum *Ulysses*"

Throughout Western European spheres of influence the night of April 30 is home to a conspicuously secular celebration. It is known in Germany as *die Walpurgisnacht* (Walpurgis Night), alternatively in the United Kingdom and the United States as Beltane or May Eve; in Italy as *la notte di Valpurga, Beltane,* or *Calendimaggio*; in Spain as *la noche de Walpurgis,* and in France as *La nuit de Walpurgis* or simply *La Walpurgis.* After Christmas and Easter it is one of the major holidays in Finland and Sweden (*VapunAatto* and *Valborgsmässoafton,* respectively). Its origins antedate written records, and it is host to a wide variety of popular and commercial revelries. Like its autumn counterpart, Halloween, it is practiced today primarily in folk and popular culture. Also like Halloween, the Walpurgis Night celebrates magic and the supernatural, the profane alternative to the predominantly monotheistic cultures of mainstream society. And it, too, is home to countless ghost stories and a wide variety of folk tales populated by witches, werewolves, and other supernatural beings.

Unlike Halloween, however, the Walpurgis Night is equally at home in cultivated and vernacular areas of endeavor. It has been the subject of paintings and other visual artworks by Albrecht Dürer, Hans Baldung Grien, Eugène Delacroix, and Paul Klee, and of ballets by George Balanchine, Boris Eikhman and Evald Smirnov, and Leonid Lavrovsky, among others. It has been used as the subject or point of departure in original films such as Wilhelm Krüger's *Le Cortège du pèlerinage des combattants de 1830 de Sainte-Walburge* (1902), Gustaf Edgren's *Valborgsmässoafton* (1935), León Klimovsky's *La Noche de Walpurgis* (1971), Carlos Aured's *El Retorno de Walpurgis* (1973; released in the United

States as *Curse of the Devil*), and David Kruschke's television horror short *Walpurgis Nacht* (2004). It has inspired poetry, drama, and other literature by a remarkable variety of authors, including Heinrich Zschokke, Theodor Storm, Bram Stoker, Ludwig Albert Ganghofer, Gustav Meyrink, Karl Kraus, Thomas Mann, Ogden Nash, and Edward Albee, as well as Goethe, whose three literary treatments are central to this book. And it has been treated in music by a number of major composers, including Loewe, Gounod, and Brahms, as well as Felix Mendelssohn Bartholdy and (perhaps) Hector Berlioz.[1]

The Walpurgis Night's artistic appeal derives in part from the pronounced cultural, historical, and political implications that have come to be inextricably bound up with it. This chapter, as the first in a book that centers on Goethe's and Mendelssohn's artistic engagements with the Night, identifies the elements of the topos as it was known to them and traces the historical sources of the legends that surround it, as well as the means by which a diabolical Sabbath atop the mountains of central Germany came to be nominally associated with an Anglo-Saxon missionary abbess. The broad scope of these issues reflects an essential feature of the Walpurgis Night: like most named calendrical events, it is far more than just an event. It is, rather, a highly symbolic cultural phenomenon—a distillation of a broad spectrum of social and ideological issues into a single time period, and thus an occasion to focus on those issues. Although obscured by the mists of time, its origins reflected the issues, ideas, and ideals that led to its emergence and cultivation. That very obscurity permits the phenomenon to be acted out, performed in divergent ways in different social and cultural contexts, and to mirror salient features of context. An examination of these performances of the Walpurgis Night in those contexts thus illuminates those salient features. Perhaps most important, artistic responses to those practices offer commentaries on the Walpurgis Night as a cultural phenomenon and on the societies that cultivate it.

Historical Context: The Old and the New

The Walpurgis Night shares with many longstanding cultural practices the general theme of a fundamental conflict between Old and New. As its long history and conspicuously secular character suggest, the Old is essentially Europe's pre-Christian religions; the new, European Christianity as a whole. The dichotomy also entails extensions (or subsets) of each of these, however. The political history by which Christianity assumed predominance as the religion of mainstream society in Western Europe aligns it with the late Frankish, Merovingian, and early Carolingian kingdoms (ca. 500–800 CE). The resultant political and religious structure, coterminous with the New generally, may be termed Western Christendom, distinguishing it from Byzantium to the East and Anglo-Saxon Christendom in the British Isles. It comprised the papal lands of the Italian peninsula, present-day France (including the west Roman empire of Gaul plus the Germanic Frankish tribes), the Low Countries, and the westernmost parts of Germany (generally extending eastward to the Rhine River), plus the Germanic tribes of the Thuringians and the Alemanni.[2]

For all its epoch-making historical import, the fusion of the Italian and western Germanic peoples under Roman Catholicism between the sixth and eighth centuries[3] was accomplished remarkably smoothly, not least of all because of a deep-seated consilience between the two groups' views of their leaders. Since both ascribed a sacral status to their leaders, who were always male and considered divinely legitimized, the tribes' acceptance of Roman Christianity entailed not only confederating with the papacy, but doing so under the common religious banner of Christ as a powerful, victory-granting ally. But this realignment also created a formidable problem, for when the Frankish king Clovis converted to Christianity and defeated his Germanic brethren in the battle of Tolbiac (Zülpich) in 496, he broke decisively with his heathen heritage in a political as well as religious sense.[4] Almost at a stroke, the non-Christian Germanic tribes to the east of the Merovingian Empire became geographic, political, and theological Others to the Christian West. Heathenism represented the Old; Christianity, the New.

The culture of the eastern Germanic tribes whose alterity was thrown into such striking relief with this political and territorial realignment underscored the momentousness of Clovis's conversion. Theirs was a politically decentralized, agrarian society that, like most Indo-European cultures, consisted of three major classes: the nobility and priests, who were considered the authorities in domestic matters; the warriors, to whom military power was accorded; and the craftsmen, servants, and slaves, responsible for the workings of daily life.[5] A rotating body of representatives from each of these groups met annually on the River Weser to settle disputes among groups. They recognized the need for an authoritative leader in time of war and chose one to lead them in those officially recognized times, but his authority lasted only for the duration of the conflict. Their family structures were oriented not around the concept of the independent individual, but around the sib (*sippia, sippa*), the community of free individuals, both living and dead, who were related through either blood or marriage.[6] Despite significant differences in worship customs and eschatology, until fairly late in their history the Germanic tribes conducted most of their worship services in the open air rather than in temples, with a special preference for hilltops, mountaintops, and other elevated sites.[7] They shared a deep reverence for the forest and a belief in women's—especially older women's—wisdom, particularly their powers for divination.[8] Sacrifice was an important part of their religious conduct; such services typically took place in sacred groves, especially when they entailed sacrifices (either human or animal).

Most profoundly problematic, however, was that the Germanic tribes were polytheistic. They divided the deities into two tribes, the Vanir (earth-gods; the progenitors of humans) and the Aesir (sky-gods).[9] Chief among the latter was Wuotan (Wotan),[10] associated primarily with the nobility. His name (the probable root of the German noun *Wut*, meaning "rage") associates him with inspired mental activity, including poetry, and strong emotional stress, including fury and rage. In order to prepare for the final climactic battle against the destructive forces of evil at the end of the world—the Ragnarök, or "Fate of the Gods"[11] —Wuotan would select the most valiant warriors from the battlefield dead and take them back with him to Walhalla ("Hall of the Slain"), where they would live in bliss and train for the final conflict. Despite his immortality and his status as the most important deity, Wuotan was untrustworthy. He was capable of changing his shape at will and often appeared in disguise among humans. He was apparently the only god to whom human sacrifices were offered; because of his association with strong emotions, war, and victorious battle, all who fell in battle (humans and horses alike) were considered sacrifices to him. It was also to him that the tribes sacrificed their prisoners after battle, usually by hanging them from trees. Because of his association with magic, Wuotan was also associated with the Germanic tribes' runes, which were used chiefly for magical and sacral purposes.

These essential tenets of the Germanic heathen Other to the Christian West are relevant for purposes of this discussion for three reasons. First, the sources that provide this information are the ones from which Goethe and Mendelssohn, as well as many of their contemporaries, obtained their information about the cultural and religious conflict between the Germanic holdouts against the ineluctable tide of Christianity and the Christian West itself. The writings of Tacitus, Orosius, Saxo Grammaticus, Müller, Görres, Barth, Leo, and Grimm decisively informed how early and mid-nineteenth-century German-speakers understood their political and religious history, and they laid the foundation for many German-speakers' views on that past well into the twentieth century.

Second, and more generally important, are the ways in which the conceptual and structural differences between nineteenth-century German-speakers' heathen forebears and their Christian adversaries would have resonated in the nineteenth century itself. The Saxons' culture was inimical to its Western adversaries' in a variety of ways, all of them fundamental: polytheism vs. monotheism; representative governance vs. divinely ordained monarchical or oligarchic rule; humans as descendants of divinity rather than creations of it; a view of nature as a domain to be inhabited rather than conquered by humanity; and the notion that life was not a thing unto itself that opened out through death into an eternity, but with death a contiguous facet of a single, unified spiritual existence that embraced all beings living and dead.[12] In each instance, the Germanic tribes' perspective offered a substantial congruence with ideas central to late-eighteenth- and nineteenth-century German culture. Certainly the idea of the tribes' representative patriarchal councils confederating and fiercely defending their ancient culture against forcible cultural and political incorporation into larger and better organized monarchies to their south and west appealed to nineteenth-century Germans laboring to rediscover a common cultural heritage under which the people of their many politically separate German-speaking states could unite as they strove for a representative, nationally unified government.

Certainly those nineteenth-century German Protestants who took patriotic pride in their "national" Lutheran creed—a significant constituency as the ideas of Friedrich Schleiermacher gained sway in the nineteenth century[13]—found it politically provocative that Roman Catholicism was the Christian denomination to which the tribes were Othered. Certainly the Saxons' societal treatment of women as the familial backbone of a patriarchal society concurred with the familial and social mores of Restoration Germany. Certainly their veneration for groves and hilltops resonated with German romantics' cultivated spiritual and artistic intimacy with their forests. And certainly the image of Wuotan as *Allvater*—an image emphasized far more in eighteenth- and nineteenth-century writings than in earlier ones—was close enough to the German romantics' monotheistic worldview to permit them to accept the heathens' polytheism as a historical prelude to their own, ostensibly more fully developed theology.

Third, the religious and other ideological chasms between the heathen and Christian practices do not just make clear the enormity of Clovis's gesture when he converted from paganism to Christianity and the depth of the antipathy between the Christian West and its heathen Others. In the context of the violence that had habitually resulted from clashes of ideas and beliefs since the beginning of the collapse of the Roman Empire, that deep antipathy in turn explains something of the urgency of the political and territorial threat posed by the adjacency of Christian and heathen cultures, especially in view of the western Germanic tribes' reputation as warriors. For any leader to hope for peaceful coexistence between two such deeply inimical cultures in that context would have been folly. The simultaneous existence of paganism and Christianity, Old and New, in the Germanic lands represented a far-reaching historical conflict that demanded resolution. That conflict came to a head during the reign of the Frankish king Charlemagne, who waged intermittent war on the Saxon tribes for thirty-three consecutive years and ultimately succeeded in converting them to Christianity, winning them as subjects of the Holy Roman Empire.

The Players, Places, and Dates

If the Franks' desire for political and territorial stability was understandable for material reasons, the issue was all the more pressing because the adherents of Europe's old heathen religions and the much newer faith of Islam were not only unreceptive to their Christian faith, but often hostile to it. These political and territorial concerns combined with the evangelizing doctrines of the Frankish Church to further mandate that the Christian gospel be spread to non-Christians everywhere, including the non-Christian Germanic tribes to the east. Last but hardly least, concomitant with these issues were the power and wealth that would attend the spread of Frankish/Roman culture: if that culture achieved its goals, those who abetted its spread would not simply have the gratification of believing that they helped to spread virtue and stability; they would also gain in authority and wealth. Altruistic and selfish interests would work not against each other, but together.

But that outcome was by no means a certainty. For one thing, by tradition the Frankish kings divided their holdings among their sons, a situation that led to the formation of many kingdoms that subdivided and confederated according to circumstance: the stability of the Frankish kingdom itself was at best provisional. Moreover, the peoples in the territories to the east were neither immune from the selfish interests that motivated the Franks nor passive. The more territorially aggressive of these eastern peoples was the Islamic Umayyad Empire, whose military expansion carried it westward across the Straits of Gibraltar and into Spain and then northward into the Frankish lands themselves; it was halted only when the Frankish king Charles Martel won the Battle of Tours in 732 and then drove the Umayyad out of Burgundy and the Languedoc in the south of present-day France. Less centrally organized but no less powerful were the Saxon tribes, whose devastation of Britain centuries earlier had earned them a reputation as ferocious warriors, a renown kept alive by the violence of their more recent harassments of the Christian churches and missionaries in the easternmost Frankish lands as well as their own. By the early eighth century Europe's Christian peoples were thus territorially and geographically divided and continually threatened by hostile non-Christians. The Saxon pagans, for their part, were often at war with each other, united only in their enmity against the Franks.

One result of this fractured political, territorial, and religious situation was the development of a deep theocratic alliance between two formidable institutions, the Frankish kingdom and the Roman Church. This alliance meant that ecclesiastical and secular magnates served together in the administration of government with the primary goal of promoting stability and prosperity in a world that since the decline of the Roman Empire had proved itself anything but immune to territorial invasion and factionalized violence. Concomitant with this development was Western Christendom's support for the evangelizing work of Anglo-Saxon (British) missionaries on the continent; in fact, for a time the Anglo-Saxon Christians had stronger ties to the Roman Church than did the Frankish Christians.[14] A third consequence—one that was unintended but probably inevitable, given the hazardous mix of material and spiritual motivations at work—was a profound bifurcation in the stratagems each party to the disputes adopted to pursue its respective causes. Christians and non-Christians alike used violence and beneficence alike to provide for the safety and stability of their respective worlds.

Out of this complicated backdrop emerged a remarkable cast of historically decisive characters. In the wings (but symbolically crucial in the eyes of later historians) were the Roman popes Gregory III (fl. 731–41), Zacharias (fl. 741–52), Stephen II (fl. 752–57), Paul I (fl. 757–67), Stephen III (fl. 768–72), and Adrian I (fl. 772–95).[15] These pontiffs urged and forged a strong Roman-Frankish theological and political alliance over the course of the eighth century by appealing to the Frankish kings Charles Martel (fl. 715–41), Pippin III (fl. 747–68), and Charlemagne (fl. 768–814) for assistance in dealing with challenges to the Roman papacy and in turn recognizing the supremacy of the Franks in temporal affairs (i.e., those involving humanity's present existence, as opposed to its heavenly existence and the afterlife, which remained the province of the Roman Church). What is more, the Roman/Frankish collaboration fundamentally altered the nature of the Frankish monarchy, changing it from a patently secular hereditary position to one that was ecclesiastical, consecrated by the pontiff, superior to all other authority within its province, and—most important—vested with divine authority. By the time Pippin III took the throne the Frankish kings' accomplishments were attributed to "the power vested by God"; those who challenged or resisted, conversely, were aligned with the forces of evil. Church and throne, long since coterminous, had become synonymous with each other and with religious verity, while all else was by its nature inimical.[16]

Closer to the center of the developing drama were the Anglo-Saxon missionaries to the continent, whose industry and religious commitment not only strengthened Roman/Frankish ties, but also brought to that enterprise two further figures of lasting historical significance: St. Boniface (ca. 680–754) and his niece, St. Walpurgis (Walburg, Walburga, Walpurga; ca. 710–79). Boniface (designated the Archbishop of Mainz and Primate of Germany on May 1, 748[17]) was a brilliant evangelizer and a master of organization; his mass baptisms reflected his success, and his efforts were doubly valuable to the Roman Church because he worked tirelessly to bring many aspects of the Frankish Church into line with their Roman counterparts—issues ranging from the celebration of Easter to monastic discipline and clerical celibacy. He also reinforced Frankish authority by establishing Christian missions within the Saxon lands, thus providing ecclesiastical centers and points of acculturation within hostile territory without (overt) authoritarian challenge. It was in response to Boniface's call for women to aid in the education of women in the Saxon lands that his niece, Walpurgis, joined his mission to the Saxon pagans in 748. By the time of her death in 779 she was widely known for the kindness and benevolence with which she treated pagans as well as Christians.

But by far the most prominent of the center-stage characters was the first son of Pippin III, Charles (b. 747), who assumed the reign of part of the Frankish lands after his father's death in 768 and eventually became known as Charlemagne (Charles the Great). Pippin's alliance with the pope had already secured papal recognition of his sons' supreme temporal authority, and Charles had demonstrated exceptional intelligence and leadership abilities on and off the battlefield when he became sole ruler of the continent's most important western lands after the death of his brother, Carloman, in 771.

Ever since Charles Martel's defeat of the Umayyad Empire in 732, the Frankish kings assumed primary responsibility for defending the Christian world from its "infidel" Others. In their view, the constant skirmishes and outright attacks on Christian establishments at the borders of the Saxon lands as well as missions and missionaries within non-Christian territories constituted a mandate to settle the peace by insisting that those currently hostile to Frankish laws be made to observe them—and since these laws were written and administered by the religious-social institution of the Church, as a practical matter that settlement required the pagans' conversion to Christianity. Because these views were generations old by the time Charlemagne succeeded to the throne, he naturally viewed his royal function as entailing responsibility for the well-being of the people of the Christian God and extending that "true" faith to the heathen as well. The most onerous of those challenges was the matter of dealing with the pagan Saxon tribes, whose human sacrifices, idolatry, and other practices were transgressions of the Christian faith, and whose aggressions included burnings of churches and missions, attacks on Christian individuals and families, and more. Charlemagne's first military engagement with the Saxons occurred in 768, and was but an overture to the more than thirty years of bloody conflict now generally known as the Saxon Wars—to which we will return presently.

In fact, the Saxon tribes, whose territories generally lay between the Rhine and Elbe rivers, were not only one of the last pockets of resistance against Romanized civilization, but also the strongest and most resilient. They had no central sovereign and designated central leaders only for the duration of a given conflict with external powers; in addition, their society was continually torn by vicious blood-feuds among sibs. Their resilience is all the more remarkable because of their lack of a functionally centralized leadership: that such a loosely organized governmental structure was able to avoid succumbing to the combined forces of a master organizer and brilliant warrior such as Charlemagne is a tribute to the tribes' ingenuity and courage.

There is, however, one named figure whose authority was generally recognized by all the Saxon tribes, and who came to personify the Saxons' religious, political, and cultural identity from both sides of the Christian/pagan divide. This individual, the last player in the cast of characters for this conflict, was Widukind (d. 804), a Saxon nobleman allied to the royal classes by birth and marriage but with the freemen and serfs in matters of law and war. Cunning and charismatic, Widukind led the Saxons in a number of revolts, rebellions, and outright battles for more than a decade. But in 785 he surrendered to Charlemagne, taking before a priest the baptismal formula devised for Saxon conversion, renouncing "the devil and his ilk," and accepting Christianity.[18] Always aware of the political potential of dramatic symbolism, Charlemagne reciprocated by confirming Widikund's possessions in Saxony—certainly a powerful incentive for the holdout Saxon pagans who had lost parents and children in the conflicts of the previous decade to accept the inevitable (i.e., Christianity), and acknowledge Frankish rule. Yet the conflicts endured for another generation, ending only after Charlemagne had broken the backbone of the remainder of the resistance by forcibly deporting thousands more Saxons from their homeland.[19]

The details of the bloody encounters are difficult to reconstruct accurately, since the Saxons' oral culture left no written records and the written histories come from self-evidently partisan Frankish scribes and chroniclers. A general description was provided by Charlemagne's friend and early biographer, Einhard (ca. 770–840), ca. 840:

> No [other] war ever undertaken by the Frank nation was carried on with such persistence and bitterness, or cost so much labor, because the Saxons, like almost all the tribes of Germany, were a fierce people, given to the worship of devils, and hostile to our religion, and did not consider it dishonorable to transgress and violate all law, human and divine. Then there were peculiar circumstances that tended to cause a breach of peace every day. Except in a few places, where large forests or mountain ridges intervened and made the bounds certain, the line between ourselves and the Saxons passed almost in its whole extent through an open country, so that there was no end to the murders, thefts, and arsons on both sides. In this way the Franks became so embittered that they at last resolved to make reprisals no longer, but to come to open war with the Saxons. . . .[20]

Even a few of the particulars help to flesh out the grim realities of Einhard's statement that the violence was perpetrated "on both sides." Already in 732, during the reign of Charlemagne's grandfather Charles Martel, the Saxon tribes burned no fewer than thirty Christian churches.[21] More notoriously, it was a group of pagans opposing conversion who killed St. Boniface ca. 754.[22] On the other hand, Boniface himself reportedly had cut down the mighty sacred oak worshipped by the Saxons near Geismar and, after they had converted to Christianity, used it in the construction of a new Christian church—an act that, even if accepted by the local Saxons (as the Frankish chroniclers recounted), was surely an affront to their neighbors who persevered in their faith and saw or heard of the missionary's destruction of their sacred symbol.

The famous incident that almost arbitrarily started the Franks' Saxon campaign occurred in 772, when Charlemagne recounted at the annual assembly of the Franks the story of the Anglo-Saxon missionary St. Lebuin (d. ca. 773), who had approached the congregated Saxons during their annual meeting, as they were worshiping the Irminsul, a great oak column representing Yggdrasill, the evergreen ash tree that connected heaven and earth and supported the universe.[23] After the missionary interrupted the Saxons' worship service and admonished them to abandon their idolatry and convert to Christianity, the infuriated Saxons nearly killed him. They were dissuaded by one of their elders, but after his departure they ravaged the territory around his mission in Deventer, also burning the church there.

These incidents had all the necessary ingredients to turn the everyday skirmishes recalled by Einhard into a full-fledged armed conflict. For the time being, however, the newly crowned king used them only for political and military capital and then retreated to consolidate his gains. By vote of the Frankish Council, his army assembled rapidly and easily took the Saxon fortress of Eresburg (present-day Marsberg), then marched from there to the grove of the Irminsul so quickly that the Saxons had no time to put together a defense or remove the treasures from the various buildings that surrounded the great column. Charles and the army stayed three days, not only destroying the Irminsul but also leveling and pillaging every structure on the site. They then moved on to the River Weser, destroying everything in their path. By the time they reached the river they found the Saxons ready to negotiate. They accepted the Frankish king's conditions and turned over twelve of their own as hostages—evidently an indication of good faith. The violence abated for a time, but at the Franks' January assembly in 775 Charles announced his decision "to attack the treacherous and treaty-breaking tribe of the Saxons and to persist in this war until they were either defeated and forced to accept the Christian religion or entirely exterminated."[24]

This potentially genocidal policy statement was merely an official milestone in a conflict that by then had already endured for generations, but it led to a further escalation of bloodshed. By far the most notorious incident in this war—exceptional in the extent of its horror but representative in its sequence of events—occurred in 782. After Charlemagne's cousin and three of his most trusted advisors had been slaughtered by a Saxon uprising (reportedly led by Widukind) in the ostensibly subdued area of Sündel, Charlemagne led a campaign back into the area, subdued the tribes, and demanded that the tribal leaders identify the ringleaders and every person who had been involved at Sündel. Widukind had in the meantime escaped, but when the Frankish king pressured them the chiefs also named some 4,500 of their tribesmen—whereupon Charlemagne had every one of these 4,500 Saxons decapitated in a single bloody day at Verden, near the River Weser.[25]

Convergence: The Naming of the Walpurgis Night

The Verden massacre occurred three years after the death of St. Walpurgis. It warrants mention here because it was a part of the Carolingian legacy of violent expansionism and suppression of Saxon culture—a culture that was widely mythologized by eighteenth- and nineteenth-century Germans. It was not only a lamentably inerasable part of the figurative lens through which those later commentators viewed their Saxon progenitors' world, but also the backdrop against which the kindness and benevolence of the saint whose name is invoked by the *Walpurgisnacht* stood out all the more starkly.[26]

The surviving evidence suggests that the Walpurgis Night acquired its name through the convergence of several figures and dates that are at turns loosely related or unrelated: a pagan goddess (or several pagan goddesses) whose history antedates the documented Walpurgis Night legends; an eponymous pagan figure associated with the Cult of Wuotan; the life and works of the eighth-century Anglo-Saxon Christian missionary who worked in Saxony; the phenomena that led to her canonization; the longstanding lore of the Brocken as a site of witches' Sabbaths; and the *Drang nach Osten* (eastward push) by which Charlemagne's empire expanded and was consolidated—and finally, the date of May 1, the date of Walpurgis's canonization, her feast day, the date of Boniface's promotion to Archbishop of Mainz and Primate of Germany, and the date traditionally assigned to the celebration of springtime.[27]

Of these convergent factors, the first two are the most obvious candidates for the demonic character associated with the popular legend of the Walpurgis Night. There is some possibility that the term's use derives from a prehistoric Germanic cult of a goddess named Walburg. The Walpurgiskirche formerly situated in Gröningen (near Magdeburg) was supposedly named after this goddess, and the Walpurgiskirche in Ypern (near Flanders) was supposedly built on the site where sacrifices to her had been made.[28] References to a pagan goddess of this name, sometimes hermaphroditic and often closely associated with phallic symbols and other fertility rituals, become increasingly prominent as one moves northward from Bavaria, extending as far as Ireland and Sweden, but a remarkable concentration of icons, sculptures, and other ritualistic symbols evoking her existed as late as the 1870s around Eichstätt—that is, in the vicinity where the Anglo-Saxon missionary also worked. The historical artifacts of this cult center around springtime and the celebration of fertility, and into the eighteenth century barren women were reputed to have used some of these artifacts to enhance their fertility.[29]

Equally possible is that the term is applied in derivation from two Old High German and Norse elements that occur in Saxon and Norse mythology in connection with Wuotan (see above): the Old High German prefix *wal-* and its Norse counterpart *val-* (to choose, select, pick out), and *burg / borg* (castle, stronghold). According to myth, Wuotan and the goddess Freia celebrated the beginning of springtime with a group of snow-white, winged virgins in a special section of Walhalla named the Walburg. But these graceful young females achieved that state of beauty through a process of transformation—for the blissful month of carnal celebrations was preceded by the stormy months of competition for the godly consort. During those preceding winter months the competitors existed as vile, deplorable creatures: the impassioned, amorous, beautiful contestants become shrieking, accursed hags. Wuotan's consort Freia becomes a Valfreia, accompanied by a host of Valkyries (*Walküre*), who (unlike the later, beautiful version of the Valkyries romanticized in the *Nibelungenlied* and Wagner's *Der Ring des Nibelungen*) wear blood-spattered helmets as they fly on winged steeds out of the evening sky, selecting those from among the battlefield dead who are to be brought to Walhalla. Sweat from the steeds' manes falls furiously to the ground; the white battle-coats of those fallen on the battlefield blow furiously about like large balls of snow; and the cold of their magical songs freezes the evening dew into frost and hailstones.[30]

In brief, the arrival of springtime signaled Wuotan's having chosen those who were to comprise the virginal consort in his carnal celebrations, and the bitter inclement weather of the winter months resulted from Valfreia's and the Valkyries' stormy selection of the candidates. The period preceding the choosing of the consort was also characterized by the appearance on earth of various grotesque creatures, some of them the Valkyries who choose from the dead for the host in Walhalla. The weather associated with the Saxon tribes' chief deity's conduct of war thus was liminally associated with the transformation that surrounded the end of winter, the thaw, and the arrival of springtime.

More easily documented are the life and works of the eighth-century Benedictine abbess Walpurgis. Although Walpurgis's biography is suffused with apocryphal anecdotes,[31] one of the remarkable events of her life may relate to the instrumental introduction that precedes Mendelssohn's setting of Goethe's cantata in Goethe's 1799 ballad "Die erste Walpurgisnacht," and one further event offers a parallel to the poem's theme of darkness and light (see chapter 3).[32] The first occurred during her passage over the English Channel in 748. According to legend, the ship carrying her and her missionary sisters was overtaken by a terrible storm that threatened to destroy them all ("doubtless," an eighteenth-century biographer tells us, "because the evil spirit is generally an enemy of human beings"[33]), but the storm abated suddenly when Walpurgis issued a contemplative prayer. The second event, known as the Miracle of Light, occurred after she had joined the monks in celebrating Vespers at the double monastery in Heidenheim. A thick darkness had descended on the buildings during the evensong, but the gatekeeper refused when asked to carry the light ahead of her and the nuns to be used in their dormitory (in accordance with the Benedictine rule). As her biographer Wolfhard puts it:

> While the [other] nuns took their evening meal as directed by the rule, [Walpurgis] went ahead to the dormitory without having eaten. There a miraculous light rose up, shining so brightly until the signal to come to Matins that its exceeding brilliance seemed to penetrate to the core of the earth. As the dedicated nuns were all marveling and rejoicing at what they beheld, they came to Mother Walpurgis and spoke to her of the eerie appearance of the light. But she, overcome with tears, turned completely to the Lord, saying: "O Lord, whom this humble maid has pledged to serve from her youth onward, thank You for the grace You have shown. You have deigned worthy to cast the comfort of Your light on this unworthy maid and on the souls of Your servants who rely on me. And You have dissolved the impenetrable darkness and its dismal frights with the comfort of Your light. This is to be attributed not to me, but to the selfless generosity of Your love and to the prayers of my brother [Winnebald]."[34]

Walpurgis died on February 25, 779. Her life of exemplary kindness—certainly not to be taken for granted among the missionaries of the day—facilitated the rapid development of a Christian cult in her name, a cult that eventually extended all the way up to the Channel and beyond. That life and the enduring affection with which she was regarded in the tumultuous century after her death led to her canonization on May 1, 870, nearly a quarter-century before the mysterious oil produced by her remains was discovered.

Eastward and Upward: The Brocken

The Walpurgis Night is celebrated throughout Western European spheres of influence, but in modern sources its seat is the Brocken or Blocksberg, the highest peak of the Harz Mountains in central Germany. A hulking mass of erratically vegetated gray granite, the Brocken rises to an elevation of 1,142 meters (3,747 feet) but its microclimate more closely resembles that of mountains of about 2,000 meters (about 6,560 feet), with snow cover from September to May and dense fog and mists as many as 300 days per year. Its altitude and atmospheric conditions produce the apparition known as the Brocken specter, Brocken bow, or (more generally) anticorona, "Bogie," mountain specter, or will-o'-the-wisp—a large, shadowy, usually triangular figure with colored illuminated rings around its upper end that appears to loom out of the mist before the observer when the sun is low, moving suddenly and erratically and confusing depth perception (see figure 1.1). The specter is actually an optical illusion produced by the observer's own shadow from behind. Because the shadow is cast on falling water droplets at varying distances from the eye, the apparition's shape fluctuates constantly, and its movement reflects the observer's own motions and the shifting of the mists. It may appear to be quite a distance ahead of the viewer, but it is actually only a few inches away. The specter is also known in German as an *Irrlicht* (literally, mad- or crazy-light). It is famous in connection with the Brocken from ll. 3860–3911 of the "Walpurgisnacht" scene in part I of Goethe's *Faust*, but it occurs wherever conditions are favorable.

The Brocken and the Harz are located between the Weser and Elbe rivers northeast of Göttingen and southwest of Berlin—east of most of the Frankish/Saxon conflicts discussed above and northwest of St. Walpurgis's domains in Heidenheim and Eichstätt.[35] This location may be partially responsible for their reputation as loci of eerie and unexplained happenings, for the Brocken was remote from all the advancing fronts of Christendom during the Carolingian era and home to the fierce Saxon tribes whose ritual sacrifices and other pagan practices, in the eyes of their Christian adversaries, immediately proclaimed their alliance with the devil. The dense forests, steep, craggy slopes, and narrow valleys of the range constituted some of the most challenging terrain faced by the advancing Christian front, which otherwise had to deal mostly with level ground and comparatively low mountains. Settlement seems to have begun only in the mid-tenth century, well after the de facto end of Charlemagne's Saxon Wars, and most of the *Oberharz* (the upper northeast end of the range) remained only sparsely populated for several more centuries. The summit of the Brocken itself was deemed unattainable to all humans except experienced hikers for centuries more. Those who reached it found a sparsely vegetated peak shrouded with mists and populated with various bizarre rock formations, among them the imposing and grotesque formations that eventually became known as the *Teufelskanzel* (devil's chancel) and *Hexenaltar* (witches' altar).

But if the difficult terrain of the Harz, its history as one of the last strongholds of heathenism, and its uncanny apparitions pointed to the Brocken as home to Christendom's enemies, this reputation was solidified by one other, far uglier cultural event: the European fascination with witchcraft and sorcery that began in the fourteenth century and culminated in the notorious witch trials of the fifteenth, sixteenth, seventeenth, and eighteenth centuries.[36] Drawing on Classical texts by Euripides, Pliny, and others who mentioned orgiastic Sabbaths atop

Figure 1.1. The *Irrlicht* (Brocken Specter or Will-o'-the-Wisp), 2003. Courtesy of Arne Danielsen.

mountains,[37] as well as the heathen tradition of open-air worship in elevated places, European folklore and literature had long identified the peaks of mountains and other heights unreachable by foot as congregating points for Satan's beasts, witches, and other creatures with supernatural means of transportation; initially at least, "Blocksberg" seems to have been a generic name for these demonic meeting-places on high.[38] The lore won the ultimate stamp of ecclesiastical legitimacy on December 5, 1484, however, when Pope Innocent VIII (fl. 1484–92) professed his belief in witchcraft, condemned it, and dispatched inquisitors to Germany to try its supposed practitioners and punish them unimpeded. Singling out Mainz, Cologne, Trier, Salzburg, and Bremen, the papal bull declared that "some parts of Northern Germany" were infested with "many persons of both sexes" who had

> abandoned themselves to devils, incubi and succubi, and by their incantations, spells, conjurations, and other accursed charms and crafts, enormities and horrid offences, have slain infants yet in the mother's womb, as also the offspring of cattle, have blasted the produce of the earth, the grapes of the vine, the fruits of the trees, nay, men and women, beasts of burthen, herd-beasts, as well as animals of other kinds, vineyards, orchards, meadows, pasture-land, corn, wheat, and all other cereals; these wretches furthermore afflict and torment men and women, beasts of burthen, herd-beasts, as well as animals of other kinds, with terrible and piteous pains and sore diseases, both internal and external; they hinder men from performing the sexual act and women from

> conceiving, whence husbands cannot know their wives nor wives receive their husbands; over and above this, they blasphemously renounce that Faith which is theirs by the Sacrament of Baptism, and at the instigation of the Enemy of Mankind they do not shrink from committing and perpetrating the foulest abominations and filthiest excesses to the deadly peril of their own souls, whereby they outrage the Divine Majesty and are a cause of scandal and danger to very many.[39]

This bull (and the notion that witchcraft and other satanic activity took place at higher altitudes) then gained further dissemination with the publication of the notorious witch-hunter's manual *Malleus maleficarum* (hammer of witchcraft) by the Cologne-based Dominican inquisitors Jakob Sprenger and Heinrich Krämer—a volume that went through some twenty-eight editions between 1486 and 1600 and eventually became accepted as the central authority on witches and witch hunts despite the proliferation of spin-off treatises.[40] Among the many enduring pernicious legacies of the *Malleus* was that it stabilized the stereotype of witches as specifically *female*.[41] The idea was not unprecedented, but it was sufficiently novel, and sufficiently central to Sprenger's and Krämer's thinking, that they explained and defended it in a separate chapter (chapter VI).[42] Here, for the first time in European history, criminal heresy becomes specifically gendered; and gender, in turn, becomes a symptom of social alterity, easily invoked by anyone with a complaint against an individual of that gender. A specious habit of antiheretical religious piety becomes the legitimizer of misogyny.[43]

The *Malleus* did not name the Brocken or any other specific elevated locale, but its insistence that witches and those possessed by devils had to fly to their destinations and its several case studies involving witches in elevated locations evidently combined with the lore concerning the witches' Sabbath atop mountains to fix this image firmly in the mind of the witch-obsessed populace.[44] In the visual arts the image of a witch flying on a broomstick or stang, encountered in manuscripts as early as 1410, became common after 1489,[45] and over the course of the next century the witches' Sabbath atop virtually any elevated location became a major theme in the visual and literary arts.[46] The Brocken, unapproachable to mere mortals, naturally assumed a prominent position among these summits, so that by 1620 the Nuremberg painter and draftsman Michael Herr (1591–1661) was able to produce his well-known copperplate of a witches' Sabbath in full swing atop that particular summit (see figure 1.2). Probably in consequence of this fascination with the idea of a demonic Sabbath on high, the witch trials soon began to include allegations and confessions to that effect, including references to the Brocken.[47] One particularly notorious incident that indicates the extent of the granite mass's notoriety was a trial held in Osnabrück in 1589. In that trial, 133 women were accused of having participated in a witches' Sabbath on the Brocken that was attended by no fewer than 8,000 witches, and at which five cartloads of wine were imbibed. All 133 were burned at the stake in a single day, except for four—reportedly the prettiest four—whom "the devil lifted up into the air and carried away before they could be put into the fire."[48]

Figure 1.2. Michael Herr, *Hexensabbat auf dem Brocken* (Nuremberg, 1620).

The Brocken and the Walpurgis Night in Literature, 1600–1800

The great witch trials peaked in the mid-seventeenth century and had generally abated by the mid-eighteenth century, having consigned tens of thousands of trials and hundreds of thousands of lost lives and ruined fortunes to the annals of history. But in the process, the Brocken, as the German-speaking lands' tallest mountain north of the Alps, had become so firmly associated with the image of the witches' Sabbath that its Walpurgis Night legends assumed a life of their own, producing a remarkable body of literature that mirrored pressing concerns of the day.

The age of the great witch hunts of course produced a great many tracts of this sort. One of the most remarkable of those that deal specifically with the Walpurgis Night in connection with the Brocken was Hans Schulze's *Blockes-Berges Verrichtung, oder ausführlicher geographischer Bericht von den hohen trefflich alt- und berühmten Blockes-Berge*, published under the pseudonym of Johannes Praetorius in 1668.[49] Fascinated with astrology, demonology, and the occult, Praetorius was the author of numerous ostensibly learned treatises in Latin and German, as well as several frankly anecdotal and fictitious collections and tales. His academic colleagues evidently harbored reservations about him, but his widely read compendium on the Brocken is credited with having affixed the name "Blocksberg" to the granite summit.[50] It also fanned the contemporary fires of heretic hunting. Written mostly in the vernacular rather than in the Latin usual in scholarly treatises of the day, it offered the literate but inerudite reader concerned with contemporary events a veritable compendium of the day's most sensational lore and learning pertaining to devilish deeds. It is a milestone in the gradual transformation of what had formerly been known as magic into sorcery and witchcraft; in the solidifying of the image of the witch as woman; and in defining all who stood outside mainstream society as inherently heretical, evil Others to society's good and noble citizens.[51]

At 582 pages, the *Blockes-Berges Verrichtung* is obviously an attempt to synthesize historical, geographic, and folk knowledge concerning the Walpurgis Night into a central comprehensive resource aimed at a broad readership. Its air of authority derives partly from its bulk; partly from its adduction of a wide array of sources ranging from the Bible and Classical antiquity (Aristotle, Plato, Caesar, Tacitus, and Pliny) through the sixteenth century (Bodin, Kornmann, Luther, and Wierus, in addition to the *Malleus maleficarum*), as well as English, French, Italian, Spanish, and Swedish ones; partly from its inclusion of extensive quotations and paraphrases in the original languages; and partly from its affectedly learned style and frequent use of acrostics (some of which mix Latin and German). For all its attempts at systematic exposition, however, it also rambles, repeats, and contradicts itself. Part I (pp. 1–86) summarizes the geography of the Brocken and the Harz as well as Praetorius's and other writers' ideas (some of them reliably reported, others quite fanciful) on the history and etymology of the Brocken. The substantially longer part II comprises eight chapters, but the chapter titles give only a general idea of the abundance of topics and themes that crop up in Praetorius's rambling prose:

> "Von den Personen, welche bey der Hexen Gasterey sich befinden lassen" (Of the persons who may be found among the witches' guests; pp. 87–201);
> "Über der Hexen-Reisefahrt" (On the witches' travel; pp. 201–48);
> "Von den Orten, da die Hexen hien fahren" (Of the places from which the witches travel; pp. 248–94);
> "Über die Mittel, Vermöge welche die Hexen zu ihren Versammlungen fahren" (On the means and abilities the witches use to travel to their gatherings; pp. 294–312);
> "Die Ursachen, warumb die Hexen zu ihren Versammlungen fahren müssen" (Why the witches have to fly to their gatherings; pp. 313–410);
> "Über die Art und Weiß, wie es mit der Hexenfahrt zugehe" (On what goes on during the witches' flight; pp. 411–97);
> "Über die Zeit, wann die Hexen ihre Blockesberges-Fahrt vor zunehmen pflegen" (Of the time when the witches are preparing for their flight to the Blocksberg; pp. 497–568); and
> "Wie lange der Hexen-Convent währe, ehe sie wieder von einander reisen" (How long the witches' convention lasts before they adjourn; pp. 569–82).

Three aspects of Praetorius's presentation of the Walpurgis Night festivities atop the Brocken are worthy of further note. For one thing, Praetorius concurs with the literature of the previous century in portraying the witches as predominantly female. In addition, the air of credibility that resulted from Praetorius's prolificness combined with the book's compilation of information from recognized sources to make Praetorius's readings of those sources and his ideas on the Walpurgis Night easily accessible to an enormous readership; this easy-access appeal was enhanced by the book's illustrations, among which the title plate ranks among the most frequently encountered in writings concerning the Walpurgis Night and the Brocken (see figure 1.3). Indeed, the title illustration visually summarizes much of the contemporary lore concerning the Brocken festivities. The formidable procession up the slopes comprises creatures both natural and supernatural, human and animal. Its participants hold and brandish prongs, pitchforks, and torches. Its attendant music is obviously loud and raucous (with bagpipes and shawms). Its activities include illicit intimacies between women and obviously male beasts. And at its head, directly behind the devil with the flaming hands, are three humans whose caps and attire reveal them to be officials of Church and state. In the lower foreground are a man holding what appears to be a homunculus aloft in a jar of some sort in his left hand and, behind him, lying on his back, the presumable source of the creature's animating spirit; further over, there is an enormous winged demon. The middleground is dominated by an enormous goat, behind which a woman engages in the homage of anal adoration. Further back and to the right, a man in a turban with a feather moves his hands above a kettle over an open flame with billowing smoke (a clear representation of Oriental alterity). And overhead we see witches on broomsticks and goats, as well as a flying goat and a woman who appears to

Figure 1.3. Title-illustration from Praetorius, *Blockes-Berges Verrichtung oder ausführlicher geographischer Bericht von den hohen trefflich alt- und berühmten Blockes-Berge* (Leipzig, 1688).

have been dropped off by it (toward the upper right). If there is any theme that emerges coherently from this dense and confused visual summary of Praetorius's monograph on the Brocken's Walpurgis Night, it is the illicit evil inherent in commingling of Self and Other.

Most of the bizarre ideas and dogmatic fantasies in Praetorius's *Verrichtung* lost their persuasive power in the course of the century following its publication. Unlike much of the contemporary literature on witchcraft, however, this book did not fade into oblivion. It remained well known into the nineteenth century, and figured as a major source for Goethe's and Heine's artistic engagements with the subject of the Walpurgis Night.[52] Because of those perhaps improbable alliances of knowledge and ignorance, superstition and art, the lore of the Walpurgis Night as a demonic sabbath attached to the Brocken remained indelibly emblazoned on the public consciousness. A bifurcation in the printed discourse on the subject resulted, mirroring the Enlightenment's conflicting rationalist and empiricist vs. sentimentalist and emotionalist impulses. On the one hand, the second half of the eighteenth century found Enlightened thinkers addressing the enduring myth either by dismissing it as simply so much fantasy, a narrative folly unbecoming to the intellect of their modern age, or by deducing a historical kernel of truth that would explain its origins and proliferation. But other writers took up the legends anew, abandoning the demonizing sociology of the treatises on witchcraft and exploiting instead the Walpurgis Night's potential for thematizing individual and societal phobias and prejudices.

One notable example of the first approach is the widely circulated *Das Buch vom Aberglauben und falschen Wahn* (The Book of Superstition and Misguided Delusion). First published anonymously in 1790 and then in an expanded version attributed to Heinrich Ludwig Fischer in 1791, the *Buch vom Aberglauben* devoted itself to debunking myths and superstitions of virtually every sort. Fischer divides the superstitious world into two classes: the deceivers and the deceived, the former being the smaller of the two.[53] He then challenges an enormous variety of widely held superstitious concepts ranging from the devil, witches, and magical herbs to the Tarot, interspersing these with more rationally oriented topics such as the power of imagination, sympathy and antipathy, and so on. A chapter on the Walpurgis Night immediately follows the sizable chapter on witches—creatures invented, he says, by "pagans and Jewry" (*Heiden- und Judenthum*)[54]—and Fischer makes clear his belief that the entire legend of the Night was promulgated and perpetuated by charlatans who took advantage of the gullibility of common folk who were familiar with the legend and susceptible to the power of imagination:

> Long ago . . . [the deceivers] realized that one could become rich from magic . . . and so they told how . . . people indentured themselves to the devil; how they were baptized and took the devil as their godfather; how afterwards every witch had to take a spirit as her husband and every warlock a female spirit as his wife; how on Walpurgis Night all the witches held a great feast with music and dance atop the Blocksberg; and more such

> absurd things. They probably also named one person or another who supposedly had already been there. But when the Walpurgis Night came (so [the deceivers] pretended), one had to be prepared for it. They gave them something to make them have vivid dreams, smeared a salve on them here and there, and generally tried to stimulate their imaginations and make them believe confidently in the entire thing. But since women are most susceptible to such jugglery and are more easily persuaded and deceived, they tried this out mostly on them. Such women would then dream of that which had so filled their soul, as is normally the case with dreams. They would imagine that they rode through the air on brooms or long spoons, and that they danced on Blocksberg, where the devil appeared in the form of a goat. Then when they awakened they would believe that all this had really occurred, recount how it had all happened to one or another of their confidantes (especially if they wanted to believe that they had seen her at the devilish wedding), and then give her some of the magic salve. This person in turn would either not dare to apologize for it and thereby confirm it (if she knew nothing about it), or she would want to take part in the festivity. When the expected night came again she would smear herself with the salve and then dream as everyone else did. . . . And this notion would pass from house to house, from one place to another, spreading ever further. The pope, the bishops, and other religious officials who heard of it would also finally come to believe that it was true, and would forbid witchery and magic on pain of death; they would probably also incite secular leaders to punish and burn those held to be witches. . . .[55]

Fischer then offers two further logical explanations for the belief in the Walpurgis Night:

> Or did the sayings about the annual witches' dance perhaps originate as follows? Shepherds in those regions are supposed to have spent the day before St. Walpurgis Day festively, often making merry and dancing well into the night. When people saw unexplained lights and moving shapes on the mountain off in the distance they arrived at all sorts of ideas, among them the odd opinion that it might have been something supernatural, witches and with them the devil, and so forth. . . . The most likely explanation is doubtless the following: a thousand years ago and more, before Christianity had been introduced into Saxony, women and girls held an idolatrous celebration atop this mountain [the Brocken] on May 1, and no men were allowed to participate in it. But when Charlemagne compelled the Saxons to accept the Christian faith the women and girls continued to hold this festival for some time, as long as they could do so at night and in secret. So the religious leaders told the people that it was an evil festival at which the devil would appear in the flesh in the form of a black goat and would make all manner of mischief with the women, who had to dedicate themselves to him and then belong to him alone, and who finally would be eternally damned. But because the women would sneak home quietly so that no one would notice it, it was said that they flew through the air to the festival on brooms and long spoons; and this, too, passed from one person to another, continuing to be repeated [even] after the celebration was no longer held.[56]

All three of Fischer's explanations for the lore of the Walpurgis Night are speculative, and all encourage its rejection by associating it with the witch hunts, which by then had been generally recognized as blights on Europe's cultural history. The first and third also perpetuate one of the most pernicious consequences of the witch hunts: the Othering of women and, to a lesser extent, peasants. Women (and girls, in the third explanation) are portrayed as both the naive victims of the quackery of pagans and Jews (another subaltern social group) and the deceivers of their husbands and other men. Alternatively, they are the exclusive participants in the heathen festivals that made it necessary for religious leaders—all of whom were men at the time—to invent the story of the witches' Sabbath in order to protect them. The fourth subaltern group (the peasantry, represented by the shepherds) plays a similar role in Fischer's second theory.

Fischer's third explanation for the legends of the Brocken and the Walpurgis Night finds the strongest basis in historical fact, and of his three it is closest to the explanations of the fabled night that would be offered by Goethe and Mendelssohn in 1812 and 1843 (see chapters 3 and 4). It is also the explanation most in touch with its time, for it had been anticipated in a regional historical guide of the Harz Mountains already in 1754, and it would also find a close counterpart in another publication issued in Berlin in 1796.

Both of these sources warrant discussion here. The earlier of the two, Rudolph Leopold Honemann's *Die Alterthümer des Harzes,* takes up the Walpurgis Night in the context of a lengthy discussion of the history of the Harz Mountains up to the fifteenth century. Honemann begins by describing the general history of the Saxon tribes' conflict with Charlemagne and their eventual conversion to Christianity, and then offers another speculative point of origin for the lore of the Walpurgis Night and the Brocken, reportedly taken from an unpublished biography of Count Julius of Braunschweig-Lüneberg (fl. 1568–89), one of the best-known rulers of the region:

> . . . In this connection it is no disservice to consider what the author of an unpublished account of the life of Count Julius of Braunschweig-Lüneberg reported concerning the origin of the familiar fairy tale that states that on the Walpurgis or Philipp Jacobi Night the witches held their meetings on the Brocken: namely, that the delusion arose from a misunderstanding of the word "Unhold" [demon]. For when the Saxons were converted to the Christian faith there must have still been many among them who did not want to abandon their heathen worship altogether, and who had become especially impatient [*ungehalten*] with Widukind because of his conversion; these were thus known as "Unholden" or "Ungehaltene." But so that no one would find them out and so that they would not fall into the hands of Charlemagne's [henchmen], these would have gone up onto the highest mountains, and therefore also up onto the Brocken, where they made sacrifices to the goddess Herda (Erth, Nerth). And because the name "Unhold" later came to mean "demon," the common man would have been tricked into believing that witches were gathering on the Brocken, just as one now points to the large stones stacked flat on top of one another that the Old Saxons formerly used as altars.[57]

In speculating that rumors of witches atop the Brocken had come from a linguistic link between the words "Unhold" and "Ungehalten" (demons and persons who had not held to their word, respectively), Honemann recalls the crude etymological speculations that had also characterized Praetorius's volume on the Walpurgis Night. His stance with regard to the lore itself could hardly be more different, however. For this account (like Fischer's third hypothesis) postulates natural historical facts as the core of the "fairy tale" of the Walpurgis Night celebrations on the Brocken: the conflict of belief between Charlemagne's Christianity, the punishments to which the heathen holdouts were subject, Widukind's conversion, and some Saxons' well-documented return to paganism after they had accepted Christianity.

A more detailed explanation of the historical origins of the lore of the Walpurgis Night appeared in December 1796, in the *Berlinisches Archiv der Zeit und ihres Geschmacks,* a serial publication compiled by Friedrich Maurer. The context in this instance is an article specifically concerning the Brocken, based (according to the subtitle) on a collection of unpublished letters concerning the Harz Mountains and the lands of the Rhineland province of Hessen.[58] After describing the geography and topography of the Brocken, Maurer takes on the legend of the Walpurgis Night, which by then had become a tale of patriotic German history:

> It occurs to me that the answer to this question [of why we encounter so many diverse traces of German idolatry precisely here in the Harz and practically nowhere else in Germany], like the key to that puzzling fairy tale of those marvelous rides through the air [that witches are supposed to make], lies in the history of Charlemagne. When this famous King of the Franks, who hungered to convert [his subjects to Christianity] as much as he hungered for conquest, stepped onto the stage of military operations in Germany, the Germans, especially the Saxons, were still free peoples filled with strength and courage, and they did not wish to be subject to any foreign dominion. As enthusiastic idolaters, they naturally valued their fathers' religion no less than their freedom. Charles summoned all his forces to conquer them. At the same time, he wanted to convert them to Christianity. This entangled him in a war that lasted thirty-three years. The Saxons were defeated many times, but after every one of Charles's victories and every peace concord they would take up their weapons anew, and after every apparent acceptance of Christianity they would revert to their idolatry. This finally aggravated Charles so much that, according to the horrible practices of the day, he resorted to force, slaughtering many who resisted baptism and laying down a law worthy of a Spanish grand inquisitor: everyone who declined to be baptized in Christ and everyone who continued to live as heathen and worship idols despite their conversion to Christianity *would be sentenced to death!*
>
> The Saxon heathen were ultimately compelled to submit to force and be publicly baptized. But in their hearts they remained heathen, and hardly had Charles and his troops withdrawn before they again were making sacrifices to their idols in the forests. Then the king had all their altars and idols destroyed, and since they were now prevented from holding their sacrificial celebrations on the lower ground they took refuge in the forests and mountains of the Harz, especially also at the summit of the Brocken, which at that time would still have been largely inaccessible, and where [their foes] would scarcely have dared to go. Nevertheless Charles, who soon learned of this, had guards posted at the paths of access to the mountains, especially the Brocken. But the Saxons, who clung to the religion of their fathers all the more diffidently (as do all who are persecuted for their beliefs), turned to guile so that they would be able to participate in their sacrificial ceremonies. They wrapped themselves in horrifying disguises and cleared the path to their idols at night by scaring the sentinels, who took flight all the more quickly at the sight of these devilish forms because those who were taking part

> in the evening procession [up the mountain] were ready for anything, armed with pitchforks and torches. If necessary they would use these to ambush and repel the Christian sentinels as well as for protection against wild animals. They may also have needed them for the sacrificial fire itself, partly for poking the fires and partly for putting wood into them; with them in hand they would dance around the sacrificial fire with feasting and merriment. Since in the Harz and especially on the Brocken there might still be snow on the ground, they may also have needed broomsticks (which the saying holds that the ladies ride upon on their way to the Walpurgis Night) for sweeping and cleaning the place for their sacrifices.
>
> The Christians of that time considered idolatry devil worship, and they were absolutely convinced that despite the Christian sentinels who were guarding the paths to the sacrificial places, the devil himself was supporting his disciples and carrying them through the air. . .[59]

Maurer notes that this explanation accords with the one offered by the author of an unpublished biography of Count Julius of Braunschweig-Lübeck[60] before moving on to link the tales of the Walpurgis Night to one of the staples of the witch-hunts' lore, the notion that some wives would steal away from their husbands during the night to partake in the demonic orgy. But since the nature of the festivity (according to his theory) was not at all demonic, any women and girls who may have stolen away during the night were doing so simply "in order to participate in the nocturnal mumming, dancing, and other joys which were perhaps not quite so decent."[61] He concludes: "Thus there came into existence that foolish belief, so murderous in its consequences, that one husband or another had a witch for a wife, one who traveled to the Brocken on May Eve in order to dance with the devil."[62]

Maurer's theory concerning the origins of the Walpurgis Night lore bespeaks the same basic impulse that motivated the explanations already offered by Honemann and Fischer: the tales originated in politics and human nature, not in the supernatural, and the lessons offered by the natural and rational explanation were more instructive than the fears and destructions that resulted from superstition. But there is also more at work here—for in this case the stories' pagan protagonists were compromised not by weakness within their number, but by the "foreign dominion" bent on forcible conquest and the eradication of their ancestral religion. The Saxons themselves were "free peoples filled with strength and courage," true to their religious ideals, and clever enough to outwit the mighty Frankish king and his troops many times. They were duplicitous only to the extent made necessary by the crimes of their Frankish adversaries, and their repeated breaches of the peace concords were understandable, since (as he later states) "they belonged to a religion as good as that of the Christians. . . . [and] Who does not cling firmly to the religion of his forefathers?".[63] And their rightfully sworn enemies were neither pagans nor Jews, but the Frankish conquerors who forcibly converted them to Christianity and annexed their lands to the Carolingian Empire.

Maurer's explanation of the Walpurgis Night thus also reveals a different sociopolitical impulse—for by late 1796 many German-speakers were anxiously facing the prospect of becoming the next province of the rapidly expanding French Empire. By 1795, Napoleon Bonaparte's armies had already conquered Luxembourg, Mannheim, and Belgium, and the earlier months of 1796 had seen further incursions into northern Italy and the German-speaking territories as well as the de facto annexation of Austria. Once again, the borders of the German-speaking lands of Europe were closing in. There was every reason for those Germans who were not yet French subjects to expect that they, like their Saxon forebears, might soon face considerable violence, foreign dominion, and compulsory abandonment of their own ways of living and thinking. The speculated historical origins of the legend of the Walpurgis Night thus offered yet another timely lesson: this time, as a warning and rallying call for readers to recognize the threat they faced and not let the fate that had befallen their forebears be repeated.

One final variety of appropriation of the Walpurgis Night for contemporary purposes must be mentioned here: its use as a subject in macabre romances. Far from contesting or attempting to rationalize the lore of the Brocken's Walpurgis Night, the authors of these contributions exploited it for its established connotations of emotional turbulence and timeless conflict between good and evil, the real and the imagined, and opposing social groups. They often used a journey up the Brocken, its slopes' well-known repute for forbidding terrain and mysterious apparitions, and its renown for inclement weather to allegorize salient aspects of the unfolding romantic drama. The lore of the Brocken thus became an emotionally and structurally important literary conceit. The most celebrated examples of this usage are of course the "Walpurgisnacht" scene from part I of Goethe's *Faust*[64] and the "Walpurgisnacht" chapter from Thomas Mann's *Der Zauberberg* (The Magic Mountain), but there are many others. One is the *Hexenfahrten und Teufelskünste, aus dem geheimen Archiv der Walpurgis Nächte auf dem Blocksberg* (Witches' Travels and Devils' Arts, from the Privy Archives of the Walpurgis Nights on the Blocksberg), written by Goethe's eventual brother-in-law, Christian August Vulpius, and published in 1797 (see figure 1.4).[65]

Vulpius's *Hexenfahrten* explicitly invokes the competing contemporary views on the origins and verity of the Walpurgis Night legends from the outset, acknowledging in the preface that there were certainly "doubters who deny the reality of merry nights on the bald summit" of the Brocken but then rejecting their doubts: "but what do the doubters matter to us—us who are convinced that our ancestors were not crazy, and who take solace in what they tell us? . . . I'll also wager, my friends, . . . that this book finds more readers than [Fischer's] *Buch vom Aberglauben* has . . ."[66]

The book itself consists of two "witches' travels" and one collection of "devils' arts," all drawing on the fanciful Walpurgis Night legends so rigorously rejected by less romantically (and superstitiously) inclined readers, including also legends of St. Walpurgis. The first of these "travels" is representative. Titled "Emilie von der Felden und Veit von der Tonne: Die Verlobung auf dem Bloxberge" (Emilie von der Felden and Veit von der Tonne: The Engagement on the Blocksberg), it is a tale of two young lovers, longtime acquaintances pure in their affection and

Figure 1.4. Title page from Vulpius, *Hexenfahrte und Teufelskünste, aus dem geheimen Archiv der Walpurgis Nächte auf dem Blocksberg* (Leipzig: Reinick, 1797).

deeply devoted to each other, separated by familial enmities and societal circumstance, and forbidden from pursuing their relationship. Desperate to find some way to meet with Emilie for even just a few hours, Veit obtains from a mysterious, fat, ugly little man two small jars containing a salve. The little man directs Veit to apply it while standing before an open window shortly before midnight on Walpurgis Night; and to send one of the jars to Emilie with the instruction that she do the same; the two will then be united for the night, able to "jest, cuddle, and amuse themselves." Standing before the windows of their homes, they follow his instructions, and find themselves magically transported through the air to the summit of the Brocken amid a host of hideous other creatures riding broomsticks and pitchforks. On the Brocken's summit they exchange rings and pledge their love to each other, but their amorous discussions are interrupted by the arrival of Satan himself in the form of a male goat (*Ziegenbock*) who advances upon them and intimates that Emilie will be his for the night. Revolted, the fair Emilie rejects Satan, who quickly realizes that they do not belong at this gathering and furiously orders the witches to "burn [the two lovers] to ashes so that not a speck remains of them, then strew the ashes to the wind, crying: 'on Walpurgis Night the supreme devil has judged justly!' "

The lovers' catastrophe is prevented, however: for just as they face certain death, the pure and noble Emilie cries out to St. Walpurgis: "Saint Walpurgis! I call on you to protect me! Stand by me! Save me from this evil! You know my innocence! Save me!" And miraculously, the saint appears bathed in brilliant light, surrounds the two lovers in a dense fog, and looks threateningly at the monsters. She uses her "heavenly powers" to transport them back to their respective homes, where they awaken safely the next day—uncertain of whether they had experienced a dream (as the doctors say) or a reality, until they discover the engagement rings on their fingers. This is the climax and the end of part I; in part II the lovers are finally united in peace.

Conclusions

As a literary artwork Vulpius's *Hexenfahrten* probably deserves the obscurity into which it has fallen. It warrants inclusion here, however, because it demonstrates the thematic potency the Walpurgis Night had accumulated by the end of the eighteenth century. As a contribution to the cultural discourse surrounding the fabled Brocken Sabbath, it incorporates many of the themes associated with the lore of the witchcraft into a prose narrative of romance between two fair youths who are unjustly kept apart by discord, ignorance, and superstition. It pits good and evil against one another as St. Walpurgis rescues the lovers from certain death at the hands of Satan's hordes, recalls her Miracle of Light as they are rescued, and explores the boundary between superstition and knowledge, illusion and reality as they and their families try to make sense of the Walpurgis Night's events and ultimately acknowledge that the supposedly imaginary night somehow enabled them to set aright the wrongs of reality. And the dramatic context for the central events of its narrative thematizes the Night's atmosphere of turbulent conflict, coming into focus in the climactic scene atop the Brocken in much the same way that the concentrated evil and inclement elements of the Wolf's Glen scene in *Der Freischütz* allegorize the evil that propels that opera's plot.

The Walpurgis Night's actual historical origins are certain to remain subjects of conjecture. That specific fact, however, is less important than the general nature of the forces that coalesced to form the legend over the course of the centuries. We may confidently assert at least that those forces sprang from the conflict between identity and alterity, and that the lore never lost its central aura of conflict even under the force of the formidable historical and ideological conflicts to which it was subject between about 800 and 1800. The lore of the Walpurgis Night is in fact an aggregate, a cumulative legacy produced through the largely arbitrary convergence of disparate ideas and facts, all subjected to human nature's astonishing capacity for xenophobia, superstition, and simple fear of the unknown.

Lest the temporal remove between the political and cultural prehistories of Goethe's and Mendelssohn's *Walpurgisnacht* treatments lull us into self-congratulatory complacence, it should be remembered that the Walpurgis Night remains affixed to deep-seated societal and historical disunity, discord, and violence. Although it has largely descended into commercialized innocuousness by now, throughout the nineteenth century and well into the twentieth it continued to occasion real violence in the form of public efforts to banish the fabled witches. The intensity and viciousness of some of those efforts reflects the strength that the Walpurgis Night's dimensions of religious and social conflict continued to exert long after its supernatural verity had been questioned and rejected in most quarters. Christian citizens in Europe used not only holy water and the fumes of incense, but also gunshots, fires, and loud noises of every sort to frighten away or otherwise rid themselves of the physical presence of witches.[67] In many instances these efforts perpetuated the cultural memory of witch hunts, witch trials, and witch burnings themselves.[68] In some places the young men of the village would assemble after sunset and crack their whips in unison with all their might, producing a sound that reputedly drove the witches away (doubtless because of the memory of the whippings that often figured in the trials of accused witches).[69] In others, villagers would assemble before the homes of suspected witches and blow upon "shawms" (*Schalmeien*) pieced together from peeled willow-wood, while in other villages they would gather and march through the streets using gunshots and the cracking of whips to frighten the witches away.[70] The sounds of clanking metal—ringing church bells, rattling chains, and scythes striking on stone—were supposed to have the same effect,[71] for they, too, sonically reminded the evil Others who lurked in, around, and above mainstream society of the famous trials in which they had been so viciously vanquished. Perhaps most ominously, children were introduced into the practices using milder counterpart activities during the day,[72] so that when they were old enough they would be prepared (or indoctrinated) to use adult means toward the same end.

These were not harmless rituals, door-to-door trick-or-treat neighborhood pilgrimages with laughing children, smiling parental escorts, and warmly lit houses offering candy and sweets. Even when they did not entail violence (as most events involving fire, whips, and guns certainly do) they were at best harassment: grim and threatening reenactments of cultural, political, religious, and social violence. Nor were they limited to society's rural, ignorant, and uneducated underclasses, for these techniques for detecting, expelling, and eradicating (perceived) alterity were developed by university-trained lawyers, physicians, scientists, and theologians. They were expounded not only in learned treatises intended for those elite classes, but also in popular plays, poems, sermons, and texts. Whether or not there were real witches in the area was immaterial, for what the ritual perpetuated and celebrated was the cultural memory, the attitude of suspicion, and the threat of reprisal for perceived alterity.[73] And as the lessons of the witch trials demonstrate, those texts' effect of using superstition disguised as knowledge in order to transform suspicion into action only concentrated conflicts of societal identity. In this case (unlike the witch trials), that concentration fell on a single night, a night that not only affected the lives of the perceived Others who had become its victims, but also became legitimized through its annual ritual enactment. That legitimacy, obtained as it was through deceptively innocuous acceptance in mainstream society, won for the Walpurgis Night considerable topical importance as an epoch-making adversarial encounter between some of the most ideologically potent symbols in European history: between religion and superstition, reason and faith; between French and German culture; between the Catholic Church and its religious opponents; and, of course, between Christians and non-Christians generally.

This is the Walpurgis Night that was familiar to Goethe and Mendelssohn, the two enlightened Romantics who stand at the center of this book. Approaching the topic across the span of two generations but from remarkably consilient social and artistic outlooks, each engaged it over a period of years in his respective art form, and each used it not only as a starting point for artistic commentary on society but also as an artistic construction of his own identity—and as a venue for offering a substantially more enlightened lesson about the adversarial symbols it evoked. Those artistic engagements are the subjects of chapters 2 through 5.

Chapter Two

Tolerance, Translation, and Acceptance

Goethe's and Mendelssohn's Voices in European Cultural Discourse to ca. 1850

> At least pave the way for a happy prosperity toward that height of culture, toward that universal tolerance of man for which reason still sighs in vain!
>
> Moses Mendelssohn, *Jerusalem; or on Religious Power and Judaism*

> Tolerance should actually be only a transitional attitude: it must lead to acceptance. To tolerate is to insult.
>
> Goethe, *Maximen und Reflexionen,* No. 151

Long after fears of demonic sabbaths atop the Brocken had been generally assigned the status of superstitious lore rather than realistic threats to the well-being of society, the Walpurgis Night continued to function as a vehicle for artistic communication on issues that were real and pressing matters of the present. By the mid-eighteenth century, it was sufficiently familiar as a cultural topos to be able to function as a point of convergence for any number of intellectual, religious, and social cross-currents. It thus naturally offered artists a means to deal literally with a calendrical and social event that was familiar even to uneducated individuals while also reflecting allegorically or symbolically on broader matters too sensitive or complex to serve this discursive function effectively. Since these convergent lines of perspective reflected their constantly changing contexts, artists' interpretations of the topic also shaped public perceptions of their artistic identity—the issues that were important to them, where they stood on those issues, and how they related to societal norms and deviations vis-à-vis those issues.

The complicated social and intellectual terrain discussed in chapter 1 thus constituted a kind of habitus[1] for the lore of the Walpurgis Night as it came to Goethe and Mendelssohn, and the ideas and issues that converged in this terrain accordingly informed the artistic and cultural identities that those two socially and politically engaged artists constructed for themselves over the course of their careers. Exploring that habitus is not just the necessary first step in exploring their respective artistic engagements with the thematic implications of the Walpurgis Night; it is crucial for understanding how this particular subject enabled them to overcome significant differences in artistic experience, religious background and outlook, and age, producing a coherent group of topically related artworks that contributed vitally to the nineteenth century's understanding of the Walpurgis Night and its thematic import.

The Social and Intellectual Terrain

The craggy, forbidding terrain of the Brocken, the Walpurgis Night's air of pervasive conflict, and the seemingly erratic convergences of competing historical currents in both make them apt metaphors for the years of the creation and early receptions of Goethe's and Mendelssohn's treatments of them. German-speakers were able to make progress in addressing and overcoming the barriers, gaps, and contradictory impulses in their political and cultural realms because of three separate but closely interrelated factors, all relevant to the lore of the Walpurgis Night and these artists' engagements with it: the great flourishing of literary culture, especially print culture, that straddled the turn to the nineteenth century; the impulse to discover and reconstruct a coherent past, both factual and mythologized, for that culture, to authenticate and perennialize it in print, and to actualize it; and the persistent presence of religion—and religious conflict—as a core issue in their cultural identity.

The first of these factors was in some ways the most far-reaching. German-speakers of the late eighteenth century devoted unprecedented amounts of time and energy to communicating their experiences and ideas via private correspondence, and Goethe's generation was the first in the German lands to experience a world with a sufficient quantity of secular readers to sustain a public literary culture.[2] This public literary culture grew exponentially during the period in question: it was the province of perhaps 5 percent of the total populace in the mid-eighteenth century, but by the end of the nineteenth century Germany represented one of the continent's most assiduously literate publics.[3] As a result the cultures of print, with all their potency as agents of social change and essential instruments of public discourse, were able to transport the vast body of generally unfocused oral and vernacular lore concerning the Walpurgis Night into literary culture, and there to transform it into a correspondingly powerful element in the emergent German sociopolitical landscape. Vulpius's *Hexenfahrten und Teufelskünste* was but one of the first manifestations of this development—one that, as we shall see in chapter 3, was an important antecedent to the vastly more powerful treatments by Goethe, among others.

More chronologically focused but no less vital to the topical character of the Walpurgis Night were literary culture's implicit but obvious aspirations to generate a nation of letters that would correspond to the nation of (oral) language that had existed up to then, and to develop a culture of corresponding ideas that somehow would not just be characteristically and essentially German, but would distill a collective German Self into a recognizable phenomenon, both historical and actual, that was distinct from the other national identities that surrounded it. Herder, Fichte, Arndt, Jahn, Riehl, and Ratzel thematized and theorized this German Self, working to articulate the terms by which it could be discerned in its past and present state. Folklorists such as Arnim and Brentano and the Grimm brothers attempted to anthologize and codify the linguistic and cultural inheritances of the *Volk*. And jurists and statesmen such as Justus Möser, Karl Friedrich Eichhorn, and Friedrich Karl von Savigny attempted to institute it in the present by means of historically based political and jurisprudential scholarship. Despite their disciplinary, philosophical, and methodological differences, these scholars' enterprises were all large-scale projects that used the comparatively new phenomenon of public literary culture in order to translate the German lands' history into an enduring body of letters representing a distinctly German identity for both future and present. The Walpurgis Night was a cultural topos immediately serviceable to these enterprises in part because of its deep roots in the German lands' past and its continued existence, evidently little altered over the years, in those same lands' present. In it, literary culture found a subject that was both already familiar even to the less-educated populace and emblematic of the historical durability central to the cultural projects of Herder, Arnim, the Grimms, and others.

The pronounced heritage of religious conflict associated with the Walpurgis Night added yet another sociological dimension to its thematic potency. For the emergence of literary culture divided the already politically fragmented German populace into two distinct subcultures: the comparatively small culture of letters, which constituted an economic and political elite, and the significantly larger one that still relied primarily or exclusively on oral communication. Religion was (after the German language itself) the most important cultural activity common to both of these classes. The specific tenets of religious belief and activities of religious culture varied immensely among regions, of course, even within the great divisions of the predominant religious culture of Christianity (both Protestant and Catholic) and the most prominent other faith, Judaism; often those of particular Christian localities retained distinct vestiges of their pre-Christian pasts.[4] Nevertheless, the Church remained one of the few institutions whose presence suffused the daily life and commercial history of both popular and elite cultures and remained foundational to the sense of identity of individuals and groups within both classes. Here, too, the lore of the Walpurgis Night was a subject not only conspicuously relevant but also familiar to German-speakers through centuries of oral heritage, and vested with issues well-suited to the active transmission of social ideas in the flourishing literary culture.

Finally, the German theological landscape of the late eighteenth and early nineteenth centuries was as deeply riven as its political and historical counterparts, fraught with competing ideas on issues ranging from the roles of religion in private and public life to the modes of transmission for religious ideas.[5] At stake here was not only the need for German literary culture to construct a coherent social history that either explained, justified, or legitimized the overwhelming social and political predominance of Christendom, but also the matter of Christianity's contemporary relationships with the continent's two principal other religions, Islam and Judaism. The issues pertaining to Islam are more straightforward, partly because the number of Muslims in the German lands during the late eighteenth and early nineteenth centuries was distinctly small and partly because there had been no real Islamic military threat to German-speaking Europe since the fourteenth century.[6] In the German lands in the late eighteenth century, Muslim alterity remained largely confined to exoticist aesthetics (as suggested, of course, by the turbaned figure in the title illustration for Praetorius's *Blockes-Berges Verrichtung*; see figure 1.3, p. 19).[7] Nevertheless, the opening up of religious discourse in the late eighteenth and early nineteenth centuries attracted some German literary luminaries to Islamic thought—most prominently the Orientalist Friedrich Rückert (who translated the complete Qur'an into German) and Goethe, who was a fervent admirer of Muhammad and many of the tenets of Islam.[8]

The matter of the roles of Jews and Judaism in the changing German society was significantly more complicated.[9] On the one hand, Judaism was the only non-Christian religion that achieved any prominence or success in contemporary debates concerning religious tolerance, and the economic, political, and social potentials for Jews in the late eighteenth and early nineteenth centuries were greater than they had ever been. In many parts of the German lands, Jews could live where they wanted, work in fields that had previously been off-limits, and practice their religion with greater freedom than had been the case at any time since the reign of Charlemagne; indeed, in an age in which state and civil legislation challenged the rights of Protestants to worship as Protestants in Catholic regions and vice versa, observant Jews retained the right to practice their religion, or not to do so, in greater measure than ever before.[10] On the other hand, proposals to emancipate or assimilate European Jewry constantly met with fierce opposition—voiced sometimes against Judaism, but just as often in ethnic terms, against Jews' fitness for citizenship.[11] In brief, given the multitude of amorphous and patently irrational rationalizations for arguments that Jews should continue to be excluded from Christian society, it is hardly surprising that attempts at legislated public emancipation on their behalf attained only qualified success. By the mid-nineteenth century the number and volume of elaborate political, religious, and (pseudo-) scientific arguments why Jews, especially observant Jews, should remain Other to mainstream society (whether the latter was Christian or secular) had swollen dramatically—a situation that certainly facilitated the resurgence of anti-Semitism in the century's second half.[12]

These tense relations between the various political and religious sects of the German lands' Jewish and Christian communities yielded a protracted, heated, and frequently brilliant discourse on tolerance in matters of identity and alterity, both religious and social, in German literary culture—themes, that is, that by now related obviously and directly to the Walpurgis Night itself. The names and ideas of the principal protagonists in this discourse in the early eighteenth century are well known. The "Pantheism conflict" (*Pantheismusstreit*) that flared up in the 1780s centered on allegations that Gotthold Ephraim Lessing supported the pantheism of the seventeenth-century rationalist Baruch de Spinoza (1632–77), a Dutch Jew; this controversy drew into its fray not only Lessing himself, but also Moses Mendelssohn, whose last work (*Morgenstunden*, 1785) was a defense of the theism of Gottfried Wilhelm Leibnitz (1646–1716). Mendelssohn himself, of course, was not only the "noble Jew" (*edler Jude*) of Lessing's *Nathan der Weise* (1779), which, set in Jerusalem during the Crusades, explicitly grapples with the social intersections of Christianity, Judaism, and Islam and constitutes one of eighteenth-century literature's greatest contributions to deist philosophy. He was also the Enlightenment's preeminent philosophical advocate of Jewish emancipation. The legacies of this sociophilosophical intercourse in turn were taken up by some of the late eighteenth and early nineteenth centuries' leading philosophers and theologians, including Fichte, Herder, Kant, and Schelling, among others.

Particularly important among these others was the preacher, classical philologist, and Protestant theologian Friedrich Schleiermacher (1768–1834), whose eloquent writings on the proper relationships between Church and state and between Christianity and other religions remained widely influential for much of the nineteenth century. Schleiermacher advocated for the right of all religions to develop freely, without interference from the state or other sociopolitical institutions. Taking his cue from Herder and speaking primarily of the *Haskalah* (especially the circle of Henriette Herz, who for Prussian anti-Semites personified the threat of emancipated Jewry[13]), Schleiermacher from 1799 to the end of his life wrote sympathetically of ancient Judaism and strongly criticized opponents of Jewish emancipation.[14] But despite the centrality of Christian-chauvinistic beliefs in his writings—he viewed contemporary Judaism as corrupted and moribund, maintained an emphatically Christological interpretation of the Old Testament, and persevered in his rejection of assertions that there was a fundamental continuity between contemporary Judaism and Christianity that justified the elimination of legislated Jewish exclusion—he continually endeavored to take Judaism seriously and remain sensitive to the concerns and perspectives of enlightened Jews, maintaining that the community of worship generated by true religion (including especially Christianity) was not imperiled by difference. Alterity does not threaten identity; it strengthens it.[15]

Schleiermacher was the preeminent theologian of his generation, and his ideas were foundational to developments in Christian/Jewish relations during the first two-thirds of the nineteenth century. His ideas on the Christological telos of the Bible and the potential of individual faith as the cornerstone of community proved foundational for the religious dimensions that German nationalism assumed as it coalesced during the mid-nineteenth century. They are also relevant for our purposes because they were strongly influenced by the ideas of Goethe and equally influential on Moses Mendelssohn's grandson Felix, who proclaimed himself a follower in November 1830—that is, at precisely the time when he developed his earliest ideas for setting Goethe's ballad "Die erste Walpurgisnacht."[16] The issues of historical, political, religious, and social identity and alterity so central to the Walpurgis Night itself and to Enlightenment discourse thus converge dramatically in the ideas of Schleiermacher, in the process forming an important bridge between the poet and the composer whose Walpurgis Night essays are the center of this book.

The Relationship Between Goethe and Felix Mendelssohn

The essentials of the relationship between Goethe and Mendelssohn are well known. The Berlin banker Abraham Mendelssohn (1776–1835) aroused Goethe's interest in the Berlin composer Karl Friedrich Zelter (1758–1832), whom he knew through the Berlin Singakademie and the salons of Sara Levy, when the two met in Frankfurt am Main in the summer of 1797.[17] After developing an acquaintance from a distance for more than two years, Goethe and Zelter first exchanged letters in August 1799. Their correspondence is in itself a remarkable phenomenon—a set of nearly 900 letters spanning a full 33 years and documenting the personal, political, and aesthetic ideas of two extraordinarily intelligent and gifted individuals.[18] The relationship assumed new importance sometime early in 1819, when Abraham and Lea Mendelssohn arranged for their eldest children, Fanny (b. 1805) and Felix (b. 1809), to begin formal instruction in composition with Zelter.[19] From this point on the gifted children of the banker who had initiated the Goethe/Zelter relationship figured prominently in the composer's and poet's letters. They were introduced to Goethe through Zelter in November 1821. Goethe was seventy-two years old, an internationally renowned icon; Felix, only twelve, a youth who had already attracted considerable attention but still very much a student composer whose first publication was nearly two years away.

From this point on, the relationship between Mendelssohn and Goethe developed on at least three levels. Most obviously, the two would carry on a surprisingly familiar correspondence and visit personally three more times between this first meeting and Goethe's death in 1832. That these meetings—in 1822, 1825, and 1830—were vitally important for Mendelssohn is obvious enough from the young composer's letters, the veneration the great poet received from the entire family, and the reports of others who were present (including Zelter, Ludwig Rellstab, Johann Christian Lobe, and Adele Schopenhauer).[20] That they were comparably important to the great poet nearly sixty years his senior is evident from the latter's (successful) attempt to persuade the youth to further extend his stay in Weimar to two weeks rather than two days,[21] as well as his gift of a bifolio for the second part of the still-incomplete *Faust* tragedy[22] and (perhaps most tellingly) his assessment that Mendelssohn's views on music were remarkably close to his own. That assessment of similarities in musical matters may have been mistaken, but it is certainly a compliment when one considers that it was based on their wide-ranging topics of conversation, which included Scotland, the Protestant theologian Wilhelm Hengstenberg,[23] Hegel's lectures on aesthetics, Hugo's *Hernani*, the theater, Walter Scott, Schiller, botany, meteorology, and attractive women, as well as music and music history.[24]

The depth of the impression Mendelssohn made on Goethe is evident from the poet's account of the composer's last visit to Weimar, sent to Zelter on June 3, 1830:

> Just now, early, at about 9:30 A.M., under the clearest of skies and amid the most beautiful sunshine, the excellent Felix, having spent fourteen enjoyable days with us and edified everything with his perfect and genial art, has departed with Ottilie, Ulrike, and the children for Jena, where he will also delight all his benevolent friends and leave for our region a souvenir that should be nobly celebrated henceforth.
>
> For me his presence was beneficial especially because I found that my relationship to music remains the same as before: I listen to it with pleasure, interest, and contemplation and I love its historical aspects—for how can we understand any phenomenon without [first] penetrating the course by which it comes to us? And above all, there was the fact that Felix shows his understanding of this gradual progression quite well, and is able to recall representative examples of every sort because of his good memory. Moving forward from the time of Bach, he brought Haydn, Mozart, and Gluck alive for me; gave me adequate instruction concerning the more modern great technicians; and finally made me sensitive to and aware of his own works. He therefore left with my heartiest blessings. . . .[25]

Less obvious but likewise important was the second-hand development of the relationship through Zelter's mediation. Well aware of the phenomenal promise of their young mutual acquaintance, the two mentors kept tabs on his development and activities, relaying greetings and news of him and each other through their correspondence. Zelter proudly reported to Goethe on his "brave and diligent" student's compositional projects, including his third and fourth operas, his various larger sacred works, and his instrumental compositions. Typical is his assessment of the young composer's growth in his fifteenth year:

> Last night Felix's fourth opera was performed *privately*, complete with dialog.[26] It's in three acts, and with the two ballets it fills about two and a half hours. The work was quite well received. The poem by Dr. Casper is also quite satisfactory, since he is a musicianly poet. I'm biased, but I can hardly suppress my marvel at how a young man barely fifteen years old can progress so rapidly. New, attractive, distinctive, and unique things abound in it—spirit, flow, repose, euphony, unity, drama. Large-scale matters [are dealt with] as if by experienced hands. The orchestral writing is interesting, [but] not overwhelming, tiresome, or simply subordinate. The musicians enjoyed playing it, but it is not at all easy. Familiar things come and go not routinely, [but] rather, from my perspective, appropriately and with appreciation. Cheer—rejoicing—without hurry—tenderness—daintiness—love—passion—innocence. The overture is a remarkable

> thing. You imagine a painter who hurls a dollop of color onto the canvas and draws the shapes with his fingers and a pencil until finally a formation appears; continually surprised, you finally glance around yourself so that you'll believe what's happening.
>
> Granted, I'm talking like a grandfather who spoils his grandson. I know perfectly well what I'm talking about, and I won't say anything that I can't back up. . . . [27]

These glowing words elicited wry envy from Goethe: "would that I could say the same," he replied, "of even one of my [court] scholars."[28] The poet also reported in 1825 that Felix's "audible and discernible" (*hör- und vernehmbare*) dedication of his Op. 3 piano quartet to him had "done [him] much good," and he later remarked that "hardly any of [his] many students had turned out so well"[29]—a real compliment especially since Felix was not a "student" of Goethe in any formal sense of the word. To the end of their lives, he and Zelter shared the news from Mendelssohn's most recent letters in their own.

Finally, there is the matter of Mendelssohn's numerous compositional engagements with poems by Goethe or attributed to Goethe. As is well known, these musical responses span virtually all the genres represented in Mendelssohn's secular oeuvre. His first published engagement was a purely instrumental one (the programmatic concert overture *Meeresstille und glückliche Fahrt* [Calm Sea and Prosperous Voyage], Op. 27);[30] his last, the second version of the secular cantata *Die erste Walpurgisnacht*, Op. 60. These two large-scale compositions are joined by the first setting of the *Walpurgisnacht* and the Scherzo from the Octet for Strings, Op. 20, which reportedly was inspired by the *Walpurgisnachtstraum* scene from *Faust I*;[31] and they frame a number of less imposing published compositional engagements: the solo songs "Ach, um deine feuchten Schwingen" ("Suleika," Op. 34, no. 4; 1837) and "Was bedeutet die Bewegung?" ("Suleika," Op. 57, no. 3; 1837–43);[32] as well as six choral songs (Op. 41, no. 6; Op. 50, nos. 1–3, and Op. 59, nos. 1 and 4). To these must be added a number of compositions that Mendelssohn withheld from publication during his lifetime. Five of these works were published posthumously,[33] and another four were completed but have remained unpublished or published only in facsimile.[34] Finally, and perhaps most tantalizingly, there is an unfinished and unpublished solo setting "Meine Ruh' ist hin" ("Gretchen"; ca. 1825) and two substantively different versions of an unfinished concert aria "O laßt mich einen Augenblick noch hier" (for bass and orchestra; 1847).

This brief inventory brings several telling facts to light concerning Mendelssohn's musical relationship to Goethe. First, he withheld more settings of Goethe than he published, and the number of settings for solo voice is surprisingly small. Second, while his settings span his creative life, those that he published all date from the relatively narrow time span of 1837–43. Third, in three instances—*Die erste Walpurgisnacht*, "Suleika," and "O laßt mich einen Augenblick"—he largely abandoned his first setting and reapproached the text using substantially different music. Finally, the number of his settings that deal with or proceed from a premise of Self vs. Other is proportionally high: the early

"Zigeunerlied" (Gypsy song), the "Türkisches Schenkenlied" (Op. 50, no. 1), all three "Suleika" settings, and both versions of *Die erste Walpurgisnacht.*

The first three of these observations are probably functions of Mendelssohn's well-known opinion that the complex sentiments of Goethe's words impeded the sort of intimately individualized communication that he considered central to musical expression.[35] The last, by contrast, suggests that he responded readily to Goethe's (and Willemer's) poetic treatments of the themes of identity and alterity. The "Türkisches Schenkenlied" and both "Suleika" texts ("Ach, um deine feuchten Schwingen" and "Was bedeutet die Bewegung") are from the *West-östlicher Divan* (1814–19). Begun as the Napoleonic Wars were drawing to a close, the *Divan* is a remarkable compendium of Middle Eastern and Western extra-biblical scripture and sensualist prose that represents one of Goethe's most explicit contributions to a "world literature" (*Weltliteratur*) that he hoped would supersede the "national literature" (*Nationalliteratur*) whose time, he felt, was nearing its end.[36] In the early "Zigeunerlied" (Gypsy song, 1771), the lyric persona is visited by seven werewolves after killing a black cat that belongs to a witch named Anne; when he is afterward visited by seven angry werewolves whom he recognizes as women from the village he calls them by name, whereupon they run howling away. Like wicked or otherwise undesirable Others elsewhere in contemporary literature, the (witch-) Gypsies of the "Zigeunerlied" are associated with animal imagery (wolves, a black cat, owls, and werewolves) and sounds (for example, "Ich hörte der Wölfe Hungergeheul, / Ich hörte der Eulen Geschrei. / Wille wau wau wau / Wille wo wo wo / Wito hu!," ll. 3–7). And the ballad "Die erste Walpurgisnacht" allots the role of Other to the characters nominally closest to the mainstream of Goethe's presumed readership—the Christian watchmen, implicitly soldiers of Charlemagne—while identifying and sympathizing with the pagans as they celebrate their ancient rites atop the Brocken. The prominence of cultural, national, literary, and ideological Others in these works—and thus in the corpus of Mendelssohn's Goethe settings as a whole—suggests that those settings represented not simply artistic engagements with alterity, but convergences of the artistic voices of poet and composer. Three convergences of Goethe's and Mendelssohn's artistic personas are especially relevant to the issues of identity and alterity in their engagements with the Walpurgis Night. These convergences center on the historical, cultural, and religious orientation of the artists and their publics.

Historical Translation: The Useful and Beloved Past

At once the most obvious and most obscure of these three points of convergence is that of Goethe's and Mendelssohn's appropriations of historical identity and alterity. Central to this attitude toward history was the notion that human society had always comprised two fundamentally opposed factions: the superstitious, narrow-minded, ascetic, dogmatic enemies of the flesh; and those who celebrated knowledge, expansive generosity, and sensual, natural beauty. This dualist view of humanity and history was what Heine, with characteristically incisive irony, invoked in his well-known polemic (1840) against the late political writer and satirist Ludwig Börne (1796–1837), who had criticized Goethe's political views:

> As in his pronouncements on Goethe, so also in his judgments of other authors, Börne betrayed his Nazarene narrowness. I say "Nazarene," to avoid either the expression "Jewish" or "Christian," although I use both expressions as synonyms to designate not a faith but a character. "Jews" and "Christians" are for me quite close in meaning, in contrast to "Hellenes," a designation I use to characterize, in the same manner, an inborn as well as learned spiritual orientation and style of thinking rather than a certain nation. That is to say: all men are either Jews or Hellenes, men with ascetic, iconoclastic, spiritual tendencies, or men whose nature it is to love life, to take pride in self-development, and to be realistic. Thus there were Hellenes in the families of German pastors, and Jews who had been born in Athens, and perhaps traced their ancestry back to Theseus.[37]

In the eyes of what Heine would term the Hellenes, then, the "Christian millennium" from roughly the eighth to the eighteenth century had been dominated by myth and superstition, whereas the more remote past—the past of ancient Greece and Rome—offered the keys for the modern world to become a rational, enlightened society and to further the progress of humanity. While the modern era, dominated as it was by ecclesiastical Christianity, was superior to the great river civilizations of the near East as well as classical Greece and Rome, its continued development required it not simply to tolerate, but to accept or even celebrate, that remote Hellenic (in Heine's sense of the word) past which it had up to then rejected or, at best, selectively assimilated.

One peculiarity of the teleology of late-eighteenth- and early-nineteenth-century cultural discourse is that of reinvigorating the present and the prospects for the future by reapproaching and appropriating the ideas and arts of the distant past. The Walpurgis Night was clearly a lively cultural topos that was prominently invested in issues of identity and alterity, and one whose historical origins had become subjects of lively debate by the late eighteenth century. Since those origins were shrouded in the mists of time, however, the Night offered later artists a useful historical subject for application to their own contemporary cultural discourse. In order to realize its allegorical potentials fully, artists needed to be cognizant of both the subject itself and the assumptions and attitudes with which their contemporaries would view it—and then to mediate between the two, translating the myth poetically so that its substance and import sent the artist's own message to contemporaries.

Goethe's brilliance as a writer combined with his lifelong fascination with languages and his didactic proclivities to produce a number of instructive writings in which he discussed these issues of translation and the problem of the translator's mediation between two cultures in general. One such instance, remarkably similar to Schleiermacher's influential and contemporaneous theory of translation,[38] is an essay written after the death of Christoph Martin Wieland (1733–1813):

> There are two maxims for translation. The first requires that the author from a foreign nation be brought over to us in such a fashion that we can regard him as one of our own. The other, by contrast, requires that we put ourselves in the foreigner's place, his circumstances, his way of speaking, his peculiarities. The advantages of each approach are familiar enough to all educated people through excellent examples. Our friend, who also in this regard sought a middle way, endeavored to combine the two; but as a man of sensitivity and taste he favored the first maxim when there was any doubt.[39]

Wieland, of course, was celebrated not least of all as the author of numerous translations of works by Greek and Latin authors and the first translator of twenty-two of Shakespeare's plays into German, as well as the author of several important original works.[40] But his translations of Shakespeare quickly came under fire for the licenses they took in endeavoring to render the plays of the English Elizabethan comprehensibly for the eighteenth-century German public, and these criticisms are certainly partially responsible for Goethe's defense of his friend's translations.[41] At the same time, Goethe reportedly expressed his private preference for Wieland's Shakespeare translations later on,[42] and his characterization of the tendency of Wieland's translations to err on the side of the reader's perspective as a sign of "sensitivity and taste" suggests that in his view the central concern of the translator as historical, linguistic, and cultural mediator was the reader's perspective.

Among the most remarkable products of Goethe's efforts to celebrate the legacies of Classical culture on their own terms by translating them into his own realm of experience are the overtly sensualist *Römische Elegien* (Roman Elegies; 1788–90, publ. 1795). Like the more subdued *Venezianische Epigramme* (Venetian Epigrams; 1790–91, publ. 1795), these poetic counterparts to the prose *Italienische Reise* were born of Goethe's first trip to Rome, and they bespeak the revelatory, even emancipatory, effect of his first immersion in the legacies of the pre-Christian cultures of Italy. The twenty poems of the *Römische Elegien* comprise a cycle of elegiac distichs in the *antike Langverse* (ancient long-verse; i.e., Classical hexameter), which Klopstock had introduced into German, familiar to Goethe in that form from Voss's translation of Homer's *Odyssey*, as well as his models in the works of Catullus, Propertius, Tibullus, Ovid, and Martial. Their subject matter likewise reflects Goethe's sense of freedom after his abrupt departure from his wearisome duties at the Weimar court and his conspicuously unwholesome affair with Charlotte von Stein there. They are love poems in several senses of the word. On the one hand, they vividly but discreetly describe Goethe's romance with an enigmatic Italian mistress referred to in Elegy XVIII as "Faustina," and their completion coincided with the commencement of Goethe's affair with Christiane Vulpius (1765–1816), whom he would marry twenty years later. But they are also poetic reflections on the sensual beauty, artistic and otherwise, of a culture inconceivably remote from the fetters Goethe had escaped—and on the joys that resulted when Hellenic and Nazarene values (as Heine would term them) were allowed to come together. Goethe explicitly articulates this joy in Elegy V, where he describes himself tapping out the "antike Langvers" on the (presumably naked) back of his mistress:[43]

Raubt die Liebste denn gleich mir einige Stunden des Tages,	If my darling deprives me of some of the daylight hours,
Gibt sie Stunden der Nacht mir zur Entschädigung hin.	She gives me the hours of night as a full compensation.
Wird doch nicht immer geküßt, es wird vernünftig gesprochen;	We're not always kissing, we carry on rational discourse;
Überfällt sie der Schlaf, lieg' ich und denke mir viel.	If she falls asleep I lie there and think a great deal.
Oftmals hab' ich auch schon in ihren Armen gedichtet	And often in her embrace I have written a poem,
Und des Hexameters Maß leise mit fingernder Hand	I have softly composed a hexameter line with my finger,
Ihr auf den Rücken gezählt. Sie atmet in lieblichem Schlummer,	Tapped out on her back. She is breathing sleepily, sweetly,
Und es durchglühet ihr Hauch mir bis ins Tiefste die Brust.	And the glow of her breath goes through me, deep into my heart.

The significance of the *Römische Elegien* for purposes of this inquiry lies neither in their intrinsic beauty per se nor in the biographical significance they held for Goethe. Rather, they are important as documents of Goethe's ideas on the poetics of translation, and on the artistic fruits yielded when the seeds of modern culture were sown in the fertile soil of historical alterity. The *Elegies'* modernity consisted not least of all in their enriching the present by synthesizing into it those noble inheritances from the past that had gone unaccepted or unacknowledged in the value systems of contemporary European society. Goethe's numerous literary engagements with historically remote subjects, fictional and factual, from within the realm of Classical antiquity as well as outside it are thus the artistic products of these ventures in historical translation: Muhammad, Ossian, Tasso, and, of course, Faust himself.

Felix Mendelssohn's approach to historical alterity was remarkably similar. Like Goethe, he received his early education mostly from privately employed instructors, with great emphasis on the Classics; and like Goethe, he cultivated his love for the rich heritage of Classical antiquity to the end of his life. By age eleven he was studying Latin six hours a week,[44] and around that time he was sufficiently well versed in Latin prosody to be able to pen a lengthy German poem titled *Paphlëis,* probably modeled on Goethe's *Achillëis, oder die natürliche Tochter* (Achillëis, or, the Natural Daughter; 1808) and comprising more than 460 lines in the same Classical hexameters of, among other works, Goethe's *Römische Elegien.*[45] In 1826 he was able to publish his German translation (completed the previous year) of a Latin popular comedy by Terence (?185–159 BCE), the *Andria*, adopting an approach to the translation that, as Barbara Kes has pointed out, represented a turning point in nineteenth-century Classical studies.[46]

Significantly, Mendelssohn's translation of the *Andria* neatly parallels the approach to historical translations advocated by Goethe in his own works of the genre (indeed, Mendelssohn sent one of the earliest printed exemplars to the poet, who promised Zelter that it would be most useful and instructive for use in the soirees of the friends of art in Weimar during the coming long winter evenings).[47] As Leon Botstein has remarked, in the first modern commentary to devote more than passing notice to the *Andria* translation, Mendelssohn's rendering did far more than simply transfer Terence's Latin text into contemporary German while using the structural and prosodic conventions of the original.[48] It also demonstrated Mendelssohn's awareness of the comedy's performance possibilities and theatrical dimensions, as well as his cognizance of his role as mediator between Terence and his own audiences. This mediatory role was particularly important because of the play's moral of reconciliation between warring families, strangers, and foreigners—and it put to the test the first of Goethe's two maxims of translation (see p. 40): whether it would be possible to transfer the ideas and poetic structures of Terence's play into German in such a fashion that both its ethical substance and its aesthetic essentials became approachable to contemporary audiences despite the historical and cultural remoteness of the original.[49] In a very real sense, this obscure document launched the lifelong project of aesthetic and cultural education and edification that came into focus in Mendelssohn's career in the mid-1830s—an endeavor that Martin Geck and R. Larry Todd have documented in their probing overviews of Mendelssohn's career, and that Leon Botstein has aptly described as "the Mendelssohnian Project."[50]

The musical applications of the Mendelssohnian Project bring into focus the relevance of the issue of historical translation for Mendelssohn's music generally, and for his *Walpurgisnacht* settings in particular. That few composers are better known for their attempts to infuse their contemporary musical idioms with historically remote ideals, styles, and techniques is well known. So is the fact that those music-historical cross-references are commonly referred to as "historicizing" or (more specifically) "classicizing," implying an at least vaguely unbecoming level of compositional reliance on established models and a concomitant lack of originality. But those gestures acquire a different significance when viewed against the backdrop of the deep spiritual and aesthetic affinities between Mendelssohn and Goethe. For Mendelssohn as for Goethe, stylistic and substantive references to historically remote models and subjects were anything but complacent or unoriginal appropriations of the established as a means of accommodating listeners' and performers' tastes. On the contrary, they were pronounced stylistic departures from the grammatical and syntactical norms of contemporary idioms, incorporated into those idioms in order to draw attention to their stylistic alterity and thus to solicit or compel interpretation from the readers and performers.[51] They acquired semiotic power precisely because of the semantic assimilation of their historical alterity into a contemporary idiom. And by challenging readers and listeners to consider what Heine would consider a Hellenic perspective—not simply to tolerate, but to accept or even celebrate that perspective—both Mendelssohn and Goethe offered what they considered the keys for the modern world to become rational, enlightened, and progressive.

Cultural and Religious Translation: Aesthetic Paganism

In some ways Mendelssohn's and Goethe's constructions of their respective cultural and religious identities could hardly be more different. Goethe came from a solidly Lutheran family and was raised as a Lutheran, but he ultimately renounced that faith for his philosophically and theologically eclectic blend of Christianity and other religions. Mendelssohn's grandparents and much of the family of his parents' generation practiced Judaism, but he and his siblings were never introduced to the faith of his forebears; they were raised Lutheran and remained devout Lutherans throughout their lives. Both artists assertively cultivated their religious beliefs in their art: Goethe frequently explored and celebrated religious systems other than Christianity, while Mendelssohn was renowned for his numerous sacred compositions celebrating Lutheran, Anglican, and Catholic Christianity. Even his psalm settings, whose Old Testament textual provenance invites association with Judaism as well as Christianity, are clearly oriented toward Lutheran audiences, while his last completed oratorio, *Elijah*, adopts what Jeffrey Sposato has termed a "strategy of dual perspective," depicting the Jews in a fashion sympathetic to the perspective of listeners attenuated to them but retaining an essentially Christological portrayal of Elijah's significance.[52] Finally, and ironically, Goethe's embracement of Hellenic subjects and views did little to impede contemporary and posthumous appreciation of his stature as a Romantic artist—albeit sometimes reluctantly so—whose cause was consistent with that of latter-day Christian culture, while Mendelssohn's firm adherence to Christianity failed to deter contemporary and posthumous critics from emphasizing or (in some cases) decrying his Jewish heritage and portraying his perceived conservatism and historicism as consequences of that heritage.

At the same time, Goethe's sympathy for religions other than Christianity—indeed, his sympathy for ideas and individuals deemed heretical by the ecclesiastical establishment[53]—and his ambivalence regarding Christianity itself were well known, while Mendelssohn's surname immediately labeled him as being of Jewish descent. (Abraham Mendelssohn urged his elder son to drop the name Mendelssohn altogether, stating that "there is no Christian Mendelssohn any more than there is a Jewish Confucius. If you are called Mendelssohn, you are *eo ipso* [by that very act] a Jew, and that is of no use to you because it is not even true."[54]) In this sense Goethe and Mendelssohn alike were Other to the mainstream of European Christendom. Consequently, their works that deal with identity and alterity posed comparable challenges of cultural and religious translation—of either translating alterity in such a fashion that readers and audiences identified with the original, challenging them to surrender their own identities and submit themselves to that Other, or discovering a "middle way."[55]

A few case studies will suffice to demonstrate how they negotiated these challenges of translation. Most broadly, Goethe's sense of alienation from his own world and his increasing fascination (especially after the death of Schiller in 1805) with ideas and systems of belief outside the realms defined by geographically, culturally, and politically immediate experience led to the formulation, after about 1826, of his idea of a transcendent *Weltliteratur* (world literature), a utopian worldwide literary culture that knew no historical, national, linguistic, or political boundaries or norms.[56] He was spurred into this program partly by the provincialism and xenophobic nationalism of many of his German contemporaries, his admiration for literary achievements from a variety of cultures (especially French and British ones) vilified or ignored by those contemporaries, and his appreciation for the fact that despite the presence of dissenters and opponents everywhere, advocacy of his works and ideas seemed to be greater in France and Britain than in the German-speaking countries. At the same time, this historically and culturally transcendent global literary culture would be one that affirmed distinct cultural traits in literature rather than subverting or deriding them, without leading to any supranational literature or canon. In this as in most other things, classical Greece served as the best model, but even in classical culture there had never yet been a true *Weltliteratur.* Goethe was convinced that the age of "national literature" (*Nationalliteratur*) was past and that the age of *Weltliteratur* was emerging.[57] He hoped and believed that the relative economic and political stability of Restoration culture would foster the emergence of his literary utopia, and he considered the comparatively cosmopolitan literary cultures of England and France as indicators of a general move in that direction.[58]

If Goethe's program for *Weltliteratur* impresses as a utopian construct whose actual implementation would be staggeringly difficult if not impossible, this impression is confirmed through his own attitudes toward one specific culture particularly relevant to the subject of this book: that of the Jews, specifically European Jews in the late eighteenth and early nineteenth centuries. On the one hand, Goethe admired the literary quality of the Psalms and the Song of Songs sufficiently to translate them into German.[59] He regarded the philosophy of Spinoza highly and returned to it throughout his life, and likewise held Moses Mendelssohn in high esteem; certainly his warm and evidently genuine friendship with the young Felix Mendelssohn, as well as his infatuation with Marianne von Eybenberg, née Meyer, testify that he did not consider Jewish descent an insurmountable liability. On the other hand, he was angered by Jewish

Emancipation Edicts and derided their pamphleteering advocates as "sanctimonious humanitarian windbags" (*Humanitätssalbader*), and his use of anti-Semitic stereotypes in the context of private communications regarding Jews who had not, as it were, distinguished themselves from their culture, obviously contravened the affirmative goal of intercultural acceptance that lies at the root of his program of "world literature."[60]

Despite Goethe's failure to follow through on his program of *Weltliteratur* completely, its goal was the artistic affirmation of intercultural dialog in the interest of the autonomy of a transcendent world culture of art and, even more generally, a mutual understanding, criticism, tolerance, and acceptance. The program thus has a clear programmatic counterpart in the Mendelssohnian Project (see above, p. 42). In Mendelssohn's case as in Goethe's, this program emerged only gradually. Although he, like Goethe, maintained a strong sense of his identity as a German artist, this self-identification, also like Goethe's, coexisted with pronounced cosmopolitan interests to the end of his life. He worked tirelessly to understand what he considered the best music, art, and literature of other cultures; read and avidly collected literature in the languages of other countries as well as literature on those countries in their original languages;[61] insisted that his music be disseminated outside Germany only when its ideas were capable of translation into that culture and acceptance on that culture's terms rather than specifically German ones; composed in English and Italian as well as German;[62] and advocated for composers and artists of other nationalities and historical periods as well as his own, so long as their works were reasonably consistent with his qualitative expectations. These cosmopolitan proclivities were present early on, inculcated in him by his upbringing and education, but they became more pronounced as he matured: his adamancy and enthusiasm for Bach's *St. Matthew Passion* were born not only of his wonder at its intrinsically musical qualities, but also of his pride in it as a masterpiece that represented the summit of German-speakers' cultural heritage,[63] and also in 1829 he both cursed (one-dimensional) "national music" (*Nationalmusik*) and conceived two of his most famously "national" works, the A-minor ("Scottish") Symphony and the *Hebrides* Overture.[64] By the mid-1840s he had acquired international distinction as a programmer and interpreter of works of virtually every European nationality, both at the piano and at the helm of the orchestra and chorus, and had lent his historical expertise also to the construction of an artistic identity for Handel that half a century later would be entirely too English and not sufficiently German for Friedrich Chrysander.[65] And like Goethe he cultivated this interpretive cultural diversity not as a polyglot or connoisseur, but as a means of enriching the cultural soil in which the seeds of creativity would fall: he expended considerable effort to bring Chopin, Liszt, and Berlioz to the Germans; Schubert to the English; Bach and Beethoven to the French and Italians; and so on. Goethe's project of *Weltliteratur* may in fact be the single most accurate way to explain the intercultural nature of Mendelssohn's re-creative persona as well as its origins.

Goethe's efforts to render cultural alterity powerless as a delimiter manifested themselves in more concrete terms in his voracious appetite for learning about alterity and his aspirations of formulating an understanding of the Other that would make sense not just as tolerance, but as acceptance. His efforts to live his philosophy of *Weltliteratur* as well as his prodigious curiosity made him a voracious devourer of writings about North and South American, Arab, Chinese, English, Finnish, French, Indian, Italian, Japanese, Persian, Scottish, Welsh, and other histories, cultures, literatures, and ideas. In many instances he translated these writings into German for inclusion in one of his or his circles' periodicals (*Chaos, Propyläen, Über Kunst und Altertum*); in others he seems to have undertaken the translation strictly for private purposes. During work on the Walpurgis Night scene for *Faust I* he checked out from the Weimar Court Library Erasmus Francisci's *Neu-Polirter Geschicht- Kunst- und Sittenspiegel ausländischer Völcker* (Newly Polished Mirror of the History, Art, and Morals of Foreign Peoples; Nuremberg, 1680),[66] one of the major works of comparative cultural studies of the early modern era and an important source of ideas on witches' Sabbaths in a variety of nations. Nor were his autodidactic enterprises limited to matters of national culture. He was equally interested—perhaps more so—in matters of religious and philosophical alterity. Although the latter efforts are partly accountable for the variety of theological influences he incorporated into his own system of beliefs, they also led to his fascination with the concept of heresy and the ideas of individuals historically deemed heretical. In his serial autobiography *Dichtung und Wahrheit,* he ascribed to this interest a real awakening of religious fervency, giving special credit to Gottfried Arnold's *Unpartheyischen Kirchen- und Ketzer- Historien, vom Anfang des Neuen Testaments bis auf das Jahr Christi 1688* (Unbiased History of Churches and Heretics, from the Beginning of the New Testament to AD 1688) and setting forth, as an example of how heretical ideas had proven foundational to his own beliefs, an unorthodox view of the Trinity and Satan:

> But I must nevertheless return to my discussion of that particular interest that inspired me in supernatural matters when I determined to develop my understanding of them as best as possible.
>
> I was significantly influenced in this by an important book that I came upon: Arnold's *Kirchen- und Ketzergeschichte.* This man is no merely reflective historian; he is at once pious and compassionate. His convictions agreed strongly with my own, and what especially delighted me about his book was that I received a favorable image of some heretics whom I had always heard described as mad or godless.
>
> A spirit of contradiction and a pleasure in paradoxes abides in us all. I studied differing opinions diligently, and since I had heard often enough that everyone has his own religion, nothing seemed more natural to me than the notion that I could create my own; this I did very comfortably. Platonism formed the foundation; hermetic, mystical, and cabbalistic ideas played their own roles; and so I constructed a world for myself that appeared quite unusual.
>
> I would certainly prefer to imagine a deity that creates itself out of eternity; but since production is inconceivable without numbers, it would have to materialize immediately

> as a second deity, which we recognize under the term of the Son. These two would then have to continue the act of production, and would thus reappear in the third one, which was every bit as alive and eternal as the whole. But with this the circle of divinity was closed, and even they would not be able to produce another who was fully their equal. Since the impulse for production continued on, however, they created a fourth one. But this one nurtured a contradiction already within itself in that it, like they, was supposed to be unconditionally yet simultaneously contained and defined by them. This one was Lucifer, to whom all creative power was henceforth extended, and from whom all remaining existence should proceed. . . . [67]

However intractable and otherwise troubling these ruminations may have been for some of Goethe's contemporary Christian readers, he maintained that he was "neither anti-Christian nor un-Christian, but decidedly non-Christian."[68]

Goethe's dedication to broadening his own understanding of ideas by systematically acquiring relevant information and studying other systems of belief would not have been alien to Mendelssohn, even though he was raised Lutheran, remained avowedly Christian to the end of his life, and pursued no such assertive exploration of religious alterity. His possession in 1844 of three collections of his paternal grandfather's writings might easily be ascribed to familial, cultural, or religious loyalty, but his close friendship with the Sanskrit scholar Friedrich Rosen (1805–37) and the titles of the specific three collections of Orientalist poetry by Rückert that he owned point to a more substantive engagement: *Die Verwandlungen des Abu Seid von Serug, oder die Maskamen des Heriri in freier Nachbildung von F. Rückert* (The Transformations of Abu Seid of Serug, or the Maskams of Heriri, Freely Recreated by F. Rückert); *Die Weisheit des Brahmanen: Ein Lehrgedicht in Bruckstücken* (The Brahmin's Wisdom: Fragments of an Educational Poem), and *Erbauliches und Beschauliches aus dem Morgenland* (Edifying and Contemplative [poems] from the Orient).[69] And despite his steadfast Lutheranism he was interested in and at least generally receptive to a number of other Christian confessions (most importantly, Roman Catholicism and Anglicanism). He also had a short-lived association with the "new Christianity" of the Saint-Simonians in Paris,[70] and by the end of his career he had sufficiently distanced himself from the anti-Semitic elements found in *St. Paul* (1836) that his final completed oratorio, *Elijah*, was able to address itself to Jewish as well as Christian audiences. His enduring success in this strategy is testified to by Alexander Ringer's account of a performance of *Elijah* given in the Oranienburgerstraße Synagogue in Berlin early in 1937. By Ringer's account (as summarized by Leon Botstein), that performance of the Lutheran Mendelssohn's strongly Christological late masterpiece achieved for the standing-room-only all-Jewish audience in Adolf Hitler's Berlin all the emotional intensity and religious fervor that one would naturally expect from "a Jewish work written by a German Jew affirming the greatness of Judaism."[71]

The most compelling parallels between Goethe's and Mendelssohn's efforts at cultural and religious translation, however, are their own creative engagements with literatures foreign to the public for which they were intended. In Goethe's case, these efforts generally take the form either of translations of other cultures' plays for production at the Weimar Court Theater, or of translations of other cultures' literature for publication independently or in one of his journals.[72] To the former group belong translations of Voltaire's *Le Fanatisme, ou Mahomet le prophète* (1799) and *Tancrède* (1800) and Euripides's *The Bacchantes* (1821–27) and *Phaeton* (1823). To the latter belong translations of all or part of Benvenuto Cellini's autobiography (1803), Diderot's *Le Neveu de Rameau* (1805), Maturin's *Bertram* (1817), Byron's *Manfred* (1820), and Manzoni's *L'Adelchi* (1826) and *Conte di Carmagnola* (1827). These translations represent a wide variety of sources ranging from Classical antiquity through French Classical and Naturalist theater to contemporary English, Italian, and Scottish poetry and prose; in many cases, their authors and subjects were invested with strong political connotations as well. Goethe's didactic attitude in bringing them before the German public is implicit but obvious: he acts as a cultural and linguistic intermediary who "translates" cultural alterity for that public, in the process adapting it so that it remains consistent with his own ideas and becomes comprehensible for his public (or, to borrow from his "maxims for translation" cited above, brings the authors of those foreign nations over to the German literary public so that it can view them as one of its own).

One of the most remarkable manifestations of Goethe's cultural and religious translations is his German rendering of Voltaire's (1694–1778) *Le Fanatisme, ou Mahomet le prophète* (Fanaticism, or, Muhammad the Prophet). In Voltaire's 1741 tragedy, the founder of Islam is portrayed as a charismatic, self-aggrandizing religious charlatan. He persuades a young follower, Séid, to murder one of his determined enemies, the Sheik Zopire, with the promise that in return he will be given Muhammad's slave girl Palmire (although the prophet has no intention of making good on this promise). Only after mortally wounding Zopire does Séid learn that the prophet's enemy is actually his own father; Palmire, his own sister. He vows to avenge his father's death by murdering Muhammad—but dies before he can do so, poisoned by Muhammad's servant Omar. Upon learning of Séid's death, Palmire denounces Muhammad to an assembled crowd in the hopes that they will recognize him for what he is and kill him. The people, however, believe his claims that righteousness is on his side and that Séid's death protected him from being murdered himself; they disperse, leaving the prophet and slave-girl alone. Before Muhammad can stop her she stabs herself to death with her brother's dagger, exclaiming "you shall rule. The world is made for tyrants" ("Tu dois régner; le monde est fait pour les tyrans"[73]). As the tragedy closes Muhammad first addresses the audience, stating that he will pay the price for his crimes with remorse, acknowledging his betrayal of God, and admonishing the fathers and children of his victims to avenge them and the heavens he has betrayed by overthrowing him immediately. But he then turns to Omar and tells him to hide the evidence of his weakness and salvage his glory; for "With God I shall rule the prejudiced universe; my empire will be destroyed if I am found out" ("Je dois régir en dieu l'univers prévenu; / Mon empire est détruit, si l'homme est reconnu"[74]).

Although Voltaire's play is (as the ordering of its title suggests) a lesson in the evils of religious fanaticism, of intolerance, and of passive compliance devoid of reason, it also characterizes Muhammad as an individual of unmitigated evil, a self-proclaimed prophet whose strongest beliefs are in himself rather than in his deity and whose strongest hunger is for power, the ruthless destruction of his opponents, and the perpetuation of his fame. This characterization posed a serious challenge for Goethe. He had translated excerpts from the Qur'an into German already in 1771–72 and also attempted his own tragedy on the subject of Muhammad (never finished). Tenets of the Qur'an inform much of the *West-östlicher Divan* (whose author "does not reject suspicions that he is a Muslim"[75]); and as late as 1819 he admitted to a Germany whose understanding of Islam was still virtually nonexistent that he "still reverently celebrate[d] that sacred night when the complete Qur'an was given to the prophet from above."[76] Thus, despite his enthusiasm for the play's moral, Goethe must have recognized Voltaire's poetic fancy. Consequently, when he translated *Le Fanatisme* for production at the Weimar Court Theater (at the suggestion of the Duke Karl August and against the advice of Schiller), he went to considerable lengths to retain the tragedy's lesson without defaming Islam or its founding prophet.[77] Some passages are excised; new passages of Goethe's own invention are inserted; the plan to destroy Zopire originates with Omar rather than Muhammad; and the verbiage that conveys the evil character of Voltaire's Muhammad is softened. In the end Goethe's prophet remains charismatic, but he is a wise and humanly fallible figure whose fatal flaws are self-preoccupation and credulousness—flaws not so different from those of his followers (or of Goethe's audiences).

This translation—for so the poet described it in his correspondence[78]—reveals the importance, for Goethe at least, of the translator's role as cultural mediator. The translator's charge was not to render literally or even faithfully from other nations to his own; it was to communicate honestly. For Goethe as for Voltaire, Muhammad personified Islam, through the Ottoman Empire the single most easily identifiable and militarily powerful Other to Western Europe at the turn of the nineteenth century. But Goethe's Other differs crucially from Voltaire's in two respects: the leader is an individual manifestation of his own people, and both Muhammad and Islam, subject to the same morals that apply to Goethe's German public, are reflections of that public itself. Goethe's translation teaches intolerance not of difference, but of fanaticism and self-preoccupation. The distinction between Self and Other is largely illusory—a lesson to which he would return in his Walpurgis Night treatments, as we shall see.

This essentially didactic attitude of functioning as a public cultural intermediary emerged in Mendelssohn's oeuvre at the outset of his career as an independent professional musician in 1833. As in Goethe's case, many of his creative mediations are translations in the usual modern sense as well as broader ones. Thus he composed songs to two poems by Byron but never considered publishing the settings in England, and he avoided the politically and personally charged Byronic persona that so attracted Berlioz, Schumann, Liszt, and (to a lesser extent) Goethe, emphasizing instead attributes that Goethe would describe as "English melancholy."[79] A similar approach to his function as musical mediator of culture obtains in the late choruses generally known under the opus number 69. These three works, all inspired by English Renaissance polyphony, were composed in English for mixed chorus with vocal soloists and organ accompaniment, intended for use in the Anglican service, and first published in that form. In the last months of his life, however, Mendelssohn decided to publish them in Germany as well—supplying German texts from the reformed Prussian agenda, applying a completely different doxology for one of the works, deleting the organ accompaniment, and rewriting the original solo passages for full chorus so that they retained the essentials of the fully composed organ part.[80] To these two cases numerous others could be added; collectively, they suggest that cultural delimiters to his own creative endeavors were so immaterial to Mendelssohn by the last years of his life that to assign a specific national provenance to the incidental music for *Antigone* or *Midsummer Night's Dream* (Opp. 55 and 61), *Elijah* (Op. 70), or the *Lauda Sion* (Op. posth. 73) is difficult or misleading.[81]

One of the most striking instances of Mendelssohn's activities as historical and cultural mediator stems, like Goethe's *Mahomet*, from the French classical theater: his incidental music for Racine's tragedy *Athalia*. This music adopts a strikingly similar approach to Mendelssohn's adopted role of public mediator between two cultures. Racine's play is adapted from the Biblical story of Athalia, queen of Judah, who usurped the throne after her husband's death.[82] In order to retain power she ordered that all members of the royal house be killed, but her son Joash escaped. For seven years of her reign, the people turned to the worship of Baal, but when Joash was revealed as the rightful heir to the throne the people revolted, overthrowing Athalia, rejecting the worship of Baal, and entering into a period of renewal under Joash's leadership.

Mendelssohn's *Athalia* was composed contemporaneously with his second setting of Goethe's "Die erste Walpurgisnacht" and the incidental music for Sophocles's *Antigone* and *Oedipus in Colonos* and Shakespeare's *A Midsummer Night's Dream*.[83] It was commissioned by the Prussian King Friedrich Wilhelm IV (fl. 1840–61), using Racine's French verses, premiered privately on December 1, 1845 (with a new German translation by Ernst Raupach of Racine's and Mendelssohn's French text), and posthumously published as Mendelssohn's Op. 74 in Germany and England in 1848.[84] On the face of things, this composition might appear to require little cultural translation, since the play's theme "that in heaven kings have a severe judge, innocence an avenger, and the orphan a father" ("Que les rois dans le ciel ont un juge sévère, L'innocence un vengeur, et l'orphelin un père"; V/8, ll. 1819–20),[85] while perhaps obscure, is hardly difficult. On the other hand, Mendelssohn here faced the issue of musically bridging the gap between the audiences of French neoclassical theater and his own audiences in nineteenth-century Prussia and England.

Mendelssohn's strategies for meeting this challenge are striking. In addition to providing a rousing entr'acte not specified by Racine (the "War March of the

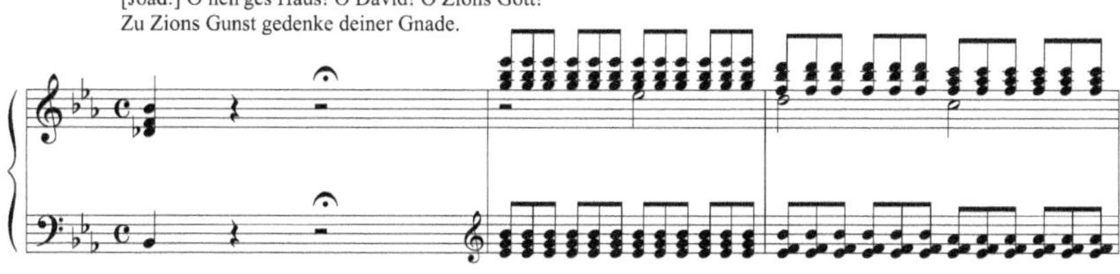

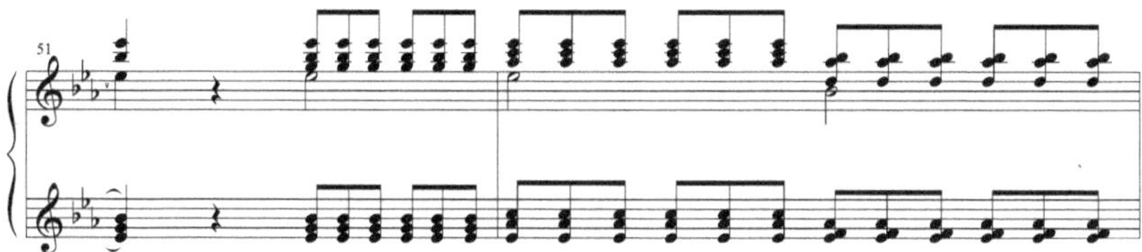

Example 2.1. Mendelssohn, Incidental Music to Racine's *Athalia,* Op. posth. 74: no. 3, mm. 45–52.

Priests," which remained extraordinarily popular into the twentieth century) and a recognizable modern framework for the whole by recalling the music of the opening chorus at the end, he inserts a setting of a modified version of the chorale "Ach Gott vom Himmel sieh' darein" near the end of No. 2 and a direct untexted quotation of the Advent chorale "Vom Himmel hoch, da komm' ich her" in No. 3, in the melodrama in which the high priest Joad prophesies the coming of the new Jerusalem (ex. 2.1).[86]

Mendelssohn's use of "Vom Himmel hoch" in the context of the *Athalia* music is a gesture of extraordinary polysemic significance. On the one hand, the chorale as a genre is contradictory if not anathematic to the tragedy's sources and historical participants (the Old Testament literary source, the Hebrew participants in the drama, and the creator and audiences of French neoclassicism). For listeners attenuated to this gestural antagonism, the scene would have been all the more provocative because the chorale solicited the sympathetic participation of protestant audiences and generated a pronounced Christological dimension absent from both the Biblical source and Racine's tragedy. By the same token, since it would have been ill-advised for the recently crowned Prussian monarch intent on sweeping religious and cultural renewal to invite comparison between himself and the play's titular protagonist, the contemporary relevance of the dramatic telos of *Athalia* for Mendelssohn's audiences certainly resided not in the play's literal subject matter or its moral warning, but allegorically in its consequences between the time of his assumption of the throne and the death of Jehoida. Celebrating the Old Testament king's strength, the house of Judah's defeat of its heathen enemies, and the renewal of the house of God, these consequences counterbalanced the Christological implications of the untexted chorale by focusing on the Old Testament, royal strength and courage, and God's protection of his chosen people and their leaders in the face of adversity. In brief, by introducing a new and potent level of anathema into Raupach's translation of Racine's adaptation of the Old Testament narrative through the untexted Lutheran chorale, Mendelssohn did more than just adopt a "strategy of dual perspective" (to borrow Sposato's phrase) that would enfranchise listeners from opposing sides of the drama's historical narrative. He also suggested the ethic of full communal participation that had played a crucial role in his invitation to join the Prussian monarch's reformist government, and that had been central to his public persona since the mid-1830s.[87]

The intensity of the religious and cultural paradox at the moment of the chorale's entrance epitomizes his didactic strategy of cultural and historical translation: it challenges listeners to formulate their own resolution of the numerous contradictory elements at hand, but it refuses to specify or dictate the nature of their emphasis. In this sense, the melodrama of Mendelssohn's *Athalia* adumbrates the composer's later fulfillment, in *Elijah* and the incomplete oratorio *Christus,* of the syncretic imperative so eloquently issued in the closing pages of his grandfather's *Jerusalem*:[88]

> Brothers, if you care for true piety, let us not feign agreement where diversity is evidently the plan and purpose of Providence. None of us thinks and feels exactly like his fellow man; why then do we wish to deceive each other with delusive words? . . . Rulers of the earth! . . . Our noblest treasure, the liberty to think, will be forfeited if you listen to [the counselors who wish to mislead you by smooth words to so harmful an undertaking]. For the sake of your felicity and ours, *a union of faiths is not tolerance*; it is diametrically opposed to true tolerance! . . . At least pave the way for a happy prosperity toward that height of culture, toward that universal tolerance of man for which reason still sighs in vain! Reward and punish no doctrine, tempt and bribe no one to adopt any religious opinion! Let everyone be permitted to speak as he thinks, to invoke God after his own manner or that of his fathers, and to seek eternal salvation where he thinks he may find it . . .[89]

♦ ♦ ♦

Racine's *Athalia,* Voltaire's *Le fanatisme,* Goethe's *Mahomet,* and Mendelssohn's *Athalia* may seem far removed from the worlds most obviously inhabited by the legends and lore of the Brocken and the Walpurgis Night. The distances among those worlds are deceptive, however; for the affinities among these works' subjects and between the two artists who dealt with them in their works are anything but remote. While abstaining from the contemporary discourses of nationalism and exoticism, both Mendelssohn and Goethe nevertheless engaged actively and creatively with the central issues of perceived essential differences between their respective audiences' Selves and their various Others—and in each case they opted not to affirm essential difference or even simply to tolerate it, but to accept it as an element consilient with their own idiom and the natural communication between themselves and their intended audiences. Moreover, in both *Mahomet* and *Athalie* they draw attention to their own translational interventions by means of ungrammaticalities vis-à-vis their respective contexts. Goethe, translating Racine's play for an audience comprised partly of rowdy students from the nearby university town of Jena and accustomed to lightweight court theatricals, and working with actors who employed only "natural" methods rather than the stylized ones essential for the serious theatrical repertoire he envisaged, wrote a work that would have required performers and audiences alike to participate in its complexities, and he assisted them in doing so by translating his original subject so that its message became intelligible and relevant to their own lives and experiences. Mendelssohn, likewise, established a pattern of adherence to his music's generic context (the Sophocles and Shakespeare incidental compositions) but employed a conspicuous stylistic ungrammaticality, the implicitly communal chorale, to solicit his audiences to bridge the gap between his source and themselves. Finally, in both instances Goethe and Mendelssohn contravened their sources, availing themselves of their established identities as social and cultural intermediaries to adopt an implicitly didactic posture and solicit their audiences to participate more fully in the works at hand—and thus to grasp their lessons more fully than would have been likely if they had been more faithful to their originals.

All this, in the context of works whose subjects revolve around a postulated enmity between Self and Other, is but a familiar application of the techniques they would use to treat the lore of the Brocken and the Walpurgis Night in the works that are the center of the following chapters.

Chapter Three

Reality and Illusion, Past and Present

Goethe and the Walpurgisnacht

By the early eighteenth century the Brocken was synonymous with the cultural topos of the Walpurgis Night, and the Harz Mountains generally had become known for their mysterious but forbiddingly rugged beauty. In a world increasingly committed to "civilization" but romantically fascinated with nature's most impenetrable domains, the Harz represented a challenge to humanity and an opportunity to contemplate the great mysteries of humankind's relationship to God and nature. The Mountains' abundant lore of ghosts, phantoms, and sundry otherworldly experiences (especially the Walpurgis Night itself) added the Supernatural to this potent mix. It is thus hardly surprising that the natural scientist, thinker, and poet Goethe dealt with the themes of the Brocken and Walpurgis Night in some way or another throughout his creative life. Drawing on a wide array of the fanciful depictions and the historical and fictitious sources discussed in chapters 1 and 2 as well as his own imagination, he touched on these themes countless times in his diaries, personal correspondence, and scientific prose, and drew inspiration from them in numerous literary productions.

A narrative reconstruction of Goethe's various lifelong engagements reveals a tightly woven web of intertextual relationships among the various literary manifestations of his interest in the legends and lore of the Brocken and the themes of Self and Other, so that the ballad "Die erste Walpurgisnacht," the *Urfaust,* the *Faust* Fragment, some of the *Faust*-related Paralipomena, the "Walpurgisnacht" and "Walpurgisnachtstraum" scenes from *Faust I,* and the "klassische Walpurgisnacht" from *Faust II* emerge as complementary literary commentaries on a central theme. Collectively, these texts reveal how his creative engagement and his international reputation combined to transform the topos of the Walpurgis Night from a widely known tale based on regional folklore into a powerful source of artistic commentary on an array of cultural, historical, and political issues.

Goethe's Engagements with the Brocken and the Walpurgis Night

The Walpurgis Night is a ubiquitous subject in Goethe's oeuvre. His earliest published engagement with it, the ballad "Die erste Walpurgisnacht" (1799), was certainly informed by his personal familiarity with the legends and lore of the Brocken, as well as his journeys to the summit in December 1777, September 1783, and September 1784.[1] The ballad also reflects his ongoing engagement with the theme of the historical and theological relationships between Christianity and other religions. The letters that document these biographical contexts offer vivid insights into the historical and symbolic import of Goethe's ballad and of the Walpurgis Night topos generally.

Although born and raised in Frankfurt am Main, Goethe was in a broader sense also a child of the Harz, for at least three generations of his paternal ancestors were born in the region and spent their entire lives there. In 1777 he made his first trip to the Brocken at the commission of the Duke Karl August of Sachsen-Weimar-Eisenach, his employer since 1775, with the charge of investigating the reestablishment of the coal mine at Ilmenau, near Erfurt. Because the novelist Goethe was already internationally famous for his epoch-making *Die Leiden des jungen Werthers* (The Sorrows of Young Werther; 1775), the *Naturforscher* Goethe made the trip incognito, traveling as Weber, a painter who had studied law. In preparation for his trip to the Brocken he reviewed Praetorius's *Blockes-Berges-Verrichtung* and perhaps also Johann Friedrich Löwen's well-known poem "Die Walpurgis Nacht," which he had known at least since he was sixteen.[2]

Goethe set out from the Weimar court in bad weather on November 29. Having endured constant rain and otherwise foul conditions for ten days, he arrived in Altenau on December 9. The following day he set out on foot for the city's *Torfhaus* (forester's house), whence he departed for the arduous climb up the Brocken with the forester Christoph Degen as a guide. The day's events were recorded succinctly but vividly in his diary and more poetically in a letter to Charlotte von Stein. The diary entry for December 10 reads:

> Early to the *Torfhaus* in deep snow. 10:15 [A.M.] set out from there onto the Brocken. Snow one ell deep.[3] 1:15 up on top. Fair, majestic moment, the whole world in clouds and mist[,] and up above everything [is] clear. What is a human that you think of? Around 4:00 head back again. In hostel with the forester in the *Torfhaus*.[4]

To Charlotte von Stein he explained the visit—especially his sense of triumph at having accomplished the ascent despite the assurances of all the locals that it was impossible, especially at this time of year:

> I want to reveal to you—do not tell anyone—that my trip was to the Harz Mountains, that I wanted to climb the Brocken. And now, Dearest, I have been up there, completely naturally, even though everyone for the past week has assured me that it's impossible.

> But the How and Why of all this I'll tell you when I see you again—[and] how gladly, I would not write just now!
>
> I would say: I have a wish for the full moon! Now, Dearest, I go out the front door, and there the Brocken stands before me in majestic moonlight beyond the spruces. I was up there today and I stood on the Devil's Altar and offered up my deepest gratitude to my God.
>
> I'll tell you the names of the places later. Just now I'm in the place they call the *Torfhaus*, a forester's hut two hours away from the Brocken.[5]

The following day he elaborated further:

> Just one more thing, for the memory's sake: as I reached the *Torfhaus* yesterday the forester was sitting there in shirtsleeves drinking his morning coffee. I spoke at length about the Brocken and he assured me that it was impossible to make the climb, and [told me] how he has often been up there in the summertime and how frivolous it would be to attempt it now. The mountains were cloaked in mist and you can see nothing, that's how it is up there now; you can't see three steps in front of your face; anyone who doesn't know exactly where he's going, etc. I sat there heavyhearted, halfway thinking that I should head back. And I felt like the king whom the prophet has shot down with an arrow and who shoots too little himself. I silently asked the gods to change this man's heart and the weather, and I was quiet. Then he said to me: now you can see the Brocken. I went to the window and it stood there before me as clear as my own face in the mirror. My spirits lifted, and I cried: And I'm supposed to not go there! Don't you have a servant, anyone—? And he said, "I'll go with you."—I scratched a drawing into [the frost on] the window as a sign of my tears of joy, and if I were writing to anyone other than you I would consider it a sin to write this. I didn't believe it [myself] until we reached the uppermost cliff. All the mists lay below us; up above it was majestically clear. All night last night until the early hours of the morning it was visible, and it was still dark when I set out at dawn this morning. . . .[6]

For Goethe, the Brocken was not only a rare constellation of fascinating natural phenomena (an aspect he would focus on in his report of his 1783 trip), but also a deeply personal, even spiritual, victory. The elements emphasized in his account to Charlotte von Stein also made their way into his literary treatments of the Brocken: a religiosity that worshipped Nature rather than God, with tongue-in-cheek hints at the legendary "witches' flight" (*Hexenfahrt*) and a flirtation with sacrilege ("I stood on the Devil's Altar and offered up my deepest gratitude to my God"); the image of light shining through the darkness; and of course the theme of humanity's capacity for overcoming superstition by reason—in this case, surmounting the Brocken's slopes during the most difficult time of year despite general assurances that the attempt was doomed to failure. Goethe managed to capture much of this symbolism in a deft pencil drawing, also completed in December 1777 (figure 3.1),[7] and equally vividly in his poem "Harzreise im Winter," also familiar in excerpt to music-lovers through Brahms's *Alto Rhapsody*, Op. 53. His commentary on the final version of that poem's penultimate stanza[8] explains it in terms of his own ascent to the peak of the Brocken:

Figure 3.1. Goethe's drawing of the Brocken (1770).

> [This stanza represents] an important, completely idealistic and indeed seemingly fantastic point whose basis in reality the poet would have to question, except that he still has a very gladdening document in his possession. I did actually stand at the summit of the Blocksberg at noon on 7 [*recte* 10] December, looking out over boundless snow between those ominous granite crags and with the most perfectly clear skies above me, out of which the sun burned mightily, so that there arose from my field-coat the familiar smoky odor of warm wool. Below me I beheld a motionless sea of clouds that covered the land in all directions and lower levels of cloud strata that suggested the mountains and valleys that lay beneath. . . .[9]

As Albrecht Schöne has demonstrated, the "social, political, moral, and poetic life" that was "bundled up into one hidden knot" in the original version of "Eine Harzreise im Winter" pronounced one further theme that is less evident in the final version of the poem, published twelve years later: the theme of the Brocken as a symbol of his own life, of nature as a prophetic allegory of a human existence independent of any deity, and transcendent of religion generally.[10] These views on the nature of humanity's relationship with God and the artistic and cultural beauties made possible outside as well as inside the theological boundaries of Christianity, so redolent of the theological controversies debated by Lessing and Moses Mendelssohn (see chapter 2), were further nurtured during his Italian journey (1786–88), during which he reveled in the opportunity to observe the legacies of Christianity and ancient paganism side by side—synchronically, as it were. After the *Roman Elegies* (1788–90) and *Venetian Epigrams* (1790),[11] they produced a densely interwoven web of impressive poetic statements dealing expressly with conflicts between Christianity and its pagan Others in mid-1797. Included among these were the little-known ballad "Der Gott und die Bajadere" (The God and the Temple Dancer, June 9) and, more notably, "Die Braut von Korinth" (The Bride of Corinth, June 5), which portrays the triumph of Christianity over paganism as an incursion into the sensual nature of humankind rather than the victory of a superior religion.[12] But these works are minor compared to another long-term artistic project that occupied Goethe during his Italian sojourn, and that also entered its final stages of maturation in that remarkable summer of 1797: his epic recounting of the *Faust* legend, undertaken as early as 1769. Goethe had conceived the *Walpurgisnachtstraum* (Walpurgis Night's Dream) in connection with the tragedy already before 1775,[13] and he included clear allusions to the Walpurgis Night and the aberrations of the Brocken already in the scene in Auerbach's Kellar of the *Urfaust* (1775, posthumously published in 1887);[14] the latter were reinforced in the *Faust-Fragment* published in 1790.[15] Although the Walpurgis Night and Walpurgis Night's Dream scenes were omitted in the *Fragment*, Goethe probably had at least some idea of their content by then, since he had already drafted the "Trüber Tag—Feld" (Dull Day—Field) scene and must have been aware of the size of the dramatic gap between the end of the Cathedral scene and the beginning of that one (ll. 3834 and 4399ff. of the final version).[16]

In fact, the compositional history of the tragedy suggests that the two Walpurgis Night scenes and the Walpurgis Night's Dream became increasingly important in his thinking about the plot of the tragedy over the course of the 1790s. He took up the idea of using them to bridge the dramatic gap after the end of the Cathedral scene anew sometime in 1786 or 1787, but had not yet worked it out when he prepared the *Faust-Fragment* for publication in 1789–90.[17] By this point his ideas for the scene had already become even more developed. Rather than further delay publication on the project (which by then was already two decades old) in order to finish crafting the bridge that would span the dramatic gap, however, Goethe decided to break off the text entirely at the end of the Cathedral scene, omitting the material that had already been completed to follow that scene in the *Urfaust*. He thus avoided the juncture altogether for the time being.

The general philo-heathen sentiment that manifested itself in Goethe's poems of mid-1797 thus offered a solution for a longstanding problem. Between then and 1801 he completed the essentials of the *Walpurgisnacht* and *Walpurgisnachtstraum* scene in *Faust I*—indeed, it was these scenes that launched this stage of work on the project, for only after they had been drafted did he turn to the "Prolog in Heaven" and the scene in the study.[18] On December 6, 1797, Goethe borrowed one of the major sources concerning the Walpurgis Night legend, Francisci's *Neu-polirter Geschicht- Kunst- und Sittenspiegel ausländischer Völcker* (see chapter 2), from the Weimar Court Library, and in a letter to Schiller dated December 20, he proposed the *Walpurgisnachtstraum* scene (as it then existed) for inclusion in the latter's 1798 *Almanach*.[19] Schiller declined to publish the scene, but since the Walpurgis Night's Dream scene coheres with the Walpurgis Night scene itself and Goethe was using the Francisci text in December 1797, the main scene probably was at least drafted in late 1797 or early 1798.

In the following year Goethe undertook a different treatment of the Walpurgis Night, and on the theme of the conflict between Christianity and paganism, penning the ballad "Die erste Walpurgisnacht" on July 30, 1799.[20] Diminutive in comparison to the formidable *Faust* project, the ninety-nine-line ballad is nevertheless revealing as a document of Goethe's personal and theological contemplations on the Brocken's most famous engagement with Good and Evil, Self and Other. It would also prove to have a prominent place in music history in settings by Karl Loewe (1833) and Mendelssohn.[21]

Goethe's smaller *Walpurgisnacht* treatment led to two of the more famous poetic/musical friendships in the annals of nineteenth-century music. On August 5, 1799, the poet wrote to the Berlin publisher and bookseller Johann Friedrich Gottlob Unger (1753–1804) praising Karl Friedrich Zelter (1758–1832) and implying that the poems of his recently published *Neue Schriften* would benefit if "that admirable artist" ("dieser fürtreffliche Künstler") were to set some of them to music.[22] Zelter, whose first published collection of songs (Leipzig and Berlin: Carl August Nicolai, 1796) had included settings of five of Goethe's poems, ventured to write to the Weimar master on August 11, thanking him for his praise and offering to send Goethe some of his more recent settings of his poems.[23] Goethe's response probably included more than Zelter would have dared to hope for:

> With sincere gratitude I answer your amiable letter, in which you would like to express to me what I have already been convinced of through your compositions: that you take a lively interest in my works and have dedicated yourself to some of them with a true aptitude. The nice thing about an active interest is that it continues to create. For if my lyric texts have given you occasion to create music, I can also say that your melodies have awakened me to lyric texts, and I would certainly find myself lifted into a lyric disposition more often than I do now if we lived closer together. You will bring me a true pleasure by sharing anything at all with me.
>
> I enclose a production with a rather unusual appearance. It came into being through the idea that one might craft dramatic ballads in such a fashion that they would offer the composer material for a larger vocal piece. Unfortunately, the present [production] is not worthy of such a great effort.[24]

The "production with a rather unusual appearance" was of course the ballad "Die erste Walpurgisnacht." Zelter thanked the poet and offered a few comments on September 21:

> I received your esteemed letter of 26 August on the 30th. "Die erste Walpurgisnacht" is a most singular poem. The verses are musical and suitable for singing. I wanted to include it in a musical setting in this letter and have worked out a good portion of it, but I cannot find the breath that breathes through the whole, so it unfortunately should be set aside [for now].[25]

Despite his disclaimer about the merits of his "unusual production," Goethe published "Die erste Walpurgisnacht" in 1800. This accomplished, he also drafted the bulk of the *Walpurgisnacht* scene from *Faust I* between November 1800 and February 1801.[26] On November 5, 1800, he dated an autograph draft for the *Walpurgisnacht* scene directly beneath l. 3911 ("Die sich mehren, die sich blähen"), and on February 9, 1801 he inscribed the date just beneath line 3935 ("Ich spüre schon die ungestümen Gäste") in the same manuscript. This document—one of only two surviving autographs for any substantial portion of the final version of *Faust I*[27]—thus establishes that these 101 lines were finished by February 9, 1801. Moreover, since the main text of the manuscript page that contains lines 3835–3911 is a clean copy in the hand of Goethe's copyist Johann Jakob Ludwig Geist (1776–1854) with autograph entries by the poet, while the remainder of the manuscript is in Goethe's own hand in the same ink as that used by Geist, we may surmise that at least those lines had already been written before November 1800.[28] Lines 3936 to 3955 (from "Wie rast die Windsbraut durch die Luft!" to "Strömt ein wütender Zaubergesang!") were begun, completed, and evidently revised on February 8, 1801. Lines 3956 to 4095 (from "Die Hexen zu dem Brocken ziehn" to "So ist die Welt auch auf der Neige") were written on either February 9 or 10, 1801.[29] The remainder of the autograph seems to have been written between February 10 and early March, and during that time period Goethe checked out numerous books pertaining to the Walpurgis Night's lore and legends—among them Praetorius's *Blockes-Berges Verrichtung* (see chapter 1).

In the meantime, Zelter was still unable to set "Die erste Walpurgisnacht" to music. On November 3, 1802, Goethe wrote that he was considering preparing a new collection of his short poems for publication,[30] and this reminder seems to have prodded Zelter into acknowledging that he had been unable to seize the opportunity presented him when Goethe sent him the *Walpurgisnacht* poem. On December 12 he wrote to the poet, acknowledging his inaction and explaining the nature of the difficulty:

> The good news that you are considering sharing some of your treasures with the world awakened me as well, and I have since tried my hand again at some of your poems. What you said to me once in connection with the "Erste Walpurgisnacht" concerning the dramatic form of romances confirmed a tendency that I had already attempted to develop in [my setting of] "Der Zauberlehrling."[31] But the "Walpurgisnacht" remained unfinished because the old played-out form of the cantata kept imposing itself on me. . . .[32]

This confession evidently satisfied the poet, who did not raise the issue of his earlier setting again. From here on, Goethe's engagement with the subject was limited to the *Faust* project.

Work on *Faust*, already generally disrupted by the Napoleonic Wars, suffered greatly beginning around 1803. But in the spring of 1806 he took up the project with renewed vigor. Between March 21 and April 25, 1806, amid the final revisions in the manuscript, he was still working on the *Walpurgisnacht* scene:

he recorded work on it on April 3, and notated its (evidently provisional) completion on April 4.[33] Part I of *Faust* was submitted to Cotta for publication in May 1806, but the Battle of Jena (October 14, 1806) and Napoleon's invasion and occupation of most of the German-speaking territories delayed its appearance until 1808.[34]

It took some time for *Faust I* to become widely known. It raised a few eyebrows relatively soon within the German-speaking countries, but only after the publication of Germaine de Staël's *De L'Allemagne* in 1813 did it begin to attract widespread attention—and then it did so primarily by strengthening the critical antagonisms between Goethe's many detractors and his admirers (see chapter 6). Its imaginative interpretation of the Walpurgis Night, along with its quirky scene of the Walpurgis Night's Dream, only contributed to the Romantic fascination with the Brocken and its famed spring Sabbath. Perhaps in response to this growing topicality, or perhaps because of the more personal friendship that had developed between Zelter and Goethe in the wake of the suicide of Zelter's step-son,[35] Zelter brought up the matter of "Die erste Walpurgisnacht" again in 1812. By now he felt he had come to terms with the poem's form but wished to know more about its historical subject; he had consulted chapter 8 of book VI of Julius Caesar's *Commentaries on the Gallic War* but found this information "insufficient and too old" for his purposes.[36] The poet replied in detail:

> But I still have to respond to your inquiry regarding "Die erste Walpurgisnacht." The answer goes something like this. Among historians there are some—and they are men to whom one cannot deny respect—who seek a real basis for every fable and every tradition, no matter how absurd, and who always believe that they have found a factual core inside the hull of every fairy tale.
>
> We owe a great deal of good to this approach, for to make prose out of such poetry requires a great deal of knowledge or indeed spirit, cleverness, and imagination, just for starters. So it is that one of the German investigators of early history has wished to discover a historical origin for the witches' and devils' ride on the Brocken, which has been known in Germany since time immemorial, in order to rescue and justify it. Thus, the German pagan priests and elders, after they had been driven out of their sacred groves and Christianity had been forced on the populace, withdrew with their faithful followers into the desolate, inaccessible Harz mountains in the early spring, so that they could offer up their prayers and their fires to the incorporeal god of heaven and earth, according to ancient custom. To protect themselves from the spying, armed converts [to Christianity] they decided that it was advisable to disguise some of their members and thereby to keep their superstitious adversaries at a distance, and thus protected by devils' masks to carry out the purest of worship services.
>
> I happened upon this explanation somewhere or other many years ago; I couldn't tell you who the author was. The idea appealed to me, and so I have made this fable-like history back into a poetic fable.[37]

If this thorough explanation provided more information than Zelter had expected, he did not show it in his response. Instead, he conveyed his gratitude philosophically:

> For the explanation of the "Erste Walpurgisnacht" you have my deepest thanks. I have truly taken it according to your description—i.e., poetically—and the historical aspect now speaks for itself. From experience I have noted that background information occasionally leads to allusions that impart to a melody a kind of clarity and truth that animate one's comprehension in such a way that part of the effort is achieved automatically. This is especially true of me, who so often requires external stimuli.[38]

Unfortunately, Zelter's response raises more questions than it answers—for although it suggests that he had finally succeeded in setting the ballad to music, no such setting survives and there is no other evidence to suggest that it ever existed. That Zelter deliberately misled his close friend, suggesting that he had set a text that he had not, is unlikely. Instead, since he neither sends his setting nor describes it in the sort of detail that by then had become customary in describing his works to the poet, it is easier to speculate that he later became dissatisfied with his effort and destroyed it. We may in any event surmise that Goethe never saw Zelter's setting, since he never referred to it in the dozens of letters they exchanged in the remaining twenty years of their correspondence. But the initiative did not fall on barren soil—for the task of setting "Die erste Walpurgisnacht" would be undertaken by Felix Mendelssohn Bartholdy in the last years of his mentors' lives. When Goethe learned in 1831 that Mendelssohn had set his poem to music, he offered his third commentary on its meaning and his compositional intentions in writing it. This time, he explained the poem in terms of its symbolic import, in the process invoking the same imagery of light and clarity that is central to the poem itself:

> With your first letter from Rome, my dear son, you brought me so much happiness that I now have every reason to express my gratitude for your second one, written from Lucerne. A letter that Zelter says you had written from Milan did not reach me.
>
> . . . It pleases me greatly that you have dedicated yourself so seriously to "Die erste Walpurgisnacht," for no one has been able to make anything out of this poem, not even our excellent Zelter. It is intended as elevated symbolism in the literal sense. For in the history of the world it must eternally be repeated that something old, established, proven, [and] reassuring will be compacted, pushed aside, dislocated, and, if not abolished, then corralled into the tightest space by emergent new forces. The middle period, in which the hatred is still capable of reacting, and still may do so, is presented here succinctly enough, and a joyous, indestructible enthusiasm flares up once again with brilliance and clarity. I'm certain you have brought life and meaning to all this. May it therefore likewise thrive in my [own] joyous pleasure.[39]

The otherwise enigmatic musical fate of Goethe's 1799 ballad and the publication of *Faust I* did not mark the end of the poet's creative engagements with the Walpurgis Night theme. In 1800 he drafted the *Helena-Dichtung*, whose essential thematic and motivic material adumbrates the "Classical Walpurgis Night" that ends the second act of *Faust II*, and on December 16, 1816, he dictated a summary of his plans for the second part that reveals his general plan to include a Classical counterpart to the Walpurgis Night of *Faust I* in the tragedy's continuation.[40]

The early 1820s saw no further work on *Faust II* (although Goethe was involved with one private and one public performance of excerpts from part I), but in the spring of 1825 he took up the project with renewed vigor.

This final chapter of the tragedy's genesis is remarkable in its compactness. Whereas *Faust I* occupied Goethe for nearly forty years from the earliest known preparatory drafts to its publication in 1808, *Faust II* was completed in only five years. In April 1827 the *Helena-Dichtung* was published as a "Classic-Romantic Phantasmagoria: Interlude to Faust," and from the summer of that year until 1831 the tragedy's completion was Goethe's main artistic project. Late in 1830 he published the first 1,424 lines of Act I, at the same time undertaking further large-scale revisions for the remainder of the work.

Finished on January 24, 1832,[41] *Faust II* was Goethe's last completed work as well as his last engagement with the subject of the Walpurgis Night. Although its genesis was neither as protracted nor as difficult as that of *Faust I*, it is significant for purposes of this inquiry because its engagement with the *Walpurgisnacht* theme is at least as important as that in *Faust I*—indeed, arguably even more so. Moreover, the years of the *Faust* tragedy's genesis witnessed several republications of the 1799 ballad "Die erste Walpurgisnacht"—and although Zelter evidently never was able to follow through on the opportunity presented by the 1799 *Walpurgisnacht* treatment, it was kept alive by his star pupil (Mendelssohn), in a remarkable manifestation of what Julie D. Prandi has termed the "kindred spirits" of poet and composer.[42]

"Die erste Walpurgisnacht"

Published in 1800 by Cotta in the seventh issue of Goethe's *Neue Schriften*, the ballad "Die erste Walpurgisnacht" (The First Walpurgis Night) is unique among his treatments of the Walpurgis Night topos in that it addresses its subject not by investing in the supernatural lore of the Brocken, but by recounting a rational and natural hypothetical explanation for that lore (see appendix 3.1, pp. 74–77). Taking as its starting point the speculative historical explanations submitted in Honemann's *Die Alterthümer des Harzes*, the 1796 *Berlinsches Archiv der Zeit und ihres Geschmacks*, and Fischer's *Buch vom Aberglauben*,[43] the ballad is based on Charlemagne's forceful imposition of Christianity on the Saxons. Goethe's evident sources for this historical starting point situate its narrative in the Harz Mountains, and its portrayal of the interactions between the pagans and the Christians suggests a time period of between 768 and 804.

The ballad's narrative is divided into two parts of approximately equal length. The first six stanzas (ll. 1–49) establish this contextual conflict and the preparations for the Walpurgis Night, and the second six (ll. 50–99) depict the Walpurgis Night itself. Stanzas 1 and 2 depict the druids' eagerness to celebrate the *Allvater* (literally, "all-father," that is, Wuotan), but in stanza 3 a man from among the people reminds them that these rites are punishable by death, and that by conducting their rites they imperil their women and children. The women echo these fears in stanza 4, but in stanza 5 one of the druids insists that "anyone who shies away from sacrifice today has earned his bondage." He then offers to surround the area with guards so that the others can worship in safety. In stanza 6 the guards disperse, but in stanza 7 one of them hatches a plan to outwit the "foolish cleric-Christians" (*dumpfe Pfaffenchristen*) by disguising themselves as "their own fabled devil" and scaring them away; these events, of course, mark the beginning of the Walpurgis Night per se. His idea is taken up by the other guards in stanza 8. But in stanza 9 the scene shifts to another druid, who laments that the situation has become so bad that they have to praise the *Allvater* under cover of darkness, asks the *Allvater* to purify their faith as "the flame purifies itself of smoke," and prays that they never lose sight of his light even if they are forced to abandon their ancient rites. Stanzas 10 and 11 then portray first a Christian guard terrified by the ruse of a pagan Sabbath carried out by the pagan guards, then the terror of the group of Christian guards as they flee in the face of the evil they believe they behold. The final stanza reverts to the pagans, who, safe from the threat of religious persecution for the time being, collectively proclaim the second druid's prayer for a pure and steadfast faith in time of adversity: "And if we are robbed of our ancient rite: who can rob us of your light!"

The poem is remarkable in several ways. Not least of all, its imagery and action invoke both sides, pagan and Christian, of the Walpurgis Night rituals cultivated in Goethe's own time, as discussed in chapter 1. The pagans' ritual fire is lit atop the highest peak, the Brocken, a practice that is consistent not only with the Walpurgis Night/Beltane fires customarily used in pagan ceremonies, but also with the contemporary use of enormous bonfires to defend against witches (or as the Swedish Walpurgis Night custom was called, "burning the witches"). On the other hand, the fact that Goethe's pagans avail themselves of a great "racket" or "ruckus" made by "wild clappers" (ll. 56, 65, 72, 85) mirrors the contemporary Christian customs of cracking whips, beating the ground and the houses with boards, firing shots, and shouting while rattling tin cans and kettles in order to chase away the witches and demons. The suggestion is clear: these protagonists are not pagan Others to the poem's intended readers; they are reflections of the readers themselves.

Although "Die erste Walpurgisnacht" is only one of Goethe's numerous writings that deal sympathetically with religions other than Christianity, it stands out as the one most obviously situated in the German-speaking countries. Its topography draws on the evocative Harz profile depicted in Goethe's 1777 drawing (see figure 3.1, p. 57): an exposed, snow-covered summit where the pagan rites are celebrated, a lower ground from which the Christian guards witness the rites and believe that they see "wolf-men and dragon-women" flying overhead, and a wooded mid-ground where the pagans live and carry out their faux-demonic ruse. The drawing itself was published only posthumously, but the ballad's titular reference to the Walpurgis Night would have easily led Goethe's contemporaries to infer the Brocken because of legends associated with that fabled night and the widespread fame of the Harz Mountains in general. For the cosmopolitan Goethe, this probably would have marked a commonality with the Egyptian, Greek, Roman, and other pagan cultures dealt with elsewhere in his writing. For eighteenth- and nineteenth-century German nationalists such as Maurer who saw the Saxon tribes' adoption of Christianity as a surrender to foreign dominion, however, it was a celebration of a noble past that also beckoned for future unity in a shared national culture.

The poem's topography is likewise symbolic. The wooded mid-ground where the pagans live and their guards carry out the ruse conceals not only the existence of the pagans but also the fact that the "wolf-men and dragon-women," along with their attendant racket, are a ruse. This symbolic middle ground possesses neither the religious fervor of the ceremonies atop the mountain nor the violence and cowardice of the Christian guards. The Christian guards, murderers of the pagans' women and children, persecute them out of ignorance and abandon their posts out of fear born of superstition; accordingly, they occupy the low ground. And what occurs atop the Brocken is not the devilish orgy imagined by the Christian guards, but a pure and noble worship service whose fire is benevolent, wise, courageous, fervent. In a word, the poem's topographical strata are commentaries on the protagonists and what they represent.

Also remarkable is the ballad's poetic technique, particularly in its diction and structure. The former category embraces not only word repetitions that emphasize the poem's main points—words and word variants such as "Flamme" (flame; seven times), "Licht" (light; twice); "Brande" (fire; once); and "Glut" (glow; once)—but also several instances of what might be termed "sound-symbolism." The central image of light (symbolizing the pagans' sacrificial fire as well as wisdom, goodness, and purity) consistently employs the back vowels "a" and "u," as well as the diphthong "ai" ("rein," "reinigt," "eilen," "heilig"), whereas the vowel "ö," sparingly used elsewhere, figures prominently in the lines entrusted to the terrified Christian sentinels ("Hölle," "-wölf," "Getöse," "Böse," etc.). And, of course, the "howl" called for in lines 58–59 and 64–65 is built into the most prominent vowels of stanzas 7 and 8: "Teufel," "Kauz," "Eule," "Heul," "Geheule."[44] (These features may reflect Goethe's hope that the poem would be set to music, since singers would naturally appreciate the distinctive effect of these recurrent sounds—especially the "au" and "eu" sounds—in prominently accented positions, as is the case in this poem.)

Moreover, into the narrative's overarching binary structure Goethe enfolds a subordinate ternary structure delineated by its sequence of dramatis personae (see figure 3.2).[45] After an introductory strophe of thirteen iambic lines of identical metrical structure declaimed by an individual pagan (stanzas 1, 5, and 9; subsection *a* in figure 3.2), each of the three sections (ll. 1–32, 33–65, and 66–99) comprises three analogous segments: a four-line modified repetition of the individual pagan's final lines, entrusted now to the group (stanzas 2, 6, and 12; subsection *b*); a counter-solo of ten to eleven rhymed trochaic lines (stanzas 3, 7, and 10; subsection *c*); and a counter-chorus of five to six lines whose content,

Dark shading = Introduction / Preparation for the Walpurgis Night
Solid shading = Walpurgis Night proper

Section 1 (ll. 1–32)	Stanza 1 a Solo 1 ll. 1–13	Stanza 2 b Chorus 1 ll. 14–17	Stanza 3 c Solo 2 ll. 17–27	Stanza 4 d Chorus 2 ll. 28–32
Section 2 (ll. 33–65)	Stanza 5 a Solo 1 ll. 33–45	Stanza 6 b Chorus 1 ll. 46–49	Stanza 7 c Solo 2 ll. 50–59	Stanza 8 d Chorus 2 ll. 60–65
Section 3 (ll. 66–99)	Stanza 9 a Solo 1 ll. 66–78	Stanza 10 c Solo 2 ll. 79–89	Stanza 11 d Chorus 2 ll. 90–95	Stanza 12 b Chorus 1 ll. 96–99

Figure 3.2. Structure of Goethe, "Die erste Walpurgisnacht," after Meredith Lee, "Poetic Intentions and Musical Production: 'Die erste Walpurgisnacht,' *Goethe Yearbook* 12 (2004):84.

meter, and rhyme echo those of the counter-solo (stanzas 4, 8, and 11; subsection *d*). The anomalous stanzas—that is, those that displace the final pagan ensemble echo of stanza 9—are, of course, those of the anomalous Others in the ballad's dramatis personae, the Christian sentinels. This structural displacement did not just facilitate a choral finale for the "larger vocal piece" Goethe envisioned in writing his poem. By disrupting the poem's otherwise regular narrative sequence it also realizes structurally a crucial feature of the narrative: the fact that the action of stanzas 8, 9, and 12 occurs simultaneously with that of stanza pair 10/11: the Saxon sentinels carry out their ruse while the rites are being conducted atop the Brocken, and their Christian adversaries presumably witness

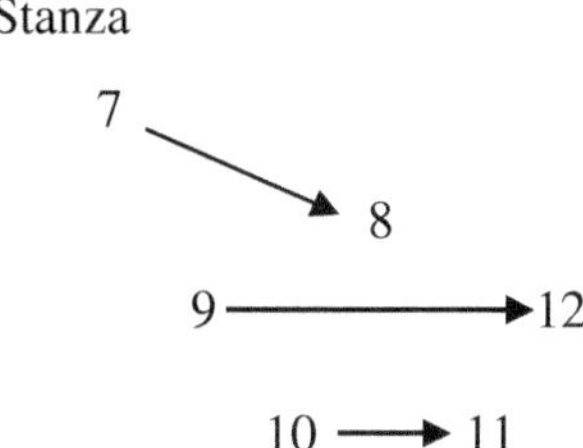

Figure 3.3. Temporal layering in second half of Goethe, "Die erste Walpurgisnacht" (by stanza).

the twin spectacles and flee while the ruse and the rites are in progress, not afterward. This structural anomaly (similar to the cinematic technique known as interfolding) reflects the narrative/diegetic anomaly of the last four stanzas as well as the alterity of the ballad's Christian sentinels (see figure 3.3).

More generally, by having its Saxon protagonists invoke values that are common to both Christianity and its pagan Others, and by casting them as monotheistic or quasi-monotheistic (praying to a single *Allvater*, even though this does not preclude their belief in other deities as well),[46] it downplays the differences between Christianity and paganism and emphasizes their theological affinities. These Christian/pagan parallels, too, are manifested in the poem's structure, for in strophes 10 and 11 the Christian sentinels speak in the same counter-solo/counter-chorus sequence employed for the pagan populace and the pagan guards in strophes 3–4 and 7–8. Moreover, the number of lines entrusted to the Christians in strophes 10–11 approximates those of the corresponding pagan strophes (11 + 6 for the Christians vs. 10 + 5 and 10 + 6 for the pagans in stanzas 3–4 and 7–8, respectively).

The larger implication of the structurally anomalous Christian stanzas, however, lies in the irony that they flee in fear of a ruse, not a reality; and that the ruse is made necessary by their incognizance of the truth that their adversaries celebrate values they themselves share. This theme of illusion vs. reality is manifested in the final chorus (stanza 12), where the metaphor of flame and smoke as symbols for light (= truth) and darkness (= ignorance) invokes values shared by many religions. The implicit admonition is that the poem's cultural alterity is self-imposed, and that the conflict between paganism and Christianity is borne of a lack of understanding that has no place in their common value-system: "The flame purifies itself of smoke: / So purify our faith! / And if we are robbed of our ancient rite: / who can rob us of your light!"

Finally, "Die erste Walpurgisnacht" stands out among Goethe's poems because Goethe explained his compositional intentions for this little poem no fewer than three times, in 1799, 1812, and 1831. The first of these letters reveals that the poem was conceived as a "dramatic ballad"—that is, a ballad whose narrative unfolds through interactive dialog without recourse to a narrative persona—and with the hope that it would be used for musical composition. In specifically musical terms, the challenges of this concept are significant. The term "ballad" specifically links the poem to works such as "Erlkönig," although that link must be qualified as applicable only to the latter's central six stanzas (i.e., those in which the father, the son, and the Erl-King speak, rather than the narrator). "Die erste Walpurgisnacht" raises practical issues in this regard, however, since it explicitly calls for choral material in strophes 2, 4, 6, 8, 11, and 12. More important is that the simultaneity of the action between stanza pairs 8/9 and 10/11 would call for an elaborate ensemble in which the various personae are entrusted with contrasting material within an overriding unity—as, for example, in the ensemble finales of Mozart, whom Goethe revered. But "Die erste Walpurgisnacht" was not intended to be staged, and the absence of a narrator together with the presence of choral material suggested the genre of the cantata—a genre to which Zelter expressed an aversion in 1802, evidently in the belief that the poet felt likewise.[47] These issues of genre and medium bedeviled not just Zelter, but also Mendelssohn, Loewe, Berlioz, and numerous other nineteenth-century composers and commentators (see chapters 5 and 6).

Goethe's two later commentaries on "Die erste Walpurgisnacht" are best viewed as a complementary pair. He attributes the content of the poem to the efforts of "one of the German investigators of early history" to "discover a historical origin for the witches' and devils' ride on the Brocken, which has been known in Germany since time immemorial, in order to rescue and justify it." Yet despite his evident skepticism concerning the efforts of those "who seek a real basis for every fable and every tradition, no matter how absurd, and who always believe that they have found a factual core inside the hull of every fairy tale," he also terms his poem "a poetic fable," thus implying that it, like most fables, illustrates a moral—often one epigrammatically expressed at the end. He then describes the nature and symbolic import of this moral in the letter he penned upon learning that Mendelssohn had completed the compositional task that had stumped Zelter for nearly forty years. The poem symbolizes an eternal historical process whereby opposing forces come into conflict and the old (in this instance, paganism) is pushed aside by the new (in this instance, Christianity). By depicting the Christian sentinels' terrified flight and granting to their pagan adversaries a momentary victory to practice their religion securely, however, he departs from his contemporaries' usual self-congratulatory diachronicity, focusing instead on "the middle period, in which . . . an indestructible enthusiasm flares up once again with brilliance and clarity" (see p. 62, above).

But this "elevated symbolism" also by definition points to some further significance—as Goethe hints in appropriating the poem's imagery of fire/light, brilliance, and clarity for the last sentence of his explanation, and by describing his own "joyous pleasure" in learning of Mendelssohn's setting in language redolent of the "joyous enthusiasm" that "flares up . . . succinctly" in the poem itself (see p. 62, above). This higher symbolic meaning, again, resides in the structurally anomalous final stanza-group. Far from adopting an anti-Christian, propagan, or other partisan religious stance, the poem articulates values common to many religions: the importance of a deep, pure, joyous faith; of steadfastness and resilience in adversity; and of communal participation in the celebration of those ideals. Only those who practice intolerance and narrow-mindedness are banished from the celebration. It emphasizes these values partly through repetition, partly through form, and partly through the use of conventional Enlightenment symbolism. The final stanza's words are repeated from stanza 9; their position at the end (a violation of the pattern of adjacent repetition practiced earlier in the poem) naturally grants them prominence; and the images of light and sacrificial fire are ubiquitous Enlightenment symbols for goodness, knowledge, truth, and wisdom.

Most important, though, is the poem's stance concerning the historical adversity between Christianity and other religions. By departing from eighteenth-century literature's usual portrayals of alterity in a predominantly Christian society, Goethe enfranchises the reader in his own skepticism regarding the wisdom of those portrayals, and indeed the degree and extent of the pagans' alterity. The Otherness of the persecuted pagans in "Die erste Walpurgisnacht" is itself an illusion. Therefore, what is necessary in the eternal historical processes of conflict, resistance, and the temporary victory of the "emergent new forces" over what is "old, established, proven, [and] reassuring" is not true alterity, but those forces' perception that it is Other. In "Die erste Walpurgisnacht" as in the *Roman Elegies* and *Venetian Epigrams,*[48] Goethe emphasizes the beauty and nobility of what stands outside the cultural and historical mainstream. But in this little poem's portrayal of the past as something indestructible and still very much a part of the present, he affirms the view of history as a phenomenon that is at once synchronic and diachronic, a view best known through the work that spanned almost all of his creative life: the *Faust* tragedy, begun by the 1770s and completed just weeks before the onset of his final illness early in 1832.

The *Faust* Tragedy

Hector Berlioz asserted that Mendelssohn's setting of Goethe's "Die erste Walpurgisnacht" had "no connection with the Witches' Sabbath in *Faust.*"[49] This statement requires qualification. It is true that the 1799 ballad does not include Faust, Mephistopheles, and the other characters of the "Walpurgisnacht" scenes from both parts of the tragedy. Nevertheless, it, too, is set in and around the Brocken (as Goethe's 1812 explanation to Zelter makes clear), and it deals substantively with many of the same issues and themes represented in those larger poetic/dramatic renderings. That the ballad was penned near the beginning of Goethe's renewed work on the tragedy that had already become his *Lebensarbeit* is no coincidence—nor is it by chance that those renewed efforts were launched by the *Walpurgisnacht* and *Walpurgisnachtstraum* scenes themselves (see above, p. 58). Instead, "Die erste Walpurgisnacht" served Goethe as a kind of compact *Vorstudie* to the Walpurgis Night episodes in the two parts of his *Faust* tragedy—one that adopts a substantially different perspective but distills many of the same issues into a smaller undertaking.

The most obvious of these issues is the matter of the location and topography of the *Walpurgisnacht* scenes, which complement each other and "Die erste Walpurgisnacht." These scenes fulfill vital symbolic and structural functions. Both are set in locales rich in symbolic import: the Brocken (*Faust I*) and the Pharsalian plain (*Faust II*). As of the mid-1790s, Goethe's Faust treatment possessed little that was imposingly celestial, demonic, or otherwise supernatural in character: it lacked the Walpurgis Night scene, the Walpurgis Night Dream, and the Prolog in Heaven, as well as Faust's opening monolog. Among Goethe's first steps in resuming work on the tragedy in 1797 was the drafting of two scenes that addressed these thematic lacunae, the *Walpurgisnacht* and the *Prolog im Himmel*, and in his work over the next three years he used these themes to bring together the *Faust* tragedy and the Gretchen tragedy within a larger dramatic and thematic framework, one that could be sustained over the span of a two-part drama and thus enable him to complete the now comparatively finite task of closing the first part.[50] That the *Prolog im Himmel* adds the celestial dimension is self-evident, and the Brocken and the *Walpurgisnacht* were obvious means of imparting a correspondingly demonic dimension.

The demonic potency of the *Walpurgisnacht* scene resides not least of all in its vivid imagery. Many of the events, sights, smells, and sounds of the scene recall the various writings about the Walpurgis Night that figured in contemporary literature (especially the books by Praetorius and Vulpius discussed in chapter 1), and some are redolent of the spectacle of the feigned witches' Sabbath in the 1799 ballad. The showers of sparks, ominously glowing ground, and unexplained lights recall the (supposedly) evil lights beheld by the Christian sentinels. The "terrible ruckus" (*entsetzliches Getöse*) of the ballad is also present, for the scene abounds with howling winds and loud, unexplained noises. In addition to the general din produced by birds, owls, crashing branches, and cracking limbs, the Brocken teems with gruesome throngs of devilish pilgrims—witches, half-witches, swine, and various unsavory figures from the Bible, history, mythology, and literature—who push doggedly on, past the plateaus where Mammon and Urian[51] preside over their own savage festivities, to the summit, the center of the night's evil: a raging magic song streams along the entire length of the mountainside.[52] The din also includes more specifically musical sounds: unidentified instruments (l. 4050), the witches' chorus (ll. 3956–4015), and the presumably crude music to which Faust and Mephistopheles dance with the young and old witches (ll. 4128–75).

But there are also important differences, and in these lie some insights into the reflexive relationship between the 1799 ballad and the final version of the scene in part I of the *Faust* tragedy. In the final version of the drama, Faust and Mephistopheles come tantalizingly close to reaching the Brocken's summit, where Satan presides over the night's gruesome festivities. They do not attain the summit, however. Mephistopheles, who brought Faust there to begin with and led him in their journey up to that point, now seeks to divert him and distract him; the Walpurgis Night ascent to the peak of the Brocken thus loses its satanic impulse. Rather than reaching the climax of evil, Faust is first lured into dancing with a young, naked witch; then he is drawn out of the revelous spirit by a vision of Gretchen with the visible stigmata of her imminent hanging; finally, he is distracted into watching an unabashedly banal satirical play, the theatrical sideshow of the Walpurgis Night's Dream. But when the Walpurgis Night scene spurred Goethe back into work on the tragedy in the late 1790s, he did intend for Faust and Mephistopheles to continue onward to the summit after the "intermezzo" (Goethe's term) that eventually became the Walpurgis Night's Dream. Once atop the Brocken, they witnessed a satanic orgy of unparalleled repugnance, grotesquery, and blasphemy—one that preserves the act of anal adoration depicted and discussed in Praetorius's *Blockes-Berges Verrichtung* (see pp. 18–20) and at the same time viciously satirizes papal homage, the Last Judgment, and (most important for our purposes) the Church's historical persecution of heretics, suspected witches, and other nonbelievers.[53]

The reasons for Goethe's deletion of the "Satan scenes" (*Satansszenen*)[54] remain unclear. Certainly they would have provided a remarkable climax to the Walpurgis Night scene, and they probably would also have saved the Walpurgis Night's Dream from the critical disdain to which it has often been subjected by presenting it not as an anticlimax, but as an interlude before the final push to the climax. In any event, the deleted scene, together with the fact that Gretchen's own circle is populated by persons subject to superstition and bigotry,[55] constitutes an important thematic link between the genuine Walpurgis Night of *Faust I* and the bluff of the 1799 ballad. The two coeval compositions function as mirror images, each finding a thematic and compositional antipode in the other. In *Faust I*—especially with the "Satan scene" intact—the Walpurgis Night is a massive procession up the Brocken, whereas in the ballad the action is predominantly downhill, from the slopes to the fields where the Christian sentinels stand their guard. In the drama, the Walpurgis Night occurs in the dramatic present; in the ballad, it is in the reader's history. In the drama the Night is the province of all things iniquitous and unearthly; the humans (Faust, the General, the minister of state, the parvenu, the author, and of course the "Proktophantasmist"[56]) are a minority, and except for Faust (who has the help of Mephistopheles) none seem likely to attain the summit. In the ballad the protagonists of Walpurgis Night are all very human: young and old, men and women, Christian and pagan, religious and military. Finally, in the drama the *Walpurgisnacht* proves to be a malignant orgy of unmitigated evil; in the ballad, it is a benign celebration of strength, courage, and devotion.

The reflective surfaces (as it were) for these mirror images are the twin issues of illusion vs. reality and the supernatural vs. the natural. Central to the identity of the protagonists in the ballad, these issues provide the mechanism for the transition into and out of the elaborate fantasy of the *Walpurgisnacht* in the play. Immediately after Gretchen's collapse in the cathedral, the Walpurgis Night begins as Faust and Mephistopheles are escorted up the slopes of the Brocken by an *Irrlicht*,[57] a phenomenon at once natural and supernatural as it mediates between those two spheres, seeming to speak, sing, and dance with Faust and Mephistopheles as it guides them onto the slope (ll. 3860–3911). The Walpurgis Night's Dream likewise distills the themes of illusion vs. reality and the natural vs. supernatural, providing the transition from the phantom vision of Gretchen and the tumult of the Brocken to the "Trüber Tag—Feld" scene. The importance of its mediatory function is underscored by the fact that it was evidently the very first product of the stage of work that resulted in the play's completion, and that Goethe proceeded directly from it to the *Walpurgisnacht* itself. And here, too, the participants are not human, at least not in any literal sense: an assemblage of characters from Shakespeare's *A Midsummer Night's Dream* and the sprite Ariel from *The Tempest,* a windmill, an orchestra of insects, a number of character types (an inquisitive traveler, an orthodox, a purist, a skeptic, a dogmatist, a naturalist, a supernaturalist, and so on)—and of course, Brocken specters and a young witch. At the same time, the subjects of the conversations and songs shared by these fanciful characters are very much a part of the real culture of the Enlightenment: art, religion, philosophy, and politics, including the revolutionary and postrevolutionary politics of the 1780s and 1790s. After bringing these issues—all of them material to the "Walpurgisnacht" ballad as well as *Faust I*—into focus, the dreamlike *Walpurgisnacht* intermezzo and all its participants finally dissolve into dust—and Faust finds himself once again in reality, facing the grim fate that befalls Gretchen because of his actions.

On the face of it, the "Classical Walpurgis Night" in *Faust II* is only distantly connected to the Walpurgis Night scene in *Faust I:* Faust has been transported from his study in the Germany of Holy Roman Emperor Maximilian I not to the base of the Brocken, but to the upper reaches of the river Peneus in the plains of Pharsalus in Thessaly (Greece), and over the course of the scene he moves not upward toward the summit, but down the Vale of Tempe to the Aegean Sea. But the chronology of the entire tragedy's composition reveals that the idea of an allegorical continuation of what became *Faust I* occurred to Goethe early on, and the essential structural principle of casting this sequel in historically and culturally transposed counterparts and complements is fully evident by the time of Paralipomenon 70 (1816), which is itself based on Goethe's previous plans (now lost).[58] Goethe himself explained this relationship in Paralipomenon 74 (the final version of his synopsis of the *Helena-Dichtung*), written in 1827. Stating that the character of Faust had now developed significantly beyond that provided for in the "crude old folk fairy tale," Goethe described his protagonist as "a man . . . who feels impatient and uncomfortable within the limits of his earthly existence"; consequently, in part II this Faust was shown in "higher regions" and "worthier circumstances."[59]

The famously philhellenic Goethe's deliberate temporal, cultural, and geographic transposition from the loosely prescribed confines of the "crude old folk fairy tale" to a series of newly invented tropes on the noble civilization and literature of ancient Greece produced another set of mirrors. The shared characters and themes between *Faust I* and *Faust II* establish them as pendants to one another, but in negating their "crude" counterparts in part I the scenes in part II also affirm those counterparts' essentials. The Faust of part II is the same self-absorbed man of learning whose profound hunger for erudition and experience requires him to break free of the circumstances that confined him in part I; the beautiful feminine object of his desires is not the humble and simple Gretchen, but the celebrated Helen of Troy; and so on. In this context, the otherwise obscure substantive relationship between the "Classical Walpurgis Night" and its modern counterpart also affirms the salient characteristics of the latter. In so doing, it also affirms both scenes' thematic connection to "Die erste Walpurgisnacht." The antithetical geographical and topographical features of the "Classical Walpurgis Night" mentioned earlier thus affirm the significance of the geography and topography of the counterpart *Walpurgisnächte* in *Faust I* and the 1799 ballad. The scene is not the remote and forbidding Harz Mountains, but Thessaly, home to three crucial battles of Classical mythology and history, the reputed birthplace of the art of war, and site of the first making of money and weapons from metals.[60] Similarly, the trajectory of Faust's classical Walpurgis Night journey is not toward a hysterical scene emblematic of hatred, banality, and unimaginable loathsomeness, but toward a majestic pageant of wholesome sensual beauty with the appearance of the nymph Galatea at the life-affirming shores of the Aegean. In this instance the journey is not thwarted; Faust does reach the goal. And aside from Faust himself its cast of characters, drawn from literature and lore rather than reality, comprises neither the bestial and half-human personages of the modern Walpurgis Night nor the familiar pantheon of Olympian deities, but the primitive demons of pre-Olympian Greek religion—demigods and demons whose abstract attributes are altogether more diffuse and, during the first part of the journey down the Peneios, less appealing.

These characters and their attributes underscore the salient features of Goethe's thinking about the Walpurgis Night as a cultural topos and subject for artistic creation. Here the theme of reality vs. illusion assumes a different guise, for the whole of *Faust II* rejects the dichotomies of past and present, myth and history. Absent those cultural, intellectual, and experiential delimiters, Goethe creates his own historically transcendent array of events and ideas, now abstracted into a bewildering wealth of ideas and themes. And in this abstract world the particular varieties of baseness that Faust encounters along the way are the same as those emphasized in the Walpurgis Night of *Faust I* and the 1799 ballad: hatred, bigotry, and narrow-mindedness. In *Faust II* the Walpurgis Night trek begins in a Classical locale synonymous with hatred, conflict, and greed.

And with the figuratively erotic climactic scene in which the homunculus smashes his glass against Galatea's shell and pours himself into the Aegean Sea the imagery of vibrant life, fiery and celestial light, and universal love recalls the pagan culture extolled in the 1799 "Walpurgisnacht" ballad. Its resplendent celebration of fertility and life born of sensuously beautiful nature parallels the pagan celebrations of fertility that gave rise to their celebrations of the arrival of spring to begin with. In a word, the telos of this Classical Walpurgis Night is strikingly similar to the values antithetical to the climax of the modern Walpurgis Night but central to the 1799 ballad.

◆ ◆ ◆

The links between "Die erste Walpurgisnacht" and the two parts of the *Faust* tragedy extend beyond their compositional histories and their self-evident commonality of location and season. If anything, they affirm each other as mirror images. But like the past and the present, the real and the unreal, the mythological and the historical, the demonic and the human in *Faust II*, and like the Christian and the pagan in "Die erste Walpurgisnacht," the alterity that exists between the *Faust* tragedy and the 1799 ballad is also largely illusory. For Goethe, the idea of the Walpurgis Night knew few barriers. Because of his considerable cultural and intellectual renown, his various artistic treatments of this idea and its attendant themes broadened the appeal and import of the Walpurgis Night in the mid- and later nineteenth century. After him, the nineteenth century viewed the Walpurgis Night not just as a folk legend about a Witches' Sabbath atop the Brocken, but as a broad topic richly invested with potential for historical, social, political, moral, and artistic commentary.

Appendix 3.1.

	Goethe	Prose Translation
	[1] *Ein Druide.*	[1] *A Druid.*
1	Es lacht der Mai.	May is laughing!
2	Der Wald ist frei	The forest is free
3	Von Eis und Reifgehänge.	Of ice and hanging hoarfrost,
4	Der Schnee ist fort;	The snow is gone;
5	Am grünen Ort	In the green place
6	Erschallen Luftgesänge.[61]	Merry songs of breezes resound.
7	Ein reiner Schnee	A pristine snow
8	Liegt auf der Höh;	Lies on the peak;
9	Doch eilen wir nach oben,	Let's hasten up there

Appendix 3.1 *(continued)*

	Goethe	Prose Translation
10	Begehn den alten heil'gen Brauch,	To celebrate the ancient holy rite,
11	Allvater dort zu loben.	To praise the father of all.
12	Die Flamme lodre durch den Rauch!	May the flame blaze through the smoke!
13	So wird das Herz erhoben.	Thus will the heart be edified.
	[2] *Die Druiden.*	[2] *The Druids.*
14	Die Flamme lodre durch den Rauch!	May the flame blaze through the smoke!
15	Begeht den alten heil'gen Brauch,	Celebrate the ancient holy rite
16	Allvater dort zu loben!	Of there praising the father of all.
17	Hinauf! hinauf nach oben!	Away! Upward to the heights!
	[3] *Einer aus dem Volke.*	[3] *A Man from Among the People.*
18	Könnt ihr so verwegen handeln?	Can you [really] behave so audaciously?
19	Wollt ihr denn zum Tode wandeln?	Do you want to stroll up to death?
20	Kennet ihr nicht die Gesetze	Don't you know the laws
21	Unsrer harten Überwinder?	Of our stubborn conquerors?
22	Rings gestellt sind ihre Netze	Their snares have been set all around
23	Auf die Heiden, auf die Sünder.	For the pagans, for the sinners.
24	Ach, sie schlachten auf dem Walle	Ah, on their ramparts they slaughter
25	Unsre Weiber, unsre Kinder.	Our women, our children.
26	Und wir alle	And we all
27	Nahen uns gewissem Falle.	Risk this in one way or another.
	[4] *Chor der Weiber.*	[4] *Chorus of Women.*
28	Auf des Lagers hohem Walle	On the camp's high ramparts
29	Schlachten sie schon unsre Kinder.	They're already slaughtering our children.
30	Ach, die strengen Überwinder!	Ah, the stubborn conquerors!
31	Und wir alle	And we all
32	Nahen uns gewissem Falle.	Risk this in one way or another.
	[5] *Ein Druide.*	[5] *A Druid.*
33	Wer Opfer heut	Anyone who shies away
34	Zu bringen scheut,	From sacrifice today
35	Verdient erst seine Bande.	Has earned his bondage.
36	Der Wald ist frei!	The forest is free!
37	Das Holz herbei,	Bring some wood here
38	Und schichtet es zum Brande!	And pile it up for a fire!
39	Doch bleiben wir	But we'll remain

Appendix 3.1 *(continued)*

	Goethe	Prose Translation
40	Im Buschrevier	In the brushy areas
41	Am Tage noch im Stillen,	During the daytime,
42	Und Männer stellen wir zur Hut	And we'll post men as guards
43	Um eurer Sorge willen.	Because of your concern.
44	Dann aber laßt mit frischem Mut	But then let us fulfill our duty
45	Uns unsre Pflicht erfüllen.	With renewed zeal!
	[6] *Chor der Wächter.*	[6] *Chorus of the Watchmen.*
46	Verteilt euch, wackre Männer, hier	Spread out here, brave men,
47	Durch dieses ganze Waldrevier	All throughout this forest grove,
48	Und wachet hier im Stillen,	And keep watch here in the quiet
49	Wenn sie die Pflicht erfüllen.	While they fulfill their [own] duty.
	[7] *Ein Wächter.*	[7] *A Watchman.*
50	Diese dumpfen Pfaffenchristen,	These foolish cleric-Christians!
51	Laßt uns keck sie überlisten!	Let's outwit them with cleverness!
52	Mit dem Teufel, den sie fabeln,	Let's frighten them
53	Wollen wir sie selbst erschrecken.	With their own fabled devil.
54	Kommt! Mit Zacken und mit Gabeln,	Come! With prongs and pitchforks
55	Und mit Glut und Klapperstöcken	And with embers and clappers
56	Lärmen wir bei nachtger Weile	Let's make a racket during our night-watch
57	Durch die engen Felsenstrecken.	In the narrow rocky stretches.
58	Kauz und Eule,	Hoopoe and owl,
59	Heul' in unser Rundgeheule.	Howl along with us.
	[8] *Chor der Wächter.*	[8] *Chorus of the Watchmen.*
60	Kommt mit Zacken und mit Gabeln,	Come with prongs and pitchforks,
61	Wie der Teufel, den sie fabeln,	Like their fabled devil,
62	Und mit wilden Klapperstöcken,	With wild clappers
63	Durch die leeren Felsenstrecken!	Through the empty rocky stretches!
64	Kauz und Eule,	Hoopoe and owl,
65	Heul' in unser Rundgeheule.	Howl along with us.
	[9] *Ein Druide.*	[9] *A Druid.*
66	So weit gebracht,	So it's come to this:
67	Daß wir bei Nacht	That we sing to the father of all
68	Allvater heimlich singen!	Under cover of darkness!
69	Doch ist es Tag,	But it is daytime
70	Sobald man mag	As soon as one desires

Appendix 3.1 *(continued)*

	Goethe	Prose Translation
71	Ein reines Herz dir bringen.	To approach you with a pure heart!
72	Du kannst zwar heut,	You can allow the enemy
73	Und manche Zeit,	Great latitude
74	Dem Feinde viel erlauben.	Today and many a day.
75	Die Flamme reinigt sich vom Rauch:	The flame purifies itself of smoke:
76	So reinig' unsern Glauben!	Thus purify our faith!
77	Und raubt man uns den alten Brauch;	And if we are robbed of our ancient rite,
78	Dein Licht, wer will es rauben!	Who would rob us of your light!
	[10] *Ein christlicher Wächter.*	[10] *A Christian Guard.*
79	Hilf! ach hilf mir, Kriegsgeselle!	Help! oh help me, my comrades in war!
80	Ach, es kommt die ganze Hölle!	Ah, all hell is coming toward us!
81	Sieh, wie die verhexten Leiber	Look how the bewitched corpses
82	Durch und durch von Flamme glühen!	Glow all over with flame!
83	Menschen-Wölf' und Drachen-Weiber,	Wolf-men and dragon-women
84	Die im Flug vorüber ziehen!	Fly about overhead!
85	Welch entsetzliches Getöse!	What a terrible ruckus!
86	Laßt uns, laßt uns alle fliehen!	Let us – let's all flee!
87	Oben flammt und saust der Böse;	Up above the Evil One flames,
88	Aus dem Boden	Out of the earth
89	Dampfet rings ein Höllen-Broden.	A hellish broth boils up around us.
	[11] *Chor der christlichen Wächter.*	[11] *Chorus of the Christian Guards.*
90	Schreckliche, verhexte Leiber,	Horrible, bewitched corpses,
91	Menschen-Wölf' und Drachen-Weiber!	Wolf-men and dragon-women!
92	Welch entsetzliches Getöse!	What a terrible ruckus!
93	Sieh, da flammt, da zieht der Böse!	Look, the Evil One flames and blisters!
94	Aus dem Boden	Out of the earth
95	Dampfet rings ein Höllen-Broden.	A hellish broth boils up around us.
	[12] *Chor der Druiden*	[12] *Chorus of the Druids.*
96	Die Flamme reinigt sich vom Rauch:	The flame purifies itself of smoke:
97	So reinig' unsern Glauben!	Thus purify our faith!
98	Und raubt man uns den alten Brauch;	And if we are robbed of our ancient rite,
99	Dein Licht, wer kann es rauben!	Who can rob us of your light!

Chapter Four

The Composition, Revision, and Publication of Mendelssohn's Die erste Walpurgisnacht

> You ask me . . . why it is that sometimes in my writings I quote examples from secular literature and thus defile the whiteness of the church with the foulness of heathenism. . . . I incline indeed to fancy . . . that in putting this question to me you are only the mouthpiece of another. . . . Please beg of him not to envy eaters their teeth because he is toothless himself, and not to make light of the eyes of gazelles because he is himself a mole.
>
> Letter from St. Jerome to Magnus, an orator of Rome

The Walpurgis Night was already heavily invested with potential for artistic commentary on cultural, political, religious, and social issues by the late eighteenth century, and it became even more so in the wake of Goethe's powerful treatments. In the German-speaking countries particularly, the ideological glorification of a pre-Christian Germanic heritage was attractive in many sectors because it effectively emancipated Christianity from its indebtedness to the "pagan" monotheism of Judaism. This movement, termed "philo-heathenism" by Jeffrey Sposato,[1] had attained a significant following by the beginning of the century and one of its most noted exponents was Friedrich Schleiermacher, among whose followers Mendelssohn counted himself in 1830 (see ch. 2, pp. 34–35). Against this backdrop, the pagan sympathies of Goethe's 1799 ballad (and, by extension, of musical settings thereof) were neither confrontational to Christian values nor provocative in their portrayal of Christian evangelizing in the Carolingian era. They simply submitted, in poetic guise, a historically based celebration of the ancestors of those latter-day Christians who were troubled by the notion that their religious pedigree resided in Judaic monotheism (or, to put it bluntly, that they were themselves essentially converted Jews).

Yet it was precisely this context that made the political implications of the Walpurgis Night and Goethe's 1799 ballad even more obvious when the poem originally sent to Zelter became the starting point for a large-scale choral/orchestral composition by Zelter's star pupil, Mendelssohn—a Lutheran in whose career the problems and potentials of Jewish sorption into Christian society converged dramatically. Goethe's unsympathetic attitude toward Jewish assimilation and his occasional anti-Semitic remarks suggest that he did not view his Walpurgis Night ballad, with its forceful question "Und raubt man uns den alten Brauch, dein Licht, wer will es rauben?" (and if they rob us of our ancient rite, who will rob us of your light?), changed to the exclamation "wer kann es rauben!" (who can rob us of your light!) in the final line, as pertaining to the assimilationist debate. And he almost certainly would not have envisioned its being set to music by the grandson of one of the Enlightenment's most eloquent advocates for Jewish/Christian assimilation. But when that ballad was set to music by a composer named Mendelssohn, how could anyone aware of the historical situation of European Jews or even of Jewry's tense relationships with contemporary Christian society fail to construe the poem's non-Christian protagonists as anything other than thinly disguised Jews? More to the point, how could Goethe's poem, when set to Mendelssohn's music, be construed as anything other than a critical commentary on Christian society's refusal to accept Judaism, and to tolerate it only on Christian terms?

These complicated convergences posed considerable risks for Mendelssohn. Despite his Lutheran faith, the composer was fully aware that his family name immediately branded him as being of Jewish descent, and he labored hard over the course of his public career to avoid self-identification as Jew.[2] By the early 1840s his fame rested not least of all on sacred compositions—including the expansively pro-Christian *Paulus*, which embodies the central tenets of nineteenth-century Pauline scholarship and resonates eloquently with Schleiermacher's theology. Nevertheless, few contemporaries would have missed the fact that by then his published sacred output included (along with *Paulus*) no fewer than four choral/orchestral psalm settings[3] —works whose Old Testament texts immediately recalled the ancestral Jewishness of their composer, and whose symphonic dimensions dwarfed all of Mendelssohn's other explicitly Christian sacred works published by the early 1840s.[4] If the nineteenth century increasingly held that scope and grandeur were functions of enthusiasm and conviction, then there was more than a little to suggest that Mendelssohn's personal sympathies lay more with Judaism than with Christianity. Perhaps most important, he must also have been aware of the deep resonance the poem's philoheathen sentiments would find in the smoldering Judeophobia of the day, especially since it portrays the evangelizing Christians not simply as adversarial Others to the Saxon heathens, but as murderous, superstitious cowards whose faith succumbs to fear in the face of the pagans' ruse. In such a context, the nobility of the pagans and the cowardice of the Christians in his setting of Goethe's "Die erste Walpurgisnacht" were decidedly problematical.

In other words, Mendelssohn certainly would not have overlooked the poem's potential for offending at least some sensibilities, and he may well have harbored some sympathy for both sides of its ethical, historical, and religious paradoxes.

The more important questions concern his understanding of the nature of his task in taking on this provocative topic—why he would risk "defiling" his hard-won reputation as a genuinely Christian voice in contemporary artistic discourse by setting to music a poem that celebrated Christianity's historical antagonists. A review of the work's genesis, performance history, and early critical reception offers some answers to these questions and insights into the development of his thinking on the problems and potentials of Goethe's ballad, as well as changes in his professional persona between the early 1830s and the mid-1840s.

The First Setting

Goethe's "Die erste Walpurgisnacht" was unwittingly set on its way toward Mendelssohn already when Goethe sent it to Zelter in 1799. Though Zelter never was able to rise to the challenge of Goethe's "poetic fable," the idea was planted in fertile soil, for he became Mendelssohn's most important composition teacher beginning in early 1819. When he formally introduced the twelve-year-old prodigy to the poet nearly six decades his senior in 1821, he initiated one of the most remarkable intergenerational artistic relationships in the annals of Western history. It is tempting to imagine that Zelter informed Mendelssohn of how his relationship with Goethe had begun and that this history then led the precocious youth to undertake the challenge his own teacher had declined.

In any case, the idea was already a "favorite old scheme" by the time Mendelssohn commenced work on the project. He evidently began composing stanzas 9 and/or 12 in Vienna in the fall of 1830, just weeks after his last visit with Goethe. He recalled the event some months later in a letter to the baritone Franz Hauser, a close friend:

> You probably still know that I once composed a passage from Goethe's "Die erste Walpurgisnacht," "Doch ist es Tag, sobald man mag ein reines Herz dir bringen," at your piano, and that I tortured you a great deal with it afterwards, playing it over and over again? The thing is now putting itself together, and I'm going to compose the entire poem as a new kind of cantata for choruses and large orchestra. It can be colorful enough, for there are majestic elements in it.[5]

But the cantata's inception also seems to have been indebted to another force: the reinstatement of the Mendelssohn household's renowned Sunday Musicales *(Sonntagsmusiken)* under the direction of Felix's older sister, Fanny Hensel, early in 1831. He reported this serendipitous influence in a letter to Hensel dated February 22:

> I cannot tell you how greatly the new Sunday Musicales please me. That is a brilliant idea, and I beg you for God's sake not to let it fall by the wayside again, but rather to commission your traveling brother to write something new for you. He will do it gladly, for he is all too delighted with you and your idea. . . . One of my pieces probably

> already owes its birth to these Sunday Musicales. When you wrote to me about [the idea] recently I wondered whether I might not be able to send you something for them, and then a favorite old scheme of mine occurred to me again—but it became so extended that I cannot [yet] give it to Emil[6] to bring along, so he will have to bring it later. Listen and marvel[!] Since I left Vienna I have halfway composed Goethe's "Die erste Walpurgisnacht," but do not yet have the courage to write it out. The thing has now taken shape but has become a grand cantata with full orchestra. It can become very merry, for at the beginning it is full of spring songs and more such things; and then, when the watchmen make a ruckus with their prongs and pitchforks and owls, there is also the witches' spookiness, and [you] know that I have a particular fondness for that. Then the druids who make the sacrifices appear in C major with their trombones, and then again the watchmen, who are afraid of them (here I mean to introduce an eerie, lightly mysterious chorus); and then finally, at the end, the complete sacrificial hymn. Don't you think that this could become a new kind of cantata? As a matter of course there is an instrumental introduction, and the whole thing is vivid enough. I think it will be finished soon.[7]

Just over a week later, on March 5, the young composer wrote to the great poet informing him of his scheme:

> I also have time during the penitential season to compose diligently and in peace. What has occupied me almost exclusively for several weeks is my music to the poem titled "Die erste Walpurgisnacht" by Your Excellency. I want to compose it as a kind of grand cantata with orchestra, and the merry beginning of spring, the witchery and devilish magic, and the recurrent solemn sacrificial chorus could provide the opportunity for the most beautiful music. I do not know whether I will succeed in doing so, but I am aware of how great the task is and of how collectedly and honorably I must approach it.[8]

By March 29, he was able to report to his family that he had made progress despite the seductive beauties of the Italian climate, and that he hoped to be able "to write the work out" before leaving. The letter also reveals that he still had no ideas for the introduction: "Once that occurs to me," he wrote, "then the thing will have come together and I will write it out in a couple of days."[9]

This prediction turned out to be premature. Nearly a month later, on April 27, he wrote from Naples to his family that he still had to "get back to [his] witches":

> This entire letter is actually cloaked in uncertainty—or rather, I am cloaked in uncertainty as to whether I should use the bass drum. "Prongs, pitchforks, and clappers" actually do make me inclined to use it, but moderation would make me disinclined. I am certainly the only one ever to have composed the Blocksberg without using piccolo, but I would be sorry to forgo the bass drum. I'm afraid that the *Walpurgisnacht* will be finished and packed up, and that I'll be traveling the countryside again and writing about God knows what, before Fanny's advice reaches me. I'm convinced that Fanny would say to use it, but I'm still undecided. A great deal of noise must be made in any case.[10]

The work's completion continued to elude him. He reported from Naples on May 10, that it was "not yet finished . . . because it [was] growing rapidly,"[11] and in an undated letter that probably stems from the summer of 1831 he ascribes its composition to Rome—also referring to it as "a grand symphony with chorus, or rather a chorus with collaborative symphony."[12] On July 13, writing to Eduard Devrient, he finally was able to issue another confident report on the composition:

> In the meantime I have also written another large composition that may also be able to have some broader effect: *Die erste Walpurgisnacht* by Goethe. I started on it just because I liked it and it spoke to me; [at the time] I wasn't considering it for performance. But now that it sits completed before me I see that it would work very well as a grand concert composition. In my first subscription concert in Berlin you will have to sing [the role of] the bearded druid priest; the choruses will be performed by [X] with the generous participation of [Y] etc., etc. I wrote the part of the priest so that it lies well in your throat, with your permission; so you'll once again have to project it. Just as it has so far been my experience that those works that I have written with the least consideration of the public have always pleased the public best, I believe it will it be that way in this instance too. I write this simply so that you'll see that I'm thinking of *practical* matters—albeit only after the fact. . . .[13]

On July 14, 1831, he reported to his family that he had worked out the conclusion of the cantata and that the following day the whole would be truly finished—except for the overture, which might take the form of either an extended symphony or "a short springtime introduction" ("eine kurze Frühlingseinleitung"). He also reported that he had improved the ending: "Now the ending has become better than even I imagined it would. The monsters and the bearded druid with his trombones that stand blasting away behind him made some royal fun for me; I spent a couple of mornings very happily with that."[14]

The following day (July 15, 1831) Mendelssohn was sufficiently confident in his new composition to inscribe the date on the final page of the score (which evidently still lacked its instrumental introduction); his diary entry for July 17 records that it had been further "tidied up" ("geputzt") by then.[15] By July 24, he had played it for Carl Mozart, who was so impressed that he suggested it should be published right away.[16] The composer, however, insisted on first trying out the new work in one of the Mendelssohn family's Sunday Musicales. As he explained in a letter from Lucerne to Devrient:

> I wish that I could *really* be with you some evening and play my *Walpurgisnacht* for you—or rather, that you could sing it for me; it lies very well for your voice. But write to me whether you can hit the high *F*—not sustained, but just for a quarter note. It occurs near the end.[17]

The following two weeks produced the most substantive information to date on the content of the work as it existed at that point: an exchange of letters between Mendelssohn and Goethe. On August 28, Mendelssohn wrote:

> I wrote to you already from Rome that I had the audacity to compose your *Erste Walpurgisnacht*; I have in the meantime finished it, while in Milan. It turned out as a

> kind of cantata for chorus and orchestra, longer and more distended than I initially envisioned, because the longer I carried it around with me the more extended, grand, and appealing the task became. Permit me to express my gratitude for the heavenly text. When the old druid brings his sacrifice and the whole thing becomes solemn and incomparably grand, there is no need to write music—it is all already so clearly present and resonant that I always sang the verses to myself without meaning to. If I can find a good chorus and an opportunity in Munich, whither I depart tomorrow, I will try to perform it there. My only hope is that people will hear in my music how deeply I have felt the beauty of the text.[18]

The elder poet responded with his third explanation of the poem's intentions—now construing it as "elevated symbolism" rather than an attempt to provide material for a large-scale dramatic work that was neither staged nor narrated, or as an attempt to return the fable-like historical conjecture concerning the Walpurgis Night's origins to a poetic fable.[19] He continued:

> . . . For in the history of the world it must eternally be repeated that something old, established, proven, [and] reassuring will be compacted, pushed aside, dislocated, and, if not abolished, then corralled into the tightest space by emergent new forces. The middle period, in which the hatred is still capable of reacting, and still may do so, is presented here succinctly enough, and a joyous, indestructible enthusiasm flares up once again with brilliance and clarity. . . .[20]

As of fall 1831, then, the *Walpurgisnacht* was sufficiently complete in Mendelssohn's view for him to write to Goethe about it and his hopes of arranging for a performance. But a significant obstacle remained, for he still had little or nothing in the way of an instrumental introduction. He was finally able to report progress on "the Saxon A-minor Overture that [was] to precede the *Walpurgisnacht*" when he wrote to Fanny on January 21, 1832, and he finished the initial version of the Overture on February 4.[21] After another pass through for revisions, he inscribed the final page of the score once again on February 13. That same day, writing from Paris, he reported on the work to his family:

> My A-minor Overture is finished; it represents bad weather. A couple of days ago I finished an introduction representing the thaw and the arrival of springtime, then numbered the pages of the *Walpurgisnacht* [i.e., the texted part of the cantata], tidied up the seven movements a little, and confidently wrote "Paris, in February" beneath "Milan, in July." I think you all will like it.[22]

Goethe never heard Mendelssohn's setting of his "poetic fable," for he died on March 22, 1832. The loss cast a shadow over Mendelssohn's spirits for months to come, and his physical well-being was compromised when he contracted cholera during the great scourge that swept Paris that spring. In mid-April he was finally able to leave for London—home to some of his more significant musical triumphs of 1829, and the final main station in his Grand Tour. There, on April 30, he performed his newly completed setting of the late poet's

Walpurgisnacht for his close friends Ignaz and Charlotte Moscheles—a performance that may account for the autograph piano-duet arrangement of the instrumental introduction (see chapter 5).[23]

But two weeks later death struck again, this time claiming the life of Zelter. This deep personal and professional loss put the young composer in a difficult position. He had spent two full years broadening his horizons, establishing strong personal and professional relationships with most of musical Europe, and preparing for a career as an independent professional musician. Particularly in London he was now the toast of musical society. But he also found himself strongly pressured to apply for the position of Zelter's successor as director of the Berlin Singakademie—a position he had little realistic hope of attaining, and one that (if attained) would leave him vulnerable to suspicions of having benefited from his family's means and influence, as well as the general prejudice that converted Jews faced in the climate of the day. That Mendelssohn was fully aware that the stolid disposition of the Singakademie would almost inevitably favor his less brilliant but more established competitors is evident from his sharp-tongued but clear-headed assessment in September 1832:

> I will be pestered a great deal about the Singakademie position, with suggestions and plans—but nothing will come of it. They will propose three candidates, including me and possibly also Schelble,[24] but if the Lord God Zebaoth himself were among the candidates the Singakademie would still choose Rungenhagen. He's old, he's honest, he's worked with them for twenty years for free, he understands little of music and nothing at all about conducting, he's good natured, and he's friendly. So the Singakademie will choose him.[25]

Misgivings aside, Mendelssohn threw himself into his candidacy once he had decided to pursue the post. Chief among the ventures intended to remind the Berliners of his talent and breadth as composer and conductor were three concerts given over the course of the winter for the benefit of the widows of the Royal Orchestra. These concerts provided the occasion, finally, for the public premiere of *Die erste Walpurgisnacht.*[26] It was performed privately on October 11, 1832, in one of Fanny Hensel's Sunday Musicales, thus realizing the composer's earlier wish to have the work performed in that venue, offering his family and friends a chance to hear the work about which they had already heard much, and giving him a chance to make practical changes and test its suitability for public performance.[27] In the concert of January 10, 1833, then, the *Walpurgisnacht* was afforded pride of place, serving as the de facto finale to the series. The impressiveness of the gesture becomes all the greater when we consider the stature of the works that preceded this finale. Featured in the series were performances of several of Mendelssohn's own major works (many of them the public and/or German premieres): the D-minor ("Reformation") Symphony,[28] the First Piano Concerto,[29] the *Midsummer Night's Dream* Overture,[30] the *Capriccio brillant,*[31] the *Meeresstille und glückliche Fahrt* Overture,[32] and the *Hebrides* Overture[33] as well as the *Walpurgisnacht.* Moreover, these compositions were placed in the company of some of the most revered composers of German musical history—J. S. Bach, Gluck, Mozart, Beethoven, and Weber.[34] The series also included an unpublished symphony by the Berlin composer Ludwig Berger, who was not only highly regarded by the local public but also one of Mendelssohn's teachers.

The gesture was more than impressive; it was audacious. In a series of concerts that coincided with his own candidacy for one of the most important musical posts in the Prussian capital, the twenty-three-year-old Mendelssohn interspersed local and world public premieres of his own works among compositions by some of the greatest geniuses of musical history—including Beethoven and Weber, the late composers whose deaths had cast a shadow over musical Europe and created a crisis for most composers of his generation. And of course the late Goethe was also represented, via the *Meeresstille und glückliche Fahrt* Overture and *Die erste Walpurgisnacht.* The potency of the gesture was not lost on Mendelssohn's contemporaries. The influential critic Ludwig Rellstab, for one, proposed in a review of the public premiere (and of the series of three concerts to which it belonged), that "[T]hese three musical evenings were more meaningful for the art than a whole year of the usual concerts."[35] If, as Wolfgang Dinglinger has proposed, Rellstab's remark reflects Mendelssohn's innovative rethinking of the conventions of concert programming, then the *Walpurgisnacht*'s position at the end of the series says much about the composer's own view of its stature as a summative finale to his compositional career up to that point.[36]

Although Mendelssohn's benefit concerts were well attended and well received, the reviewers consistently reminded readers of the composer's youth and suggested that the music, despite its merits, was not devoid of signs of his youthfulness. Rellstab commented with regard to the first concert (and the "Reformation" Symphony in particular) that

> We would prefer it if the composer would adhere less to colossal things than to beautiful essentials; if his instrumentation were not so overly rich; and finally if he would err more on the side of melodiousness and less on the side of harmonic and bold beauties. He also rarely shows us fair skies; it is almost always stormy or tempestuous. But falling into excess is characteristic of youth and springtime, and perhaps we may expect more settled days from the more advanced seasons of life. Some reminiscences of Weber's *Euryanthe* (third act) and on the whole a recreation of the forms cultivated in Beethoven's late years also cannot escape mention.[37]

Rellstab also discussed the *Walpurgisnacht* in greater detail in a review of the concert of January 10:

> The second half of the concert comprised a longer musical composition by Herr Mendelssohn for voices and orchestra. The composer's subject was provided by Goethe's poem "Die erste Walpurgisnacht," which explains the historical circumstances behind the magic festival at the peak of the Blocksberg and thus (or perhaps nevertheless) is romantic. In a grand instrumental introduction, which to us seemed too long, the

composer offers an image of the whole. In this section the composer was inspired by essentially the same challenges that Spohr had to address in his *Faust* and (after him) Weber in his *Freischütz*.[38] We would have some objections to the treatment of the text (although this would involve too much detail for these pages), but the work is equally rich in individual beauties, fantastic moments, and bold combinations; the choruses are particularly effective. So disruptive were the overly crowded hall—in the lower level there was hardly even standing room left—the considerable heat, and the early departure of some listeners that this reviewer, too, left early (after the original and fantastic chorus "Kommt mit Zacken, kommt mit Gabeln") in order to reserve for himself the freer enjoyment of the conclusion at some future occasion. We therefore do not permit ourselves to judge the whole. We did, however, get the impression that up to that point the work dispensed with the cantilena that is so necessary for the voice, and for which the poem provides not a few opportunities. . . .[39]

A correspondent for the Leipzig *Allgemeine Musikalische Zeitung* was also impressed, but more frank in voicing his conservative objections:

> . . . The second part of the concert was filled by a new cantata by Felix Mendelssohn-Bartholdy: "Die erste Walpurgisnacht," a poem by Goethe that is more fantastic than lyrical. In this composition, with its almost excessive orchestral outlay, we see the composer rich in musical invention for instrumental works, often in ways approaching Beethoven's last works. This was evident already in the very long introduction. Some vocal solos for the tenor (Herr Mantius) were original and melodious, and the choruses were for the most part appropriate to the subject—unearthly, bizarre, and vigorous. But on the whole this grand vocal piece, excellently performed by the large orchestral forces of the Royal Kapelle, was not as generally effective as expected. This probably is attributable to the lack of pronounced melody, the poem itself, and the too obvious reliance of [the music] on modulations and instrumental effects. This third concert was exceedingly well attended. . . .[40]

The concerts—especially the one that included the *Walpurgisnacht*—made a lasting impact on members of Mendelssohn's immediate circle of family and friends. Eduard Devrient, who performed the role of the druid priest in the private and public Berlin performances, was so impressed that he suggested that a "dramatic [i.e., staged] performance" would be very effective—an idea that he eventually made good on (see chapter 6).[41] The composer's mother, Lea, implicitly praised the cantata (along with Mendelssohn's other original works performed in the series) when she sized up developments in the ongoing contest for the Singakademie directorship in a letter to the violinist Ferdinand David shortly after the premiere: "Felix's three benefit concerts for the fund of the widows of the orchestra are now over, and they aroused much enthusiasm and interest. If he and his compositions are too original for *le gros de public*,[42] they nevertheless aroused true enthusiasm among those whose tastes concur with his own; through them he has won a multitude of fans."[43]

Even more impressed was Fanny Hensel, who came to know the work—perhaps by singing the part of the old pagan woman in the "Könnt ihr so verwegen handeln" section (stanza 3 of Goethe's poem)[44]—during her time with Felix in the summer of 1832. Writing in May of 1833, Hensel described the cantata as "one of the most interesting pieces of music that there is" ("eins der interessantesten Musikstücke die es giebt").[45] She also confided to her diary that Lea Mendelssohn had been singing part of the "Kommt mit Zacken" chorus (stanzas 8 and 9 of Goethe's poem) sometime in mid-May 1833. With tongue-in-cheek humor, Fanny reports that her son, Sebastian (then nearly three years old), heard his grandmother's tune and asked who had written it—whereupon Lea answered that it was by Goethe, who had written "a great many songs" ("Der Goethe hat ja sehr viel Lieder gemacht").[46]

Hensel retained her enthusiasm about the *Walpurgisnacht* long after the Berlin premiere. Writing to Mendelssohn in Düsseldorf (where he had taken the position of Municipal Music Director) in late February 1834, she enthused to him about the cantata, asking whether and when he planned to perform it there and requesting that he send her the score for a few weeks.[47] She repeated the request shortly after he had taken up his new position as Kapellmeister of the famed Gewandhaus Orchestra in Leipzig in 1835, and referred to it again (in an allusion to the Finale of Beethoven's Ninth Symphony) early in 1836.[48] Although there seems to be no surviving documentation of when Fanny came into possession of the manuscript for the early version, she clearly did so—for her penciled handwriting is present on several pages, including some containing material deleted in Mendelssohn's script (see chapter 5).

And what of Mendelssohn's own use of the early version after the public premiere? In April 1834 he was still planning to perform it in Düsseldorf and then to publish it. In response to Hensel's February 1834 request that he send her the score he wrote on April 7:

> I cannot send you the *Walpurgisnacht* just now because it will probably be given in our next concert (on May 4, hopefully in fair weather). I am inclined to publish it soon in score etc., even though I now see that I will have to write almost all of it out once again because the instrumentation is poor. But I really appreciate the fact that I understand this better now.[49]

As it turned out, the composer's characteristic self-doubts got the better of him. He did not conduct the 1830–33 version of the *Walpurgisnacht* in any documented concerts from his Düsseldorf years.[50] When he moved to Leipzig in August 1835 he took the score along with him but left the original parts behind in Berlin, with the instruction that they be sent to him in due course.[51] This situation suggests that the envisioned improvements were sufficiently limited that they could be worked out in the score and then transferred to the original parts if a Leipzig performance could be arranged, but that idea, too, came to nothing. Sometime in the late 1830s Mendelssohn discussed the work with Robert Schumann, and he may have shown him the score at this point. On a loose leaf gathered up with the notebook that contained the other sketches for a biography of Mendelssohn, Schumann noted that

> I asked him about his setting of Göthe's [*sic*] "Walpurgisnacht," which he had composed much earlier. "The first part he now would find dislikable; the second part, on the other hand, pleased him a great deal." "He wanted to wait for the time at which he could write a new first part for it." Softly [something illegible] he told me of a letter he had received from Goethe concerning the poem.[52]

This information permits secure conjecture on several points concerning the status of the *Walpurgisnacht* cantata at that point in Mendelssohn's career. As late as 1837 he was still sufficiently convinced with his earlier setting to discuss it with Schumann, and he still thought of the work as comprising two large parts rather than the nine shorter movements of the final version. Finally, at least the bulk of his reservations concerned part I (stanzas 1–6 of Goethe's poem).

In any event, Schumann's and Mendelssohn's 1837 exchanges concerning the original version of the *Walpurgisnacht* are the latest surviving indications of Mendelssohn's active circulation or discussion of the original version. For the time being, his evident bid to succeed where his teacher had failed and to address the compositional challenges posed by Goethe's ballad had yielded little success. The *Walpurgisnacht* had parted ways with several major compositions that had accompanied its initial composition and been premiered during the years surrounding its own premiere. The *Calm Sea and Prosperous Voyage* and *Hebrides* Overtures, begun in 1828 and 1829 respectively, had been published in 1832–35; the First Piano Concerto, composed in 1831, had been published in 1832; and the Octet and A-major Quintet for Strings, begun in 1825 and 1826, respectively, had been published in 1833. Most important, the oratorio *St. Paul*, begun late in 1831 and premiered in 1836, was published in 1836–37, firmly establishing Mendelssohn as a composer of large-scale choral/orchestral works and emblazoning on his artistic persona a profoundly Pauline Christian confessional. But like several other significant works written during that remarkably creative period (among them the "Reformation" and "Italian" Symphonies), the *Walpurgisnacht* languished in an uncomfortable no-man's-land: completed, substantially revised, performed publicly, and at least moderately well received, but now consigned to the composer's desk drawer because of his penchant for revision.

Unlike the "Reformation" and "Italian" Symphonies, however, the *Walpurgisnacht* would be resuscitated in the 1840s. This time it would finally become suitable, in the eyes of its composer, for representing him in print to the broader musical public.

Fruition: The "Walpurgisnacht" of the 1840s

By the time *Die erste Walpurgisnacht* reappears in the surviving letters, Mendelssohn had attained the noon of his fame. For more than a decade his repute as a pianist, director, and concert programmer had been steadily broadening, and he had achieved celebrity around the continent and in England.

Since 1835 he had been Kapellmeister of one of Europe's finest orchestras and had become a widely sought-after conductor of music festivals. He had already worked in the service of two kings and won the admiration of Queen Victoria and the Prince Consort Albert. By the time of the *Walpurgisnacht*'s completion he would have added a third royal appointment to this list,[53] and by the time of its publication his professional standing was further enhanced by his role as de facto organizer and founder of Germany's first conservatory of music, whose doors opened on April 3, 1843.[54] And of course he was by now a composer of international renown, creator of acknowledged masterworks in virtually every available genre. In other words, to the extent that one's professional identity is a function of recognition and breadth of contribution, this Mendelssohn was a different figure than the admittedly brilliant but somewhat sheltered and completely unestablished twenty-three-year-old whose cantata had been performed in Berlin in 1833.

Accordingly, the composer now found that the work as he had previously introduced it was no longer representative—and the process of revision as it unfolded between 1842 and 1844 became far more extensive than anything he had likely envisioned in the early 1830s. He mentioned it in passing (and half-jokingly) in a letter to Friedrich Kistner on June 17, 1839,[55] and offered a more substantive reflection on its standing in a letter of November 18, 1840, to his friend Karl Klingemann in London:

> In the concert for the elderly and ailing musicians to be given here at the end of the month my *Lobgesang* is to be performed; I have now undertaken to present it not in the imperfect form that was given in Birmingham due to my illness,[56] and that gives me plenty to do. . . . Incidentally, you have a great deal to answer for with the excellent term that you discovered,[57] for I am not only sending that piece out into the world as a symphony-cantata, but also am seriously considering resuming work on the *Walpurgisnacht*, which has been sitting there idly for a long time, under that nomenclature. It's odd that when I first got the idea for it I wrote to Berlin that I wanted to write a symphony with chorus, then later couldn't get my courage up for that because the three movements[58] would be too long as an introduction—and yet I still felt that something was lacking with a mere introduction. Now the symphony movements can be included according to the original plan, and then the whole thing can be published. Do you know it, then? I don't believe that it's very good for performance, but I nevertheless like it a great deal.[59]

For all its optimistic tone, this letter evidently produced no direct results, for the project was still incomplete when the idea turned up again more than two years later. On November 28, 1842, he wrote of the plan to his mother, Lea: "I would now very much like finally to make the *Walpurgisnacht* into a symphony-cantata. This was my original intention but nothing came of it because I lacked the courage to make it so."[60]

After a hiatus of nearly a decade, the rehabilitation of the *Walpurgisnacht* progressed rapidly—and as the changes advanced, Mendelssohn clearly began to assert the distance between his first setting of Goethe's ballad and its new incarnation. He completed the autograph orchestral score for the revised version sometime in December 1842,[61] and by the 11th of that month the revisions were sufficiently complete for him to write of the project in detail, in the past tense, and with conspicuously ironic references to Christian religious traditions:

> On the 21st or 22nd we will give a concert here for the king. . . . [I]n the second half my *Walpurgisnacht* will be resurrected, albeit in a rather different habit than the previous version, which was fed all too generously with trombones and rather scrappily written for the voice. But for this I was obliged to write out the entire score again from A to Z [and] insert two new movements, to say nothing of the remaining tailoring.[62]

But circumstances once again conspired against progress on the revision project. The composer's mother died on December 12, 1842, and the arrangements for the funeral, the considerable work in dealing with the estate, and Mendelssohn's general state of mind made further work on the *Walpurgisnacht* (as well as its inclusion on the program of the royal concert) impossible. By the time he resumed work on the project he was able to report to Fanny:

> The business matters and (external) labors are pressing down hard on me once again and making me fairly desolate. On the other hand, writing music in the little room I've set up precisely for that purpose is my best means of consolation and relief. Fortunately, as I've already written to you, I had rewritten the entire *Walpurgisnacht*, but only the four-part choral material because it was to be sung in a week and the rehearsals had already begun. But the whole of the orchestral material still had to be written out, and the multitude of little details that had to be entered were, as I've said, the first and only things that really (not just apparently) occupied me. Now it is finally finished, and I believe that even you, who knew the earlier one so well (better than any soul other than myself), will be amazed at how much better the whole thing is now. I cannot now bear even to think that anyone knows it in its first version; everything that was good in that one has been retained and has only now attained its rightful significance, since the defective and inadequate material has now been deleted and replaced.[63]

A more specific report of the activities involved in these preparations was written to Klingemann several days later:

> A few days before the 11th [of December 1842] I had starting doing what I had long since planned, writing out my *Walpurgisnacht* anew. I had [already] had the vocal parts from the entire thick score written out and copied and had already rehearsed them, since they were to be given during the King's visit. Then I was called to Berlin, and having been interrupted for weeks I've now once again begun writing the instrumental parts.[64]

Fanny, however, was unconvinced (a response she admitted was typical of her reactions to Felix's revisions):

> I'm also very curious about your revisions in the *Walpurgisnacht*. You know how difficult it is for me to adjust to revisions, but I'll do my best. If only you've retained my lovely

> alto solo—that gave me great pleasure as a young woman playing an old woman. The memory of such triumphs doesn't [just] disappear.[65]

The essentials of the remainder of the *Walpurgisnacht*'s history are familiar from standard accounts. Late in January 1843 Mendelssohn and the directors of the Gewandhaus concerts programmed the work for the subscription concert of February 2. Mendelssohn was conducting the chorus and orchestra in a rehearsal (one of only two) when Hector Berlioz, who had heard the early version in Rome in the spring of 1831, arrived in Leipzig, where Mendelssohn had arranged for him to conduct two benefit concerts in February. The revised version was premiered under Mendelssohn's direction as the close of a concert given on February 2, 1843, with Sophie Schloss, Maria Heinrich Schmidt, Wilhelm Pögner, and August Kindermann as vocal soloists. The program for the concert included, beneath the soloists' names, an explanatory note enclosed in quotation marks and parentheses, and probably authored by the composer himself:

> ("In the last days of paganism in Germany, the druids' sacrifices were subject to punishment by death at the hands of the Christians. Nevertheless, at the beginning of springtime the druids and the populace sought to regain the peaks of the mountains so that they could make their sacrifices there, and to intimidate and chase off the Christians (usually through the latter's fear of the devil). The legend of the first Walpurgis Night is supposed to be based on such attempts.")[66]

The cantata also won the enthusiastic endorsement of Berlioz, who described it as follows in his *Voyage musical en Allemagne et en Italie* (first published in French and German later in 1843 and then reprinted, with further annotations, in his *Memoirs* in 1865):[67]

> The Subscription Concerts Society which [Mendelssohn] had mentioned . . . is a large and flourishing organization with a magnificent choir, a first-rate orchestra, and a hall, the Gewandhaus, which has perfect acoustics. It was in this spacious and splendid building that I was to give my concert. I went straight there on alighting from the coach, and came in on the middle of the final rehearsal of Mendelssohn's new work, which is a kind of oratorio on Goethe's *Walpurgisnacht*. I was at once astounded by the quality of the voices, the responsiveness of the singers, and above all the grandeur of the work.
>
> I am strongly inclined to regard it as the finest thing that Mendelssohn has done.[68] . . . One must hear Mendelssohn's music to realize what scope the poem offers a skilful composer. He has made admirable use of his opportunities. The score is of impeccable clarity, notwithstanding the complexity of the writing. Voices and instruments are completely integrated, and interwoven with an apparent confusion which is the perfection of art. I would especially single out, as superb examples of two diametrically opposite genres, the mysterious scene of the posting of the sentinels and the final chorus, in which the voice of the priest rises solemnly and serenely at intervals above the din of the decoy demons and sorcerers. One does not know which to praise most in this finale, the orchestral or the choral writing, or the whirling momentum and sweep of the whole.[69]

Berlioz was not the only one impressed. The premiere of the *Walpurgisnacht* was such a success that the directors of the Gewandhaus concerts considered a repeat performance in a benefit concert to be given on February 23.[70] The critic Oswald Lorenz, writing in the *Neue Zeitschrift für Musik,* called the work "an extraordinarily lovely thing, a cantata—or rather a ballad, as [the composer] would prefer to call it. It has been a long time since I heard anything so fresh and healthy, anything that brought such joy to one's heart."[71]

Despite this warm reception, Mendelssohn still had doubts about the work's viability for publication; to his close friend Ferdinand Hiller he wrote on March 3, 1843: "I have rewritten the *Walpurgisnacht* anew from A to Z. It is practically a new piece and a hundred times better [now]. But I still have doubts about whether I'll have it published."[72] Finally, the composer resolved to bring out the work in the summer of 1843. On July 14, he wrote to Friedrich Kistner asking whether he was still interested, and on July 15 he completed another series of revisions in the orchestral score, adding this date to the date of December 1842 already inscribed on its final page. At around the same time he wrote out the first piano-vocal score for the entire work.[73] He sent the latter to Kistner on July [17], at the same time informing him that he was having a separate manuscript of the orchestral score prepared by a copyist.[74] That manuscript, to be used for the engraving of the parts and score, was sent to Kistner on August 15.

In preparing the cantata for publication Mendelssohn decided to replace the anonymous prose explanatory note used for the Leipzig premiere. After a title page that reads "*Die erste Walpurgisnacht* / *Ballade für Chor und Orchester*/gedichtet von Goethe / componirt von / F M B / op. 60 / Clavier = Auszug," the second page of the autograph piano-vocal score, held in the Museum of Educational Heritage (Tokyo), begins by quoting an excerpt from Goethe's letter of September 9, 1831, to Mendelssohn (see figure 4.1). The page then lists the dramatis personae in an organizationally practical order: the choruses in order of appearance (chorus of the druids and the pagan populace—chorus of the druid watchmen—chorus of the Christian watchmen) followed by the soloists in order of appearance (an old woman from the people—a druid—a Christian watchman—the druids priest—a druid watchman). In parentheses the page then states: "after this comes the text as it is given on last year's concert program, but without the prefatory note" ("hierauf kommt der Text wie er auf dem vorjährigen Concertzettel steht, jedoch ohne die Vorbemerkung"). Mendelssohn subsequently revised the sequence of presentation for the dramatis personae in red crayon, so that the new order presents the soloists first in order of dramatic prominence (the druids' priest—a druid—a Christian watchman—a druid watchman—an old woman from the people), followed by the choruses in order of appearance (chorus of the druids and the pagan populace—chorus of the druid watchmen—chorus of the Christian watchmen).

As Hiromi Hoshino has demonstrated, Mendelssohn continued to revise the *Walpurgisnacht* in ways that would require changes in the orchestral score and

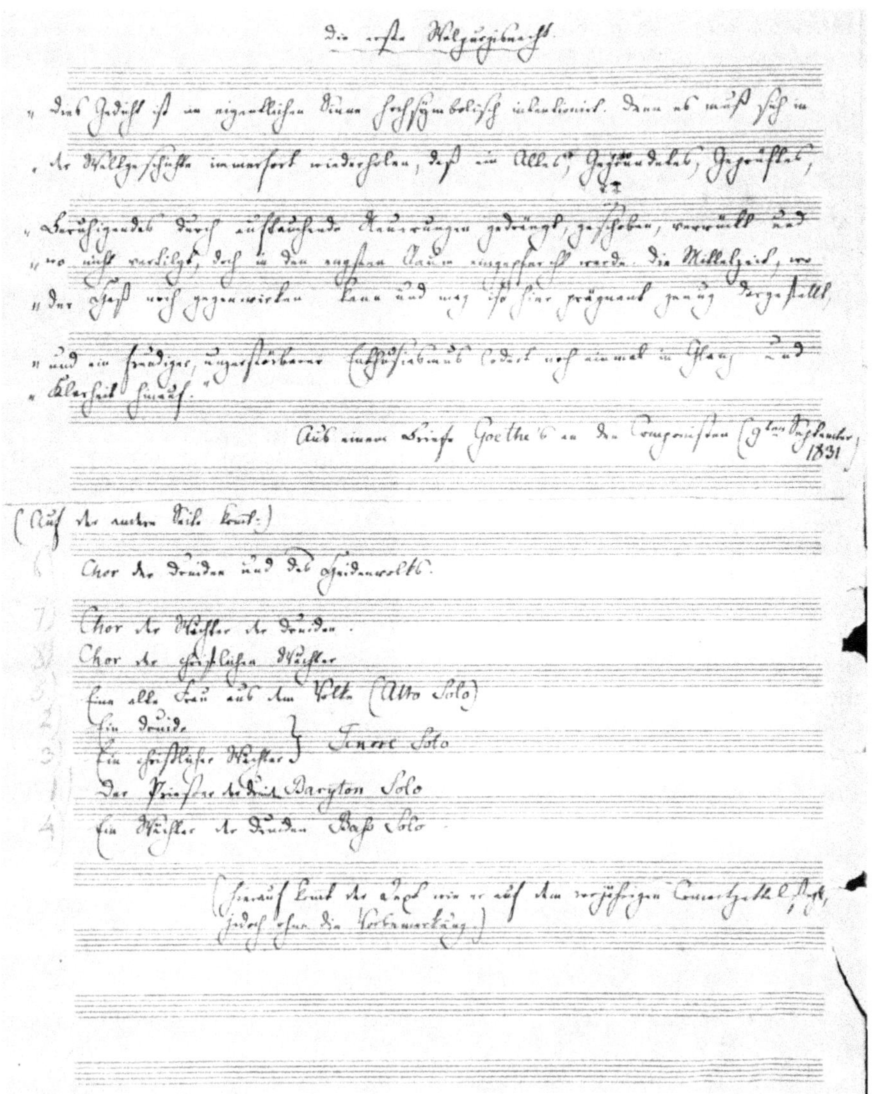

Figure 4.1. Mendelssohn, autograph prefatory page to piano-vocal score of *Die erste Walpurgisnacht,* Op. 60. Courtesy of Museum of Educational Heritage, Tokyo.

orchestral/choral parts as well as the piano-vocal score after the autograph for the last-named was completed.[75] By late November 1843, however, the proofs for the piano reduction were ready for correction[76] and he had arranged for the work to be published in England by his preferred publishers there, Ewer & Co.

(London), and distributed by his preferred French publishers, Benacci & Peschier (Lyons).[77] On January 14, 1844, as arrangements were being made for a performance by the Hamburg Musikverein, Mendelssohn wrote to inquire as to the publication dates, and the publisher responded the following day that the release date had been set for February 1.[78] The piano-vocal score and vocal parts were published ca. February 1, but at that point the full score and orchestral parts were "still in progress" ("noch in der Arbeit").[79] Having received three exemplars of the piano-vocal score on his birthday and a presentation copy, Mendelssohn enthusiastically commended the publisher on his work on February 4, 1844:

> Dear Herr Kistner,
> Please accept my warmest gratitude for the superb production on my *Walpurgisnacht*, of which I received three exemplars yesterday followed by the splendid presentation copy today.[80] Your understanding of how to adorn these things and how [the result] is at once clear, delicate, and functional is truly unique! Many, many thanks for that. I require no more exemplars of either the vocal parts or the piano-vocal score beyond those that you so kindly sent, and if I should later need them I would remember your kind offer and take advantage of it. If Herr Otten in Hamburg and the Zwiebrücken Musikverein have by chance contacted you regarding vocal parts etc., please do me the favor of complying with their requests as soon as possible.[81]

On February 14, Mendelssohn asked Kistner about the progress on the score and orchestral parts for the cantata, and three days later the publisher responded that the engraving would be finished early in March.[82] The proofs for the score were sent to the composer on March 16, and the score and parts were released in mid- or late April.[83] Mendelssohn's setting of Goethe's ballad had finally been "sent out into the world" after a gestation that spanned more than thirteen years.

If Mendelssohn still harbored reservations about the position his newly completed ballad would occupy in the musical world, they may have been assuaged by Julius Becker's lengthy review of the piano-vocal score, published in two installments in the *Neue Zeitschrift für Musik* on February 26 and 29, 1844.[84] Becker's review ranks Mendelssohn's cantata among the most significant artworks of the present, also identifying as germane to contemporary discourse many of the issues that have dominated discussions of the cantata ever since.[85] It begins with an epigraph excerpted from stanza 2 of Schiller's "An Goethe, als er den Mahomet von Voltaire auf die Bühne brachte" (To Goethe at the occasion of his staging of Voltaire's *Mahomet*[86]):

> Wir können muthig einen Lorbeer zeigen,
> Der auf dem deutschen Pindus selbst gegrünt.
> Selbst in der Künste Heiligthum zu steigen
> Hat sich der deutsche Genius erkühnt,
> Und auf der Spur des Griechen und des Britten
> Ist er dem bessern Ruhme nachgeschritten.[87]

(We can bravely display a laurel that greened on Germany's Pindus itself. The German genius dared to climb even into the sanctuary of the arts, and, following in the path of the Greek and the British one, strode on to greater fame.)

This epigraph is followed by an introductory segment that amounts to a justification for the remarkable length of the review, ascribing to its subject an ironically sacred stature and proposing that the work merits lasting fame:

> Revealed in a masterpiece of art, the highest idea of the beautiful permits analysis only up to a certain point, and the attempt to infuse into such a work as a *triumvirate* the holy *trinity* of truth, beauty, and goodness is largely the province of those abstract speculations that all too easily lose any meaning for art and specifically for musicians. On the other hand it remains certain that the greater an artwork is, the greater the response it elicits from our artistic consciousness. Thus, the more decisively and significantly it strikes us, the more decisive and significant are the judgments we naturally pronounce on it. . . . The truth always sooner or later emerges victorious from struggle! In this regard Mendelssohn Bartholdy also shares the fate of all preeminent spirits of his time!
>
> Turning now, after these introductory remarks (which at any rate seem to us like a word spoken in due season), to his last-published work, *Die erste Walpurgisnacht*, we do not in fact know to which of the familiar genres of vocal composition we should assign this tone-poem, superb in its invention as well as its execution. . . . This much is certain: that the designation "oratorio," which an enthusiastic Hector Berlioz applies to the *Walpurgisnacht* (obviously for lack of a better term), is not appropriate simply because the oratorio, strictly speaking, belongs only in the church, and the term "secular oratorio" is justifiable only if the concept of the oratorio denotes only the external musical form, "secular" applying to its subject matter, which must be anything but sacred. The term "cantata" is even less adequate because in that genre the lyrical predominates, whereas the epic is more prominent [here]. . . . Although the present work greatly exceeds the meaning of "ballad" as we musicians understand it, this term is probably the most meaningful, all the more so because the poem is so designated. If the musician requires a special term to distinguish it from the familiar ones, perhaps "concert ballad" would be the most appropriate.[88]

Becker closes the first installment of his essay by quoting the printed score's excerpt of Goethe's letter of September 9, 1831, to Mendelssohn, noting the work's remarkably long instrumental introduction, and proposing that the Introduction's length and complexity are justified because they adumbrate the "elevated import of the work as a whole" ("die hohe Bedeutung des ganzen Werkes").[89] The bulk of the second installment comprises a detailed description of Mendelssohn's setting, associating the Introduction with "that holy spirit of order that, as Novalis would put it, 'lets chaos shimmer through its clearly woven fabric' " and quoting a translated version of Berlioz's assessment.[90] Becker's conclusions, however, are especially noteworthy for their articulation of many of the issues germane to this problematical composition:

> Thus the exalted master greets the German genius anew with this work, having already braided a laurel into the fadeless crown of glory of the poet-heroes of Germany and

> Britain as composer of *Antigone* and *A Midsummer Night's Dream.*—Rejoice in that, my Germany, and consider that it was one of your greatest poets who uttered the words given as a motto at the outset of this article, just as this is also true of one of your greatest tone-poets, Mendelssohn Bartholdy![91]

For all its panegyrical tone, Becker's review is important not least of all for the insights it provides into the issues Mendelssohn's contemporaries would have found in his setting of Goethe's ballad. Submitted by one of Germany's greatest living composers, *Die erste Walpurgisnacht* was a "sublime" interpretation of a text on that subject by one of her greatest poetic voices. It affirmed German-speakers' cultural identity by celebrating the Saxons' pre-Christian past. It transcended contemporary theoretical and aesthetic genre delimitations and achieved what Becker considered an unprecedented unity of poetic and musical spirit. It built on the scenic and dramaturgical accomplishments of Mendelssohn's celebrated incidental music to Shakespeare's *A Midsummer Night's Dream* and Sophocles's *Antigone.* Perhaps most important, the epigraph extracted from Schiller's "An Goethe" engaged the issue of alterity to the mores and beliefs of mainstream Christian society: for as discussed in chapter 2, Voltaire's *Mahomet*—especially in Goethe's "translation"—is a searing critique of fanaticism and superstition of the very sort that figures so prominently in Goethe's ballad concerning the conflict between Christianity and paganism in the Harz Mountains. In this light, any contradiction implied by Mendelssohn's decision to celebrate "the foulness of heathenism" in the same sacred idiom cultivated for the glorification of Christianity in *St. Paul* and his other earlier sacred music becomes understandable and obvious: the composer of music for the great plays of Shakespeare and Sophocles has joined forces with Goethe, Schiller, and Voltaire on one of the pressing social and cultural issues of the day: the issue of religious and social tolerance and acceptance.

The revised version of *Die erste Walpurgisnacht* quickly became more popular than Mendelssohn had predicted. Although the compositional context for the first version reaffirms its authority as a compositional compeer to the *Hebrides* Overture and the most important musical stepping-stone to his first international triumph in choral/orchestral composition, *St. Paul,* the published version claims unquestionable authority as the better representation of his compositional persona as it had developed by the early 1840s. At the same time, Mendelssohn's two *Walpurgisnacht* settings are more than case-studies in the evolution of the music he created in response to Goethe's culturally charged "poetic fable," more than documents of a changed source of musical and poetic utterance, from the voice that speaks in the "Reformation" Symphony, the *Hebrides* Overture, the G-minor Piano Concerto, and *St. Paul* to the one that speaks in the "Scottish" Symphony, the E-minor Violin Concerto, the C-minor Piano Trio, and ultimately *Elijah.* Above all, they are revealing testimonies of Mendelssohn's self-identification as a musical translator of the mid-nineteenth century's discourses of identity and alterity, tolerance and acceptance.

Chapter Five

The Sources, Structure, and Narrative of Mendelssohn's Walpurgisnacht *Settings*

Mendelssohn's letters concerning the final version of *Die erste Walpurgisnacht* make clear that the differences between it and the version of 1831–33 were crucial. In this instance there is no doubt that in retrospect Mendelssohn regarded these two versions as different stages in the life of a single work-concept rather than autonomous texts validated by their respective contexts.[1] Nor is there any question but that he considered the later version superior once it had been completed. Nevertheless, through the mid-1830s he intended to revise rather than rewrite the early version, and as late as August 1835 he expected these revisions to be sufficiently noninvasive that he could enter the changes into the parts used for the 1833 premiere. Only after he had actually begun the revision process did the new version begin to depart radically from the old one. By January 1843 he could "no longer bear to think that anyone [knew] it in its first version," and by March 1843 he had come to think of it as "practically a new piece."[2] Foundational to these revisions as well as Mendelssohn's ultimate decision to publish the work were the historical and symbolic programs discussed in chapters 3 and 4.

Because of the wealth of surviving information concerning Goethe's and Mendelssohn's ideas concerning the Walpurgis Night as cultural and artistic topos, because of the extensive changes Mendelssohn's setting underwent between 1831 and 1844, and because Mendelssohn explicitly distanced the revised version of *Die erste Walpurgisnacht* from its early version, this chapter treats those two versions of the ballad as separate settings. Their shared features reveal what he considered successful about the early setting throughout the work's life span, while the differences between the version that he had come to consider "defective and inadequate" by the early 1840s and its eventual replacement offer useful insights into his development as a composer and the changes in his professional standing over the course of that decade. More generally but no less importantly, they reflect changes in his understanding of Goethe's treatments of the Walpurgis Night topos and its potential as a source of artistic inspiration over the course of those years.

Mendelssohn's Settings of Goethe's Ballad: A Synoptic Overview

Mendelssohn's two settings of "Die erste Walpurgisnacht" possess a similar tonal organization (see figure 5.1). After a lengthy instrumental introduction beginning in A minor, both introduce the first stanza of Goethe's text in A major, a key frequently associated with springtime in Mendelssohn's music. Stanzas 2 through 4 center on F-sharp minor, A major, and D minor, while stanza 5 (one of two that were completely replaced in the final version) is in A minor with prominent recourse to E minor. The cadence into stanza 6 turns to E major as the pagans agree to post sentinels around the mountain to safeguard those carrying out the worship service at the summit, and E major remains the key as the preparations for the night close and the guards spread out along the wooded slopes. The first part of stanza 7 (the beginning of the Walpurgis Night proper) is set as a recitative that modulates from E minor to G minor (conspicuously absent up to this point), where one of the pagan guards proposes the ruse to scare away the "foolish cleric-Christians" (*dumpfe Pfaffenchristen*) and the key remains G minor as his idea is taken up by the other sentinels. The music swerves abruptly to the dominant of A minor as the ruse itself begins, and this remains the key of stanza 8 as a whole (although there are also prominent excursions into E minor, B-flat major, and G minor). The ruse ends with a massive deceptive cadence on the submediant (F major) for an instrumental interlude, but with stanza 9, A minor returns, moving to C major as the druid's thoughts turn from regret that it has become necessary to worship secretly to the central prayer for their faith to be purified by the *Allvater*'s light as the fire is purified of smoke. Both versions of the Christian guards' stanzas (stanzas 10 and 11), the other passage entirely reconceived in the final version, center on the new keys of C minor and F minor and turn to C major as the guards flee, and C major remains the tonal center for the final pagan hymn (stanza 12).

In sum, both of Mendelssohn's settings reflect a large-scale tonal organization that moves from A minor through A major to E major and closes in the relative major of the original tonic (see ex. 5.1). In both versions the first part traces the movement from *A* (minor and then major) to its dominant, while F-sharp minor is strongly associated with the pagans and their culture. And in both versions Walpurgis Night itself moves from G minor for the planning of the ruse, through A minor for a more elaborate phase, to the closing paean in C major, with the instrumental interlude between stanzas 8 and 9 set in F major and the Christian sentinels' music in its parallel minor and C minor.

As Mendelssohn's eventual vehemence in rejecting the first setting would suggest, however, there are substantial differences in the two versions' execution of this tonal plan. The more important of these will be discussed under "Structural Revisions," below. For the moment it will suffice to note that the plan operates around four principles that are easily explained in terms of Goethe's ballad. The material that represents the pagans' actual or genuine existence generally is

Goethe	(stanza / ll.) Voice	1 1–13 Ein Druide	2 14–17 Die Druiden	3 17–27 Einer aus d. Volke	4 28–32 Chor der Weiber	5 33–45 Ein Druide	6 46–49 Ch. der Wächter	7 50–59 Ein Wächter	8 60–65 Ch. der Wächter	9 66–78 Ein Druide	10 79–89 Ein christl. Wächter	11 90–95 Ch. der christl. Wächter	12 96–99 Ch. der Druiden
FMB	Mvt	Einleitung						No. 2					
1833	Scoring	Ein Druide (T solo)	Ein Dr. (T solo /Chor der Druiden (TTBB)	Eine alte Frau (A solo)	Ch. der Weiber (SSAA) / Eine alte Frau (A solo)	Ein Dr. (T solo)	[Ch. der Wächter] (TTBB)	Ein Dr. (T solo) (ll. 50–53) / Ein Dr. Männerch. (T, TTBB) (ll. 54–59)	[Ch.] (SATB)	Ein Dr. (B solo) / [ch.] (SATB)	Ein [christl.] Wächter (T solo)	Ch. der [christl.] Wächter (kleinerer Ch.) (TTBB)	Ch. der (Frauench. + Der ganze Männerch.)
	Key	A	f♯	A–d	g–d - a	a –V/e	E	e–g–G E–V/a	V/a– a–V/a	F–a–C	c	f–V/f	C

FMB	Mvt	No. 1	No. 2	No. 3	No. 4	No. 5	No. 6	No. 7		No. 8	No. 9
Op. 60	Scoring	Ein Druide (T solo) / Ch. des Volks (SA) / Ch. der Druiden und des Volks (TB)	Eine alte Frau aus dem Volke (A solo) / Ch. der Weiber aus dem Volke (SSAA)	Der Priester (Bar solo) / Ch. der Dr. (TTBB)	Ch. der Wächter der Dr. (SATB)	Ein Wächter der Dr. (B solo) (ll. 50–53) /Ch. der Wächter der Dr. (TTBB) (ll. 54–59)	Ch. der Wächter der Dr. und des Heidenvolks	Der Priester (Bar solo) / Ch. der Dr. und des Heidenvolks	Ein chr. Wächter	Ch. der chr. Wächter	Der Prister (Bar solo) / allgem. Ch. der Dr. u. des Heidenvolks
	Key	A/f♯	A–d–g– d–V/a	a–C–e	E	e–g–G– E–V/a	V/a–a	F–a–C		V/f– f–C	C

Figure 5.1. Structural overview of Mendelssohn's settings of "Die erste Walpurgisnacht" (texted portion) (cf. Figure 3.2).

Example 5.1. Tonal organization of Mendelssohn's settings of "Die erste Walpurgisnacht": (a) 1830–33 version; (b) Op. 60.

presented as a function of A major and F-sharp minor (the transition to springtime, stanza 1, and stanza 2). Stanzas 3 and 4 establish the alterity of the pagans whose intimidation has made them hesitant to pursue the old ways, focusing on D minor with prominent recourse to G minor (the latter especially in stanza 4). These dark tonal areas are aptly mirrored through Mendelssohn's isolated use of C minor and F minor in the Christian watchmen's stanzas (10 and 11). The textual components that somehow reflect the interaction or conflict between the pagan and Christian are set to keys that mediate between these two sets of tonal axes: fluid movement between A minor and C major for the druid priest's admonitions about the necessity of remaining true to the faith in the face of adversity and encircling the forest in order to preserve this religious freedom (revised version of stanza 5 and both versions of stanza 9); E minor and E major for the pagan men's adoption of the idea (remainder of stanza 5); G minor for some of the sentinels' idea to carry out the ruse (stanza 7); and A minor for the ruse itself (stanza 8). The same is true of the most explicitly transitional material: the pagan sentinel's idea for the ruse (stanza 7) moves from E minor through A minor to G minor, and the instrumental interlude between the end of the mid-ground pagan ruse (stanza 8) and the ceremonies atop the Brocken (stanza 9) mediates between these two with F major. Finally, the material that deals with the free religious celebration of the metaphorical light of the *Allvater*—that is, the theological common ground between the pagan and Christian cultures represented by the ballad's protagonists—is associated with the key of C major, which offers significant tonal common ground for both (at the levels of the mediant, submediant, and root vis-à-vis the pagan tonal areas and the root and dominant vis-à-vis the Christian ones).

The supple but tightly woven tonal structure of *Die erste Walpurgisnacht* provides the foil for a remarkably diverse assemblage of themes and stylistic references. The programmatic designations of the two main sections of the introduction augur the centrality of contrast for the work as a whole. The first of these, labeled *Das schlechte Wetter* (The Bad Weather), uses the stylistic vocabulary familiar from the fourth movement of Beethoven's "Pastoral" Symphony and Mendelssohn's own contemporaneous *Hebrides* Overture (see ex. 5.2a). The second section, labeled *Der Übergang zum Frühling* (The Transition to Springtime, ex. 5.2b) transforms the thematic incipit of the first into a radiant A-major theme that becomes the main idea of stanza 1 (ex. 5.2c). This strophe begins with a tenor solo and then includes the chorus as well as the solo.[3] Stanza 2 is also a responsorial setting, beginning with a tenor solo before the entry of the men's chorus (ex. 5.2d). But the pagans' enthusiasm is abruptly interrupted when one of them—designated "an old woman from among the people" by Mendelssohn—warns of the consequences if their Christian adversaries catch them engaging in the practice (stanza 3). For this stanza, which is at once a reminder and a foreshadowing of the pagans' eventual fate, the tempo slows and the solo part is given to an alto (ex. 5.2e)—a role Fanny Hensel evidently performed when the early version was performed in Berlin on October 11, 1832.[4] The music of stanza 4 is an extension of stanza 3, assigned to the women's chorus as in Goethe's ballad.

Example 5.2. Mendelssohn, *Die erste Walpurgisnacht*, Op. 60: Essential thematic material of introduction and stanzas 1–4: (a) Introduction, "Das schlechte Wetter," first theme (mm. 4–8); (b) Introduction, "Der Übergang zum Frühling" (mm. 360–62); (c) No. 1 (mm. 8–13); (d) No. 1 (mm. 94–98); (e) No. 2 (mm. 3–9).

As already noted, the first and revised conceptions of stanza 5 were completely different. In the 1830–33 setting Mendelssohn cast this strophe as a tenor solo, *Allegro vivace*—an angry rejection of the idea that the pagans should weigh the consequences before conducting their sacred rites (ex. 5.3a). But in the revised version he reconsidered the *Affekt* of this movement, setting it for baritone solo (labeled *der Priester* / the priest) and adopting first an attitude of devotion (ex. 5.3b) and then one of resolve. The latter is signified through a quickening of the tempo and the introduction of insistent dotted-eighth-note–sixteenth-note repeated patterns (ex. 5.3c). Once the critical decision to post guards has been made, the pagans' mood brightens. Amid fanfare-like calls in the brass and winds, the voices of the male chorus depict the guards cheerily spreading out along the hillsides (stanza 6; see ex. 5.3d).

The music of the Walpurgis Night proper reveals some of Mendelssohn's most assertive interpretive interventions—instances where the music seems to depart from the forms and stanza groupings of the poem. As noted in chapter 3, stanzas 7 and 8 of the poem follow the pattern of solo/choral response employed in the previous stanza pairs. Mendelssohn, however, compresses the first half of stanza 7 (ll. 50–53) into a brief recitative and sets the remaining five lines of that solo stanza as an extended crescendo for solo voice and male chorus, based on a G-minor march-like tune whose consequent phrase features a chromatically descending melodic cell (ex. 5.4a). According to the established pattern and the roles specified by the poem, stanza 8 would be the male chorus's response to stanza 7, and would use essentially the same thematic material. Instead, it is autonomous and uses the full chorus. It is also the lengthiest of all the musical numbers, extending over 286 measures in the first setting and 306 measures in the final one and tracing the broad outlines of a fully developed sonata form based on an A-minor theme first introduced by the women's chorus (ex. 5.4b).[5] And it is followed by another passage not specifically called for by the poem: a *fortissimo* orchestral interlude based on a flickering figure originally introduced as a woodwind accompaniment in the second half of stanza 7 (ex. 5.4c). By the end of this interlude the scene has changed to the Brocken's summit, where the druid priest presides over the pagans' solemn ceremonies (stanza 9; see ex. 5.4d). For stanzas 10 and 11 the scene changes to the poem's other topographical extreme, the low ground occupied by the Christian watchmen, where the two versions provide substantially different music for the solo watchman's panicky report of the horrors he believes he witnesses and the other Christian watchmen's echo (ex. 5.4e–g). The pagans' worship, meanwhile, has proceeded undeterred: the druid priest's hymn returns to the foreground in stanza 12, taken up in a radiant C major by the full chorus (ex. 5.4h–i).

The final feature of the thematic structure of *Die erste Walpurgisnacht* that warrants mention here is that it represents an extended essay in thematic transformation and organic development within a multimovement cyclic form.[6] This overarching structural coherence is achieved through the use of two contrasting melodic cells. The first of these cells is recognizable by its characteristic pitch contour (usually $\hat{5}$–$\hat{1}$–$\hat{2}$–$\hat{3}$, ascending), its tendency to begin on an upbeat (often with a repeated note), and its placement at the outset of themes, stanzas, or especially important lines of text (see ex. 5.2a–d, 5.3d, 5.4a, 5.4d, and 5.4h). The second one is best described as a chromatic descent in the minor mode, usually beginning on $\hat{2}$ or $\hat{6}$ (see ex. 5.4a and 5.4c). This technique—arguably a worthy compeer to Berlioz's and Liszt's better-known essays in thematic transformation—not only provides Mendelssohn's settings with a large-scale coherence of the sort essential to his mature style as well as that of Goethe, but also represents the key to understanding Mendelssohn's early designations of *Die erste*

Example 5.3. Mendelssohn, *Die erste Walpurgisnacht:* Essential thematic material of early and revised versions of stanzas 5 and 6: (a) 1830–33 version: I: 667–77; (b) Op. 60: No. 3 (mm. 1–10); (c) Op. 60: No. 3 (mm. 22–26); (d) Op. 60: No. 4 (mm. 14–16).

Example 5.4. Mendelssohn, *Die erste Walpurgisnacht:* Essential thematic material of stanzas 7–12: (a) Op. 60, No. 5 (mm. 17–26); (b) Op. 60, No. 6 (mm. 39–49); (c) Op. 60, No. 7 (mm. 1–4); (d) Op. 60, No. 7 (mm. 29–32); (e) 1830–33 version, No. 2 (mm. 463–64); (f) Op. 60, No. 8 (mm. 2–6); (g) Op. 60, No.8 (mm. 14–17); (h) Op. 60, No. 9 (mm. 5–9); (i) Op. 6, No. 9 (mm. 18–25).

Walpurgisnacht as "a new kind of cantata" and his eventual linking of it with the symphony-cantata *Lobgesang*, Op. 52.[7] This technique was one of several issues that Mendelssohn grappled with as he struggled to perfect his setting between 1831 and 1843.

Doch ist es Tag, so - bald man mag ein rei - nes Herz dir brin - gen.

Hilf, ach hilf mir, Kriegs - ge-sel - le! Ach, es kommt die gan-ze Höl-le!

Hilf, ach hilf mir, Kriegs-ge - sel-le! Ach, es kommt die gan-ze Höl - le!

Schreck-li-che, ver-hex-te Lei - ber, Men-schen-Wölf und Dra-chen - Wei - ber!

Die Flam-me rei-nigt sich vom Rauch, so rei-nig' un-sern Glau - ben!

Example 5.4. (*continued*)

The Musical Sources and the Revision History

The surviving manuscript sources for Mendelssohn's settings of *Die erste Walpurgisnacht* document the issues involved in his protracted struggle to come to terms with Goethe's 1799 ballad and its subject. The circumstances of the work's genesis naturally group the sources into two broad classes: those that pertain to the early setting and those that pertain to the final one. Each of these groups includes a variety of classes of sources: sketches, drafts, one autograph full score, and a set of parts, plus the first printed editions of the orchestral and choral parts, piano-vocal score, and full score of the final version. These sources are summarized in tables 5.1 and 5.2 (pp. 108–11).

The three sets of sketches are useful in several regards. Most obviously, they are musical counterparts to the paralipomena for Goethe's *Faust*—documents that reveal early stages of the ideas for the thematic and motivic material and the planning of the version of 1831–33. Some of these ideas were rejected outright; others were adapted for use in later versions; and a few achieved definitive form already in these early notations.[8] They also offer a glimpse into the creative workshop, particularly when coupled with the correspondence discussed in chapter 4.

One example of these insights must suffice for this brief discussion. Page 41 of Sk2 includes nine complete measures of score for the early version of Mendelssohn's setting of stanza 6 (see figure 5.2), analogous to mm. 16–23 of No. 4 in the final version. The paper type, writing implement, and voice leading show that this page originally followed directly from the last measure of p. 62 of the composing score (AS1), but Mendelssohn broke off the notation of this page about three-fourths of the way across the staves, evidently setting the page aside for use as scratch paper and replacing it with what is now p. 63/67 of AS1. Eventually he used the page for sketches for other parts of the cantata, including the "bad weather" of the introduction, the original version of the preceding stanza (stanza 5), the second half of stanza 7, and stanza 8. Additionally, p. 39—now the first leaf of the bifolio but surely the second one before Mendelssohn rejected the page—includes several monetary computations and diary-like jottings: an annotation in the upper left-hand corner (evidently written before the sketches for the second half of stanza 7, since the musical notes work around the verbal ones) refers to "Tasso; Goethes Tasso, Gluck." And on the lower right-hand side, near the sketches for no. 8, are the annotations "Mechetti. 150 / Br[ief] v[on] Marx / ŏ angekomm[en] / Br[ief] an Goethe?"

Mendelssohn was sufficiently confident in the cantata as a whole to inscribe and date the final page of its texted portion on July 15, 1831. The score passage of Sk2 had obviously been written and rejected before that, but when did the on-the-fly rejection of the score occur, and when were the sketches written? Since Mendelssohn's letters make clear that the content and extent of the introduction were still undetermined in mid-1831 and his first confident report on the overture dates from January 21, 1832 (when he described it as "the Saxon A-minor

Table 5.1. Sources for 1830–33 Version of Mendelssohn, *Die erste Walpurgisnacht*

Siglum	*Location, description*
Sk1	*Oxford, Bodleian Library, Mus. M. Deneke Mendelssohn c. 47, fol. 29r.* Sketch, 4 measures, for strophe 6 (mid-October 1830).
Sk2	*Staatsbibliothek zu Berlin–Preußischer Kulturbesitz, Mus. ms. autogr. F. Mendelssohn Bartholdy 18, pp. 39–42.* Sketches for the instrumental introduction and an incomplete page of score for nine measures of stanza 6 ("Verteilt euch wackre Männer hier"). The page of score was written and removed from AS1 before July 15, 1831. The sketches for the Introduction almost certainly date from between then and January 1832.
[*AS1a]	Autograph beginning of the instrumental introduction, with slow beginning (Andante) in G minor, 3/4, 138 mm; incomplete (between July 15, 1831, and February 13, 1832). In private possession.
APf1	*Staatsbibliothek zu Berlin–Preußischer Kulturbesitz, 2 an: Mus. ms. autogr. F. Mendelssohn Bartholdy 49.* Holograph arrangement for piano duet four hands, corresponding to "bad weather" and "thaw" of AS1. Edited and partially reproduced in facsimile in my edition of the first complete version (Madison, WI, A-R Editions, [2007]).
AS1	*Krakow, Bibliotheka Jagiellońska, Mus. ms. autogr. F. Mendelssohn Bartholdy 37.* Autograph full score with additional markings in other hands; 66 oblong leaves, in green binding and within a librarian's case. Its first page with notated music bears the inscription "H.d.[m.]" ("Hilf du mir," roughly trans. as "Help thou me"), which Mendelssohn typically inscribed when beginning serious work on a composition. Autograph page numbers originally ran from 1 (the first page) to 123, but this sequence was disturbed by the removal of subsequent pages. There is also a set of page numbers in the script of Albert Kopfermann, former head of the Music Division of the Königliche Bibliothek zu Berlin (now the Staatsbibliothek zu Berlin–Preußischer Kulturbesitz). In this chapter both page numbers are cited when applicable, with Mendelssohn's and Kopfermann's paginations separated by a slash (e.g., "p. 49/53"). The leaves evidently were originally arranged as a regular series of bifolia, but the structure is now irregular in places due to the removal of individual leaves and the insertion of various paste-overs. At least two further paste-overs have been separated from the volume

Table 5.1. *(continued)*

Siglum	Location, description
	entirely—evidently before it passed into the possession of the Berlin Staatsbibliothek; see [*AS1b] and *AS1c.
[*AS1b]	Residue of the glue from the underside of this lost manuscript is present on p. 97 of *AS1*. The manuscript itself is lost. It was almost certainly autograph and must have transmitted material pertaining to stanza 8, but otherwise nothing is known of its content or structure.
*AS1c	*Paris, Bibliothèque Nationale de France (Bibliothèque du Conservatoire), Ms. 207*. One single sheet in full score transmitting an early version of the close of stanza 9 and beginning of stanza 10. The paper, ink, and writing utensil of *AS1a are identical to those of the main *Notentext* of AS1, clearly indicating that it was a part of that autograph's compositional history. Moreover, the first measure of *AS1a follows directly from the penciled corrections to the last undeleted measure of AS1 p. 112, and the last notated measure of fol. 2v of *AS1a leads directly into the first measure of AS1 p. 114, the recto side of which (p. 113) retains signs of a now-deleted paste-over. These notational linkages confirm that *AS1a was at some point either a part of AS1 or intended to be so.
[*AS1d]	Full-score fragment(s), autograph, with original close of stanza 9 and beginning of stanza 10, continued from p. 105/112 of AS1. Lost. All that may be conjectured about the content of this source is that it followed the *ante correcturam* reading of AS1 p. 105/112 and was replaced by *AS1c.
*AP1	*New Haven (Connecticut), Yale University Music Library, SC Ma21 / M522 / Er87*. Autograph tenor part with no title or other heading and many deletions and corrections. This manuscript transmits an early version of the tenor part, beginning at I: 399 and extending through the original version of the Introduction to No. 2 (II: 25).
[AP2]	Autograph tenor part headed "Ein Druide"; fair copy with no corrections or changes, corresponding to the "Druide" part for the early version as given in AS1. Lost.

Table 5.1. *(continued)*

Siglum	*Location, description*
[A/CP]	Parts for other soloists, chorus, and orchestra used for the performances in Berlin (November 11, 1832, and/or January 10, 1833). Some of these parts may be autograph (as AP1 and AP2 are) or contain autograph corrections and changes.

Table 5.2. Sources for final version of Mendelssohn, *Die erste Walpurgisnacht,* Op. 60

Siglum	*Location, description*
Sk3	*Staatsbibliothek zu Berlin–Preußischer Kulturbesitz, Mus. ms. autogr. F. Mendelssohn Bartholdy 19, pp. 67–68, 71–77, 79–86.* The sketches on pp. 67–68 are written upside down on a rejected and only partially completed page of full score for Mendelssohn's setting of Psalm 95 ("Kommt, laßt uns anbeten"), Op. 46, which was composed in 1839–42 and published in 1842.
Sk4	*Bodleian Library, Oxford, MS M. Deneke Mendelssohn c. 22, fol. 6r.* Sketch for stanza 10.
AS2	*Musikbibliothek der Stadt Leipzig, PM 143.* This full-score autograph copy was the source for the performances and editions of Op. 60. Its first page with notated music bears the inscription "H.d.m." It consists of the full score plus an appended score with additional music for piccolo, three trombones, bass drum, and cymbals. The paper types in this autograph reveal three major stages of revision: Stage I: pp. 37–60 (stanzas 1–5); pp. 65–80 (end of st. 7 and beg. of 8), 105–7 (most of st. 12). Stage II: Overture pp. 1–4, 9–20; pp. 61–64 (end of stanza 6 and beg. of st. 7), 81–84 (mid. of st. 8), pp. 91–96 (m. 4 of stanza 9 to end of stanza), appended score. Stage III: Overture pp. 5–8, 21–35; 85–90 (end of stanza 8 and beginning of interlude); 97–104 (st. 10–11, beg. of st. 12); 113–14 (pic, tbn, bd, cym for end of st. 8).
*AS2a	*Staatsbibliothek zu Berlin–Preußischer Kulturbesitz, Mus. ms. autogr. F. Mendelssohn Bartholdy 56.* Autograph full-score fragment for st. 8. Bears autograph pagination "85–88" in Mendelssohn's

Table 5.2. *(continued)*

Siglum	*Location, description*
	hand. The lower margin bears the inscription "Herrn Landsberg zum Andenken an gute alte Zeit und an Felix Mendelssohn Bartholdy. Leipzig 4ten Sept. 1843."
[*AS2b]	Lost. End of stanza 11 and beginning of stanza 12.
[*AS2c]	Lost. Choral score produced ca. December 14, 1842.
[CP1]	Choral parts for revised version based on [*AS2c], produced between December 14 and 21, 1842.
[*AS2x]	Lost pages originally included in Stage I of AS2 but removed.
[*AS2y]	Lost pages originally included in Stage I and/or Stage II of AS2 but removed.
[CS1]	Copy of full score made by Eduard Henschke, based on AS2. Lost.
APf2	*Tokyo, Museum of Educational Heritage at Tamagawa University.* Autograph piano-vocal score based on AS2, produced in late spring/early summer of 1843. This autograph is now available in full-color facsimile, ed. Hiromi Hoshino (2005).
*AB	Pierpont Morgan Library, New York. Albumblatt, US-NYpm, Morgan Collection.
EPfG	First German edition of piano/vocal arrangement, published by Kistner, Leipzig [1844]. Fol., engr., Plate no. 1400; 91 pp. Introduction arr. for pf duet. See Ward Jones, *Catalogue,* Vol. III, 105–6 (item 373).
EPfE	First English edition of piano/vocal arrangement, published by Ewer & Co., London [1844]. Fol., engr., 87 pp. Words in English (trans. William Bartholomew) and German. Introduction arr. for pf duet. See Ward Jones, *Catalogue,* Vol. III, 106 (item 375).
EPvG	First edition of German vocal parts, published by Kistner, Leipzig [1844]. Fol., engr., pl. no. 1401. See Ward Jones, *Catalogue,* Vol. III, 106 (item 377).
EPvE	First edition of English vocal parts, published by Ewer & Co., London, [1844]. No extant exemplar currently known.
EPo	First edition of orchestral parts, published by Kistner, Leipzig [1844]. Fol., engr., pl. no. 1402. Partial set survives in GB-Ob; see Ward Jones, *Catalogue,* Vol. III, 106–7 (item 376).
ESG	First German edition of full score, published by Kistner, Leipzig, [1844]. Fol., engr., pl. no. 1403, 163 pp. See Ward Jones, *Catalog,* Vol. III, 105 (item 371).

Figure 5.2. Staatsbibliothek zu Berlin—Preußischer Kulturbesitz, Mus. ms. autogr. F. Mendelssohn Bartholdy 18, p. 41. Used by permission.

Overture that [was] to precede the Walpurgisnacht"[9]) we may provisionally assert that the sketches were written late in 1831 or early 1832. But the reference to Mechetti, Marx, and Goethe on the lower right-hand side provide another clue—for Mendelssohn did indeed write to the poet on August 28, 1831 (see chapter 4, pp. 82–83), and on that date he also wrote to the Viennese publisher Pietro Mechetti reminding him that the agreed-upon honorarium for the rights to several of his compositions was 150 Gulden.[10] The sketches for the "bad weather" portion of the Overture, the original version of stanza 5, the second half of stanza 7, and stanza 8 thus seem to have been written ca. August 1831. That date provides a provisional *terminus ante quem* for the writing and replacement of the original reading for the beginning of stanza 6.

On the face of it, these observations offer little more than an interesting tale for those already curious about the genesis of the work or Mendelssohn's creative process in general. But they also demonstrate that Mendelssohn did not sketch the whole and then realize and revise it in score, but moved fluidly between advanced stages of work (writing out the full score) and "precompositional" stages: stanza 6 was composed before stanza 5, and the overture was sketched, written, and rewritten after the texted part of the cantata had been provisionally completed. This recursive creative process does not just rescue the sketches from a presumedly isolated position with regard to the finished product; it places them and other rejected or prefinal materials in the white heat of the compositional forge. Even the earliest sketches for the *Walpurgisnacht* (Sk1) demonstrate that it and the *Hebrides* Overture are compositional and conceptual siblings, despite their different genres and the substantial chronological gap between their respective final versions.[11] In brief, the oneness of the various source classes means that the variants they transmit are invested with broad meaning for our understanding of the *Walpurgisnacht* as a whole.

The same is true of the remaining manuscripts for the early setting. The manuscript arrangement of the Introduction for piano duet (see figure 5.3) is clearly a composing score: the Secondo part is provided only sketchily and is mostly incomplete, and the two pianists' parts are written above one another in four sequential staves rather than on facing pages (the practical convention for this medium). This arrangement was almost certainly prepared and used for one or both of the private performances in 1832 (see chapter 4, pp. 83–84). It is clearly based on the orchestral score (AS1) as it existed at that point but does not reflect all of the deletions and other changes now present in that score. APf1 thus establishes a *terminus ante quem* of April 1832 for some of the variants transmitted in the full-score autograph of the introduction and a *terminus post quem* of October 1832 for others. (The chronology would of course be more precise if the date for the notation of APf1 were ascertained, but the available evidence does not permit this.) Additionally, the fact that Hensel's ideas for reviving the family's Sunday Musicales reportedly provided the initial impetus for Mendelssohn's composition of the early setting—and that it was evidently performed in that venue with piano rather than orchestral accompaniment—combines with the care Mendelssohn invested in preparing the keyboard arrangement of the final version to corroborate the artistic validity of the piano-vocal reduction.[12]

The interrelationships between the two remaining incomplete orchestral scores and the orchestral composing score (AS1) likewise offer more than just curiosities. As shown and described before it disappeared into private possession, the early score for the Introduction ([*AS1a]) began with a slow introduction in G minor before moving to C major.[13] This version differs from all other surviving versions not only in its overall gesture—for in no other version does the work open with a slow introduction—but also in its tonal structure: it is difficult to envision the cantata without its paradigmatic tonal progression from A minor to C major.

The relationships between the orchestral composing score (AS1) and the surviving and lost full-score fragments are more complicated. The composing score must have included another version of the close of stanza 9 (source [*AS1c]) that was subsequently removed and replaced by another close for that stanza. In all probability, that replacement page was the fragmentary full score now held in the Bibiliothèque Nationale de France (source *AS1c), whose initial measure follows the corrected reading of the last undeleted measure of stanza 9 in AS1. To

Figure 5.3. Staatsbibliothek zu Berlin—Preußischer Kulturbesitz, 2 an: Mus. ms. autogr. F. Mendelssohn Bartholdy 49, p. [5]. Used by permission.

complicate matters further, residual glue on the next page in AS1 (p. 106/113) indicates that that page was at some point deleted and replaced by a paste-over, but there is no sign of glue on *AS1c—an indication that yet another version of the beginning of stanza 10 existed at some point but is now lost (source [*AS1d]). To determine the precise chronological, philological, and musical relationships between these four sources is impossible on the basis of the available evidence; all that is clear is that *AS1c represents a revised version of the original close of stanza 9 and beginning of stanza 10—perhaps, but not necessarily, the definitive revision for the cantata's early version. Nor is it possible to determine precisely when *AS1c was removed, although the presence of Mendelssohn's autograph signature at the end of the first recto side shows that he removed it himself and gave it to someone as a gift after it was of no more use to him.

Once again, the import of these revisions extends beyond the sources and chronology of the work itself, for the passage in question represents one of the most important moments in the plot of the poem—the point at which the perspective shifts from the pagans' ceremonies atop the Brocken to the Christian guards' superstitious fear on the lower ground before the slopes. For all their lacunae, the sources reveal that one of the largest compositional challenges for Mendelssohn in the early 1830s lay in one of this poem's most problematical structural and narrative features.[14] Against this backdrop, his replacement of stanza 10 with entirely new music in the final version assumes a new significance as a continuation of his extended efforts to find a compositional solution to that feature—and his solution in the final version becomes all the more remarkable.

The revisions of the early 1840s reveal the musical substance behind Mendelssohn's 1843 assertion that "everything that was good" in his first setting of Goethe's 1799 ballad had "attained its rightful meaning" through the replacement of "the defective and inadequate material" from the early version (see Table 5.2).[15] Clearly, the early setting of Goethe's ballad is a chronological and qualitative compeer to the *Hebrides* Overture, the D-minor ("Reformation") Symphony, both versions of the A-major ("Italian") Symphony, and *St. Paul*; and Mendelssohn's overall satisfaction with that version endured for some time: even after moving to Leipzig he suggested to Robert Schumann that most of the revisions were needed in the "first part" (i.e., the Introduction and stanzas 1–6).[16] Nevertheless, he became increasingly dissatisfied with it as he turned to the revision project in practical rather than abstract terms—so that revisions of the early 1840s reveal increasingly pronounced rethinkings of his approach to the work. By early 1844 a revised version that originally had remained fully vested in the early setting had come to differ significantly in its completion of the problematical instrumental introduction, its music for every stanza of Goethe's ballad, its interpretation of the relationships of individual stanzas to one another, and its overall musical structure. By the end of these late revisions, the only feature of the original setting that remained fully intact was its distillation of the premises and import of Goethe's poem into musically compelling terms.

The sources for Mendelssohn's second *Walpurgisnacht* setting reveal that he was still struggling with many of the same issues that had troubled him from the outset—the "bad weather" part of the introduction, the problematical stanza 3, the second half of stanza 8 (see ex. 5.4c, above), and the transition between the scenes depicting Christian guards' panic and flight and the pagan ceremonies atop the Brocken—but the sketches reveal him working on most of the rest of his concept as well. And once again, the evidence suggests a highly recursive revision process that became more extensive and complicated than originally envisioned—a situation entirely characteristic of Mendelssohn. This second phase of the *Walpurgisnacht*'s genesis and source situation has been well served in studies by Douglass Seaton, Christoph Hellmundt, Peter Krause, and Hiromi Hoshino;[17] however, none of those studies has fully correlated the extant sketches, the three surviving complete autograph scores, and the two surviving autograph full-score fragments with the extant correspondence. The following account consolidates those studies' findings, focusing on matters that offer corrective and supplemental information that relates directly to the points to be discussed later in this chapter.

Although Mendelssohn's letters reveal that he was "seriously considering resuming work on the *Walpurgisnacht*" as early as November 1840, he evidently got around to the project only about two years later.[18] In late November or early December 1842 he took up the project in earnest. The initial steps in this overhauling were almost certainly taken with AS1 at hand: working from that score and writing on a discarded leaf from his setting of Psalm 95 (Op. 46, 1839–42), Mendelssohn first notated a tempo sequence for an overture in 3 parts, then sketched the segments from stanzas 1–5 that he wished to overhaul (see figure 5.4) as well as an extended sketch for stanza 12.[19] He then produced several separate continuity drafts:[20] one for the end of stanza 2, all of stanzas 3 and 4, and the beginning of stanza 5;[21] one for the end of stanza 5 and the beginning of stanza 6;[22] one for the second half of stanza 7, moving from the last two words of the recitative (l. 53) through the G-minor *Männerchor* setting of the remainder of stanza 7;[23] and one for the end of stanza 9 and all of stanza pair 10/11.[24] Sometime in the midst of these labors he also sketched a new version of the end of the overture.

These reworkings' concentration on stanzas 1 through 6 is consistent with Schumann's note of ca. March 1837 that by then Mendelssohn had come to find "the first part" (stanzas 1–6) "dislikable," while the second part "pleased him a great deal" (see chapter 4, p. 88). The strategy they suggest for the overture reflects a significant rethinking of the cantata's opening: it was to comprise a clear set of three movements, as in the *Lobgesang*, and an abrupt interruption of the "bad weather" rather than the gradual abatement depicted in AS1. Although these revisions' reliance on ideas transmitted in AS1 is still obvious, they were evidently sufficiently different for Mendelssohn to pursue the work's rehabilitation. His letters suggest that they were used along with AS1 as the basis of a new choral score (source [*AS2c]) that he had produced in December 1842, as well as a set of parts (source [CP1]) that were used in the ongoing preparations for the performance planned for December 21. By December 11, the entire score had been written out again "from A to Z," complete with a "two new numbers" (i.e., a new version of stanzas 5, 10, and 11).[25] This evidently complete new score comprised the pages identified in table 5.2 as Stage I of AS2, plus the lost pages identified as [AS2x]. Mendelssohn was sufficiently confident in it to copy the dates of completion from the final page of AS1 onto its final page, adding a final "wiederum beendigt Leipzig 1842 (im December)" (finished again in Leipzig, 1842 [in December]). But this version of stanzas 10 and 11 (worked out on pp. 83–84 of Sk3) was not the final revision; instead, it was a reworking of ideas from *AS1c, which was itself a revision of ideas first transmitted in AS1.

Had matters continued uninterrupted, Mendelssohn's second *Walpurgisnacht* setting would have been premiered on December 21, 1842, in a version that was still rather close to that represented in AS1. By the time he was able to gather his thoughts and spirits and return to work on current engagements after the death of his mother on December 12, however, he had reconsidered part of the overhauling undertaken in 1842 and entered into yet another stage of revision. These changes (reflected in pp. 71–72 of Sk3 and Stage II of AS2) resulted in the addition of piccolo, bass drum, and cymbals, the use of trombones in stanza 8, and the removal and replacement of more pages (source [*AS2x] in table

Figure 5.4. Staatsbibliothek zu Berlin—Preußischer Kulturbesitz, Mus. ms. autogr. F. Mendelssohn Bartholdy 19, p. 68 (inverted). Used by permission.

5.2) from the score completed in December 1842. This is the version of *Die erste Walpurgisnacht* that was premiered in the Gewandhaus under Mendelssohn's direction on February 2, 1843, winning the enthusiastic praise of Berlioz and generating excitement in far broader quarters (see chapter 6).

The remarkable proliferation of minute and far-ranging variants introduced between the premiere and the publication of the *Walpurgisnacht* is familiar to those acquainted with the publication histories of Mendelssohn's works. Mendelssohn made substantial alterations in the composition while preparing the piano-vocal arrangement (source APf2), also transferring these revisions into the full orchestral score. When he received the manuscript that was to be used as the engraver's copy (i.e., the *Stichvorlage*, source [CS1]) back from the copyist he made yet more changes (comparatively relatively minor ones) to that score—but these changes could not be entered into the autograph piano-vocal score, since it was already at press. And in going through the first set of proofs in November 1843, he not only corrected errors but also made yet more substantive changes—without, however, transferring these back into the autograph for the piano-vocal score. Still more revisions followed in the proofs for the orchestral score, which Mendelssohn received on March 16, 1844, and most—but not all—of these were transferred back into AS2.

The extensiveness of this third major stage of revisions to Mendelssohn's second setting of the Goethe's "Walpurgisnacht" ballad is conveniently reflected in its basic statistics. It accounts for thirty-six of the 114 pages in AS2, all of the forty-eight pages in APf2, the removal of sources *AS2a, [*AS2b], and [*AS2y], and three sets of proofs. It forms the direct basis of the German piano-vocal and full scores and the indirect basis of the English piano-vocal score and the first set of German parts. Perhaps most important, it required the production of at least one more sketch (Sk4) reflecting a major component of the poem that had given Mendelssohn problems since the early 1830s: the musical material for the "Christian" stanza 10.

The ultimate product of this convoluted publication history was an impressive array of early editions: first out, evidently ca. February 1, 1844, were the German and English piano-vocal scores and vocal parts (the English sets based on the proofs for the German version and containing the German text along with William Bartholomew's English translation). These were followed in mid- or late April by the orchestral parts and the full score (see chapter 4, pp. 93–94). In addition, Mendelssohn's copyist, Eduard Henschke, made an arrangement of the entire piano-vocal score for piano duet, and this was issued ca. 1845 after being proofed and approved by the composer in November 1844.[26] Mendelssohn also caught a misprint in the first German edition of the piano-vocal score sometime after its first printing, marking it in red chalk in one of his exemplars at some point. This error was evidently reported to Kistner, who released a new micro-edition with the correction entered.[27] Finally, he received a separate presentation copy, which he at some point inscribed and gave to his wife, Cécile.[28]

The complexity of the genesis, source situation, and revision history of *Die erste Walpurgisnacht* no doubt largely accounts for the fact that it has yet to be published in an authoritative critical edition.[29] This complexity extends far beyond the sources, however, and beyond the complexities of Goethe's ballad, also encompassing issues of musical form, narrative, and genre.

Structural Revisions

The familiar observation that Mendelssohn was a master of form is often qualified with a suggestion that the form and content of his works were somehow incongruous, that his structural proficiency came at the expense of correspondingly worthy Romantic musical ideas. The backhanded compliment has been challenged in recent decades, and *Die erste Walpurgisnacht* is but one of many works that refute it. Indeed, the cantata's synthesis of its musical and textual elements and implications confirms Mendelssohn's modernity and corroborates the notion that he was very much a child of his own time—a notion that finds abundant support in contemporary responses to his music and career but is incompatible with portrayals of him as an awkwardly retrospective pseudo-Romantic who failed to come to terms with the values and challenges of the mid-nineteenth century.

Mendelssohn's *Walpurgisnacht* settings certainly reinforce his generally acknowledged mastery of large-scale structure, and their complicated geneses and source situations probably affirm contextually the nature of his aspirations in setting Goethe's ballad "collectedly and honorably."[30] These considerations, however, are largely matters of biography and circumstance. They cannot substitute for a critical assessment of his efforts to synthesize the various dimensions of Goethe's poem and submit his own musical contribution to the broader discourse surrounding the Walpurgis Night as cultural topos. Mendelssohn's two settings offer useful critical insights into the structural, narrative, and symbolic dimensions of his reading of the ballad and its subjects.

As shown in figure 5.1 (p. 99, above), Mendelssohn's early and revised settings are similar but not identical in their large-scale organization. The version of 1830–33 explicitly recognizes only two parts: the *Einleitung* (Introduction, comprising the instrumental introduction and stanzas 1–6) and "No. 2" (stanzas 7–12). This organization reflects the background structure of the poem's narrative, for what eventually became known as the Walpurgis Night was the pagans' worship and the attendant hoax on the slopes of the Brocken—not the events recounted in the first six strophes. Accordingly, each of the cantata's two parts reveals a coherent tonal structure consistent with this poetic metastructure (see ex. 5.1, p. 100). The *Einleitung* moves from A minor through A major to their mutual dominant, E major, as the guards spread out on the wooded slopes of the mountain. This tonal structure, which parallels the preparatory function of the first six stanzas, is tonally resolved with the return to A minor in stanza 8 (the full-scale ruse). But this resolution is ensconced within the large-scale tonal and textual drama of stanzas 6–12: the recitative (ll. 50–53) provides the transition from E major to G minor, which is solidly established as the key associated with the idea of the pagan ruse. But unlike part I, which tonally emphasized the lack of dramatic resolution of the first six stanzas by outlining a background-level half cadence, part II reflects the closure provided as the pagans atop the Brocken celebrate the *Allvater*, moving from G minor to

G major over the course of stanza 7, and ultimately resolving to C major (stanzas 9 and 12).

Mendelssohn's second *Walpurgisnacht* setting does not label this background-level structure, though it retains most of its features. Instead, it emphasizes smaller units within the poem—only rarely the stanzas per se, and more often stanza groups whose texts express shared basic ideas that are in turn manifested in the tonal structures, themes, and role casting of Mendelssohn's music. Thus, stanzas 1 and 2 both depict the pagans on the wooded slopes, celebrating the arrival of springtime and eagerly anticipating the opportunity to praise the *Allvater* in the pure whiteness of the snow that still caps the peak of the Brocken. These two stanzas together comprise No. 1 of the revised setting. Accordingly, they share the overall key center of A major and emphasize F-sharp minor when the textual emphasis is on the pagans' religious fervor rather than the radiant greens of spring; their lyrical tenor solo writing and frequent stylistic invocations of choral part-songs stylistically invoke youth and springtime. Stanzas 3 and 4 (the poem's counter-solo and counter-chorus reminding the personae of previous stanzas that their planned celebrations will likely have terrible consequences and endanger the lives of them all) comprise the whole of No. 2. These stanzas balance the youthful ardor, expansive melodies, vibrant textures, and quick tempo of No. 1 by introducing "an old woman from among the people," a slower tempo (Allegretto non troppo), a conspicuously narrow-ranged and predominantly conjunct melody, and a subdued accompaniment. A major is also present here, but it functions as a pivot to the more somber key of D minor. Stanza 5 of the poem becomes No. 3 of the cantata, entrusted to the solo druid priest and a men's chorus and moving fluidly between A minor, C major, and E minor. The last of these provides a pivot to the setting of stanza 6 (No. 4) in E major, which again emphasizes the collective through its use of a chorus of druid watchmen as well as the *Frauenchor*.

The subgroupings within the original part II (stanzas 7–12) follow a similar pattern. Stanza 7 becomes No. 5, although it is entrusted to the entire group of pagan guards rather than just one of them (as specified by the poem); as already noted, the key of this stanza is G (minor and then major). Stanza 8 becomes No. 6, a conspicuously symphonic and developmental movement in A minor for the full chorus and orchestra with piccolo and expanded percussion section, and by far the longest and most difficult number in the cantata. The ceremonial activities atop the Brocken are the focal point of No. 7, which begins in F major and returns to A minor for ll. 67–69 of stanza 9, before moving to C major for the balance of the strophe. *C* provides a tonal orientation for the remainder of the cantata: the Christian guards' stanzas, both using *C* as a springboard for F minor, are grouped together as No. 8, while No. 9 returns to C major for stanza 12.

Mendelssohn certainly did not undertake the renumbering of the movements in his second *Walpurgisnacht* setting casually; he must have known that this semantic reorganization would obscure the stanza organization of the text as well as its larger bipartite structure. By foregrounding smaller units within the overall structure, however, he facilitated recognition of important dramatic and musical elements and poetic and musical cross-references less prominent in the original bipartite organization. The central stanzas of the introduction (stanzas 3 and 4) differ pronouncedly from their framing stanza pairs not only in their voicing (they represent the pagan populace as a whole, including the women), but also in their import: surely the practical and ultimately well-founded fears voiced in those stanzas represent a different emotional and spiritual realm than the springtime merriment and religious fervor expressed in stanza pairs 1–2 and 5–6. In Mendelssohn's first setting this difference is highlighted by his decision to change the persona of stanza 3 from Goethe's "a man from among the people" to "an old woman from among the people" and the flat-key emphasis of both stanzas 3 and 4, but this crucial dramatic difference is subsumed into the overall tonal plot of the introduction. The revised version highlights this crucial dramatic and musical alterity by recognizing this stanza pair as a separate movement (No. 2). Similarly, by conjoining the two stanzas depicting the Christian guards into a single movement discrete from the rest in the second setting, Mendelssohn emphasizes that this movement possesses its own stable tonal center that has played no role in earlier movements and reminds performers that the watchman in stanza 10 is not the same voice that appears in stanza 7 (see discussion in chapter 7, pp. 210–13). And by separating the solo druid priest's movement in the first part of the plot (stanza 5) he encourages performers and listeners to appreciate the crucial textual, tonal, and thematic connections between that stanza and stanzas 9 and 12—connections that may otherwise be obscure because a great deal of music intervenes between stanzas 5 and 9.

But the recomposition of stanza 5 also had further consequences. In the first setting it is entrusted to tenor solo—the same tenor, evidently, who had initiated the youthful revelry of spring and exhorted the pagan populace on to worship in stanza 1—and set as an *Allegro vivace* rage aria in A minor (see ex. 5.3a, earlier). If any doubt existed concerning the source of this druid's ire, it is dispelled in the aria's mid-section, which quotes the distinctive accompaniment from strophe 3 at the phrase "um eurer Sorge Willen" (because of your concern, l. 43; cf. ex. 5.5 and ex. 5.2e, earlier). The mocking tone of this reference seems to confirm the youth and impulsiveness of the druid of stanza 5, and thus to place him and other youthful members of the pagan populace in opposition to the voices of the "old woman from among the people" (as Mendelssohn designated Goethe's druid of stanza 3) and the other women.

In the final version stanza 5 is prefigurative rather than retrospective. Mendelssohn casts its dramatic persona not as an impetuous youth, but as a "bearded druid priest" (as he put it in his letters), written for solo bass, with support from the men's chorus for ll. 36–38 and 44–45 (see ex. 5.3c–d, earlier).[31] This recasting—another license taken with Goethe's poem—eliminates the original druid's vehement and mocking rejection of the old woman's warning, bridges the bipartite structure of the poem's narrative, and musically aligns the meaning of stanza 5 with stanzas 9 and 12 rather than 1 and 2.

Example 5.5. Mendelssohn, *Die erste Walpurgisnacht:* Original setting of l. 43 (1830–33 version).

One further difference between the two settings cannot go unmentioned here: the ways in which each deals with the last stanza's closing recollection of the themes of identity, alterity, and conflict (l. 98) and the celebration of light symbolically construed (l. 99). In both settings, the stanza as a whole is set in a resplendent C major, and in both it uses not only the full orchestra but also the full chorus. But the two settings reveal Mendelssohn exploring substantially different strategies for musically realizing this imposing final dialectic. After an original version that placed little emphasis on the poem's final line,[32] he reconsidered the absence of conflict in these lines and pasted a new bifolio over the original continuation of the *Animato,* in the process inserting a forceful reminder of the conflict expressed in l. 98 into the pagans' hymn (ex. 5.6a, pp. 124–30). He retained this music in the continuity draft for this passage in Sk3, but in the final version he moderated his approach somewhat. There, Mendelssohn's *Walpurgisnacht* dispenses with the inserted obsession on l. 98 ("und raubt man uns den alten Brauch"). Instead, its final hymn presents a modified recapitulation of the music to which ll. 76–79 were set just before stanza 10. The result is that the final pages offer a close that is at one more compact and more dramatic—for now the music does achieve resolution, and (perhaps more important) this resolution coincides with the crucial textual change from "wer will es rauben" (who *will* rob us of that) to "wer kann es rauben" (who *can* rob us of that) (cf. ex. 5.6b, pp. 130–33 and mm. 438–54 of the final version[33]).

And what of the instrumental introduction, which cost Mendelssohn so much trouble in completing his musical *Walpurgisnacht?* Readers familiar with the final version know that it suggests but does not confirm a sonata form. As shown in figure 5.5, it highlights distinct themes associated with the tonic A minor and its minor dominant (E minor), follows these with a developmental middle section in two parts, obviously prepares a return to the tonic, and then presents the main theme in the tonic. This recapitulation, however, remains dramatically unfulfilled after the climactic arrival at F major just before the second part of the development section (ex. 5.7, pp. 137–38). The "bad weather" theme never regains its full severity; by m. 237 the horn/bassoon call that disrupted the return of the main theme in A minor has disintegrated to a wistful *pianissimo*; and the second theme never returns in the tonic. In brief, the horn/bassoon call that thwarts the climax of the inclement development also disrupts the sonata process, robbing the recapitulatory process of its force and thus clearing the way for the remarkably unlearned canonic "transition to springtime" in A major (a passage whose freshness would still resonate in Brahms's Second Symphony more than forty years later).[34]

Mendelssohn arrived at this strategy only in the last year of the *Walpurgisnacht*'s fourteen-year genesis. In the first setting, the "bad weather" section was cast as a full-fledged sonata form that recapitulated both main themes and then cadenced emphatically on the tonic A minor before gradually yielding to the warmth of the coming springtime (see figure 5.6, p. 139). In this version as in the final one, F major represents a critical point of arrival in the development section. Here, however, that arrival is followed by a retransition that is still developmental in character. This passage intensifies rather than interrupts the bad weather, building first to a new climax and then dropping off mysteriously before returning to the emphatic reprise of the main theme at m. 219 (ex. 5.8, p. 140).

If the sketches are any indication, Mendelssohn discarded the idea of a full-fledged sonata-form introduction as soon as he returned to the cantata in the winter of 1842–43. Nevertheless, he tried to rehabilitate elements from the earlier version, assimilating their recapitulatory function into a concept that had already come to feature the dramatic intrusion of the calls in the tenor register. In the sketch that survives on p. 72 of Sk2, the F-major climax (extending from the end of staves 3/4 to the beginning of staves 5/6) disintegrates into a return of the original second subject, now beginning in F minor and moving to a second prominent arrival on B-flat major, where the call intrudes. By the eighth measure of staves 11/12 the second subject is back again, now in the tonic A minor (though its inherent instability precludes any real sense of tonal arrival). The last two notated measures of this sketch mark the return of the main theme in the tonic.

On the whole, this sketch suggests the same general goals achieved in both the version of 1830–33 and the final version. The differences between the sketch and the final version become instructive in this context. Common to all are the idea of the introduction as an A-minor sonata form that yields to A major; an emphasis on F major and B-flat major as mediators between those two large-scale tonal determinants; and the idea of a weakened or obfuscated reprise. What is at stake, au fond, is the rhetorical force of the gestures that relate this overture to its immediate and broader contexts. The first of those contexts—that is, this particular setting of Goethe's ballad—centers on narrative issues, while its broader semantic and semasiological contexts center on the "elevated" symbolic imports of the poem and the *Walpurgisnacht* topos generally.

Example 5.6. Mendelssohn, *Die erste Walpurgisnacht:* Successive revisions of end of stanza 12: (a) 1830–33 version, mm. 532–69 (*post correcturam*); (b) No. 9 (mm. 11–43; after *APf2*).

Example 5.6a. (*continued*)

Narrative Issues in "Die erste Walpurgisnacht"

Goethe's description of his "Die erste Walpurgisnacht" as a "dramatic ballad" reveals his awareness that the poem raised issues that were specifically narrative in

Example 5.6a. (*continued*)

nature, and his statement that he had created it with the specific idea that "they would offer the composer material for a larger vocal piece" (see p. 59, above) suggests that he understood at least something of the nature of the challenges these issues would raise for composers. Zelter, too, would not have overlooked the

Example 5.6a. (*continued*)

problem posed by the diegetic simultaneity of stanza-pairs 8/9 and 10/11 (representing pagan and Christian soloists and choruses, respectively). Whether this narrative complication was one of the specific issues that thwarted Zelter's efforts to set the ballad to music is unclear from his letters. But both versions of Mendelssohn's cantata suggest that he was aware of the specifically musical ramifications of the

Example 5.6a. (*continued*)

poem's narrative structure—and that he viewed some of these challenges as problems likely unforeseen by the poet; others, as opportunities to express musically the central ideas he found in the poem.

Clearest among the poem's issues that posed musical problems not hinted at in Goethe's remarks concerning the ballad are several aspects of its casting and

Example 5.6a. (*continued*)

role distribution. The participation of women's voices is a general problem of this sort. Strictly speaking, Goethe's poem provides for the use of women in only five lines (the "Chor der Weiber," stanza 4), for in Goethe's usage, as elsewhere in nineteenth-century Germany, the term "druid" denoted a male pagan.[35]

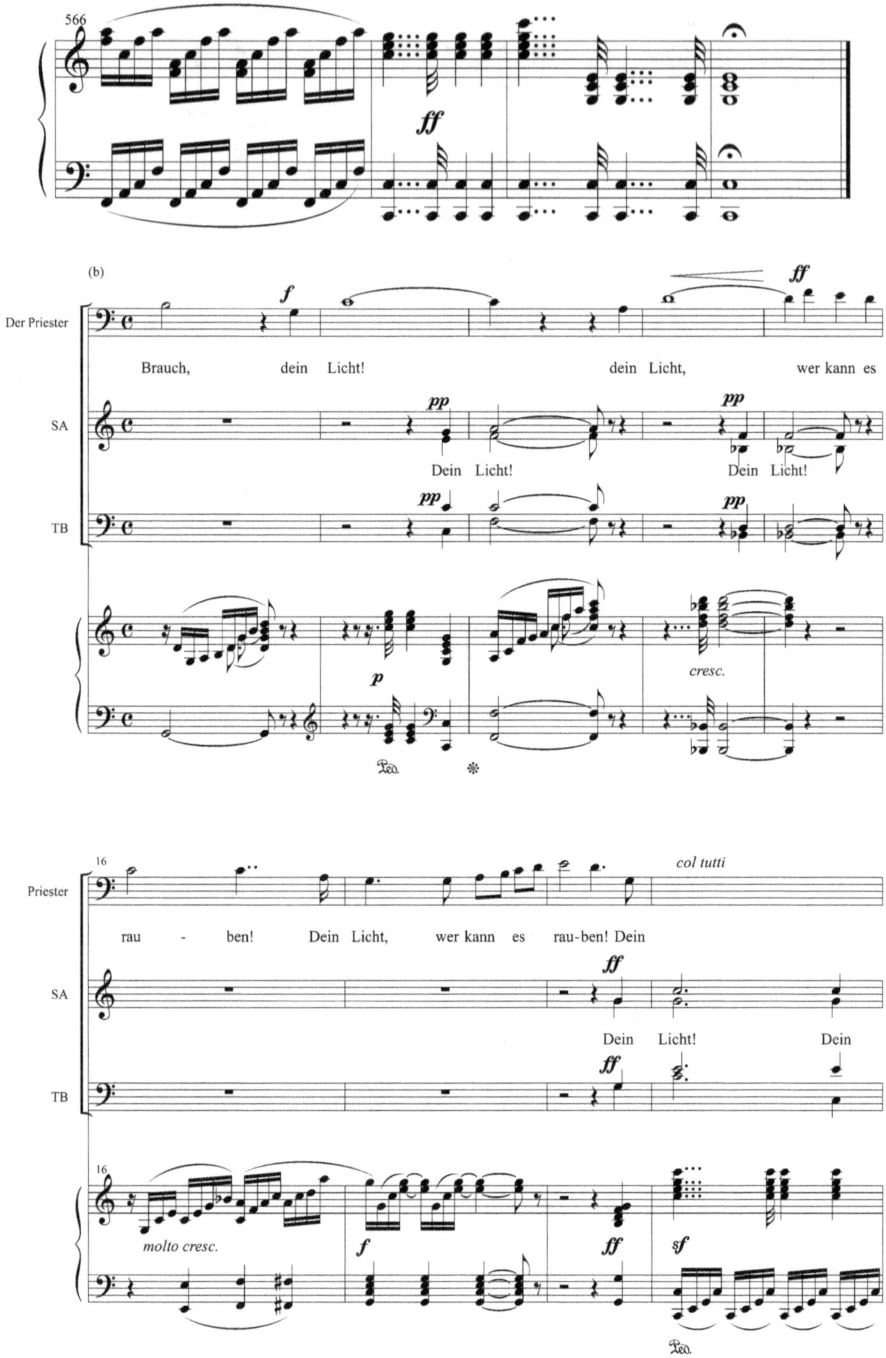

566

ff

(b)

Der Priester

f *ff*

Brauch, dein Licht! dein Licht, wer kann es

SA

pp *pp*

Dein Licht! Dein Licht!

TB

pp *pp*

p *cresc.*

Ped.

Example 5.6b. (*continued*)

Example 5.6b. (*continued*)

Mendelssohn's use of the *Frauenchor* both separate from and in conjunction with the *Männerchor* in the final version of stanzas 1, 2, 6, 8, 9, and 12 (Nos. 1, 4, 6, 7, and 9) thus represents a significant departure from the role casting specified by the poetic source—one that portrays the pagan populace as more heterogeneous than Goethe evidently envisioned (and perhaps also throws the narrow-mindedness of the exclusively male Christian sentinels into even sharper relief).[36]

The idea for this compositional intervention is evident already in the 1830–33 *Walpurgisnacht.* In the first six stanzas of that setting Mendelssohn retained Goethe's use of the men's chorus for all except stanza 4. He adapted the casting of the choral roles in part II of that version to make for a more musically viable ensemble, however, introducing the women's voices in stanzas 8 and 12, and in the last line of stanza 9 (l. 78)—but still distinguishing, in stanza 12, between the

Example 5.6b. (*continued*)

"Chor der Druiden" and the "Frauenchor."[37] In addition, although he originally scored lines 72–76 of stanza 9 (which in the poem is given to a solo druid, as is the rest of the stanza) for baritone solo and four-part men's chorus, he eventually revised this passage in pencil, reassigning the choral response to the entire chorus in octaves.[38] This alteration clearly was made at an extremely late date—probably when Mendelssohn first returned to the project of revising the cantata in the early 1840s—but the idea of compressing the responsorial texture that

Example 5.6b. (*continued*)

Goethe creates between stanzas 9 and 12 into each of those stanzas, with the full chorus participating in each, was in any case retained and extended in the second version.[39] The result is not only a scoring that would prove more satisfactory for the full chorus—one cannot help but wonder whether Mendelssohn had the issue of the role of the *Frauenchor* in mind when he said that the early setting was "rather scrappily written for the voice"[40]—but also a rather more balanced portrayal of the roles of men and women, priests and populace in the pagan culture the poem celebrates.

The balance between male and female participation certainly also accounts for Mendelssohn's recasting of stanza 3 in both settings of *Die erste Walpurgisnacht*. Here, too, Goethe assigns this stanza to a druid (i.e., a male pagan, obviously not the one to whom stanza 1 was given), and thus consigns the

Example 5.6b. (*continued*)

women's role to that of echoing the fears of a minority of the male populace. But Mendelssohn directed in both versions of the cantata that the stanza should be sung by "eine alte Frau aus dem Volke" (an old woman from among the people) and scored the stanza for alto or mezzo-soprano solo, as was traditional with operatic roles for old females.[41] In reassigning this role he both created a more balanced scoring for performers and drew on a persistent theme in the lore concerning European paganism—for, as shown in chapter 1, the Germanic tribes typically viewed old women as sources of wisdom and prophecy, and this stereotype belonged to the frequently troped themes of nineteenth-century lore concerning the distant Germanic past. The recasting of stanza 3 had a strong basis in the history and lore of Goethe's ballad, albeit not in the poem itself.

The recastings in the final setting were not limited to gender reassignments, however. As already mentioned, Mendelssohn reassigned stanza 5—which Goethe entrusted to "Ein Druide" (probably a member of the same youthful group that had celebrated the arrival of spring in stanza 2, if not the same druid who had proclaimed that arrival in stanza 1) to "Der Priester der Druiden" (the druids' priest), a personage who first appears in stanza 9 of the poem. Similarly, stanza 7 is given to a tenor solo in the first setting, but to a bass solo in the final version. Stanza 8 is specified as belonging to the "Chor der Wächter der Druiden und des Heidenvolks" (chorus of the druid watchmen and the pagan folk) rather than Goethe's simple "chorus of the watchmen." (For Goethe there was no need to specify that these watchmen were pagans, since the Christians had not yet been mentioned in the ballad.) And stanza 12 is reassigned to "Der Priester" and the "Allgemeiner Chor der Druiden und des Heidenvolkes" (general chorus of the druids and the pagan folk).

Equally significant are Mendelssohn's various ways of addressing the poem's most important problem that was clearly intended by Goethe: the dramatic simultaneity of stanza pairs 8/9 and 10/11. Stanza 9 vacillates between A minor (the key of stanza 8) and C major (the first appearance of this tonal center), using A minor for the lines that deal with darkness, struggle, or conflict (ll. 66–68 and 72–74) and C major for the lines that emphasize the symbolic image of light (ll. 69–71 and 75–77). At the same time, stanza 9 vividly depicts "the bearded druid with his trombones that stand blasting away behind him,"[42] using sharply dotted rhythms in the trombones at the outset of the stanza in the final version and throughout the minor-mode material in the version of 1830–33 (ex. 5.9a, p. 144). In the original version of stanzas 9 and 10—the only stanzas that adopt the perspective of the Christian sentinels—these two elements, the insistent reiteration of the pitch *C* and the trombone blasts, figure decisively in the accompaniment (ex. 5.9b, pp. 145–46). In the final setting of the Christian watchmen's stanzas, the pagans' pitch-goal *C* provides a remarkably persistent pedal point, even when it is dissonant with the remainder of the melodic and harmonic fabric, and the accompaniment features fleeting references to the thematic material of stanzas 7 and 8 (ex. 5.9c, p. 146). By working the defining features of these pagan stanzas into the accompaniment of the stanzas declaimed by the Christians in the stage time of the poem, Mendelssohn clarifies that those Christian stanzas occur simultaneously with the pagan ruse and the ceremonies atop the Brocken, not afterward.

Finally, the role assignments and the pan-diegetic processes of Mendelssohn's setting of the poem's concluding pagan and Christian stanzas underscore one further fact that emerges from Goethe's and Mendelssohn's comments concerning their respective engagements with the Walpurgis Night topos: for poet and composer alike, the ballad's characters were distillations of broader collectives in a (conjectural) historical drama of "elevated" symbolic import. In that context, the element of time within the poem/cantata must be understood in relation to its broader historical context. The subject of the ballad is not the events that transpire within it, but the relationships among its dramatic personae and their roles in the processes by which those events unfold. These dramatic personae represent the main players in a great historical drama whose significance lies not least of all in its relationship to the present.

Exposition					Development		Recapitulation (truncated)	
Introduction	1st theme	Trans.	2nd group (fm. 1st theme)	Cl. gr. (fm. 1st theme)	(Developmental) (new theme)	retransition	1st theme	Coda
a	a	a–e	e	e	e–F	F → V/a	a	a
1–4	5–32	32–51	52–94	94–111	112–88	188–238	239–301	301–

Figure 5.5. Structure of "Bad Weather" portion of Introduction to Mendelssohn, *Die erste Walpurgisnacht*, Op. 60.

Example 5.7. Mendelssohn, *Die erste Walpurgisnacht*, Op. 60: Disruption of F-major climax of development in Introduction (mm. 173–94). *Source*: EPfG.

One prominent shared characteristic of the two main versions of the instrumental introduction readily points to Mendelssohn's cognizance of these issues: the overture functions neither simply to distill the elements of the drama into an instrumental prelude nor to introduce the drama. Instead, it is at once a concise presentation of the symbolic elements of the drama to come, the first term of the dramatic argument, an adumbration of the salient processes by which the drama unfolds, and a distillation of the musical means employed in the ensuing texted portions. Individually, these features are familiar enough from elsewhere in Mendelssohn's oeuvre. Certainly the Overture to *St. Paul* compactly presents at least some of the primary symbolic values and dramatic processes of the oratorio's plot, and certainly the Op. 61 version of the *Midsummer Night's Dream* Overture condenses the musical means of the following incidental numbers into a concise

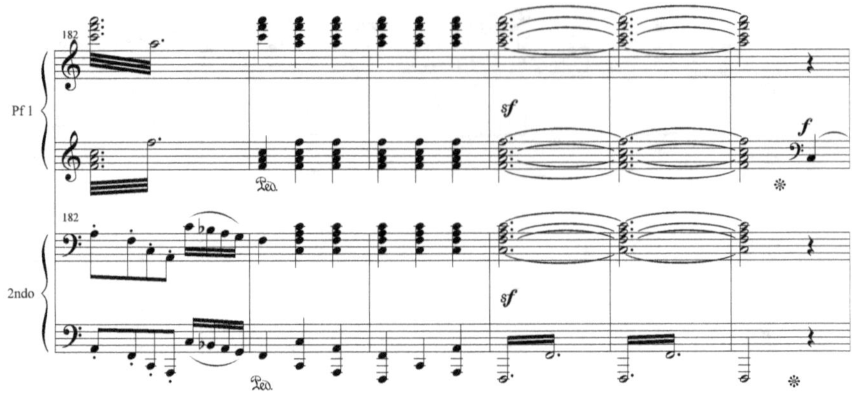

Example 5.7. (*continued*)

narration of the play's salient elements as Mendelssohn considered them. In these instances as in most other overtures to cantatas, oratorios, and incidental music, however, the overture is extrinsic to the diegetic time of the play itself. *Die erste Walpurgisnacht* stands apart from these as the first instance in which the overture unfolds *within* the diegetic time of the plot itself. This inclement weather and this thaw belong first and foremost to the experience of the poem's/cantata's protagonists rather than that of the performers and listeners.

The concept was hardly without precedent, of course.[43] But the introduction to *Die erste Walpurgisnacht* is a remarkable instance because the passage of time in which it participates is itself a symbolic process. And of course, this introduction (unlike, for example, Haydn's overture to *The Creation*) initiates the process of thematic transformation by introducing the thematic substance of that process. Equally remarkable is that the thematic raw material presented in this overture was arrived at only reductively—that is, the material that develops out

Exposition					Development		Recapitulation		
Introduction	1st theme	Trans.	2nd gr.	Cl. gr. (fm. 1st theme)	(Developmental	retransition)	1st theme	2nd gr.	Cl. gr.
a	a	→	e	e	e–F	F → V/a	a (2nd inv.)	a (2nd inv.)	a (root pos.)
1–4	5–32	32–49	49–84	84–98	98–184	185–228	228–53	254–85	286–

Figure 5.6. Structure of "Bad Weather" portion of Introduction to Mendelssohn, *Die erste Walpurgisnacht* (1830–33 version).

Example 5.8. Mendelssohn, *Die erste Walpurgisnacht* (1830–33 version): Close of development and arrival of recapitulation in Introduction (mm. 179–223). *Source*: APf1; some material in 2ndo supplied editorially.

Example 5.8. (*continued*)

Example 5.8. (*continued*)

Example 5.8. (*continued*)

Example 5.9. Mendelssohn, *Die erste Walpurgisnacht:* Pan-diegetic material in stanzas 9, 10, and 11 (a) 1830–33 version, stanza 9 (II: 433–39); (b) 1830–33 version, stanza 11 (II: 495–99); (c) Op. 60, stanza 10 (No. 8, mm. 2–11).

of it in the texted movements had already been composed by the time Mendelssohn decided on the content and nature of the Introduction.[44] The considerable effort he devoted to developing and underscoring the affinities among the thematic materials thus attains special significance as a compositional effort whose goal was not simply the organic unity of the cantata as a whole, but a musical response to the idea that underlay its content.[45] The most important large-scale moments in these processes, discussed earlier in this chapter, are sustained

Example 5.9. (*continued*)

by a series of more localized transformations. The following remarks focus on interactions between the two principal melodic cells in several of their more localized transformations.

As noted earlier, the chromatically descending melodic cell (cell *y*; see Exx. 5.4a and c, above) acquires obvious motivic importance only in the setting of stanzas 7–12 (the Walpurgis Night proper). This does not mean, however, that the cell is absent or only incidentally employed earlier in the cantata. It emerges already in mm. 7–12 of the "bad weather" introduction, embedded in two layers in the *C–B–B-flat–A–G-sharp / A–G-sharp–G–F-sharp–F–E* of the alto and bass lines (ex. 5.10a, p. 147). A more forceful statement occurs in mm. 164–68, in the series of syncopated suspensions in the violins just before the dramatic interruption of the development (ex. 5.10b). However innocuous these two presentations may

Example 5.9. (*continued*)

Example 5.10. Mendelssohn, *Die erste Walpurgisnacht,* Op. 60: Chromatic descents: (a) Introduction, mm. 7–12; (b) Introduction, mm. 164–68; (c) No. 1, mm. 127–36; (d) No. 2, mm. 18–26.

appear, they suffice to distinguish the chromatic descent from its context, to suggest it as a figure that overlays a substantially quicker rhythmic background, and to associate it with inclemency, strife, and struggle. These characteristic associations are absent from the pagan merriments of stanza 1, but with the appearance of the choral declamation of stanza 2 "Die Flamme lodre durch den Rauch" in No. 1, the flame's symbolic purification of itself from smoke, allegorizing the pagans' yearning for purity, freedom, and knowledge even in the face of adversity, results in a recollection of the chromatic descent in the men's chorus (see ex. 5.4c). In the revised setting of stanza 3 it occurs at the old woman's poignant reminder that the Christians have slaughtered the pagans' fathers and children (ex. 5.10d), a passage that Mendelssohn specifically sketched in Sk2. In the first part of the cantata, this motive, rhetorically significant of strife and inclemency, is carefully kept separate from material that underscores the affects indigenous to the pagans' culture, with its religious fervor and exultant celebration of the freshness of springtime.

That situation changes as a direct conflict between the pagans and their Christian adversaries approaches. As already noted, the cell reemerges as the pagan guards hatch their plan to outwit their Christian counterparts, and its importance in the G-minor march-like theme of stanza 7 is now asserted through its repetition four times in direct succession (see ex. 5.4a, earlier). It

Example 5.11. Mendelssohn, *Die erste Walpurgisnacht,* 1830–33 version: Recapitulation in setting of stanza 8, featuring stretto of cell *y* (II: 306–77).

takes on a life of its own at the recapitulation in the setting of stanza 8—first as the consequent phrase to the main subject of that stanza and then as a dense stretto that takes over completely, leaving the thematic material autochthonous to stanza 8 behind (see ex. 5.11). In the early setting, the importance of the material

Example 5.11. (*continued*)

is underscored by the remarkable cadential approach to this A-minor recapitulation. Having crafted an exposition that establishes a fifth-related tonal axis for the movement, Mendelssohn closes the development by tonicizing the lowered second scale degree (B-flat) and returns directly from that tonally remote position

Example 5.11. (*continued*)

to the tonic A minor in second inversion. The chromatic subject of the stretto naturally stands out after such a jarring return (a matter that Mendelssohn struggled with),[46] and the irreverent imitation that constitutes this climax further emphasizes its contextually established connotation of conflict as well as a more general affect of *Teufelsspuk.*

Example 5.11. (*continued*)

The original reading of the revised version (transmitted in *AS2a) offers another version of this passage, and the final version, evidently arrived at only after the premiere and as Mendelssohn was preparing the score for publication, offers yet another strategy (ex. 5.12, pp. 155–58). Common to all these versions is the idea that cell *y* would be a defining feature of the culmination of the pagan ruse in stanza 8.

Example 5.11. (*continued*)

As one would expect, cell *y* plays no role in stanzas 9 or 12: its attendant air of conflict is as emotionally remote from the single-minded purity of the ceremonies atop the Brocken as the mid-ground ruse and the panic of the Christian guards are geographically remote from those ceremonies. The cell is germane to stanzas 10 and 11, however, and it accordingly reappears there in the early setting, in a brief but prominent statement in combination with the main theme

Example 5.11. (*continued*)

of the stanza pair, as the Christian guards exclaim at the "Schreckliche verhexte Leiber" (horrible bewitched corpses, l. 90) and then take up the solo Christian sentinel's suggestion that they flee (ex. 5.13, p. 158).

The narrative function of the main melodic cell (*x*) derives not least of all from its contextual relationship to cell *y*. A central theme of "Die erste Walpurgisnacht" is that the celebration of light (symbolizing goodness, purity,

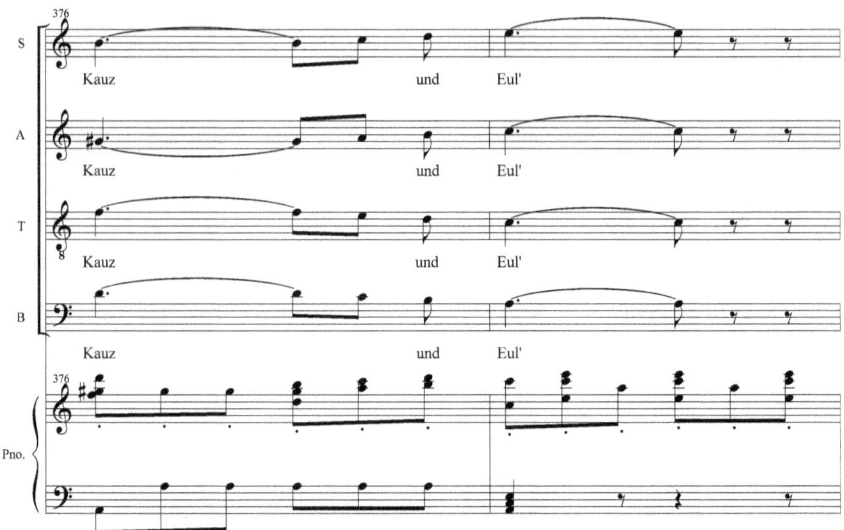

Example 5.11. (*continued*)

truth, and wisdom) is attained through the elimination of darkness (symbolizing confusion, ignorance, malevolence, and conflict): "Die Flamme reinigt sich vom Rauch: so reinig' unsern Glauben!" (The flame purifies itself of smoke: Thus purify our faith!). Given this theme, it is significant that the two cells appear in the same movement only when that movement is in the minor mode: this is true not only of the introduction but also of Nos. 2, 5, and 6, as well as the original version of what became No. 8. Moreover, cell *y* becomes increasingly remote as the transformations of cell *x* move increasingly in the direction of the pitch *C*. That pitch is the subsidiary goal of the cell in the Introduction (ex. 5.2a), but here *C* functions as the mediant, subservient to its tonal context of A minor. By stanza 9 the motive has been resituated into C major, and the original emphatic association of the motive with A minor has yielded to one where *C* is the tonal goal, even though it is achieved only in the middle of the phrase (see ex. 5.4d, earlier). The same tonal orientation and thwarted realization of the goal occurs in the original and revised versions of the Christian sentinels' music in the setting of 1830–33 (ex. 5.14a–b, p. 159). And by the time the pagans have eradicated the threat of the Christian guards (No. 9) motive *x* is able to sustain its drive forward, ultimately achieving the goal of *C* that previously has been either denied or subverted (ex. 5.14c). In a word, the thematic cells' struggles for primacy work in tandem with their respective transformations to allegorize the struggle between the poem's pagan and Christian protagonists—and thus to manifest the "elevated symbolism" that underlies the poem's central purpose.

Example 5.12. Mendelssohn, *Die erste Walpurgisnacht*, Op. 60: Recapitulation in setting of stanza 8, featuring stretto of cell *y* (No. 7, mm. 239–79). *Source*: EPfG.

Example 5.12. (*continued*)

271
S
A
T
B
wil - den Klap - per - - stöc - - - - - - - - -
ken Kommt mit wil - den Klap - per -
ken Kommt mit wil - den
Kommt

Example 5.12. (*continued*)

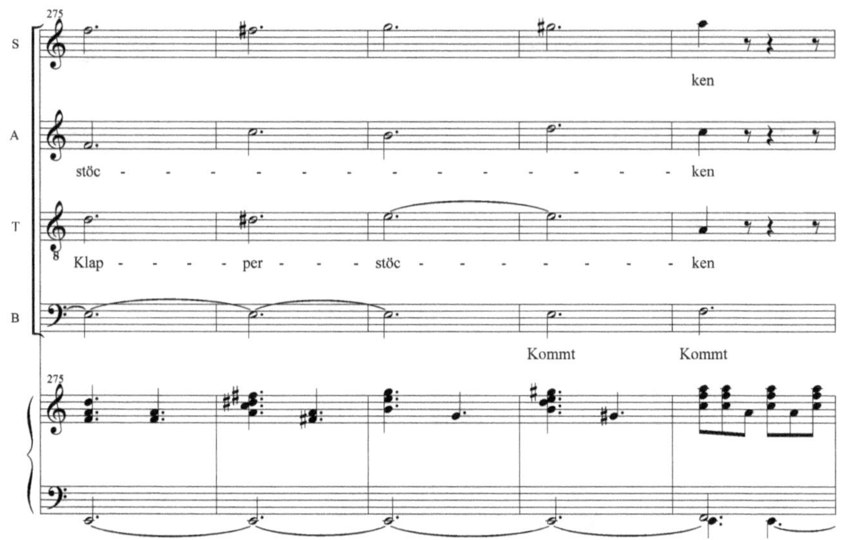

Example 5.12. (*continued*)

Example 5.13. Mendelssohn, *Die erste Walpurgisnacht,* 1830–33 version: Cell *y* in setting of stanza 11 (No. 2, mm. 500–502).

Conclusions: "Hochsymbolisch intentionirt"

What exactly is the "elevated symbolism" of Goethe's "Die erste Walpurgisnacht," and is it the same as or different from that of Mendelssohn's cantata? How, in turn, do both relate to the historically based explanation Goethe offered to Zelter in December 1812 and the briefer but equally historical explanation printed in the concert programs at the cantata's premiere?[47]

Example 5.14. Mendelssohn, *Die erste Walpurgisnacht:* Transformations of cell *x*, resituated from *A* to *C:* (a) stanza 10, original setting in 1830–33 version; (b) stanza 10, revised setting in 1830–33 version; (c) stanza 12 (Op. 60, No. 9: mm. 5–12).

Goethe scholarship has devoted little attention to the first two questions, concentrating instead on the Walpurgis Night scenes in *Faust I* and *Faust II.* Mendelssohn scholarship has arrived at widely varying answers. Carl Dahlhaus suggested that the poem appealed to Mendelssohn because of its complicated treatments of narrative and historical time. Richard Hauser viewed the cantata as a half-hearted, unimaginative, and kitschy musical setting of the ideas behind Goethe's poem.[48] For Douglass Seaton, the poem's treatment of the theme of the struggle for religious freedom offered Mendelssohn an opportunity to

Example 5.14. (*continued*)

cultivate his gifts for large-scale organic unity, brilliant orchestration, programmatic composition, and musical exploration of the Romantic fascination with the supernatural.[49] Michael P. Steinberg, Heinz-Klaus Metzger, and Leon Botstein have read the cantata's version of the poem's pagans as thinly disguised European Jews and the cantata itself as "a Jewish reference," "a Jewish protest against the domination of Christendom" and "an expression of Mendelssohn's sympathy for his Jewish heritage."[50] Julie Prandi and Meredith Lee have emphasized the artistic and cultural empathy that existed between Goethe and Mendelssohn, viewing poem and cantata as different media symbolically celebrating the Enlightenment values shared by poet and composer.[51] Similarly, John Toews has found in the revised version "a conscious reaffirmation of [Mendelssohn's] fidelity to what he saw as the universalism of Goethe's aesthetic and historical stance, and his loyalty to a type of religious truth that was accessible through enlightened feeling and that outlived the particular rituals and dogmas in which it first appeared in space and time."[52] And Jeffrey Sposato, pointing to the anti-Semitic implications of the texts in some of Mendelssohn's contemporaneous works, has suggested that Goethe's ballad appealed to Mendelssohn's interests in the supernatural and served as a vehicle for exploring the philo-heathen proclivities that also manifested themselves in *St. Paul*.[53] For all their merits, however, none of these arguments has adduced the full body of available evidence to formulate a coherent understanding of how the 1799 ballad relates to Goethe's own experiences on the Brocken, the lore surrounding the mountain, the Walpurgis Night material in the various *Faust* texts, the two explanatory notes Mendelssohn disseminated pertaining to the cantata, the ways in which the cantata changed over the course of its genesis, and the correlation between these changes and those in Mendelssohn's own professional and artistic persona between 1830 and 1844.

Taken together, that evidence indeed portrays the poet and the composer as kindred spirits and the cantata as a compelling testament to their deep-seated affinities. For to identify precisely the import of "elevated symbolism" is ultimately impossible: such a limited symbolic reading would be anathema to the concept of *hochsymbolisch*. What is possible is to observe that both Goethe's ballad and Mendelssohn's cantata affirm the fundamental affinity between Goethe's three literary engagements with the topos of the Walpurgis Night: all symbolism possesses no stable inherent meaning. Instead it relies on the enfranchisement of readers or listeners to participate in the processes that the artwork uses to describe the symbolism, to identify the issues at stake, and to construe its import according to their own experiences—an experiential dialectic of individualized communal piety much like that to which Schleiermacher's *Gemeindetheologie* exhorted Christians. Read literally, "Die erste Walpurgisnacht," the *Walpurigsnacht* and *Walpurgisnachtstraum* scenes in both parts of the *Faust* tragedy, and *Die erste Walpurgisnacht* all center on dichotomies between Self and Other, Christian and non-Christian, good and evil, the real and the imaginary. Their subject is neither the dichotomies themselves nor the precise nature or value of any one of the opposing forces. Rather, their subject is the process that leads to the reader's realization that these are not dichotomies, mutually exclusive subclasses, but dualities, individual parts of a coherent whole. What matters is the integrity of that whole and the inherent affinities that unite its constituent parts. The process of coming to that realization, of discovering how Goethe turned the "fable-like history" back into a "poetic fable," is the path to light to which the poet and the composer both invite.

Chapter Six

At the Crossroads of Identity

Critical and Artistic Responses to Goethe's and Mendelssohn's Walpurgisnacht *Treatments*

To view Goethe's and Mendelssohn's artistic engagements with the theme of the Walpurgis Night from a latter-day perspective is deceptively simple. Figuring centrally in the foreground are the colossus of the Walpurgis Night scene in the first part of the *Faust* tragedy and the final version of Mendelssohn's cantata, which, while dwarfed by Goethe's Walpurgisnacht treatment in *Faust I,* nevertheless ranks among the most-performed choral/orchestral compositions worldwide. Surrounding these are Goethe's 1799 ballad on the subject, which is known primarily through Mendelssohn's music, and the "Classical Walpurgisnacht" of *Faust II,* whose reception even today might be reasonably compared with the reception of the works from Beethoven's late Vienna period prior to the 1860s. Finally, somewhere on the peripheries are the *Walpurgisnachtstraum* scene from *Faust I,* the reportedly analogous Scherzo from Mendelssohn's Octet for Strings (Op. 20) and the orchestrated version of the latter from the London version of Mendelssohn's C-minor Symphony, Op. 11, and Mendelssohn's first setting of Goethe's 1799 ballad.[1]

That image becomes plainly one-dimensional if one considers the two artists' Walpurgis Night treatments in the context of their creators' biographies and reception histories, and still more so in the context of other nineteenth-century artistic engagements with the Night as cultural topos. These contexts add color, depth, and perspective to the image of the artistic contributions discussed in the previous paragraph. For if the Walpurgis Night had become integrally bound up with societal and political issues by the time Goethe came to it, his creative engagements with it also made it into a legitimate subject of artistic discourse. Its identity as Mendelssohn took it up was thus not least of all a function of Goethe's artistic identity, and because of parallels in Goethe's and Mendelssohn's respective professional identities between ca. 1820 and 1850, their two personas converge on the topic of Walpurgis Night:[2] both use its accumulated connotations of wide-ranging social and political issues and conflicts between Self and

Other, Christian and non-Christian, good and evil, the real and the imaginary as means of enfranchising readers and listeners in the process of realizing the Night's moral imports. As a result, the critical receptions of Goethe's and Mendelssohn's Walpurgis Night treatments also offer a microcosmic view not only of them as artists and social and cultural figures, but also of issues that defined the identities of their critics in their own changing historical contexts. Their convergent artistic identity in treating the Walpurgis Night vests the subject with an even greater power as a lens for viewing the issues and ideas that defined European society of the early and mid-nineteenth century.

This chapter represents a long look through that lens, one that endeavors gradually to bring those defining issues and ideas into focus by relating them to the issues, ideas, and artworks discussed earlier in this book. I begin by reviewing the essentials of nineteenth-century critical receptions of Goethe and Mendelssohn, then focus on significant aspects of the critical receptions of their respective *Walpurgisnacht* treatments with an eye to the issues discussed previously. The image that ultimately emerges is more than a little ironic, for as the original intersection of Goethe's and Mendelssohn's self-constructed artistic identities receded into the historical distance critics not only lost sight of the original subject itself, but also lost their appreciation of its import with regard to identity and alterity. The Walpurgis Night as an inspiration for socially engaged artistic discourse—the original thematic Self for Goethe's and Mendelssohn's treatments viewed synchronically—thus becomes Other over the course of their reception histories.

The Critical Receptions of Goethe and Mendelssohn in the Nineteenth Century

The close artistic and personal relationship between Goethe and Mendelssohn has become a staple of critical writings on both. Their biographers consistently note their personal acquaintance as well as Zelter's role as intermediary. The stories of Mendelssohn's success at tutoring the sage of Weimar in music history, from the works of Bach through Mozart and Beethoven to works by himself and his contemporaries, are the stuff of scholarly and popular accounts as well as fiction. Goethe's profound interest in history and historical processes is observed as a corollary to Mendelssohn's own interest in music history and his contributions to the formation of the concept of a musical canon. His admiration for Classical antiquity, like his classicizing values in general, are obvious counterparts to Mendelssohn's knowledge and love of Classical languages and literature and his own artistic cultivation of ideas, styles, and techniques from earlier repertoires. Finally, critical commentaries on the two and their relationship observe the aesthetic tension between these historical impulses and both artists' prominence in their own contemporary Romantic world.

The parallels between Mendelssohn's and Goethe's careers are nothing short of remarkable, given the substantial differences in their ages. Both had acquired an extraordinary international reputation by their mid-twenties, Goethe through *Götz von Behrlichen* and *Die Leiden des jungen Werther* and Mendelssohn through his landmark performances of Bach's *St. Matthew Passion* in 1829 and the publication of his Octet for Strings (Op. 20) and his already-acclaimed *Midsummer Night's Dream* and *Hebrides* Overtures (Opp. 21 and 26) in 1832–35. Both possessed a deep sense of German cultural identity, and this self-image fueled their later efforts to use art as a tool for a large-scale cosmopolitan social project aimed at upholding the ideals of *Bildung* and high moral and aesthetic standards in the face of certain corrosive aspects of Romanticism (xenophobic nationalism in Goethe's case, empty virtuosity and dilettantism in Mendelssohn's). Both were firmly convinced of the enduring value of the great art of the past, both in itself and as a source of inspiration and ideas for the present. And by the ends of their lives both had become central figures in European cultural politics—figures whose numerous admirers and comparatively few detractors were equally ardent, but whose significance and contributions could be neither denied nor ignored.

At the same time, the relationship between Goethe and Mendelssohn figures more prominently in the Mendelssohn literature than in its Goethian counterpart. This is to some extent natural, since Goethe's life was substantially longer and Mendelssohn entered into it only in the poet's last twelve years. But the disparity also owes to another, considerably more complex factor: the disparity in their critical and aesthetic reception histories. The reverence with which many or most Europeans regarded Goethe during the mid- and later nineteenth century prevented his love for the Classics and his contempt for many aspects of Romanticism from undermining his central position in the then-emergent canon of German cultural luminaries; but during precisely the same years Mendelssohn's position as a contributor to the compositional discourse of music history was aggressively challenged: he was increasingly viewed as epigonal, a composer who never quite succeeded in outgrowing the archetypal "period of imitation" and consequently remained unbecomingly reliant on models from the past. The critical constructions of both artists' identity and historical significance thus changed dramatically over the course of the nineteenth century. For late nineteenth- and early twentieth-century commentators, Mendelssohn's artistic stature was buttressed by his artistic and personal affinities with Goethe, but Goethe needed no such buttressing. Mendelssohn thus figures less prominently than any number of comparatively minor figures in many accounts of his life and works.

The critical receptions of Mendelssohn and Goethe became more complicated between their deaths and the founding of the German Reich in 1871. In some quarters Goethe was increasingly embraced both abroad and within the German-speaking countries over the course of the late 1830s and the 1840s. For these admirers, many of them members or extensions of the liberal Goethe-cult of Rahel Varnhagen von Ense, née Levin (1771–1833), and her husband Karl August (1785–1858), he was a cultural and intellectual luminary, one whose legacies would enduringly benefit literature, politics, and intellectual culture.[3] Equally prominent until the 1870s was an anti-Goethe faction that held that Goethe's advocacy of Classical antiquity and opposition to progressive nationalism had been part of a larger betrayal of the function of art as idealized poetry in favor of an all-too prosaic reality. This faction comprised an improbable agreement between individuals who still held that Goethe's art was corrupt and immoral, and young progressives—most prominently, the *junges Deutschland* (young Germany) movement. Heinrich Heine (1797–1856), who in 1827 had likened Goethe to an Olympian deity who "[saw] everything with his clear Greek eye," drew on Friedrich Schlegel's well-known 1794 declaration that Goethe was the poet who articulated "an entirely new period in the history of art"[4] when he asserted already in 1828 that "[his] old prophecy that the period of art that began at the cradle of Goethe [would] end beside his coffin seems close to its fulfillment. Today's art must be disposed of entirely because its principles are based on the old, now-rejected regime and have their roots in the holy Roman imperial past."[5] Heine's deft correlation of art, politics, and historical progress became a central tenet of mid-century Goethe criticisms, and the years surrounding the 1848 revolutions teem with epithets such as Gottfried Keller's "Goethe-Philister" and "Goethe-Pedanten," terms that relegate Goethe's art to the past and argue for the urgency of new artistic direction because of the urgency and turbulence of the political present.

These developments all have clear parallels in the early decades of the posthumous reception history of Mendelssohn, who died in November 1847, just weeks before the onset of the great revolutionary tide that would sweep Europe beginning in January 1848. On the one hand, the third quarter of the century witnessed the growth of a Mendelssohn cult whose enthusiasm bordered on idolatry, especially in England, where his music had been slow to catch on until the early 1840s, but where the composer Charles Edward Horsley (1822–76) in 1872 would describe Mendelssohn's works as "his monument," leaving them "to the admiration of all who would learn what is good and great in music" while describing the composer as "in all relations of life . . . humanly speaking perfect."[6]

Other currents in postrevolutionary culture claimed Mendelssohn not as a hero, but as a victim, producing an anti-Mendelssohn faction whose vitriol bordered on calumny. Because his surname immediately and indelibly associated him with the idea of Jewish assimilation into Christian culture, he personified racial and political alterity to the anti-Semitic elements of revolutionary culture—an Otherness that found some of its most repugnantly eloquent expression in Wagner's notorious essay "Das Judenthum in der Musik" (Jewry in Music; 1850) and Franz Liszt's less well-known but equally influential chapter on Jewish attributes and influences in his *Sur les Bohémiens et de leur musique en Hongrie* (On the Gypsies and Their Music in Hungary; 1859).[7] Because he epitomized success in the cultural climate of Restoration Germany and personified many of that culture's values, he was a natural target for post-1848 cultural progressives who viewed the world of the *Vormärz* as a betrayal of the liberal and democratic ideals that had spawned the French Revolution a generation earlier. And his complicated cultivation of closely interdependent but seemingly contradictory

"Classical" and "Romantic" stylistic impulses in his own music became a sign of historical recidivism, a retreat from an ostensibly more wholeheartedly Romantic genius that had spawned early masterworks such as the A-minor String Quartet (Op. 13) and the *Midsummer Night's Dream* and *Hebrides* Overtures. This perceived recidivism was also, in the eyes of contemporary science, an inevitable consequence of his Jewish heritage, as was his mastery of "external form" in the supposed absence of a corresponding richness of ideas or depth of emotional expression.[8]

Only in the 1870s did a marked divergence in Goethe's and Mendelssohn's posthumous reception histories emerge, as critical opposition to Goethe all but disappeared while Mendelssohn's advocates increasingly lost ground to his detractors. The ascendant nationalist discourse of the 1860s combined with the post-Hegelian dialectical advocacy of Goethe's classicism as a synthesis of polarities to render him more German and less the province of the rest of the world in the eyes of his biographers and critics, despite his emphatically cosmopolitan aesthetic outlook.[9] Earlier disputes regarding his contributions thus yielded to a generalized but highly heterogeneous Goethe cult: any number of contradictory ideas and aesthetic impulses in the late nineteenth century claimed their roots in his ideas and most other aspects of his diverse output. Concurrently Mendelssohn, whose cosmopolitan success never impeded his dedication to the cause of German music and public perception of him as the quintessential German composer, became less genuinely German and more obviously Jewish in the eyes of his critics—with all the liabilities that contemporary culture ascribed to that cultural identity.

The bifurcation in Goethe's and Mendelssohn's reception histories was augmented by changing views of their relationship to posterity and developments in their respective provinces of scholarship. Goethe, like Beethoven, became widely viewed as the prophet of the modern world, while Mendelssohn became little more than a historical throwback, useful to the present for his rediscovery of the musical past but never quite able to rise to the challenges that historical knowledge posed for one's identity as a truly great contributor to artistic progress. This view of Goethe's greatness was facilitated by the vastly improved knowledge and appreciation of his creative life, his artistic persona, and the texts of his works—a knowledge that resulted from a dramatic surge in primary-source studies concerning him during the last two decades of the nineteenth century. The same years witnessed a pronounced downturn in such studies concerning Mendelssohn, so that late nineteenth-century commentaries become increasingly derivative, less aware of the breadth of his creative life and his artistic persona, and more one-dimensionally dependent on the prevalent conventional wisdoms.

These changes in reception history reveal more than just how views of Goethe, Mendelssohn, their respective works, and their artistic and personal relationships have changed through history. They also parallel changes in critical receptions of the two artists' respective Walpurgis Night treatments, and thus provide a convenient reflection of changing societal attitudes toward the issues that had become intimately associated with the Walpurgis Night as a cultural topos by the time Goethe and Mendelssohn took it up between 1799 and 1844. Moreover, since the issues of identity and alterity central to the mid- and later nineteenth century's cultural polemics also informed the changing constructions of Goethe's and Mendelssohn's cultural identity during those years, it is hardly surprising that those issues also figure prominently in the critical receptions of both artists' *Walpurgisnacht* treatments. Goethe's ballad, which almost entirely escaped critical notice during his lifetime,[10] first received critical acclaim through Mendelssohn's cantata. The composer's revised *Walpurgisnacht* setting, for its part, was initially viewed as a demanding and provocatively original work that demonstrated both his own innovative spirit and his profound artistic empathy with the illustrious poet—but Romantic innovation and spiritual empathy receded from critical view as his reputation declined; eventually, the work became merely "genial" and "ingratiating," in some ways naive rather than insightful—the artistic compeer of neither its textual source nor (especially) the poem's authorship.

The Reception of Goethe and His *Faust* up to 1832

Goethe's status as a towering figure who could not be bypassed in the world of letters was firmly established already by the 1780s, but the generally unquestioned esteem that he now enjoys as sovereign deity of German literary culture came into existence only quite late. During his lifetime and for some decades thereafter his titanic status entailed a great deal of ambivalence and outright enmity. Having effectively set in motion currents that would become central to German literary Romanticism with his Storm and Stress masterpieces of the 1770s (especially *Götz von Behrlichen,* 1773; and *Die Leiden des jungen Werther,* 1774), by the turn of the nineteenth century he was deeply disappointed with many of the currents he had unleashed. Yet he was also widely regarded, in part because of those currents, as a force of artistic, moral, and social corruption. In the meantime, working with Friedrich Schiller, he had founded the aesthetic school generally known as Weimar Classicism and developed his philosophy of a supranational *Weltliteratur* (world literature), a philosophy that alienated him from the ardent nationalism of most German Romantics and European Romanticism generally. By the last decade of his life he felt less accepted by his German contemporaries than by their British, French, Italian, and Russian counterparts.[11]

The significance of these developments becomes clearer against the backdrop of the reception history of the two parts of Goethe's *Faust* tragedy and their respective Walpurgis Night elements. Although Friedrich Schelling (1775–1854) observed already of the *Faust-Fragment* (which included neither the Walpurgis Night nor the Walpurgis Night's Dream material) that the character of Goethe's

Faust was a specifically German manifestation of "the inmost, purest essence of our age" ("die innerste, reinste Essenz unseres Zeitalters"),[12] the complete Part I of the tragedy attracted surprisingly little public critical notice inside Germany until mid-century. The most important early review of Part I, written by the Dresden archaeologist and critic Karl August Böttiger (1760–1835) and published in 1809, offers high praise for Goethe's recounting of the legend as a whole (particularly in comparison with the "philosophical and therefore boring" contemporaneous version by K. C. L. Schöne),[13] but withholds approval of the *Walpurgisnacht* and *Walpurgisnachtstraum* scenes, which he found disruptive to the narrative and "highly displeasing" to his "moral sensibilities."[14]

Elsewhere on the continent Goethe's *Faust* fared little better during the first two decades of the century. The last years of the Napoleonic wars placed vast strains on the community of letters in France; public notices of things German were few and highly critical. The French-Swiss political commentator Benjamin Constant (1767–1830) described the *Fragment* in his journal on February 12, 1804, as "a derision of the human race" ("une dérision de l'espèce humaine"), and in 1816 Auguste de Saint-Chamans (1777–1860) regretted that "that composition of human horrors, diabolical merriments, and poetic lunacy" had not been left in the marionette theater.[15] By the early 1820s, however, French cultural relations with the German-speaking countries were sufficiently improved that a number of translations began to appear. Initially, these translations were quite free, essentially treatments of Goethe's drama as a highly malleable substance to be truncated, rearranged, or otherwise adapted to fit the conventions of the French theater (a trend that was somewhat understandable because of the extraordinary length of the German original; after all, Goethe himself made extensive changes for the performances with which he was involved[16]). Most important among them were the free translation published in 1823 by the diplomat Louis Sainte-Aulaire (1778–1854) and the more literal one published in 1825 by Philipp Albert Stapfer (1766–1840).[17]

But by far the most influential advocate for Goethe during the century's first two decades was Germaine de Staël (1766–1817), whose *De l'Allemagne* (On Germany; 1810–13) stands as one of the nineteenth century's most impassioned efforts to introduce German culture to France.[18] Because of de Staël's association with the resistance to Bonaparte, publication of *De l'Allemagne* was banned in France; the emperor had all known copies of the first French edition seized and destroyed. It was finally published in 1813 in both French and English editions in London, where it immediately garnered attention in part because of its status as a document of a French émigrée's ideas on a topic that was politically sensitive to the emperor who was the national enemy. (The success and influence of her account are testified to by the fact that it sold 1500 copies in just three days.[19]) Free publication in France occurred only after Napoleon's demise.

De l'Allemagne offers a wide-ranging survey of German literature and its history, including a description and detailed synopsis of *Faust I*. De Staël states that the play as a whole "cannot be exceeded in boldness of conception"[20] and includes among its highlights a free translation of most of ll. 4183–4210 (the appearance of the vision of the hanged Gretchen and the beginning of the transition to the Walpurgis Night's dream) and a description of the "Sabbath of Witches" (le sabbat de sorcières; i.e., the Walpurgis Night), which she describes as "truly the saturnalia of genius" ("vraiment les Saturnales de l'esprit"), a "whirlwind of all that can be thought or said, when images and ideas rush headlong, confound themselves, and seem to fall back into the abysses from which reason has called them" ("[le] tourbillon de tout ce qu'on peut imaginer et dire, quand les images et les idées se précipietent, se confondent, et semblent retomber dans les abîmes dont la raison les a fait sortir").[21]

De Staël's description of *Faust I* is significant not only because of its enthusiastic celebration of Goethe at a time when such endorsements were not to be taken for granted, but also because of its emphasis on its grotesque and inherently evil elements: in her view, Mephistopheles was "the hero of the piece . . . the Evil Being *par excellence,* before whom all others . . . are only novices"; yet he, unlike the Satan of Dante and Milton, was "a civilized devil . . . awkward without timidity, disdainful without pride."[22] And because of his character, which "supposes an inexhaustible knowledge of social life, of nature, and of the marvelous,"[23] the drama as a whole became "a nightmare of the imagination . . . that redoubles its strength. It discovers the diabolical revelation of . . . that incredulity which attaches itself to every thing that can ever exist of good in this world."[24] Goethe's frank exploration of intense evil in the context of a plot that celebrates the tensions between evil and good, knowledge and innocence, and the supernatural, the divine, and human nature thus became a celebration of the ignoble attributes themselves. By casting the poem in this fashion, de Staël reaffirmed by exaggeration the offensiveness of Goethe's text for some sensibilities while also extolling the aesthetics of the grotesque in a fashion quite inconsistent with his own views, especially later in his life.

Finally, de Staël's remarks on Goethe and German literature generally are notable for what they do *not* say. Her discussion of German poetry ranges across a considerable expanse of Goethe's oeuvre and names several works emblematic of the sort of aesthetic paganism discussed in chapter 2: the *Roman Elegies,* "Die Braut von Korinth," and "Der Gott und die Bajadere."[25] She also commends Germans (both "the populace" and "men of more enlightened minds"[26]) for their willingness to step outside the intellectual and moral framework of Christianity, reasoning that "though Christianity opposes all groundless fears, popular superstitions always have some sort of analogy to the prevailing religion."[27] She also discusses, in the context of her praise for Goethe's humor, "Der Zauberlehrling" (The Sorcerer's Apprentice), which Goethe consistently published along with "Die erste Walpurgisnacht." Yet while the "Walpurgisnacht" ballad hovers remarkably close to the surface in de Staël's discussion of Goethe and German poetry, it is never mentioned—another indication of its minor or inferior status in the eyes of Goethe's and Mendelssohn's contemporaries.[28]

The English reception of *Faust I*, strongly informed by de Staël's characterization, was both aided and complicated by English readers' prior familiarity with Christopher Marlowe's celebrated *Tragical History of Doctor Faustus* (1588, publ. 1604) and by Goethe's controversialness in England prior to that point (itself a function of the political dimensions that his name had quickly assumed vis-à-vis events in France since about 1790).[29] By the mid-1790s English literary culture acknowledged him, along with Lessing and Schiller, as a leading voice in German letters, a successor to Wieland (whose affinity with Laurence Sterne appealed to English readers), and an improvement on the rather stale dramas of Solomon Gessner (1730–88) and August von Kotzebue (1761–1819).[30] But it remained aloof toward German literature and German culture generally well into the nineteenth century. *Götz von Behrlichen* and especially *Werther* had attracted considerable insular attention from the beginning. On the whole, however, Goethe as an author was considered pernicious and immoral—an "apologist of suicide"[31] who represented ethical turpitude and (ironically enough) English Jacobinism.[32] Even Coleridge and Wordsworth, both of whom were fascinated with Goethe, were unable to come to terms with his work. Coleridge argued that he "lacked religion" and was not a good poet because of his supposed immorality, and he later planned to write his own *Faust* (to be titled *Michael Scott*) with a substantially redefined character of Faust and significant dramatic differences.[33] Wordsworth, for his part, found in the Goethe of *Wilhelm Meisters Lehrjahre* "a profligacy, an inhuman sensuality . . . which is utterly revolting."[34]

Goethe's *Faust* was able to make headway in part because England's alliance with Prussia in the defeat of Bonaparte substantially diminished English reservations toward Germans and their culture, and in part because of the English version of de Staël's *De l'Allemagne*. De Staël's "satanic"[35] misreading of Goethe's text corroborated his detractors' suspicions of his immorality, but it also won enthusiastic converts to his cause by offering writers such as Blake, Byron, Keats, and Shelley a new literary model for an escape from neoclassicism and the confines of conventional literary moralizing.

English critical responses to Part I of Goethe's *Faust* generally took the form of either critical notices concerning the work, or translations of all or part of it. The earliest critical notice, published in the *Monthly Review* in 1810 (three years before de Staël's *Germany* was published), singles out the Walpurgis Night scene as a "scene of enchantment [that] is described with a force of imagination and a truth of psychology which aspire to vie with Shakespeare,"[36] thus placing both play and author in eminent company. Otherwise, however, the reviewer sides with the detractors who questioned Goethe's moral propriety, calling the play "trash" and "an uncouth though fanciful mixture of farce and tragedy, of profaneness and morality, of vulgarity and beauty, of obscenity and feeling."[37] Other early nineteenth-century English reviewers found Part I of Goethe's tale incomplete and morally ambivalent—although it seems safe to assume that at least some of these reservations were born of frustrated expectations produced by readers' prior acquaintance with the tragedy of sin and damnation offered in Marlowe's more straightforward and frankly moralistic version.

The most strikingly positive review of Goethe's Part I, published anonymously in 1820,[38] defers judgment on the moral issues of the play, suggesting that criticism had to "be silent" on that point until Faust's fate was revealed in the drama's completion and acknowledging "numerous and transcendent beauties" along with many other greatnesses.[39] But this reviewer finds fault with Goethe for one point central to this book: the Walpurgis Night scene, which he considers gratuitous and disruptive to the plot:

> . . . Unfortunate, abused Margaret!—she groans under the weight of her desperation, and Faustus appears to have discarded her entirely from his thoughts. Conducted by Mephistopheles, he attends the nocturnal concave [*sic*], or sabbath of Witches on Walpurgisnight [*sic*]—and engages with them in their malign and brutal joys, and rites. However imaginative, and full of smart repartee and satire, this picture of the riot of St. Walpurgo [*sic*] may be, we must nevertheless blame the poet for having thus placed it in a part of his work, where it interferes most unpleasantly with an interest of a higher and more powerful nature—we mean the pathos of the situation in which the unhappy, but still amiable, Margaret is placed. How could Goethe have thought it possible to make us relish this fantastic extravagance, these mad subtleties of a poignant intellect, at the moment when he has so forcibly excited out pity, and with this passion filled our hearts. In this scene, he appears to us to consult propriety, and the wishes of his readers, only when, at the conclusion, he introduces the apparition of a female—pale as death—whom Faustus instantly recognizes to be his Margaret.[40]

Although the anonymous 1820 review of *Faust I* is by far the most perceptive and receptive of the English-language commentaries published up to then, its anonymous author clearly finds the Walpurgis Night scene excessive. The same is true of an even more thoughtful and sympathetic review by the brilliant Scottish writer, journalist, and mathematician Thomas Carlyle (1795–1881), an acquaintance of Goethe whose English translations of *Wilhelm Meisters Lehrjahre* and *Wanderjahre* would advance Goethe's cause considerably in Britain.[41] Like the anonymous 1820 reviewer, Carlyle cannot quite accept the Walpurgis Night scene. After stating that "[i]t is impossible to convey any idea of this extraordinary convention [of the Walpurgis Night revelry on the Brocken], or of the plan which Goethe has taken to depict it," he admits that the "*Saturnalia* of poetry as well as of witchcraft . . . wavers between sense and utter nothingness, and leaves an impression like the first dawnings of thoughts in the mind, before they can at all be converted into propositions capable of being contradicted or affirmed."[42] And he, too, finds the Walpurgis Night and Walpurgis Night's Dream scenes somewhat gratuitous: "Faust mingles in this satanic revelry more than we could wish; yet he soon grows tired of it; and we can almost pardon him for having snatched a few moments of enjoyment, or at least forgetfulness, from a source however mean, when we reflect that they are the last allotted to him."[43] Together, these two essays not only sustained English interest in Goethe and kept his *Faust* saga alive, but also led to a series of translations that struggled mightily to come to terms with Goethe and the German Faust more frankly and perceptively than had been done before.

As of the early 1820s, then, Goethe's Walpurgis Night treatments had largely failed to succeed: the 1799 ballad was lingering in obscurity, and the *Walpurgisnacht* of *Faust I* had won French critical approval only in the context of de Staël's fanciful rendering of the play's plot. Goethe, with his keen interest and substantial ability in the visual arts, surely would have regarded with satisfaction the fact that the success of the scene (and of the play as a whole) was abetted at around this time by a set of illustrations. These illustrations, prepared by Friedrich August Moritz Retzsch (1779–1857), were published at the suggestion of Goethe himself, who had resisted the notion of publishing illustrations to his play until he saw Retzsch's drafts in Dresden in 1810.[44] Published as a series of twenty-six etchings of important scenes in 1816, they are remarkable for the tension that resulted from the taut crispness of their flowing lines and the absence of any emphasis on light and shadow. Among these illustrations were two of the Walpurgis Night scene. The first (figure 6.1) concerns the beginning of the scene (approximately ll. 3835–70), and depicts the obviously evil Mephistopheles beckoning upward on the Brocken as a seemingly bewildered Faust looks on. The illustration includes not only the *Irrlicht* (in the lower left-hand corner cf. fig. 1.1, p. 14), but also the "Gegend von Schierke und Elend,"[45] complete with all manner of aberrant animal-like creatures (a distinctly malicious horned snake atop the boulder behind Mephistopheles, an owl beside the fir tree in the upper right, a toad in the lower left, and two unidentifiable but hideous creatures on the ground in the lower left and lower right), and a multitude of witches flying overhead on domestic items (broomsticks and rugs or blankets), goats, and pigs. In keeping with the powerful and paradoxical directional pull of the narrative in Goethe's text,[46] the lines of the drawing display a massive upward sweep among all the animate creatures, from the lower right to the upper left; the only exception is the skeleton-like creature flying in the upper left-hand corner, which seems to be beckoning the others onward and upward. At the same time, Retzsch reflects the scene's enormous tension by contrasting the animate figures' upward motion with the conspicuous stasis of the environs: the massive boulder that dominates the middle ground and the strong vertical lines of the fir trees.

Even more impressive is Retzsch's illustration of the tumult further up the mountain (figure 6.2), corresponding to ll. 4041–4213 of the play. As in the previous illustration, the scene retains a strong upward and leftward pull. Now, however, the overall sense of direction is weakened by numerous stationary groups of misbegotten creatures engaged in drinking, dancing, and illicit sexual activity. Nor does Retzsch forgo Goethe's inclusion of the seemingly respectable figures. Toward the rear of the left foreground, taller than the surrounding group of dancing figures, is the capped and bearded "Proktophantasmist"; further up, center in the middle ground, are two other respectable humans

Figure 6.1. Morris Retzsch, *Illustrationen zu Goethes Faust* (1825): First illustration of *Walpurgisnacht.*

(evidently the minister and the general; ll. 4076–83); and behind them, strolling and engaged in conversation, are two courtly figures (the author and the parvenu; ll. 4084–91). Most powerful, though, are the figures of Mephistopheles and Faust, whose gaze and stance are directed against the flow of the scene and supported by other, more subtle diagonals from the lower left toward the upper right (the gaze of the Proktophantasmist in the lower left, the line of the right arm of the naked woman dancing with the monk in the middle ground). Faust points upward and to the right, where the apparition of Gretchen stands motionless, isolated from the action by a lonely and erratically foliated fir tree, the foreshadowing line of the hangman's noose clearly visible around her neck, as Mephistopheles tries to redirect his attention to the devilish Walpurgis Night revelries. This illustration is remarkable not only for its overall spatial retention of the narrative sequence (the upward sweep is coordinated with the sequence of characters, so that the distinguishable characters and events that occur later in the text are also higher in the illustration), but also for Retzsch's re-creation of the disruptive effect of the appearance of the Gretchen apparition in the lines of his etching.

Retzsch's illustrations for *Faust I* marked the first unqualified success for the work; Percy Bysshe Shelley, for one, found the Walpurgis Night scene incomprehensible

Figure 6.2. Morris Retzsch, *Illustrationen zu Goethes Faust* (1825): Second illustration of *Walpurgisnacht.*

until he saw Retzsch's rendering.[47] They were reprinted numerous times in Germany, and Johann Peter Eckermann (1792–1854), Goethe's friend and colleague at the Weimar court, may have echoed Goethe's own views in 1829 when he commented on their usefulness as the basis for "the actions, gestures, and appearance [*Physiognomie*] of the individual characters" in staged productions of the play.[48] They were used as the basis for Hermann Neefe's stage design of the first public performance of *Faust I* (given in Braunschweig on January 19, 1829), as well as for an 1838 Coburg performance of *tableaux vivants* with spoken excerpts from the play.[49] They also contributed to the contemporary English and French reception of *Faust I.* In 1820 (the same year as the anonymous appreciative review from the *London Magazine*) they were recopied by the English illustrator Henry Moses (ca. 1782–1870), and republished with explanatory excerpts in English translation by George Soane (1790–1860).[50] Moses's copies were in turn reprinted and reviewed in numerous subsequent English publications as late as 1879. They quickly became so well known that already in

1821 the *European Magazine and London Review* commented that what had "most contributed to render 'Faust' more popular in England, [was] the series of beautiful Outlines by Retzsch, which delighted all those who read the tragedy, and made those who had not anxious to peruse it."[51]

In France, too, Retzsch's etchings quickly found their mark. They were copied in new engravings by Pierre Antoine Branche (1805–?) and published early in 1828 and then already later that year in a second version, with a supplemental analysis of the play by Elise Voïart.[52] Their influence is felt in the seventeen lithographs for *Faust I* by Eugène Delacroix (1798–1863; see figures 6.3 and 6.4). Delacroix had seen and admired Retzsch's etchings already by 1821, and in 1828 he published his own renderings as part of a new edition of the French translation by Stapfer first published in 1825.[53] Goethe reviewed and approved two drafts for this series and announced them in 1827 in *Über Kunst und Altertum*, describing Delacroix as "an artist whose decisive talent no one denies, but whose wild manners, when he uses them, by no means tend to agree with the turbulence of his conception, the turmoil of his composition, the forcefulness of his positioning, and the rawness of his colors" and continuing: "But for that reason he is precisely the man to immerse himself in Faust and in all likelihood to produce pictures from it that no one else could have conceived."[54] He clearly was not disappointed when the new edition appeared in 1828:

> Here, in a fantastical product between heaven and earth, between the possible and the impossible, between the crudest and most tender, and between any other opposites one might possibly imagine, Herr Delacroix seems to feel at home and proceed as if on his own turf. The impressive luster [of this edition] is thus muted and the spirit transported from the world of the clear letters into a dusky world, and the ancient sense of a fairy-tale-like narrative returns to the fore. . . .[55]

The reasons for Goethe's admiration are readily evident from Delacroix's two illustrations of the Walpurgis Night scene. In the first (figure 6.3), he dispenses with the whirlwind of misbegotten creatures that populated the sky and earth in Retzsch's etching, retaining only Mephistopheles, Faust, and a pair of serpents. The terrain no longer resembles the rugged landscape of the Brocken; it is closer to what one might expect in the French Alps (a reasonable change, given the edition's presumable readership). The erratically spaced and oddly pitched fir trees of Retzsch's etching are replaced by a single ancient, mighty oak. Faust's expression is no longer hapless or curious, but possessed of its own anger or evil. Most important, the powerful sweep from the lower right to the upper left of the picture is retained, now emphasized through the texture of the strokes and the gradual darkening of the scene as the eye follows the sweep from the light ground beneath Faust's left foot into the black recesses of the tree's foliage. The picture retains a powerful tension despite the drastically reduced cast, in part because of the dramatic interplay of darks and lights, but also because of the tension built into the exaggerated stances of the characters.

Figure 6.3. Eugène Delacroix, first illustration of *Walpurgisnacht* for translation of Goethe's *Faust* by Albert Stapfer (1828) (cf. Figure 6.1).

Figure 6.4. Eugène Delacroix, second illustration of *Walpurgisnacht* for translation of Goethe's *Faust* by Albert Stapfer (1828) (cf. Figure 6.2).

The depiction of the end of the Walpurgis Night (fig. 6.4) reveals a similar reinterpretation. Here, too, the numerous abominable characters represented in Retzsch's illustration are reduced to the group of serpents, lizards, and toads in the lower right-hand corner, the two demons opposite them, and a group of shadowy dancing figures down the hill behind them. As in Retzsch's illustration, the sense of upward sweep is preserved, chiefly through the texture, but it is weakened by a series of forceful contrasting lines (most prominently, the right arm and left leg of the front demon and the line extending upward though the boulder before Faust, through the front side of his and Mephistopheles's figures). And the animate cast is reduced to the three essential figures: Mephistopheles, Faust, and the apparition of Gretchen, floating suspended from the hangman's noose held by the winged demon behind her, with her breasts exposed and her eye sockets black and lifeless.

Together, these illustrations combined with the sometimes misguided but often enthusiastic critical comments of reviewers and the spate of unabashedly free translations to heighten general interest in part I of Goethe's *Faust* tragedy over the course of the 1820s. (Though it must remain a matter of speculation, it is tempting to imagine that the pronounced upswing in public acceptance in the mid-1820s played a role in Goethe's return to work on his *Lebensarbeit* in the last few years of the decade.) These developments in turn led to a new series of translations that deliberately aspired to address the inaccuracies, inadequacies, and omissions of earlier attempts. In France, the most important of these, published in 1828 by Gérard de Nerval (1808–55), impressed Goethe.[56] In England, the issues that continued to challenge English readers during this early struggle to come to terms with the first part as a whole are more vividly reflected in the translation of the Walpurgis Night scene by Percy Bysshe Shelley (1792–1822).

Shelley's "May-Day Night" was penned in the first two months of 1822 and published posthumously in 1824 in the *Liberal*, the journal conceived by Byron, Hunt, and Shelley himself as a vehicle for their controversial writings and a counterweight to the conservative tone of established literary journals in England.[57] It is the final product of Shelley's longstanding fascination with Goethe in general and *Faust I* in particular.[58] Already in 1815–16, shortly after the publication of de Staël's *Germany* but well before there was any strong insular consensus affirming *Faust*'s worthiness as a successor to *Werther*, Shelley undertook a literal translation of ll. 243–1213 of the poem (i.e., from the beginning of the "Prolog in Heaven" into the scene in Faust's study). His immediate impetus for returning to the project of translating the play seems to have been his receipt of a copy of the Retzsch illustrations with Soane's selective translations on January 12, 1822; he wrote that Retzsch's etchings were "worthy of Göthe" but found Soane's translations of the excerpts "miserable."[59] Work on the project was closely bound up with his project of translating into English Calderon de la Barca's *El mágico prodigioso* (The Wonder-making Magician; 1637), itself thematically close to the *Faust* legend. On April 10, he reported that he had "(imagine my presumption) translated several scenes from both as the basis of a paper for our journal [the *Liberal*]."[60]

Shelley's plan to publish his *Faust* translation in the *Liberal* and his inclusion of the "Prolog in Heaven" and the Walpurgis Night scene—that is, the two scenes that had never before appeared in English translation—suggest that the project aimed to confront English readers' sensibilities head-on, and thus to compel them to come to terms with *Faust I* in its totality. The version ultimately published in the *Liberal*, which reflects changes made by Mary Shelley and/or Hunt, backs off from a number of these difficulties, evidently in the interest of prudence and propriety. Some such instances are relatively minor,[61] but others renege on Shelley's clear efforts to preserve at least something of the vulgarity of the German original. One such instance occurs in the lewd quatrains exchanged by Faust, Mephistopheles, an old woman, and a young girl in ll. 4128–43. The version published in the *Liberal* simply summarizes this provocative scene in rather innocuous terms: "(Faust dances and sings with a girl, and Mephistopheles with an old woman)."[62] Shelley's fair-copy manuscript, however, includes ll. 4128–43 in a translation that, while not as forcefully prurient as Goethe's original, at least preserves its suggestive quality:[63]

Goethe (*GA* 5: 272)	*Shelley*
FAUST mit der Jungen tanzend.	Faust (dancing[)]
4128 Einst hatt' ich einen schönen Traum:	I had once a lovely dream
4129 Da sah ich einen Apfelbaum,	In which I saw an apple tree,
4130 Zwei schöne Äpfel glänzten dran;	Where two fair apples with thier [*sic*] gleam
4131 Sie reizten mich, ich stieg hinan.	To climb & taste attracted me.
DIE SCHÖNE.	The girl.
4132 Der Äpfelchen begehrt ihr sehr,	The little apples you desired
4133 Und schon vom Paradiese her.	From Paradise came long ago;
4134 Von Freuden fühl ich mich bewegt,	With you I feel, that if required,
4135 Daß auch mein Garten solche trägt.	Such still within my garden grow.
MEPHISTOPHELES *mit der Alten.*	Meph[istopheles]
4136 Ein hatt ich einen wüsten Traum;	I had once a ghastly dream
4137 Da sah ich einen gespaltnen Baum,	In which a shattered tree did seem
4138 Der hatt ein ungeheures Loch;	To bear a X X upon its bough
4139 So groß es war, gefiel mir's doch.	Twas like—you understand me now.
DIE ALTE.	Old Woman
4140 Ich biete meinen besten Gruß	My best kiss & this to boot
4141 Dem Ritter mit dem Pferdefuß!	To the Knight of the Cloven Foot
4142 Halt Er einen rechten Propf bereit,	*X X X X*
4143 Wenn Er das große Loch nicht scheut.	*X X X X*

That Shelley's translation remained unfinished is unfortunate, for it represents the strongest credible effort at acknowledging the textual and artistic integrity of a work that in the early 1820s was still regarded as more eccentric and difficult than successful. Efforts to coax a translation out of Coleridge, which the London publisher John Murray had begun already in 1814 in the wake of the success of de Staël's *Germany*, ran aground on his rejection of the work's suitability.[64] Frances Leveson Gower's (1800–57) complete translation of Part I, published in 1823, is at best a qualified success, since it willfully omits sizable stretches of material, including most of the Walpurgis Night scene, for "considerations of decency."[65] As a result, by the mid-1820s the appetite and interest of at least the more learned portions of the English literary public had been whetted, but only those with a strong command of German had any means of reading the work in even a reasonably reliable version.

The reception history of the "Classical Walpurgis Night" from *Faust II* has been rather more muted. On the one hand, the fact that the second part of the tragedy was published only after Goethe's death and nearly a decade after the emergence of a recognizable consensus that the scene and the play as a whole were not merely eccentric poetic rubbish spared it the sort of critical disdain and willful textual mangling suffered by its earlier counterpart. Almost from the beginning, the scene's complicated allusive and allegorical webs, its equally complicated relationship to its "romantic" counterpart in *Faust I*, and the nature of its structural and textual relationships to Classical models have fascinated scholars. On the other hand, Part I overwhelmingly dominates discourse on the Goethe/*Faust* engagement—and thus, by extension, on the two Walpurgis Nights. Just as the pointed and not entirely unfounded 1833 criticism of the influential literary historian Wolfgang Menzel that in *Faust II* Goethe had (as eloquently summarized by Arthur Henkel) "betrayed his original Faust . . . by bestowing on him an impenitent apotheosis in a Christian heaven"[66] did not hinder Part II's relatively smooth acceptance as a counterpart and completion to Part I, neither has the "Classical Walpurgis Night" ever really gained acceptance as a genuine Walpurgis Night: it is identified as such only because of Goethe's application of the epithet, and it seems to have exerted little influence on readings or assessments of its predecessor. This was the status of the Walpurgis Night as a cultural topos when Goethe took up the topic anew in the second part of his telling of the tragedy, and when Mendelssohn announced to the great poet that he had undertaken to set his 1799 ballad on the subject to music.

Critical Responses to Mendelssohn's Second Walpurgis Night Setting

Readers familiar with Mendelssohn's cantata primarily from its rather marginal status in the latter-day canon may be surprised at the degree of attention it attracted in the mid- and later nineteenth century. Nineteenth-century performance reviews, like their modern counterparts, often commented on the music at hand only perfunctorily, very generally, or indirectly (or not at all), concentrating instead on the performance itself. But reviewers of performances of *Die erste Walpurgisnacht* often discussed the work itself at great length. The reasons for this exceptional practice are unclear, although it seems plausible that the stature of poet and composer contributed to the reviewers' decisions. The fact is convenient, however, for these lengthy and detailed commentaries highlight several important aspects of how nineteenth-century performers and audiences responded not only to *Die erste Walpurigsnacht* itself, but to the poet, the composer, and the position of the poem and the cantata in the oeuvres of their respective creators. Most important, they reveal much about the nineteenth century's attitudes toward the cantata's textual themes.

One remarkable feature of the early reviews is that they consistently rank *Die erste Walpurgisnacht* at or above the level of compositional achievement of *St. Paul*, as Mendelssohn's greatest composition or very nearly so: Berlioz was by no means alone in his 1843 judgment that it was "the finest thing that Mendelssohn [had] done."[67] To judge from the contemporary press and the number of documented contemporary performances, its position in its oeuvre remained unchallenged until the completion and publication of *Elijah* in 1847, and it remained a staple of most orchestras' and choruses' repertoire to the end of the century—long after the onset of widespread skepticism about Mendelssohn and his music.

This enthusiastic reception was evident even before the *Walpurgisnacht* was published. The first performance made news around Europe—including two most peculiar reports that circulated in the British and Parisian press. On February 28, 1843, an otherwise unidentified correspondent named "F. B. J." reported breathlessly to the *Musical Examiner* (London):

> I write to let you know that a new choral composition by Dr. Mendelssohn has obtained immense success. It is a musical illustration of Goethe's ballad, entitled *Die erste Walpurgisnacht*. This is, beyond a doubt, one of the most original and striking compositions of the celebrated author of *Paulus*, and it will materially add to his fame. It was played, for the first time, at the last *abonnement* [*sic*] concert here, under the direction of the composer. The overture, a duet, a quartet, a quintet, and the final chorus were, each and all, enthusiastically encored.[68]

Essentially the same report—now embellished to state that the overture, and so on, had been encored "two, three, and even four times" (!)—appeared anonymously in the *Revue et gazette musicale de Paris* on March 5,[69] and that review was then taken up elsewhere in the British musical press, translated back into English and further embellished.[70]

Clearly, these early notices made up in enthusiasm for what they lacked in factual accuracy, since the cantata includes no duet, quartet, or quintet, and its continuous structure precludes stopping for encores. Nevertheless, "F. B. J." and his anonymous tropers provided two useful bits of insight on the contemporary reception of Mendelssohn's *Walpurgisnacht*. First, Mendelssohn's doubts regarding its suitability for performance and publication notwithstanding, it created an immediate sensation—so much so that musical correspondents lapsed into fiction in reporting on its premiere. Second, and more important, it did so not least of all as a successor to *St. Paul*, thus eclipsing several other choral/orchestral compositions of the late 1830s and early 1840s—not only the settings of Psalms 42 and 95 (opp. 42 and 46), but also, and more strikingly, the symphony-cantata *Lobgesang* (Hymn of Praise, Op. 52), which had been received with great acclaim in England and Germany. What is more, these reports show, perhaps surprisingly, that the *Walpurgisnacht*'s glorification of pagan Others to Europe's mainstream society was not an obstacle to its success. In view of the Walpurgis Night's longstanding status as a festival of evil and Goethe's residual controversialness even amid widening recognition of his greatness, it could by no means be taken for granted that a musical setting of a minor Goethe poem celebrating paganism would be accepted, much less acclaimed, in the mid-1840s. Given Victorian England's reputation for religious dogmatism, one might expect that these risks would be particularly evident there. In the event, however, the English reception of Mendelssohn's *Walpurgisnacht* reveals precisely the opposite.

Mendelssohn conducted the Philharmonic Society of London in the English premiere on July 8, 1844,[71] using the text provided by Mendelssohn's preferred English translator, William Bartholomew of Ewer & Co., London (see chapter 7). The reviewers again made liberal and not entirely faithful use of each other's words in reporting on the work, but their comments make clear that it was well received. At the same time, the detailed description of the poem's plot and the fact that the explanatory notes on the plot were republished separately suggest that the poem required some explanation for English audiences. The *Musical World* (London), quoting "the admirable account from the pages of a morning contemporary,"[72] reported:

> The *First Walpurgis Night,* performed for the first time in this country, is a musical version, by Dr. Mendelssohn, of Goethe's magnificent poem, wherein the derivation of the German superstition of witches and evil spirits haunting the Harz mountains on the night of the 1st of May, is taken as the basis of the narrative. The legend is said "to have originated in the heathen time, when the Christians tried by force to prevent the Druids from observing their accustomed rites of sacrificing in the open air and on the hills. The Druids are said to have placed watches round their mountains, who, with their dreadful appearance hovering round the fires, and clashing their weapons, frightened the enemy, and the ceremonies were proceeded with." The translation of Goethe's words is by Mr. Bartholomew, who has succeeded in rendering them very closely, preserving at the same time their sonorous oddities, and no little of their dramatic quaintness. The music is as original as the poem, and reflects its characteristics with an effect both startling and extraordinary. It opens with an overture in A minor, descriptive of a storm, and the approach of spring, piled upon a ground work of rolling violoncello passages, leading to a brisk allegro in A major. The character is vague and broken, but it is altogether a grand instance of that bold descriptiveness of invention which belongs exclusively to Mendelssohn. A light chorus in A [No. 1] follows in praise of spring, swelling in body and majesty as the resolution of the Druids and the people to commence the holy sacrifices, is expressed. "An aged woman," in an allegretto air in D minor [No. 2], indicative of trembling alarm, warns the multitude of the murderous snares preparing for them by the Christians; succeeded by a wailing female chorus, extremely dramatic and effective. The Druid priest checks the incipient impulse to neglect the rites, and orders the sacred pile to be prepared [No. 3]. This air, an andante in A minor, with its interspersed chorus declamatory of fearlessness[,] is bold and striking, and leads to a chorus of Druid guards, in E, descriptive of vigilance and precaution, and the dispersion of the band among the passes of the glen [No. 4]. This, a passage singularly expressive of stealthy motion, was enthusiastically encored. A solo intimates the intention of the Druids to mimic the demons in order to terrify their Christian assailants; and then occurs a wonderful chorus in G minor, upon which Mendelssohn

> has expended all his strength. It suggests the rushing of men "in and out each rocky hollow;"[73] and abounds in the most extraordinary harmonic devices, illustrative of terrible and scaring figures [Nos. 5 and 6]. It is wild, fearful, and grotesque, and if put upon the stage, and well enforced by scenic accessories, would be tremendously grand and startling. Like the scherzo in the *Midsummer Night's Dream*, it is crowded with supernatural fancies. The cries of owls and ravens mingle with the bellows of hobgoblins; and the music is full of fantastical motion, indicating the darting, fluttering, and grimacing, of thousands of ugly, misshapen creatures. It is a chorus of great difficulty, varying often in time and character; but it was extremely well executed. A solo by the priest prefaces another chorus by the Druids [No. 7], being an address to their deity, as the smoke of the sacrifice ascends to Heaven—from which, it will be remembered, Goethe derives a moral. A "Christian guard" here sings an agitated solo in C minor, in which he expresses his terror at seeing the supposed demons; and he is joined by a chorus of his comrades, describing also their superstitious dread, as well their determination to escape by flight [No. 8]. A triumphant chorus by the Druids, in C major, terminates the scene [No. 9]. The whole was efficiently performed by the singers—Miss A. Williams, Miss Dolby, Mr. Allen, and Herr Staudigl, executing the solo parts. The goblin chorus took every body by surprise, and well it might.[74]

This review was followed by another one, more detailed in description of the poem's premise, in *The Musical Examiner* two days later. Notably, the *Examiner*'s review incorporates some elements from Celtic and fairy mythology (such as the description of the pagans' sacrificial fire as "blue fire")—presumably in order to make it easier for readers to identify with the subject of the poem:

> The grand feature of the concert was the *First Walpurgis Night.* Of this, the latest work of Dr. Mendelssohn, though we may not yet agree with some critics, who entitle it his greatest work, we are happy to speak in terms of unqualified praise. The fine poem of Goethe, which forms the basis on which Mendelssohn has erected his splendid musical drama, is founded on an old legend of the Hartz [*sic*] mountains. The early Christians, as they grew more numerous and powerful, were decidedly averse to the religious ceremonies of the Druids, and tried all in their power to prevent their celebration. The first of May, the *fête* of St. Walpurgis, was also the epoch of a great festivity among the Druids. The latter, unable to offer incense to their idols in the light of day, were compelled to resort to night worship—and as a stratagem to prevent iuterruption [*sic*], great numbers of them, grotesquely attired, uttering strange noises and playing fantastic gambols, with the assistance, we suppose, of some of the combinations of tortured flame, termed by the moderns *blue fire*, contrived to scare away their ignorant Christian persecutors—whose religious zeal, though proof against all human power, shrank instinctively from whatever seemed to issue from the world of phantoms, in which the superstitions with which their cradle teemed had nurtured them.
>
> Against these, their faith in the great teacher was of no avail, and the Druids, laughing in their sleeves, performed their *mystic* ceremonies in safety. Goethe seemed to think this poem well suited to music, and recommended it to Dr. Mendelssohn in a letter. The musical adaptation of the poem is a splendid triumph of genius. . . . Nothing can be more dramatic, picturesque, and poetically faithful than the whole of this. Its performance was generally admirable, and the enthusiasm with which it was received by the audience exceeds all description. . . . [Messrs.] Staudigl and Allen,

> Misses Dolby and A. Williams, were admirable in their solos and concerted *morceaux*. Miss Dolby, especially, was a charming old woman, but not at all fitted to scare away the Christians.[75]

Nor were affirmative responses to Mendelssohn's *Walpurgisnacht* limited to Victorian England. Even in Vienna, where Mendelssohn was generally received more cautiously than elsewhere, the *Walpurgisnacht* met with resounding success. The extent of this success is testified to by a lengthy review by H. Adami first published in the *Wiener Theaterzeitung* and reprinted in the *Signale für die musikalische Welt*:[76]

> *Die erste Walpurgisnacht* is a true epoch-making work in the world of the arts, and one that may after careful consideration be termed Mendelssohn's greatest composition. I was somewhat skeptical of the assessment of the imaginative and enthusiastic Berlioz that I read several months ago in the *Journal des débats*, for the enthusiasm that gives power and life to the composer is at best unbecoming to the judge of art, and one must proceed soberly if one is to submit a sound judgment. But this time Berlioz did not overstate his case. In the musical world there has long since been only one predominant opinion concerning Mendelssohn's essential musical technique, excellent orchestration, interpretive genius, and intimate acquaintance with all the means of composition, and other periodicals have missed no opportunity to do all in their power to spread his fame. We who are accustomed to Mozart and Beethoven actually were not very impressed with him; his greatest work, the oratorio *St. Paul*, seemed rather too long to us, despite its many beauties, and his *Midsummer Night's Dream* Overture succeeded because of its excellent performance in the Philharmonic concerts. We found it difficult to warm to his strict, almost puritanical attitude, which was obviously based on the genius of old J. S. Bach. Amid all the movement in the accompaniment and amid all his rich employment of his artistic resources, we found lacking that breadth of musical ideas to which we have become accustomed, or by which we have become spoiled, and above all that compelling warmth that propels Beethoven's works in particular and makes them especially impressive. In the *Walpurgisnacht* Mendelssohn has proceeded hand in hand and completely in step with old father Goethe, and behold! He succeeded in his gambit, creating a work that will and must resonate around the world. Anyone who has immersed himself in this majestic poem and come to understand it, even if he is himself no artist, has already created a work of art—only internally, of course, but his soul is edified by it and soars high above the realm of daily existence. Goethe has been called a heretic because he did not suffer the usual canned formulas, the power plays, the cry of "get up so that I can sit there." But he penned the beautiful verses:
>
> Die Flamme reinigt sich vom Rauch.
> So reinig' unsern Glauben!
> Und raubt man uns den alten Brauch
> Dein Licht, wer kann es Rauben![77]

After quoting the excerpt from Goethe's letter to Mendelssohn of September 9, 1831, printed in the score,[78] Adami continued with enthusiastic praise for the composer such as seldom encountered in the Viennese press up to that point:

> Mendelssohn has set this world-subject, with its sublimely serious and humoristic parts, in a genuinely poetic fashion, and the musical poem carries throughout the imprint of a masterwork. The attractive constituent parts are tied together in their essence; the solo voices and chorus are used in effective alternation; the melodies are new, evocative, and always appropriate to the words; the whole is dominated by a rich, luxurious variety; everything [in the vocal parts] can be heard throughout despite the busy and always clear figurations in the instruments; and the work is an outpouring—or rather, the beautiful course of a broad river along the sides of its pleasant banks as it passes on its way into the enormous, peaceful, sun-strewn sea, where the idea can gratefully come to rest as it gazes into infinity, enjoying the miracles of creation. With every measure one senses that this material speaks to the individuality of this composer, and his effort adorns his head like a shimmering crown of laurel. Another composer may have gotten a different idea for the overture; but the depiction of the transition from winter to spring is a part of Mendelssohn's individuality, and his depiction succeeds; I do not wish to argue with him about it. The first chorus with tenor solo [No. 1] is fresh and uplifting, as is the stretto filled with effects. The song of the old woman with women's chorus [No. 2] is characteristic; the melody sung by the Druid [No. 3] is sublime, and the wonderful chorus "Verteilt euch, wackre Männer, hier" [No. 4] is even more effective. The next chorus, "Kommt mit Hacken [*sic*] und mit Gabeln" [Nos. 5 and 6] is truly genial. What variety! What effects! How intelligent the instrumentation, the distribution of the parts! Earnestly and with inmost fierceness the Druid sings the words "So weit gebracht" etc. [No. 7]. The [Christian] guards flee, and the words already quoted above constitute the imposing finale, the keystone of the whole. I say again that this work, which poses no insurmountable difficulties, will be very well received everywhere and, I hope, also frequently performed. It was received with due appreciation, and with great applause at the close. The fact that the applause was not always loud after the individual movements probably owes to the way the cantata is structured, [since] it forms a [single] whole and contains no separate arias, duets, or choruses that seem to say to the public (most of whom are distracted): "this is the end; applaud now." The poem and the music are deep and require inmost perception, which is not always possible for the audience in the case of a brand new work.[79]

Like the English critics, Adami notes that there was at least some attempt at applause before the conclusion of the performance. This remark may make some sense of the English reviewers' remarks about movements being encored—for it is easier to imagine audience applause and perhaps even cries of "encore" as individual movements were ending and new ones beginning (much as happens today after solos in jazz performances) than to imagine the conductor (especially the composer!) halting midway through the work and repeating the preceding movement before continuing on. That nineteenth-century performances encountered premature applause and perhaps cries of "encore" seems clear, given the consistent reports to that effect; that segments of the music were actually repeated is less so.

Finally, Mendelssohn's second setting of *Die erste Walpurgisnacht* found staunch advocates even in France—a peculiar fact in part because of the French musical public's rather slow acceptance of Mendelssohn's vocal music, but especially because one would not expect a French audience, predominantly Catholic, to sympathize readily with a work celebrating Saxon pagans who (if one considers the poem's conjectural historical context literally) fell victim to the cruelties of Charlemagne. Nevertheless, while enthusiastic responses in France were fewer and less influential than in England and the German-speaking countries, they were by no means rare. Both aspects of this reception may have been the product of the French translation that circulated in the 1840s and early 1850s.[80] This translation, prepared by Edouard Bélanger (known not least of all for his well-disseminated translations of songs by Schubert and Beethoven), evidently recognized the cultural disjunctions that the original text of the *Walpurgisnacht* would have faced among French audiences. Rather than sealing its negative fate in that fashion, Bélanger adopted a substantially more daring strategy: to completely recast the poem's persecutors and persecuted (Self and Other) in roles more readily approachable to French audiences. The Saxon pagans became Roma Gypsies; their Christian adversaries, archers engaged in the then (apparently) still-legitimate "sport" of Gypsy-hunting.

Bélanger's gambit seems to have gone unchallenged for some time. In 1853, however, the eminent critic Léon Kreutzer took him to task in the *Revue et gazette musicale de Paris,* blaming the reportedly "very cold" reception of the "quite remarkable" composition by Mendelssohn on the damage the text inflicted on the sense of the entire composition.[81] Kreutzer begins by summarizing the argument of Goethe's poem, then goes to the heart of the significance of the ballad's provocative portrayal of the conflict between the pagans and Christians:

> Such is the most remarkable subject of this ballade by Goethe. Is it an inherited tradition? Does Goethe here permit himself to criticize the cult of Christianity? I know not. But what I cannot figure out is the peculiar way in which M. Bélanger has translated this ballade. In plotting the first few movements of his composition Mendelssohn sought to achieve an original and stern character that expresses the dark recesses of the pagan forests that surround those austere druids in their white robes and golden sashes. With a stroke of the pen M. Bélanger has caused those druids and their forest to disappear—and with what sort of people has he replaced them? You guessed it: Gypsies. As for the Christian soldiers, they will become archers. Archers are not rare; they are found everywhere. For their part, the druid guards in the forest will be transformed into necromancers and sorcerers. These changes do away with the character of the work completely: this is particularly important in the *witches' Sabbath,* which becomes nothing more than a pleasantry, a nice game played by frightened soldiers, and it definitely compromises the name of the great German poet.—I do not ask that Christianity interfere in this ballad, or that its humoristic elements be mixed with its grandiose ones. I ask only that we be allowed to keep our druids and that they be given something better than archers as enemies upon whom to cast their spells. Archers and Gypsies! I'll come back to that. . . .[82]

Having effectively thrashed Bélanger's adaptation of Goethe's text, Kreutzer devotes most of the remainder of his review to enthusiastic praise for most of Mendelssohn's music. After stating that the introduction "abounds with new and picturesque effects," he continues with an admonition to the Parisian public to study the music and take its lessons to heart:

> It is an icy northern winter. The fir trees melancholically shake the powdery snow off their branches, and the frost has been caught off-guard and frozen in mid-fall; all is night and silence in the heart of the forest, and a pale sun casts a feeble light over the clouds laden with rime and hail. How does Mendelssohn's music express all this? Go hear it for yourself. If it impresses you also, that will confirm it more successfully than will studying the composer's means for producing [the effect].[83]

Likewise important is Mendelssohn's setting of stanzas 7 and 8 (No. 6):

> The veritable scene of the witches' Sabbath that follows is, after the overture, the most important movement. The secret of this picturesque music is its choice of means of producing effects, its able distribution of timbre. In movements of this sort melody is incapable of conveying the idea. Harmony, rhythm, and above all mixtures of sonorities—these are the resources at the composer's disposal. Mendelssohn has used them deftly. Thus, nothing is more thrilling than the effect of the *pianissimo* bass drum and cymbals with which that grand scene begins; this produces a truly funereal effect. . . . The moon seems obscured by some mystery; the forest is populated by strange and dreadful phantoms. With the whistling accents in the violins the swarms of horse-mounted sorcerers descend onto their familiar broomsticks; with a murmuring in the basses and the dull roar of the trombones the graves come into view as they expel their pale inhabitants; with a cry from the piccolo a demon gives the signal for the hellish round-dance. The valley had been deserted; now, it swarms with nameless creatures. With the first chords an owl, annoyed at all the uproar, takes flight from a hollow in an old tree-trunk; we hear the sinister beating of his wings muffled by their thick plumage. How is this effect obtained? By a bassoon, an instrument whose timbre in the middle range is dull, almost hideous, sounding a series of prodigiously fast repetitions of a single pitch: these are the rushed beatings of the wings of our owl, who discreetly finds his refuge in some more tranquil place.[84] Such is my own interpretation of the most bizarre passage in the movement. I believe it is a good one; perhaps my neighbor has another one which he believes equally good. I would be sorry to learn that I am wrong, however, for I believe that this new actor is playing a role as unforeseen as it is interesting. . . .[85]

Perhaps most interestingly, Kreutzer devotes considerable energy and wit to mocking the Parisian public for its ignorant and superficial response to this "most remarkable" work. His annoyance is understandable: because of the absence of pauses between movements, many listeners had difficulty following the progress of the composition even though the movements were listed in the program. Consequently, many believed that the setting of stanza 6 (No. 4: "Verteilt euch, wackre Männer, hier") was the scene of the feigned witches' Sabbath and marveled at the "picturesque nuance" with which Mendelssohn depicted the infernal scene. Remarking that those in the boxes scarcely knew to offer more than timid applause after the work's final chords had sounded, he fires one parting salvo: "One would have to give up on Mendelssohn's ballad and box it up if one did not know the Conservatoire's public, which is very finicky and very skittish in its feigned knowledge, but fundamentally very good-natured once it is satisfied that it can approve of a work without compromising the fairness and infallibility of its opinions."[86]

The wit, sarcasm, and intensity of Kreutzer's review of this 1853 performance of *Die erste Walpurgisnacht* recall his own, Berlioz's, and Mendelssohn's earlier criticisms of the Parisian public's unsympathetic response to Beethoven's music. This resemblance also bespeaks another peculiarity of the cantata's early reception: the poem's "elevated symbolism," as explained in the letter from Goethe quoted on the frontispiece of the first editions, eluded comment from English and French reviewers. For all its ardent advocacy of Mendelssohn's music, its unstinting ridicule of Bélanger's translation, and its biting satire of the public's complacency, Kreutzer's review shies clear of any symbolic intent. That fact did not escape the notice of a contemporary German reviewer who praised Kreutzer for his efforts to advocate for the *Walpurgisnacht* despite Bélanger's translation, the indifferent performance, and the unsympathetic public but noted that he had "denounced the translator's stupidity without himself having grasped Goethe's actual idea."[87] (Readers interested in the French translation may be interested to know that sometime later in the 1850s, 1860s, or 1870s a new, essentially literal French translation of Mendelssohn's cantata, prepared by Victor Wilder, was published by J. Maho, Paris.[88])

One further observation concerning the critical reception of Mendelssohn's second *Walpurgisnacht* setting is necessary: German-language reviewers consistently interpreted the cantata in terms of the work's "symbolic" import, while American, English and French critics comment on that import scarcely or not at all. The reasons for this disparity are obscure, since the relevant excerpt from Goethe's letter of September 9, 1831, to Mendelssohn were included in translation in the contemporary English and French editions. The preview of the work that attended the Boston premiere in *Dwight's Journal of Music* in 1862 is representative. Although the anonymous reviewer describes the individual movements in considerable detail and specifies that the translation used was that of William Bartholomew (which did include Goethe's explanation of the poem's "elevated symbolism"), he omits any reference to symbolic content. Instead, after describing the cantata as "a most successful musical translation of Goethe's curious poem," he explains the work in terms of its literal subject:

> Walpurgis figures in the German calendar as the female Saint who converted the Saxons from their Druidical faith to Christianity. The deities of the heathen worship became the devils and witches of the Middle Age tradition; and as Venus was still fabled and believed to hold her court in the heart of a mountain in Thuringia, so the witches and evil spirits of the Northern mythology were supposed to hold their infernal "Sabbath" on the night of the first of May, on the summit of the Harz mountains. With what wild imaginative art Goethe has conjured all its elements together in the famous scene in "Faust!" (Shelley's free translation admirably preserves the spirit of it). Goethe made a poem out of every thing that interested him; it was his way of solving intellectual and moral problems, of reaping and laying up the fruits of his inquiries. So besides the scene in "Faust," he has embodied in a separate little poem, "The First Walpurgis Night," his idea of the manner in which the tradition of the "Witches' Sabbath" may have originated. May Day Eve is dedicated to St. Walpurgis, and naturally the mob of

> outcast evil spirits chose her night to make a great stir. The idea is, that the Druids fled to the mountains, to pursue their ancient rites, unmolested by their Christian presecutors [*sic*]. To avoid detection, which would be death, they took advantage of the superstition of their enemies, and set guards about all the approaches to the place, who dressed themselves up like demons, and ran through the woods with blazing torches and hideous noises, frightening the Christians away.[89]

By the 1870s the cantata's symbolic import had become so remote that the composer's friend Julius Rietz (1812–77) elected to omit it in the edition of the *Walpurgisnacht* he included in the series of *Mendelssohn's Werke* published by Breitkopf & Härtel between 1874 and 1877. Since the Rietz edition has served as the main source for almost all subsequent editions, this ill-advised editorial decision probably contributed to the disassociation of Mendelssohn's music and Goethe's explanation of the text's serious purport, so that by the end of the century, awareness of the cantata's serious dimension seems to have all but disappeared from critical consciousness. Even the thorough and overwhelmingly sympathetic overview of Mendelssohn's music by George Grove and the enthusiastic and detailed discussions by Hermann Kretzschmar and Siegfried Ochs fail to mention this aspect of the work.[90] The situation is unfortunate, for the disappearance of general awareness of that crucial dimension of the *Walpurgisnacht* coincided precisely with more general acceptance of the notion of Mendelssohn's musical superficiality, a notion that led to the virtual cessation of credible scholarship concerning his works until the sesquicentennial of his birth in 1959.[91]

Staged Performances

The interpretive reception history of Mendelssohn's setting of Goethe's ballade is also remarkable in one further regard: it mirrors the nineteenth century's increasing fascination with staged drama. The leader in this trend was Eduard Devrient, for whom the role of the druid priest was originally written. Devrient recalled in his memoirs (1869) that already around the time of the Berlin premiere of Mendelssohn's first setting he had suggested that the work would fare well as a staged rather than concerted production:

> Between November and January he gave four [*sic*] concerts in the concert hall of the Schauspielhaus, and among others of his compositions that were given was the first performance of *Die erste Walpurgisnacht*, which he had already extensively revised. Already then I vividly envisioned the impression that would necessarily be made by a dramatic [i.e., staged] performance of this cantata. When I told Felix of this, he responded thoughtfully, "Possibly; try it sometime." "I will," I answered, "as soon as I have a stage at my disposal."[92]

Devrient eventually made good on his word. Already widely recognized as a director and theater critic, he earned international renown with his milestone

Geschichte der deutschen Schauspielkunst (History of German Theater, 3 vols.; 1848), and was appointed director of the Court Theater in Karlsruhe in 1852. He was granted virtually unlimited organizational and artistic license for reviving and reforming the theater and opera, and quickly succeeded in gaining renown for his insistence on the integrity of ensemble work, his productions of Gluck, Mozart, Goethe, and Shakespeare, and his resistance to excessive displays of individual actors' virtuosity. *Die erste Walpurgisnacht* was first staged on May 10, 1860, and was so successful in this version that it became a staple of the theater repertoire for some time thereafter.[93]

However peculiar the idea of a staged production of Mendelssohn's setting of Goethe's ballad may seem to modern readers, it evidently caught on among contemporaries. The Karlsruhe performances—which, like most performances of that theater by then, tended to set the professional standard—were imitated in Vienna and Paris, among other places. Critics generally responded favorably to these performances, commenting approvingly on the drama and the vividness of Mendelssohn's music, just as in concerted performances. The idea of staging the work raises several difficult logistical problems, however—most prominently, the matter of how to deal with the interfolding of sequential and simultaneous narrative space in the ballad's second half (the Walpurgis Night proper). As discussed earlier, the plot of the poem requires that the Christian guards' stanza pair (strophes 10 and 11; No. 8) occurs simultaneously with the pagan watchmen's ruse (stanza 8; No. 6) and the pagan populace's ceremonies atop the Brocken (stanzas 9 and 12; Nos. 7 and 9), and in his second setting Mendelssohn goes to some lengths to achieve this pan-diegetic effect musically (see chapter 5, pp. 125–35). But in a staged production this temporal layering is more complicated, since the action of all three layers presumably continues equally while the musical representation privileges the layer in the foreground at a given point in the poem.

Ironically, modern readers would be left entirely to conjecture as to how nineteenth-century productions negotiated these problems if not for a detailed account of one staged production of *Die erste Walpurgisnacht* left by a commentator who hardly numbers among Mendelssohn's partisans: the critic Richard Pohl (1826–96), best known for his intrepid advocacy of the ideas of Liszt, Wagner, and the New German School during the 1850s and 1860s, the years in which Mendelssohn's reputation was most relentlessly attacked. In 1862, in the context of a review criticizing what he (rightly) feared would become a trend of quasi-operatic staged productions of cantatas and oratorios, Pohl provided a detailed description of such a production given in Leipzig, also identifying the logistical and dramaturgical problems that arose in such a production.[94] The essentials of his account are as follows:

- The production uses a divided stage, with foreground and background level at different heights.
- During the "bad weather" portion of the Overture, the curtain remains down.

- At the "transition to springtime" (mm. 360ff.) the curtain rises. Warriors and other members of the pagan populace are asleep on the ground in the front (lower) portion of the stage; one by one, others arrive to awaken them, gradually filling the front portion of the stage.
- At stanza 1 a solo Druid enters the stage, and he and the other pagans sing the solo/chorus No. 1 (stanza pair 1–2). In the final measures of the movement, at the words "Hinauf! So wird das Herz erhoben!" some of the warriors and other pagans move to the rear (upper) portion of the stage, where they begin constructing an altar.
- Meanwhile, the remainder of the pagan populace listens anxiously as the old woman warns them of the probable consequences of their pursuit of the ancient rites (stanza pair 3–4; No. 2). While the druid priest reproaches them (No. 3), those in the background begin piling wood on the altar and ceremoniously dedicating it. One of the warriors proposes posting sentinels, and this is followed by No. 4 (stanzas 5–6), during which some of the sentinels, whom Pohl describes as "extras" (*Statisten*), disappear offstage.
- Prongs, pitchforks, clappers, and torches are brought onstage for "the famous witches' chorus" (the second part of No. 5 and No. 6; stanzas 7 and 8). During this portion of the cantata the extras run around the stage.
- At the beginning of No. 7 (stanza 9) the fire atop the altar is lit, and the pagan populace gradually moves to the rear of the stage, gathering around the altar.
- At No. 8 the chorus of Christian guards appears at the front of the stage and wants to storm the assembled pagans, but the sight of "wolf-men and dragon-women" frightens them away. The work closes with the pagans assembled around the altar.

Pohl's criticisms of staged productions of the *Walpurgisnacht* offer several useful insights into the role it had come to play in musical life by the 1860s. As a practical matter he objects that the limitations of the stage hamper the realism of any such production. Because the size of the stage makes it impossible for the chorus to spread out as the text demands during the chorus "Verteilt euch wackre Männer hier," the staged action comes to a standstill precisely when the text requires motion. Similarly, the difficulty of the "Kommt mit Zacken und mit Gabeln" chorus requires the singers to remain stationary, with their torches and pitchforks uncomfortably close, while the motion "through the narrow rocky hollows" ("durch die engen Felsenstrecken"), entrusted to the extras, is conspicuously static, again cramped by the size of the stage. In the particular case of *Die erste Walpurgisnacht*, additional problems are posed by the fact that stanza 12 (No. 9) is a continuation of stanza 9 (No. 7, after the end of the 2/4 time): both "belong together musically and poetically."[95] Although Mendelssohn remained true to Goethe by retaining the poem's introduction of what Pohl calls the "intermezzo" of the Christian guards' stanzas between the two—a poetic element that he deems "unnecessary" ("unnöthig")[96]—less piety in setting the poem would (he says) have been beneficial to the music and clarified the dramatic situation. More generally, he observes that the great advantage of oratorios and cantatas is that "they leave it to the fantasy of the auditor to imagine scenic aspects and thus to envision things that cannot be presented in reality. . . . All musical and poetic means can overlap one another unencumbered by time and space."[97]

Most important for understanding the position of Pohl's critique in the reception history of Goethe's and Mendelssohn's *Walpurgisnacht* treatments are the reasons for his fundamental objection to staged productions of concerted works. Concerted music was inherently epic in nature, he says, whereas the modern age demanded that staged musical productions be dramatic. Practical dramatic issues such as those posed by Devrient's staging of *Die erste Walpurgisnacht* were tolerated and even understandable during the Classical era, but by the 1860s the age of musical drama had become sufficiently advanced that such productions represented nothing more than failed experiments—attempts by "classicists" to enrich the operatic repertoire while avoiding the endeavors of "Wagner and his school" at any cost, and to avoid acknowledging that Mendelssohn had become a thing of the past.[98]

Indeed, as *Die erste Walpurgisnacht* gradually succumbed to the downward drag on Mendelssohn's reputation during the 1860s and 1870s, only one feature continued to be singled out for praise as being consistent with the progressive ideas of that age: the vividness of the instrumental introduction as descriptive music. Even Pohl, whose article above all aims to consign Mendelssohn's *Walpurgisnacht* to an earlier music-historical age apart from the progressive ideas of his readers' present, acknowledged this in a footnote,[99] but other writings on the work more readily explore the significance of this finding. Also in 1862, Friedrich Zauder, in the first monograph on Mendelssohn's *Walpurgisnacht,* comments on the remarkable length of the introduction (it occupies about twelve of the forty-five minutes required for a complete performance, he says), but he especially commends Mendelssohn for its vividness as program music:

> What he presents to us is no ordinary bad weather, nothing trivial such as we encounter in the streets of our cities; nor is it those cold and damp days full of thick fog that we encounter in rural areas before the beginning of spring, such as Haydn shows us at the beginning of *Die Jahreszeiten.*[100] These are the winter storms, the cloudbursts, the mountain torrents and tempests of the rocks and cliffs of the Harz Mountains, of the Brocken. Now the basses roar, now the flute whistles, now the winds storm with mighty interjections; now the flute flashes like lightning and the timpani threaten powerful thunder strokes; sudden dissonances cut through the icy cold; rapid repeated notes trickle like rain; brisk figures cascade like water from on high. Occasionally a sudden quiet spell intervenes as if some rocky crag has broken the force and the drive of the storm for a moment, or as if our ears have found a respite from the storms and the rain in some recessed crevice and hear the storm and rain only muted, from a distance.[101]

Most important, however, is Zauder's observation that the introduction to *Die erste Walpurgisnacht* dispenses with the "potpourri-like" convention of employing the best thematic material from the ensuing music and instead undertakes to prepare the listener psychologically and emotionally for the drama that follows.[102] That this foreshadowing applies to the introduction's stormy weather as an adumbration of the poem's social, religious, and cultural conflicts is obvious. But for Zauder the means by which the "transition to springtime" sets in are equally significant. Although the gesture has a gentle precursor in Haydn's *Jahreszeiten,* there the temporary struggle between the inclement and vernal impulses is announced and explained by the voices, whereas in Mendelssohn's *Walpurgisnacht* it plays out in the instruments alone. Moreover, in the parlance of the day such dramatic interruptions were indicators of the sublime, and of course the attainment of sublime spiritual exaltation is the telos of poem and cantata alike. Finally, as Juliette L. Appold points out in her recent dissertation, Mendelssohn's correspondence amply demonstrates his view of landscape and weather as allegories for human states of mind, especially religious and ethical ones.[103] The introduction to the cantata—clearly labeled in two contrasting sections—thus not only depicts the "Schirke und Elend" of the setting and adumbrates the work's overall affective or emotional progress from conflict to sublimity, but also intimates the earthbound nature of the former and the spiritual and religious significance of the latter.

These observations are self-evident enough. But Zauder, writing in 1862, seems to have been one of the last commentators to note the dramatic and spiritual significance of the *Walpurgisnacht*'s introduction: later authors continue to note the conspicuous length of the introduction and the pictorial vividness of its "bad weather," but they began to overlook Mendelssohn's symbolic treatment of the emotional and spiritual landscape and weather during precisely those years in which later composers exploited that symbolism in their own music. Mendelssohn was relegated to the musical past by later commentators' incognizance of his originality and their implicit denial of his relevance to the ideas that would become crucial for future composers such as Gustav Mahler and Richard Strauss (both of whom admired his music).

Finally, the significance of the disparity between Pohl's and Zauder's aesthetic valuations of Mendelssohn's *Walpurgisnacht* setting is evident in their discussions of the nature and importance of the change of scene between stanzas 8 and 9 (the beginning of No. 7). This moment marks a critical juncture in the poem's symbolic topography and its central play on the conflict between illusion and reality: it accomplishes the scenic transition from the mid-ground ruse of a witches' Sabbath to the true solemn ceremonies on high, thereby gradually leaving behind the feigned demonic element for true spiritual exaltation.[104] Pohl proceeds from a generally unsympathetic view (and an evident misunderstanding of the plot of Goethe's poem[105]), and thus finds that the entire cantata runs afoul of its poetic subject from the onset of the pagan ruse. Zauder, by contrast, recognizes the scenic import of the beginning of No. 7, focusing on the musical means of realizing an implied but crucial diegetic shift and observing its musical parallel to the beginning of the pagan scene:

> The last of the (as always) thrice-repeated [exclamations of] "Kommt" at the close of the number leads directly into No. 7, just as the last "Kommt" of No. 5 carried over into No. 6. Here, too, there follows an instrumental movement, [this one] comprising twenty measures (counting its first measure with the final "Kommt"). Externally this one, like its earlier counterpart, provides an introduction to the next number; in its content, however, it has much more in common with the preceding movement and takes more from it than it brings into the new one; in any case, it provides the transition. The idea that a movement as extended and highly developed as the previous one [No. 6] requires special parts to tie it to its neighboring movements seems very well taken. This is achieved very cleverly here. Not only does the 2/4 time, which had occurred several times in No. 6 (while the vocal parts remain firmly in 6/8) gradually take over toward the end, occurring six and five measures from the end and then in the last two measures, before No. 7 *L'istesso Tempo* finally begins, but the figure that dominates this new beginning is brought back from two movements earlier, No. 5 (and not No. 6), so that we are led out of the wild No. 6 just as we were led into it before. The peculiarity of this scene is thus properly emphasized for the listeners so that we become aware that we are returning to the path we left earlier on. In the *diminuendo* of the last four bars of this orchestral transition, during which we hear all the instruments (piccolo, bass drum, and cymbals) characteristic of the preceding scene for the last time, as if from afar, and out of which the timpani roll that led into No. 6 now leads us, the scene fades just as in the *dissolving views* and a new one appears before us: namely, the scene of the druids' sacrificial site where the sacrifice is made to the all-father by the priest and the pagan populace. Suddenly an *Andante maestoso* in 4/4 time presents itself, and this constitutes the real No. 7.[106]

One might of course object that the passage Zauder discusses here is short and untexted, and thus inconspicuous as a carrier of musical or dramatic meaning. On the other hand, Mendelssohn's inclusion of the entire passage in both settings of Goethe's text suggests that he considered it integral to his musical conception of the poem (certainly more so than his original settings of stanzas 5, 9, and 10), and its diegetic function in the context of the poem as well as its crossfading of thematic and motivic material associated with discrete elevations in the topography of the plot represent important—perhaps unprecedented—efforts to deal with those issues in symphonic contexts.[107] Equally apt is Zauder's likening of the effect of the pan-diegetic beginning of No. 7 to the "dissolving views." A variety of the pre-cinematographic "magic lantern,"[108] "dissolving views" were scenes projected using two or more projectors or lenses to slide between alternate versions of the same image (such as one during the day and one at night). The effect of poem and music, in this instance, is visual—another manifestation of Mendelssohn's by-now well-documented visual imagination.[109] And his musical realization of this effect is not only remarkable in itself, but also important as a milestone among nineteenth-century attempts to deal with the problems of musical and dramatic time. Finally, the mere fact that he recognized the poem's pandiegetic qualities and devised a means of realizing them musically, while other, purportedly more dramatically inclined later contemporaries failed to perceive or deal with them is significant with regard to later constructs of his artistic identity and historical significance. Far from "turning the actual situation of Goethe's play on its head," as Pohl suggests,[110] Mendelssohn devised a way to realize the poem's essential temporal confluence in the closing stanzas (see chapter 5, pp. 129–35). Zauder recognized the importance of this feature already in 1862, but later commentators, probably influenced by familiar post-Wagnerian critiques that Mendelssohn lacked dramatic ability, have overlooked it entirely. They have thus overlooked a compelling musical gesture that, once recognized, makes fully evident the temporal confluence of the poem's closing stanzas—and of Mendelssohn's musical suggestion that the religious gap that separates the poem's pagan protagonists and their Christian antagonists, like the dissolving views themselves, is illusory.

Conclusions: The Convergence of Identity and Alterity

One final observation must be submitted in the interest of demonstrating the irony of the above. This irony surrounds the critical reception of Mendelssohn's *Walpurgisnacht* in the context of mid- and later nineteenth-century critical discourse. As noted above, one of the work's most enthusiastic admirers was Berlioz—whose own celebrated "Witches' Sabbath" was conceived, revised, and completed contemporaneously with Mendelssohn's cantata. The affinities those two works exhibit in dealing with their common subject becomes obvious even with just a perfunctory review. Both rely on the juxtaposition of sacred and profane, and both characterize the profane by colorful instrumentation with added percussion and emphatically heterogeneous timbres, abrupt and occasionally audacious harmonic turns, and seemingly trite lyricism in brisk tempo. But there is one important difference, for Berlioz's witches remain vile and grotesque, while Mendelssohn's pagans, in keeping with the meaning of Goethe's poem, are only deceptively evil during their ruse, and are otherwise courageous, noble, and pure. What is profane, pagan, and intolerable to Christianity in the *Symphonie fantastique* possesses no attributes of nobility, no legitimate position in a grand historical narrative: the quasi-autobiographical narrative persona of that work, and thus the agnostic Berlioz himself, still views the participants in his witches' Sabbath as grotesque. By contrast, in his own *Walpurgisnacht* the devoutly Lutheran Mendelssohn reserves for the pagan enemies of Christianity the same affect of grand spiritual exaltation that he had also applied with resounding success in *St. Paul*.

In brief, then, the approach to identity and alterity in Berlioz's witches' Sabbath remains grounded in its own contemporary mores, while that of Mendelssohn's *Walpurgisnacht* not only steps outside those values, but also solicits listeners and performers to do the same. It is Mendelssohn—so often accused of conforming to the social and religious mores of mainstream society, and of ducking the social issues of his age, and consequently Othered in critical discourse concerning religious, social, and artistic identity in nineteenth-century music—who adopts a critical and aesthetic stance that challenges listeners to question those contemporary mores directly. Even today, and even in sympathetic commentaries, he comes off as a figure who is ill at ease with modernity and with any sort of challenge not rooted in the past; his artistic persona is thus all the more obviously remote from the sympathies of latter-day commentators and performers. Yet the Mendelssohn of *Die erste Walpurgisnacht* speaks, with Goethe, in a voice that resonates more with latter-day ideas on social identity and alterity than it did with those of his contemporaries and later generations. His Otherness to the nineteenth-century music with which most latter-day musicians identify is an anachronistic construct, a function of the identities of those narrow-minded, intolerant contemporary and later observers who overlooked or refused to accept the challenges he issued. And in musically realizing Goethe's artistic engagements of the moral imperative of religious, cultural, and societal conflicts between Self and Other, Mendelssohn speaks with a voice that not only tolerates alterity, but fully accepts it.

Chapter Seven

Performing Identity and Alterity

Die erste Walpurgisnacht
Then and Now

The historical, religious, and societal conflicts reflected in the various texts discussed here, as well as the works themselves, all stem from European culture of the nineteenth century and earlier, but the body of readers, listeners, and performers to whom these texts address themselves is considerably broader. Latter-day readers are not simply auditors to the extensive literary, musical, and visual discourses that center on the Walpurgis Night; we are participants in them. Our voices commingle in discourse with other voices whose physical sources of enunciation are long dead, but whose ideas remain alive and vibrant. Goethe's 1799 ballad, his *Faust* tragedy, and Mendelssohn's cantata on the subject of the Walpurgis Night are thus works whose musical as well as textual contents are subjects very much the province of our own time—subjects that we address each time we read, study, discuss, or perform those works.

With this perspective in mind, it seems appropriate to conclude this discussion of historical and artistic engagements with the Walpurgis Night topos with a few remarks concerning the performance of Mendelssohn's cantata. The problems that the performance-centered issues of tempo, language, and ensemble placement and disposition raise in this work shed more light on the conflicts between New and Old, Self and Other that are central to the poem and Mendelssohn's cantata, as well as on the broader import of *Die erste Walpurgisnacht* as an enduring, socially conscious artistic realization of the moral of Goethe's "poetic fable."

Tempo

In the fourth letter of his *Voyage musical en Allemagne et en Italie* (Musical Voyage in Germany and Italy), written in 1843 and republished in his *Memoirs* in 1869, Berlioz recalled an 1831 discussion with Mendelssohn concerning the metronome:

> One day I had been speaking of the metronome and its utility.
>
> "What is a metronome for?" exclaimed Mendelssohn. "It is a most useless instrument. A musician who cannot guess the time of a piece at first sight is a blockhead."
>
> I could easily have answered that there were a good many blockheads, but I held my peace. . . .
>
> One day [Mendelssohn] asked me to show him the score of my *King Lear* overture, which I had just finished writing at Nice. First he read it over slowly and attentively, and then, just as he was about to play it on the piano (which he did with matchless ability), "Give me the exact time," said he.
>
> "Why should I? Did you not say yesterday that any musician who could not guess the time of a piece at first sight was a blockhead?"[1]

Together with Wagner's later criticisms of Mendelssohn's tempi[2] and the instances in which Mendelssohn's tempo markings are inconsistent with latter-day conventions, this account seems to have generated a conventional wisdom that holds that Mendelssohn's tempo indications should be taken with a grain of salt; that his metronome markings in particular are of little use; and that his tempi in performance were too quick and inflexible for most of the Romantic repertoire. There is, however, a great deal to suggest that this conventional wisdom, rather than Mendelssohn's approach to tempo, is unrealistically inflexible and in need of modification.

To begin with, Mendelssohn was not alone in his view that good musicians would find verbal tempo expressions more useful than metronome markings as tools for decoding the performance cues provided by notation: most performers viewed tempo not in strictly chronometric terms (which is all that the metronome addresses), but as the product of a fluid intersection of a variety of values reflected in the notation. The "blockheads" may have required metronome marks to prevent serious misreading, but sensitive nineteenth-century performers generally based their views concerning the time of music on intersections among four distinct aspects of notation: meter, note values, incidence of rapid note values, and types of rhythmic figuration.[3] Small note values pass more quickly in the context of meters with higher denominators than they do in ones with lower denominators: in a 3/4 allegro, eighth notes (and consequently the beats themselves) are faster than those in a 3/2 allegro but slower than those in a 3/8 allegro. Moreover, the pulse of a given tempo designation in triple meter was assumed to be faster than that of the same tempo designation in a duple meter. Finally, the choice of tempo designation reflects the fastest generally encountered note value, so that a piece in which eighth notes are prevalent will tend to receive a slower tempo designation than one in which sixteenth notes are prevalent, even though the beat in the former may be quicker.

Moreover, as Siegwart Reichwald has recently shown,[4] Mendelssohn's exchange with Berlioz most likely reflects the circumstances under which it occurred rather than a substantive ignorance on Mendelssohn's part. His correspondence and others' reports consistently show that his views on tempo were based on his careful study of compositions, especially with regard to their form and their inner logic. He held that musical notation, well rendered, functioned as a symbolic system that conveyed the composer's intention; understanding of this intention, however, was possible only after careful study of the score. His question to Berlioz was simply a matter of convenience—one that was also understandable, given Berlioz's idiosyncratic approach to musical form and Mendelssohn's evident lack of prior familiarity with his music itself.[5]

Finally, an overview of Mendelssohn's correspondence and publications from the 1830s and 1840s reveals that he gradually became more convinced of the usefulness of the metronome over the course of his career. The published editions of the early 1830s offer metronome markings in only one instance: the *Midsummer Night's Dream Overture*, Op. 21 (published in 1832–35).[6] In 1835, after having to turn over the rehearsal of his *Melusine* Overture to a musician about whose sensitivity he evidently harbored reservations, the timpanist Friedrich August Grenser (1799–1861),[7] he included metronome marks in all his published ensemble compositions. The first such instance is *St. Paul*, Op. 36 (published in 1836–37); the last, *Elijah* (which appeared in print shortly before Mendelssohn's death). His setting of Psalm 42 seems to have marked a turning point: the choral and orchestral parts, piano-vocal arrangement, and full score were published in mid-1839 without metronome markings, but after hearing performances with "horrifying" tempi he wrote to the publisher later that year stating that he would like to have the proper metronome markings "made known," sending specific metronome markings for each movement and asking the publisher to check them against other metronomes to ensure that his own was accurate.[8] Thereafter, he included metronome marks in all his ensemble compositions.

All this leaves unaddressed the supposition that Mendelssohn's tempi were too rigid in the eyes of his contemporaries, and that modifications of the pulse within passages in a governing tempo were infrequent or lacking altogether. These criticisms, however, are seldom encountered during Mendelssohn's lifetime, and it is probably no coincidence that they proliferated during the period when (a) the conductor's prerogative for rubato for purposes of "expressive depth" was increasingly emphasized; and (b) Mendelssohn and other composers of Jewish descent were by increasing consensus regarded as inherently incapable of anything more than expressive (and hence artistic) superficiality accompanied by impressive but inexpressive musical ideas. In fact, several contemporaries later recalled his "blend[ing of] one subject to another without forcing the passage in the smallest degree,"[9] and public as well as known private communications produced during his years of public performance yield little that would suggest the complete absence of rubato in his music making. If one considers the tetracarpellary matrix of tempo-affecting parameters discussed above in tandem with the frequency of changes in rhythmic figuration that coincide with important structural junctures, often in tandem with verbal tempo indications, it seems clear that subtle but noticeable internal tempo modifications were an integral part of Mendelssohn's approach to the time of music—less than that to which later performers and listeners became accustomed, but fully in keeping with the general tastes for tempo modification in ensemble music at the mid-nineteenth century.[10]

Mendelssohn provided precise tempo and metronome markings for the published editions of the final version of *Die erste Walpurgisnacht.* These markings, given in the orchestral score, the German and English piano-vocal arrangement, and the choral parts, were entered sometime between the completion of the respective autographs and the appearance of the editions themselves. Since Mendelssohn not only oversaw the production and proofs of these editions, but also described the German piano-duet arrangement as "superb," the metronome markings were certainly not introduced by the publishers without his permission. Indeed, since they are absent in the surviving autographs but included in editions that he carefully proofread, they belong somewhere among the latest revisions, specifically those introduced in November 1843 (since they are included in the editions of the piano-vocal arrangements as well as the orchestral score).[11] Up to that point the difficult score had been rehearsed and performed only under Mendelssohn's own direction. But precisely at the point when the question of how others—the "blockheads," as it were—would have to negotiate it, he introduced the metronome markings. We may thus assume that the markings were both authorized and carefully chosen.

But how reliable and practical are they? Working from the scores' metronome prescriptions and rounding up to the nearest 5 seconds in the event of impractically precise durations (e.g., 3′50″ instead of 3′47″ for No. 6), they produce a composition of about 30 minutes' duration, distributed as follows:

Overture, "Das schlechte Wetter":	6′00″ (Allegro con fuoco, 3/4, 𝅗𝅥. = 60)
Overture, "Übergang zum Frühling":	2′00″ (Allegro vivace non troppo, quasi l'istesso tempo, **C,** 𝅗𝅥 = 96)
No. 1 (Stanza 1):	1′50″ (L'istesso tempo)
No. 1 (stanza 2):	1′40″ (Allegro assai vivace, ¢, 𝅗𝅥 = 160)
No. 2:	1′40″ (Allegretto non troppo, 3/4, ♩ = 138)
No. 3 (stanza 5, ll. 33–43):	2′20″ (ll. 33–43: Andante maestoso, **C**, ♩ = 80; più animato poco a poco; ll. 44–45: ♩ = 112)
No. 4:	1′40″ (Allegro leggiero, ¢, 𝅗𝅥 = 88)
No. 5:	2′35″ (ll. 50–53: Recit, 3/4 [no further specification]; Repeat of ll. 52–53: Andante, (3/4), ♩ = 104; ll. 54–59: Allegro moderato, **C**, ♩ =144)
No. 6:	3′50″ (Allegro molto, 6/8, 𝅗𝅥. = 88)
No. 7: (instrumental interlude)	0′25″ (L'istesso tempo, 2/4, 𝅗𝅥 = 88)

No. 7 (stanza 9):	2′50″ (Andante maestoso, **C**, ♩ = 72)
No. 8:	1′00″ (Allegro non troppo, **C**, 𝅗𝅥 = 92)
No. 9:	2′10″ (Andante maestoso, **C**, ♩ = 80)

On the whole this duration is close to that found in modern performances,[12] an observation that suggests that Mendelssohn's metronome markings are quite reasonable. But disparities in tempo emerge if one compares some of Mendelssohn's tempo designations with those found in modern performances. The disparities in stanzas 1, 6, 7, 10, and 11 (Nos. 4, 5, and 8) are unremarkable, although some performances take stanzas 10 and 11 somewhat quicker than indicated. His markings for stanzas 9 and 12 (Nos. 7 and 9) are slower than most currently available recordings, although not by much (and some performances take those movements even slower). And those for stanzas 3–5, though noticeably quicker than many latter-day performances, are still plausible.

This leaves the instrumental introduction, stanza two (the second half of No. 1), and stanza 8 (No. 6), whose tempo indications are considerably quicker than most modern performances. I have never heard a performance that sustained or even attempted the introduction's specified "bad-weather" tempo of 𝅗𝅥. = 60 (although Catherine Rose Melhorn reports that she observed it, in accordance with Siegfried Ochs's indications);[13] most performances average about 𝅗𝅥. = 48–52 for the bulk of this section, losing some speed after the interruption from the horns and bassoons in mm. 187ff. (despite the *a tempo* designation). The disparity continues in the transition to springtime (mm. 360ff), which most recordings take at about 𝅗𝅥 = 84 rather than the specified rate of 𝅗𝅥 = 96. The obviously brisk specified tempo of 𝅗𝅥 = 160 for stanza 2 rarely if ever comes closer than 𝅗𝅥 = 120, and thus that stanza usually lasts about 2′30″ rather than 1′40″. Finally, some performances start stanza 8 (No. 6) at the specified rate of 𝅗𝅥. = 88, but few manage to sustain that speed; many soon slip into a more comfortable tempo, even after beginning more slowly than Mendelssohn directed.

The fact that the slow and fast tempo variances compensate for each other, so that neither affects the length of the work as a whole, might be taken to indicate that the degree of variance is ultimately immaterial—perhaps the product of the sort of casual or half-serious approach to metronome markings so colorfully recounted by Berlioz. I would argue, however, that with the possible exception of the "transition to springtime" the movements in which modern convention errs on the side of slowness are precisely the ones in which the plot of the work's poetic text mandates a sense of urgency, an urgency that derives from the exertions of conductor and players alike and comes across to listeners as not just "quick," but "as quick as possible," probably as a result of some sort of affective or emotional duress and possibly with the risk of losing control. Certainly the pagan populace's rush to celebrate their ancient rites atop the mountain, sufficient to make them lose sight of the law against that practice and the risk of loss of life that it would entail, even though it had already cost them "their fathers and children," argues for a tempo for stanza 2 that is not just buoyant and lively

(Allegro vivace), but *quite* (*assai*) buoyant and lively. Such breakneck youthful excess is, of course, precisely the old woman's charge against the pagan youth.

The modern convention of having that "old woman" simply hobble along at a reasonable or comfortable rate for an old woman is likewise improbable; for the lack of a transition between Nos. 1 and 2 makes clear that the old woman's entrance is an interruption (something that is unlikely to occur suddenly when an elderly person is moving at a slow tempo). Since the woman is acting under the emotional duress of recalling painful memories and forecasting dire consequences, the affect of the movement should reflect this fact; the disparity between Mendelssohn's prescribed tempo and conventional modern tempi suggests that this is one performance parameter that should be used to achieve his desired effect. The same is true of No. 6, which often lapses into what Philip Radcliffe (in connection with the A-major Symphony) called "the too-comfortable jog-trot into which 6/8 time is liable to lead Mendelssohn."[14] The urgency with which the pagan guards undertake their ruse is self-evident, but the movement's musical complexity, technical difficulty, and colorful scoring suggest that the demanding metronome marking is an admonition of sorts—a prod for performers to push well beyond what is comfortable. Finally, the same view argues for the temporal urgency of the "bad weather" portion of the introduction. The need for a sense of urgency is readily evident from the key, the tempestuous melodic and thematic material, and the movement's function as an instrumental adumbration or allegory of the political, historical, and religious backdrop for the text. Here, too, however, the depth and intensity of that conflict calls for extraordinary means. As in No. 6, a tempo that is uncomfortably fast can not only convey that programmatic intensity, but also enhance the effect of the movement's metrical disruptions and the kaleidoscopic effects of its orchestration.

Language

Modern performers and commentators generally assume that music should be performed in the native language of the composer, and that translated versions are artistically inferior even when they were prepared with the composer's full participation. The assumption often fits well enough. As I have argued elsewhere, however, it is decidedly awkward in Mendelssohn's case.[15] This is so partly because of his views on the nature of text/music relationships, partly because of his exceptional linguistic proficiencies, and partly because of the degree of his participation in producing most of the translated editions that appeared during his lifetime. If anything, by privileging the "original" tongue—a concept that is often unclear in his case—at the likely expense of the interpretive enfranchisement of the listener in such instances, we contravene rather than adhere to the composer's firmly held convictions concerning the expressivity of texted music. The same, perhaps surprisingly, is true of "literal" translations.

The final version of *Die erste Walpurgisnacht* is arguably one such instance, although the complications that pertain to it are also instructive. The contemporary French translation by Edouard Bélanger, which recast the poem's pagans as Gypsies and its Christians as Gypsy-hunters, was evidently produced without Mendelssohn's knowledge or participation. As noted in chapter 6, it was ridiculed in the French press by the eminent critic Léon Kreutzer—but a contemporary German critic, while concurring with Kreutzer in condemning Bélanger's adaptation, also asserts that Kreutzer himself had not grasped "the actual idea" ("die eigentliche Idee") of Goethe's poem as it is explained in the excerpt from his letter of September 9, 1831, to Mendelssohn printed in the published score.[16] This exceptionally negative critical reception (which mixed glowing remarks on Mendelssohn's music with general denunciation of the Gypsies-vs.-archers version of the text that accompanied it in performance) illustrates the importance of both the text and its contemporary context. On the one hand, since there can be little doubt that the predominantly Catholic French audiences of the 1840s and 1850s would have found little sympathy or empathy for the *Walpurgisnacht*'s Saxon pagans, Bélanger's idea to recast the roles of Other and Self as more familiar "parallel" protagonists is understandable. At the same time, the German critic was correct that Kreutzer's more literal explanation of the historical basis of the poem betrayed no cognizance of the poem's "elevated symbolism," a fact that suggests that Bélanger's adapted translation failed in its attempt to convey the poem's import by removing the contextual obstacles that would result from a literal translation. But the problems only multiply when one considers that Kreutzer's supposedly superficial reading of the poem concurs precisely with the historical explanations that Goethe offered to Zelter in 1812, as well as the one Mendelssohn offered in the printed program for the work's premiere: the German critic may have grasped the poem's symbolic import, but he, too, missed the conjectured historical foundation that formed the basis of that symbolism.

A different situation obtains in the case of William Bartholomew's English translation. By the time of this edition's publication, the London-based firm of Ewer & Co. had become Mendelssohn's preferred English publisher, led by Edward Buxton. Bartholomew, as the firm's main in-house translator, was thoroughly familiar with Mendelssohn's exacting standards of translation. He had produced the English translations of the symphony-cantata *Lobgesang* (Op. 52) and the Op. 41 and Op. 50 part-songs, as well as those of the incidental music to *Antigone* (Op. 55) and the so-called Gutenberg cantata. The latter two were particularly arduous undertakings, involving extensive and detailed correspondence between composer and translator and numerous revisions and rethinkings concerning the approach to the translated text. By position and experience, then, Bartholomew's English translation of *Die erste Walpurgisnacht* is at least potentially viable as an alternative version in the English-speaking world.

The *Walpurgisnacht* is also exceptional among the English translations of Mendelssohn's works of the 1840s, however. After the international stir the work made at its premiere, Mendelssohn evidently offered the English publication rights to Buxton sometime before July 11, 1843, suggesting that he read the poem first. Buxton, who evidently had a German background and spoke and wrote German fluently (including the German script), eagerly accepted the offer on July 14.[17] He showed Bartholomew a literal translation later that summer, and Bartholomew reported to Mendelssohn on August 23, that he "saw nothing in it which may not be made understandable to the English."[18] He continued,

> If on talking it over with him, you would wish me to *try* my hand at it, I will with pleasure make the attempt; if I fail, or you wish any other to do it, so long as the piece itself be made available, never mind by whom, so that it be well done, for I wish all your music to become the common stock of England as well as Germany.[19]

Mendelssohn and Buxton probably discussed "the English edition, translation, etc." during Buxton's visit to Leipzig late in 1843,[20] and the assignment did go to Bartholomew. But during the lag time before the publication, English interest in the work had accelerated so much that Mendelssohn's earlier London publisher, Novello, began conspiring to snatch up the English rights if they had not already been taken.[21] On December 20, Buxton, having heard of these plans and anxious to establish his copyright, sent Bartholomew's English translation to the work's German publisher, Kistner, so that it could also be included in the German plates if so desired—a remarkable step indeed, for Buxton had not yet officially purchased the rights to the piece.[22] He further explains:

> I beg to say, that if you have no objection to sell me the work I will publish it in Clavier Auszug [i.e., in piano-vocal reduction], in which case you might get Mr. K[istner] to defer his publication a short time if not already done.[23]

The remainder of the cantata's English publication history seems to be the product of crossed lines of communication. Buxton wrote again on January 2, asking Mendelssohn to send "the music to [Bartholomew's] words as [Mendelssohn] promised" so that he could publish the work.[24] In the meantime, however, Kistner had at Mendelssohn's request sent a second set of German proofs to the composer, including one to be sent to the English publisher; these Mendelssohn received and sent to Buxton by January 4, 1844.[25] But since the German edition had progressed significantly farther than the English one and Mendelssohn and Buxton had not discussed whether the English text should be included beneath the German one in the score, the composer elected to have the German edition published without additional English text underlay.[26] The English edition, by contrast, included the German text beneath the English one.

By agreement between Mendelssohn and both publishers, the piano-vocal arrangement and vocal parts were published on February 1. About six weeks later, Bartholomew, in a rare moment of self-effacement, sent Mendelssohn a disclaimer regarding his translation:

> Your "Walpurgis Nacht" is now published; & I hope . . . it will be pretty free from errors.
>
> I regret that more time was not allowed me for my adaptation; which in consequence of that which I sent to Germany not being returned when the German corrected proofs were sent here, was done in the greatest haste to make the publication a valid copyright on the day appointed. As a translated poem, looking at it with a reference to its great original, I fear it will not satisfy you: for there were many words I could not render literally; and which in some cases had I done so, would not have aided the whole: so I wrote by compensation. Again too, my endeavours to keep the picture words in the same places as in the German, fettered me. I mention this to extenuate the faults you may detect in the performance of a task—not the easiest I ever encountered.[27]

Bartholomew's trepidation is understandable. Still smarting from the protracted and agonizingly detailed work in creating texts for *Antigone* that would mediate successfully between Sophocles, Tieck, Mendelssohn, and the English public, he had under considerable temporal duress prepared for that same public a translation of a poem based on German history by the author who was by consensus Germany's most provocative author—a poem, moreover, that touched on issues that were decidedly sensitive in contemporary society, by no means to the advantage of Christianity.

Mendelssohn's response to Bartholomew's disclaimer (if he responded at all) is lost. But if the public response to the English premiere of the *Walpurgisnacht* is any indication,[28] the English translator had indeed succeeded in making Goethe's poem understandable to the English, as promised in his letter of August 23, 1843. The accomplishment is remarkable not only because of the compact complexity of Goethe's poem, but also because Bartholomew's engagements with the Gutenberg *Festgesang* revealed him to be most eager to indulge in the theological chauvinism characteristic of Victorian Christianity—that is, unlikely to respond well to this poem's philo-heathen sympathies.

What Bartholomew had in his favor was the poem's emphasis on religious themes that are common to paganism as well as Christianity, its general historical background, and its (presumably unintentional) use of protagonists appropriate to British as well as German audiences' frame of reference. Despite many differences, the parallels between the Celtic religious forebears of Bartholomew's British audiences and their Germanic counterparts are numerous and substantive: both religious cultures included druids; both deeply venerated the forests and conducted their sacrificial religious ceremonies in the open air on hilltops and in groves; and both suffered protracted violent conflicts with their Christian adversaries before their eventual relegation to historical and religious alterity.[29] The cultural memory of this conflict had also been vividly revived by the pseudo-Celtic Ossianic fever that swept Europe in the late eighteenth and early nineteenth centuries. Because of these parallels, English audiences' knowledge of their own country's centuries of religious strife—both between paganism and Christianity, and between Protestantism and

Catholicism—would have provided them all the tools necessary to grasp the poetic argument, empathize with its theme of the conflict between identity and alterity, and appreciate Mendelssohn's musical enactment of those ideas.

Despite his disclaimer, Bartholomew was generally successful in exploiting these Celtic/Germanic cognates while also setting the "picture words" and essential ideas of Goethe's poem to Mendelssohn's music. One such example is the prophetic alto solo of strophe 3 (No. 2), which manages to retain a similar poetic structure while also placing conceptually and affectively comparable words in parallel places:

18 Könnt ihr so verwegen handeln?	Know ye not a deed so daring,
19 Wollt ihr denn zum Tode wandeln?	Dooms us all to die despairing?
20 Kennet ihr nicht die Gesetze	Know ye not it is forbidden
21 Unsrer harten Überwinder?	By the edicts of our Foemen?
22 Rings gestellt sind ihre Netze	Know ye, Spies and snares are hidden
23 Auf die Heiden, auf die Sünder.	For the sinners call'd "the Heathen"?
24 Ach, sie schlachten auf dem Walle	On their ramparts they will slaughter
25 Unsre Väter, unsre Kinder.	Mother, Father, Son and Daughter!
26 Und wir alle	If detected,
27 Nahen uns gewissem Falle.	Naught but death can be expected.

Although Bartholomew alters the stanza's rhyme scheme from *aabcbcdcdd* to *aabcbbddee*, this does not affect the textual congruence with the rhyme schemes of Mendelssohn's musical phrases (the musical phrase pairs still align with textual phrase pairs). The weakest point in the stanza from a structural perspective occurs in ll. 20–23, which replace Goethe's set of three *c*-rhymes, two *b*-rhymes, and one *d*-rhyme with another 3-2-1 set (*b*, *d*, and *c*, respectively). The noun "Tode" (death) in l. 19 is replaced, quite naturally, by the verb "die" on an affectively dissonant *F* (the seventh of the fully diminished seventh chord) in m. 686 (ex. 7.1, m. 7). The final syllables' rhyme and the syntactical analog between the two words that bring the enmity between the two main groups of protagonists into focus is likewise preserved, paralleling Mendelssohn's setting of those lines as a sequence (*Überwinder*–*Sünder* and "Foemen"–"Heathen"; see ex. 7.1, mm. 12–13 and 17). And, of course, the line whose affective center is *schlachten*, rendered literally as "slaughter," still coincides with the chromatic lament in mm. 18f. The latter change makes it necessary to change Mendelssohn's *unsre Väter, unsre Kinder* (literally, "our fathers, our children") to "Mother, Father, Son, and Daughter," in the interest of the rhyme, but since *Väter* was already Mendelssohn's alteration of Goethe's *Weiber* this change is of little consequence. Least literally rendered are the strophe's last two lines (ex. 7.1, mm. 34–49), which Goethe uses to emphasize that the careless actions of a few will endanger the entire pagan community. Bartholomew sacrifices this emphasis on the collective *uns* (which provides a useful transition to the "chorus of the women" in stanza 4), but his emphasis on death as the only predictable consequence of the

Example 7.1. Mendelssohn, *Die erste Walpurgisnacht*, Op. 60: No. 2, mm. 3–49, in original German and with English translation by William Bartholomew. *Source*: EPfE.

pagans' pursuit of their ancient rites is probably justifiable, given the stanza's prophetic import.

Equally important at the end of No. 9 is Bartholomew's preservation of a parallel to the text's crucial change of verb from *will* (will) to *kann* (can) in the poem's final line. Except for this verb, ll. 96–99 of Goethe's text are a literal repetition of ll. 75–78. Mendelssohn musically emphasizes this change from the unrounded close front vowel ɪ to the rounded back vowel ɑ by making *kann* the first musical high point of No. 9, at a massive sustained subdominant chord with a renewed *fortissimo* (ex. 7.2). Unable to render the difference literally, Bartholomew seized an opportunity presented by the quatrain's modification at

Example 7.2. Mendelssohn, *Die erste Walpurgisnacht*, Op. 60: No. 9, mm. 18–28, in original German and with English translation by William Bartholomew. *Source*: EPfE.

its second statement. The last two lines of stanza 9 translate *und raubt man uns den alten Brauch: dein Licht, wer will es rauben?* as "our customs quell'd, our rights withheld, Thy light shall shine for ever!" The end of stanza 12 takes advantage of the fact that the English "Thy Light," unlike the German *dein Licht*, does not repeat its vowel sound, translating the final line pair as "Though Foes may cloud or quell our light; Yet Thine, Thy light shall shine for ever!" Bartholomew's modification is more syntactically invasive than Goethe's, but it affects the sense of

Example 7.2. (*continued*)

the final line little—and it emphasizes Mendelssohn's formidable musical climax by aligning it with a vowel whose resonance approaches that of the crucial *kann* in Mendelssohn's and Goethe's version.

Whatever its defects, then, there is good reason to consider Bartholomew's English version of *Die erste Walpurgisnacht* artistically viable. Although the English text does not render the poetic original literally, Mendelssohn's correspondence with Bartholomew and other translators reveals that literal translations are essentially incompatible with his views on the nature of verbal and musical expression.[30] Moreover, Bartholomew's text not only effectively coordinates the poem's essential ideas with Mendelssohn's music, but also successfully negotiates what is probably the crucial feature of both vis-à-vis their poetic import: the depiction of spiritual affinities between the pagans and their Christian adversaries through role reversal. The resounding acclaim afforded the cantata in the Victorian world—a world that might quite reasonably be expected to be inimical to such philo-heathen sentiments, and that still harbored decided reservations about Goethe because of his religious unorthodoxy—further testifies to the composer's and translator's success in conveying the poem's provocative message concerning identity and alterity to English performers and audiences—who were in many ways themselves Other to the poem's originally envisioned readership.

Roles and Disposition of Forces

Modern performance conventions present a problem with regard to the role assignments in *Die erste Walpurgisnacht.* Today the work is usually performed with three vocal soloists: an alto for the role of the "old woman from among the people" in strophe 3 (No. 2), a tenor solo who plays both the druid in strophe 1 (No. 1) and the Christian guard in strophe 9 (No. 8), and a baritone or bass solo who doubles as the druid priest (strophes 5, 9, and 12; Nos. 3, 7, and 9) and the druid watchman (strophe 7; No. 5). But the reports and surviving programs of performances given during Mendelssohn's lifetime (including those under his direction) reveal that the latter two roles were to be cast for two different soloists: a baritone for the role of the druid priest and a bass for the druid watchman (see figure 4.1, p. 93).

These role assignments are critical to the realization in performance of the geographic aspect of the poem's plot, as well as the topographic symbolism so important to both Goethe's poem and Mendelssohn's cantata. Although the composer tampered with the casting of Goethe's poem by reassigning strophe 3 to "an old woman from among the people" rather than "a man from among the people," this change reinforces the work's basis in the lore of the Saxon pagans, as well as creating a female role (see chapters 1 and 5). By contrast, the modern convention of conflating the roles of the druid priest and the druid watchman contravenes the plot of the ballad, which requires that the action unfold on three geographic levels: the ceremonies atop the Brocken (where the priest leads the faithful in their worship), the Christian guards' post at the lowest level, and the mid-level slopes where the pagan guards hatch their plan and carry out the ruse; the last, of course, is where the druid watchman (bass solo) operates. Since the ballad's topographic strata are poetic critiques of the character and attributes of the three main groups of protagonists, conflating the roles of the priest and the druid watchman also compromises this symbolic function.

Similarly, on the title pages Mendelssohn carefully designates three distinct choruses: the *Chor der Druiden und des Heidenvolks* (Chorus of the Druids and the Pagan Populace), the *Chor der Wächter der Druiden* (Chorus of the Druid Watchmen), and the *Chor der christlichen Wächter* (Chorus of the Christian Watchmen). In contradistinction to modern performance conventions, the plot and geography of the poem require that the last of these comprise only some of the men of the chorus, not the entire group, probably one smaller than the other male choruses;[31] and that they *not* participate in the various pagan

Figure 7.1. Biblioteka Jagiellońska, Krakow, Mus. ms. autogr. F. Mendelssohn Bartholdy 37, pp. 115/122. Used by permission.

choruses—at least those before No. 9 (see below). Moreover, the plot of the poem suggests that the chorus of the druid watchmen in nos. 3, 4, and 6 should be entrusted to another subchorus comprising *some* of the men of the chorus of the druids and the pagan populace; this subchorus is a counterpart to the chorus of the Christian watchmen. Finally, then, Mendelssohn assigns No. 9 (stanza 12) to an *allgemeiner Chor der Druiden und des Heidenvolks*, meaning that the entire pagan populace (the women's chorus, the chorus of the druid watchmen, and the remainder of the men from the chorus of druids) unites in hymnic praise—evidently for the first time in the cantata.

Does this mean that the chorus of the Christian watchmen has to sit out the final paean? Strictly construed, yes—but as shown in figure 7.1, the beginning of this chorus in the autograph full score of the 1830–33 version includes the designation *Der ganze Männerchor* (the complete men's chorus) in addition to the designations *Chor der Druiden* and (at the beginning of the staff) *Frauenchor* (women's chorus). This peculiarity (which may or may not have carried over into Mendelssohn's plan for the later setting) would concur with the obviously greater musical appeal of involving the entire chorus in this solemn number to suggest that the composer may indeed have wanted the entire ensemble to be involved in these majestic final minutes of the cantata. Moreover, the first editions make clear that the solo tenor (rather than the solo bass) performs a dual role: as the Druid of No. 1 (stanza 1) and the Christian guard of No. 8 (stanza 10). This role reversal not only spans the pagan/Christian divide, but in so doing also concurs with the 1833 autograph's specification that *Der ganze Männerchor* be included in the final movement.

The last point raises one further important issue concerning the disposition and arrangement of the vocal forces—namely, whether they should be positioned in an arrangement that has since become more-or-less standard, or in some special configuration that reflects conventions of Mendelssohn's day and/or the specific plot of this text. As is well known, one of the few consistent features of nineteenth-century orchestral/choral plans was that the chorus was placed in front of the orchestra rather than behind it (as is now customary). In the German-speaking countries this arrangement typically positioned the sopranos and tenors to the conductor's left and altos and basses to the conductor's right as late as the 1880s and 1890s.[32]

The special casting features of *Die erste Walpurgisnacht* also raise the possibility that the vocal forces were separated in a fashion comparable to Berlioz's arrangement in performances of his "dramatic symphony" *Roméo et Juliette* (1839–46)—a concerted work that is contemporaneous with the *Walpurgisnacht* and likewise makes much of the distinctions and oppositions among the various forces who are united in the end.[33] If so, the Christian *Männerchor* (which Mendelssohn in 1830–33 specified as "smaller") would be spatially separated from the remainder of the chorus, and the several constituent groups of the pagan choruses would likewise be spatially and acoustically distinct, presumably with the four soloists near their respective choirs. The effect of the sudden entrance of the complete choral and solo ensembles of the pagans at the beginning of the final number would have been most dramatic in this instance—especially if it also included the chorus of the Christian guards.

The latter scenario may seem unfounded, since the plot of the poem depends on the opposition between the Christians and their pagan adversaries. But one peculiarity of Mendelssohn's role specifications at least raises the possibility: the fact that the solo tenor functions as both the druid of No. 1 and the Christian guard of No. 8. In one sense this dual function, most practicable in concerted performances because of the absence of costumes, violates the dramaturgical principle of opposition between the Christians and pagans in the cantata. But it is probably more practical (at least from the perspective of planning) than hiring two separate tenors, one to feature in less than two minutes' worth of music near the beginning of the work and the other to feature in about one minute's worth of music near the end. Most important, however, is that this apparent role violation in fact underscores the central point of both poem and cantata: the need for enmity between the Christians and pagans, like the lore of the Walpurgis Night itself, is an illusion, the product of ignorance and intolerance rather than irreconcilable conflicts in religious belief. By changing from a pagan persona to a Christian one the solo tenor dramaturgically realizes this poetic message before it is stated as such in the final movement. Similarly, by joining with the combined pagan choruses in the final triumphant hymn, the chorus of Christian guards would realize in performance the process of overcoming fear, hatred, and superstition and joining with their former adversaries in collective celebration of their mutual *Allvater*. The collective attainment of that all-illuminating metaphorical light, which Mendelssohn musically renders in the idiom of grand spiritual exaltation so familiar today from *St. Paul*, *Elijah*, and the orchestral psalms, is the goal that poem and cantata alike set for performers and listeners.

In three important recent essays, Leon Botstein has urged modern listeners, performers, and commentators to approach the life and the music of Mendelssohn not with anticipation of finding a genial, clever, and often brilliant compeer to a supposedly greater depth and spirituality in Beethoven, Schubert, Schumann, and Wagner.[34] Instead, Botstein argues, Mendelssohn's music can be grasped and appreciated only if we assume—as his public evidently did—that that music "creates the space for the listener to become aware of his or her own need for engagement."[35] The composer wins his authority as the source of musical utterance not by declaring its import, but by enfranchising his performers and listeners in realizing it; and this collective or even communal participation becomes all the more important when the music is as overtly rooted in the great questions of human beliefs and human coexistence as is that of *Die erste Walpurgisnacht*. If we approach this music as we typically approach the music of those other just-named masters—if we erect the stage's figurative fourth wall and view what transpires behind it from the perspective of those who expect Mendelssohn to produce a clever entertainment of little spiritual import—we will neither grasp the moral of Goethe's poetic fable nor participate in the elevated symbolism of the processes that transpire in it and Mendelssohn's music. Mendelssohn's setting of Goethe's poem will then emerge as a historically based fable of human weakness rather than a symbolic contribution to artistic discourse that centers on the historical, social, and religious potency of the events, issues, and ideas that have converged on the theme of the Walpurgis Night.

Those words are addressed to performers as well as listeners and commentators. For in order to realize the import of the final chorus of *Die erste Walpurgisnacht* performers must use Mendelssohn's musical setting of the meaning of Goethe's text not to emphasize the differences that are the source of the historical, societal, and religious divisions that underlie the work's narrative in the first eleven stanzas, but to overcome them. That final chorus implores voices and instruments, young and old, Christian and heathen, Self and Other, performers and auditors to transcend the conventional roles and performative spaces that divide them, and to converge in a new communal space where fear, hatred, ignorance, and superstition, like the smoke of the pagans' sacrificial fires, are banished by the purifying flame and the light of mutual toleration, acceptance, and universal truth.

Epilog: Convergences

> In New York there are ninety different Christian denominations, each of which recognizes God and the Lord in its own way without being at all disconcerted by the others. In the natural sciences, indeed in every area of inquiry we must advance so far; for what sense does it make that everyone speaks of liberality while wishing to hinder others from thinking and speaking in their own ways?
>
> — Goethe, *Maximen und Reflexionen,* No. 709

With these words the pantheist Goethe, who referred often enough to the Enlightenment proverb that "every human has his own religion"[36] and described himself as "neither anti-Christian nor un-Christian, but decidedly non-Christian,"[37] expressed admiration for a spirit of religious tolerance that he saw as feasible (if also not yet assured) in the young United States, also proposing such ideological pluralism as a goal for all areas of inquiry and endeavor. But Goethe was also well aware of two paradoxes that had been forcefully articulated by Montesquieu, whom he greatly admired: first, that throughout history tolerant spirits have continually been compelled to use force to defend tolerance against intolerance, and thus to become intolerant themselves; and second, that the development of the civilization he and his contemporaries so ardently embraced was irrevocably rooted in violence and religious intolerance, while history's religiously tolerant societies had been predominantly nomadic and idolatrous—"primitive" in the contemporary parlance. When the Lutheran Mendelssohn, celebrated grandson of Europe's preeminent advocate of an assimilated Jewish/Christian society, elected more than a decade after the poet's death to replace his original historical explanation of the origins of the Walpurgis Night legend with an excerpt from Goethe's letter explaining the "elevated symbolism" behind the cantata's text, he implicitly challenged performers and listeners to do what Goethe solicited in his *Walpurgisnacht* ballad and Montesquieu had proposed in chapter 13 of *The Spirit of the Laws,* Book XXV:[38] to recognize the moral imperative of Goethe's "fable-like history" (Montesquieu's "most humble remonstrance") and then to discern an Enlightened path—a path that would lead not only to religious, intellectual, and social toleration, but to acceptance and recognition.

This book is the product of a number of remarkable convergences. The naming and explanation of the Walpurgis Night resulted from the convergence of the religious and political conflict of Charlemagne's Saxon wars, the benevolence of St. Walpurgis, Christian hagiography, pagan cults, superstition, and reason. The literature and music around which this book centers resulted from the convergence of the lives and ideas of a pantheist poet/scientist and a Christian composer/conductor sixty years his junior. And the Night's stature as a theme for socially conscious artistic discourse resulted from the convergences of their respective engagements with it as a cultural topos in different media and substantially different artistic and social contexts. By problematizing the epic historical clash of societies and beliefs that supposedly generated the lore of turbulence and conflict indelibly associated with the Walpurgis Night, Goethe solicited readers to overcome not only the barriers recounted in that history but also those that led them to identify with any particular party to that conflict: for those partisan perspectives impeded celebration of the great historical, religious, and societal dialectic of which those conflicts are one part. Mendelssohn, in turn, took the ballad and his audiences' familiarity with the conflicted literature and lore of the Walpurgis Night itself as starting points for his own musical realization of the moral of Goethe's "poetic fable." He stepped outside his own identity as an ardent Christian of Jewish descent and drew inspiration instead from the challenge to transcend ideological, social, and religious barriers, conveying an emphatically spiritual message neither specifically Christian, nor Jewish, nor Muslim—a message that was, in a word, heathen. In so doing he undertook for himself as composer and for his music as artistic discourse the same challenge that Goethe's poem continues to issue to its readers.

Appendix A

Original Texts of Select Lengthy Documents Originally Written in Languages other than English

Original Texts of Lengthy Translations in Chapter 1:

Note 55: Fischer, *Das Buch vom Aberglauben*, 125–27: "Vor Zeiten . . . schwatzten [die Betrüger] ihnen vor, daß man durch Zauberei reich werden, und . . . so erzählten sie ihnen, was dabei vorgehen müsse: Daß man sich dem Teufel mit seinem Blut verschreibe, daß man umgetauft werde und dabei einen Teufel zum Pathen bekomme; daß hernach jede Hexe einen Geist zum Bräutigam, und jeder Hexenmeister eine Geistin zur Braut haben müsste; daß auf Walpurgis die ganze Hexenzunft einen prächtigen Schmaus mit Music und Tanz auf dem Blocksberg halte—und dergleichen albernes Zeug mehr. Sie nannten auch wol einen und und den andern, der schon dabei wär. Wenn nun der Walpurgisabend kam; so gaben sie vor, man müsse dazu vorbereitet werden, gaben ihm etwas ein, davon er lebhaft träumte, bestrichen ihn hie und da mit einer Salbe, und suchten überhaupt seine Einbildungskraft auf alle Art zu erregen, und ihm die ganze Sache gewiß zu machen. Weil aber die Weiber am geneigtesten zu solchen Gaukeleien sind, und sich leichter überreden und irre führen lassen, so probirte man das vornemlich mit ihnen. Eine solche Frau träumte dann in der Nacht von dem, wovon ihre Seele so voll war, wie es bei Träumen gewöhnlich ist. Da dünkte es ihr, als ritte sie auf einem Besen, oder einer Ofengabel durch die Luft und tanze auf dem Blocksberg, wo der Teufel in Bocksgestallt [*sic*] erscheine. Erwachte sie nun wieder, so glaubte sie, es sey alles wirklich geschehen, erzehlte dieser und jener Vertrauten, besonders wenn sie dieselbe auf der Teufelshochzeit gesehen haben wollte, wie alles zugegangen sey, und gab ihr auch von der Hexensalbe. Diese, wenn sie gleich nichts davon wußte, wagte es entweder nicht, sich zu rechtfertigen und Anzeige davon zu thun; oder sie wünschte an diesem Fest Antheil zu nehmen. Kam nun die erwartete Nacht, so beschmierte sie sich auch mit Salbe, und glaubte und träumte wie jene. . . . Und dieser Glaube gieng von Haus zu Haus, von einem Ort zum andern immer weiter. Der Pabst, die Bischöfe und andere Geistliche, welche davon hörten, meinten endlich auch, es sey wahr, und verboten das Hexen und Zaubern bei Lebensstrafe; reizten auch wol die weltliche Obrigkeit, diejenigen zu bestrafen und zu verbrennen. . . ."

Note 56: Fischer, *Das Buch vom Aberglauben*, 129: "Oder ist nicht die Sage von dem jährlichen Hexentanz auf dem Blocksberg vielleicht auf folgende Art entstanden? Die Schäfer in jenen Gegenden sollen ehedem den Tag vor Walpurgis festlich zugebracht, und oft bis in die Nacht fröhlich gewesen seyn und getantzt haben. Da man nun in der Entfernung Lichter und hüpfende Bewegungen auf dem Berg sah, welches man sich nicht erklären konnte, so gerieth man auf allerhand, unter andern auch auf die sonderbare Meinung, daß es etwas übernatürliches, Hexen, mit ihnen der Teufel u. s. w. sey; . . . Die wahrscheinlichtste Erklärung hievon ist ohne Zweifel folgende: Vor tausend Jahren und drüber, ehe das Christenthum in Sachsen eingeführt war, wurde auf diesem Berge am ersten Mai ein heidnisches Götzenfest von Weibern und Mädchen gehalten, wobei keine Mannsleute seyn durften. Als nun Kaiser Carl der grosse die Sachsen nöthigte, den christlichen Glauben anzunehmen, blieben die Weiber auf dieses Fest noch lange so erpicht, daß sie es heimlich und des Nachts feierten. Die Geistlichen sagten daher den Leuten: es wäre ein Teufelsfest, wo der Böse in Gestalt eines schwarzen Bockes leibhaftig erscheine, und mit den Weibern allerlei Unfug triebe, die sich ihm verschreiben müßten, ihm nun eigen angehörten, und endlich ewig verdammt würden. Weil sich aber Sie Weiber heimlich dahin schlichen, daß es niemand merkte; so sagt man, sie ritten auf Besen und Ofengabeln durch die Luft dahin. Dieser Glaube gieng hernach von Mund zu Mund, und erhielt sich auch, seitdem jenes Fest nicht mehr gefeiert wird . . ."

Note 57: Honemann, *Die Alterthümer des Harzes*, vol. 1, 11–12: "Hiebey ist nicht undienlich zu gedenken, was der Verfasser einer ungedruckten Erzehlung des Lebens Herzogs *Julii* zu Braunschweig und Lüneburg von dem Ursprunge des bekannten Mährchens, daß in die Walpurgis oder Philippi Jacobi Nacht die Hexen auf dem Brocken ihre Zusammenkünfte hielten, berichtet hat; daß nemlich dieser Wahn aus einem Mißverstande des Wortes *Unholden* entsprungen sey. Denn, als die Sachsen sich zum christlichen Glauben bekehren lassen, wären noch viele unter ihnen gewesen, die ihren heidnischen Gottesdienst nicht gänzlich hätten verlassen wollen, und besonders über dem Wittekind, seiner Bekehrung halber, ungehalten geworden wären, die man daher Unholden, oder ungehaltene, genannt. Um aber von niemand erkannt zu werden, und denen von Kayser Carl dem Grossen Fehm-Richtern nicht in die Hände zu gerahten, hätten dieselbe auf die höchsten Berge, und folglich auch auf den Brockensberg, sich begeben; woselbst sie der Göttin *Herdä*, auch *Erth* oder *Nerth* genannt, geopfert; und, weil der Nahme *Unhold* nachgehends einen Hexenmeister hätte bedeuten müssen, wäre von dem gemeinen Manne vorgegeben worden, daß die Hexen auf dem Brockensberge zusammen kämen. Wie man denn auch noch grosse und oben platte in der Ordnung gesetzte Steine auf dem Brocken zeiget, welche denen damahligen Unholden Sachsen zu Altären gedienet haben sollen."

Note 59: "Der Brocken: (Aus einer Sammlung ungedruckter Briefe, über den Harz, und die hessischen Lande." *Berlinisches Archiv der Zeit und ihres Geschmacks* 2 (1796): 535–37: "Die Antwort auf diese Frage ['warum wir gerade hier, und sonst in Deutschland fast nirgends, so zahlreiche und mannichfaltige Spuren deutschen Götzendienstes, antreffen sollen?'], und der Schlüssel zu dem räthselhaften Mährchen von jenem wundervollen Luftritte, liegen, dünkt mich, in der

Geschichte Karls des Großen. Als dieser berühmte Frankenkönig, mit eben so vielem Bekehrungs- als Eroberungsgeiste, die kriegerische Schaubühne in Deutschland betrat, waren die Deutschen, namentlich die Sachsen, noch freie Völker voll Kraft und Muth, die sich durchaus keiner fremden Herrschaft unterwerfen wollten. Als eifrigen Götzdienern lag ihnen aber die Religion ihrer Väter, nicht weniger als ihre Freiheit, am Herzen. Karl bot alle seine Kräfte auf, sie zu überwinden. Zugleich wollte er sie zum Christenthum bekehren. Dies verwickelte ihn in einen Krieg, der über drei und dreißig Jahre dauerte. Oft wurden die [p. 536] Sachsen geschlagen; aber nach jedem Siege Karls, und nach jedem Friedensschlusse, griffen sie immer wieder zu den Waffen; und, nach jeder scheinbaren Annahme des Christenthums, kehrten sie zum Götzendienste zurück. Dies erbitterte Karln zuletzt so sehr, daß er, nach damaligen schrecklichen Begriffen, Gewalt brauchte, viele, die sich nicht wollten taufen lassen, niederhauen ließ, und ein Gesetz gab, daß dem Feuereifer eines Spanischen Großinquisitors angemessen ist. Alle diejenigen nämlich, welche die christliche Taufe anzunehmen sich weigern, oder unter dem Christen-Namen sich verstellen, und trotz deu Bekenntnis des Christenthums fortfahren würden, als Heiden zu leben und Götzen zu dienen, *sollten mit dem Tode bestraft werden*!

"Die heidnischen Sachsen mußten zwar endlich der Gewalt weichen, und öffentlich die Taufe annehmen; allein in ihren Herzen blieben sie Heiden, und wenn sich Karl mit seinem Kriegsheere kaum zurückgezogen hatte, opferten sie in den Wäldern wieder den Götzen. Der König ließ darauf alle ihre Altäre und Götzenbilder zerstören; und da sie nun in der Ebene gehindert wurden, ihre Opferfeste zu feiern, so nahmen sie ihre Zuflucht zu den Waldungen und Gebirgen des Harzes, namentlich auch zum Gipfel des Brocken, der damals noch wenig zugänglich seyn mochte, und wo man, sie zu verfolgen, sich schwerlich getraute. Indessen ließ Karl, der bald Nachricht davon erhielt, an den vorzüglichsten Opferfesttagen, die Zugänge zu den Gebirgen, namentlich zum Brocken, mit Wache besetzen. Allein die Sachsen, welche, wie alle wegen des Glaubens Verfolgte, der Religion ihrer Väter um so eifriger anhiengen, sannen auf List, an den Freuden ihrer Opferfeste Theil nehmen zu können. Sie verkleideten sich in scheuß- [p. 537] liche Larven, und bahnten sich den Weg zu ihren Götzen, indem sie des Nachts die Wachen erschreckten, die beim Anblick dieser Teufelgestalten um so geschwinder die Flucht ergriffen, da die Theilnehmer der nächtlichen Opferzüge, auf alle Fälle gefaßt, mit Heuforken und Feuergabeln bewaffnet waren. Diese gebrauchten sie, im Nothfall, sowohl zum gewaltsamen Bestürmungen und Verdrängen der christlichen Wache, als auch zum Schutze gegen wilde Thiere. Vielleicht bedurften sie ihrer auch beim Opferfeuer selbst, theils zum Nachlegen des Holzes, theils zum Herausziehen der Feuerbrände, mit welchen in der Hand sie, in Schmauß und Fröhlichkeit, um das Opferfeuer herumtanzten. Da auf den Höhen des Harzes, wenigstens auf dem Brocken, am Feste der ersten Mainacht, gewöhnlich noch Schnee liegen mochte, so bedurfte man vielleicht der Besen, auf deren Stielen die Sage die Damen der Walpurgisnacht reiten läßt, zum Fegen und reinigen des Opferplatzes.

"Die damaligen Christen hielten den Götzendienst für Teufelsdienst, und glaubten nichts gewisser, als daß der Teufel selbst, trotz der mit christlichen Wachen besetzten Zugänge zu den Opferplätzen, seine treuen Anhänger unterstütze, und durch die Luft hinauf führe. . . ."

Original Texts of Lengthy Translations in Chapter 2:

Note 25: Letter from Goethe to Zelter, June 3, 1830 (*GA* 21: 907–8): "Soeben, früh halb 10 Uhr, fährt, beim klarsten Himmel, im schönsten Sonnenschein, der treffliche Felix, mit Ottilien, Ulriken und den Kindern, nachdem er 14 Tage bei uns vergnüglich zugebracht und alles mit seiner vollendeten liebenswürdigen Kunst erbaut, nach Jena, um auch dort die wohlwollenden Freunde zu ergötzen und in unsrer Gegend ein Andenken zurückzulassen, welches fortwährend hoch zu feiern ist.

"Mir war seine Gegenwart besonders wohltätig, da ich fand, mein Verhältnis zur Musik sei noch immer dasselbe; ich höre sie mit Vergnügen, Anteil und Nachdenken, liebe mir das Geschichtliche, denn wer versteht irgend eine Erscheinung, wenn er sich von dem Gang des Herankommens [nicht] penetriert? Dazu war denn die Hauptsache daß Felix auch diesen Stufengang recht löblich einsieht und, glücklicherweise, sein gutes Gedächtnis ihm Musterstück aller Art nach Belieben vorführt. Von der Bachischen Epoche heran hat er mir wieder Haydn, Mozart und Gluck zum Leben gebracht, von den großen neuern Technikern hinreichende Begriffe gegeben, und endlich mich seine eigenen Produktionen fühlen und über sie nachdenken machen; ist daher auch mit meinen besten Segnungen geschieden. . . ."

Note 27: Zelter to Goethe, February 8–10, 1824 (*MA* 20.1: 785–86): "Gestern Abend ist Felixens vierte Oper vollständig nebst Dialog unter uns aufgeführt worden. Es sind drei Akte die nebst 2 Balletten etwa 2½ Stunden füllen. Das Werk hat seinen hübschen Beifall gefunden. Auch das Gedicht von Dr. Casper ist geschickt genug da der Poet musikalisch ist."

"Von meiner—schwachen Seite kann ich meiner Bewunderung kaum Herr werden, wie der Knabe der so eben 15 Jahre geworden ist mit so großen Schritten fortgeht.

"Neues, Schönes, Eignes, Ganzeignes ist überall zu finden. Geist, Fluß, Ruhe, Wohlklang, Ganzheit, Dramatisches. Das Massenhaften wie von erfahrnen Händen. Orchester interessant nicht erdrückend, ermüdend nicht bloß begleitend.

"Die Musici spielen es gern und ist doch eben nicht leicht. Das Bekannte kommt und geht vorüber, nicht wie genommen vielmehr an seiner Stelle willkommen und zugehörig. Munterkeit, Jubel, ohne Hast, Zärtlichkeit, Zierlichkeit, Liebe, Leidenschaft, Unschuld.

"Die Ouvertüre ist ein sonderbares Ding. Du denkst Dir einen Maler der einen Klacks Farbe auf die Leinwand schmeißt, die Masse mit Finger und Pinsel austreibt woraus zuletzt eine Gruppe an den Tag kommt daß man, fort und fort überrascht, sich endlich nach einer Begebenheit umsieht weil ja geschehen sein muß was wahr ist.

"Freilich spreche ich wie ein Großvater der seine Enkel verzieht. Ich weiß wohl was ich sage und will nichts gesagt haben als was ich zu beweisen wüßte . . ."

Note 39: Goethe, "Zu brüderlichem Andenken Wielands" (*GA* 15: 1086): "Es gibt zwei Übersetzungsmaximen: die eine verlangt, daß der Autor einer fremden Nation zu uns herüber gebracht werde, dergestalt, daß wir ihn als den Unsrigen ansehen können; die andere hingegen macht an uns die Forderung, daß wir uns zu dem Fremden hinüber begeben und uns in seine Zustände, seine Sprachweise, seine Eigenheiten finden sollen. Die Vorzüge von beiden sind durch musterhafte Beispiele allen gebildeten Menschen genugsam bekannt. Unser Freund, der auch hier den Mittelweg suchte, war beide zu verbinden bemüht, doch zog er als Mann von Gefühl und Geschmack in zweifelhaften Fällen die erste Maxime vor."

Note 67: *HA* 9: 350–51: ". . . allein ich muß demohngeachtet wieder zu jenem Interesse zurückkehren, das mir die übersinnlichen Dinge eingeflößt hatten, von denen ich ein für allemal, insofern es möglich wäre, mir einen Begriff zu bilden unternahm.

"Einen großen Einfluß erfuhr ich dabei von einem wichtigen Buche, das mir in die Hände geriet, es war Arnolds 'Kirchen- und Ketzergeschichte.' Dieser Mann ist nicht ein bloß reflektierender Historiker, sondern zugleich fromm und fühlend. Seine Gesinnungen stimmten sehr zu den meinigen, und was mich an seinem Werk besonders ergetzte, war, daß ich von manchen Ketzern, die man mir bisher als toll oder gottlos vorgestellt hatte, einen vorteilhaftern Begriff erhielt.

"Der Geist des Widerspruchs und die Lust zum Paradoxen steckt in uns allen. Ich studierte fleißig die verschiedenen Meinungen, und da ich oft genug hatte sagen hören, jeder Mensch habe am Ende doch seine eigene Religion, so kam mir nichts natürlicher vor, als daß ich mir auch meine eigene bilden könne, und dieses tat ich mit vieler Behaglichkeit. Der neue Platonismus lag zum Grunde; das Hermetische, Mystische, Kabbalistische gab auch seinen Beitrag her, und so erbaute ich mir eine Welt, die seltsam genug aussah.

"Ich mochte mir wohl eine Gottheit vorstellen, die sich von Ewigkeit her selbst produziert; da sich aber Produktion nicht ohne Mannigfaltigkeit denken läßt, so mußte sie sich notwendig sogleich als ein Zweites erscheinen, welches wir unter dem Namen des Sohns anerkennen; diese beiden mußten nun den Akt des Hervorbringens fortsetzen, und erschienen sich selbst wieder im Dritten, welches nun ebenso bestehend lebendig und ewig als das Ganze war. Hiermit war jedoch der Kreis der Gottheit geschlossen, und es wäre ihnen selbst nicht möglich gewesen, abermals ein ihnen völlig Gleiches hervorzubringen.

"Da jedoch der Produktionstrieb immer fortging, so erschufen sie ein Viertes, das aber schon in sich einen Widerspruch hegte, indem es, wie sie, unbedingt und doch zugleich in ihnen enthalten und durch sie begrenzt sein sollte. Dieses war nun Luzifer, welchem von nun an die ganze Schöpfungskraft übertragen war, und von dem alles übrige Sein ausgehen sollte. . . ."

Original Texts of Lengthy Translations in Chapter 3:

Note 5: Letter of December 10, 11, 1777, to Charlotte von Stein (translated from *GA* 18: 383): "Ich will Ihnen entdecken (sagen Sies niemand) dass meine Reise auf den Harz war, dass ich wünschte den Brocken zu besteigen, und nun liebste bin ich heut oben gewesen, ganz natürlich, ob mir's schon seit 8 Tagen alle Menschen als unmöglich versichern. Aber das Wie, von allem, das warum, soll aufgehoben seyn wenn ich Sie wiedersehe. wie gerne schrieb ich ietzt nicht.

"Ich sagte: ich hab einen Wunsch auf den Vollmond!—Nun Liebste tret ich vor die Thüre hinaus da liegt der Brocken im hohen herrlichen Mondschein über den Fichten vor mir und ich war oben heut und habe auf dem Teufels Altar meinem Gott den liebsten Danck geopfert.

"Ich will die Nahmen ausfüllen der Orte. Jezt bin ich auf dem sogenannten Torfhause, eines Försters Wohnung zwey Stunden vom Brocken.

Note 6: Letter of December 10, 11, 1777, to Charlotte von Stein (translated from *GA* 18: 384): "Nur ein Wort zur Erinnrung. wie ich gestern zum Torfhause kam sas der Förster bei seinem Morgenschluck in Hemdsermeln, und diskursive redete ich vom Brocken und er versicherte die Unmöglichkeit hinauf zu gehn, und wie offt er Sommers droben gewesen wäre und wie leichtfertig es wäre iezt es zu versuchen—Die Berge waren im Nebel man sah nichts, und so sagt er ists auch iezt oben, nicht drey Schritte vorwärts können Sie sehn. Und wer nicht alle Tritte weis pp. Da sas ich mit schwerem Herzen, mit halben Gedancken wie ich zurückkehren wollte. Und ich kam mir vor wie der König den der Prophet mit dem Bogen schlagen heisst und der zu wenig schlägt. Ich war still und bat die Götter das Herz dieses Menschen zu wenden und das Wetter, und war still. So sagt er zu mir: nun können Sie den Brocken sehn, ich trat ans Fenster und er lag vor mir klar wie mein Gesicht im Spiegel, da ging mir das Herz auf und ich rief: Und ich sollte nicht hinaufkommen! haben Sie keinen Knecht, niemanden—Und er sagte ich will mit Ihnen gehn.— —Ich habe ein Zeichen ins Fenster geschnitten zum Zeugniss meiner Freuden Trähnen und wärs nicht an Sie hielt ich's für Sünde es zu schreiben. Ich habs nicht geglaubt biss auf der obersten Klippe. Alle Nebel lagen unten, und oben war herrliche Klarheit und heute Nacht bis früh war er im Mondschein sichtbaar und finster auch in der Morgendämmerung da ich aufbrach."

Note 9: Translated from *HA* 1: 398: "Ein wichtiger, völlig ideell, ja phantastisch erscheinender Punkt, über dessen Realität der Dichter schon manchen Zweifel erleben mußte, wovon aber ein sehr erfreuliches Dokument noch in seinen Händen ist. Ich stand wirklich am siebenten Dezember in der Mittagsstunde, grenzenlosen Schnee überschauend, auf dem Gipfel des Brockens, zwischen jenen ahnungsvollen Granitklippen, über mir den vollkommen klarsten Himmel, von welchem herab die Sonne gewaltsam brannte, so daß in der Wolle des Überrocks der bekannte branstige Geruch erregt ward. Unter mir sah ich ein unbewegliches Wogenmeer nach allen Seiten die Gegend überdecken und nur durch höhere und tiefere Lage der Wolkenschichten die darunter befindlichen Berge und Täler andeuten."

Note 24: Letter from Goethe to Zelter, August 26, 1799 (translated from *GA* 19: 384–85): "Mit aufrichtigem Dank erwidere ich Ihren freundlichen Brief, durch den Sie mir in Worten sagen mochten wovon mich Ihre Kompositionen schon längst überzeugt hatten: daß Sie an meinen Arbeiten lebhaften Anteil nehmen und sich manches mit wahrer Neigung zugeeignet haben. Es ist das Schöne einer tätigen Teilnahme daß sie wieder hervorbringend ist; denn wenn meine Lieder Sie zu Melodien veranlaßten, so kann ich wohl sagen daß Ihre Melodien mich zu manchem Liede aufgeweckt haben und ich würde gewiß wenn wir näher zusammen lebten öfter als jetzt mich zur lyrischen Stimmung erhoben fühlen. Sie werden mir durch Mitteilung jeder Art ein wahres Vergnügen verschaffen.

"Ich lege eine Produktion bei, die ein etwas seltsames Ansehen hat. Sie ist durch den Gedanken entstanden: ob man nicht die dramatischen Balladen so ausbilden könnte daß sie zu einem größern Singstück dem Komponisten Stoff gäben. Leider hat die gegenwärtige nicht Würde genug um einen so großen Aufwand zu verdienen."

Note 25: Letter from Zelter to Goethe, September 21, 1799 (*MA* 20.1: 8–13 at 13): ". . . Ihren mir höchst schätzbaren Brief vom 26 August habe ich am 30 erhalten. *Die erste Walpurgisnacht* ist ein sehr eignes Gedicht. Die Verse sind musikalisch und singbar. Ich wollte es Ihnen in Musik gesetzt hier beilegen und habe ein gutes Teil hineingearbeitet, allein ich kann die Luft nicht finden die durch das Ganze weht und so soll es leider noch liegen bleiben. . . ."

Note 32: Letter from Zelter to Goethe, December 12, 1802 (*MA* 20.1: 28–30 at 29): "Die angenehme Nachricht, daß Sie im Begriff sind, der Welt von Ihren Schätzen mitzuteilen hat mich auch wieder erweckt und ich habe mich seitdem wieder an Ihren Gedichten versucht. Was Sie mir einst, bei Gelegenheit der *ersten Walpurgisnacht,* von der dramatischen Form der Romanzen geschrieben, bestätigte mir eine Neigung, die ich schon im Zauberlehrling zu entwickeln versucht hatte. Die Walpurgisnacht blieb aber des wegen unfertig, weil sich mir immer die alte abgetragene Kantatenuniform aufdrängte.. . ."

Note 37: Letter from Goethe to Zelter, December 3, 1812 (*MA* 20.1: 301–4 at 303–4): "Nun muß ich noch Ihre Anfrage, wegen der ersten Walpurgisnacht erwidern. Es verhält sich nämlich folgendermaßen. Unter den Geschichtforschern gibt es welche, und es sind Männer, denen man seine Achtung nicht versagen kann, die zu jeder Fabel, jeder Tradition, sie sei so phantastisch, so absurd wie sie wolle, einen realen Grund suchen, und unter der Märchenhülle jederzeit einen faktischen Kern zu finden glauben."

"Wir sind dieser Behandlungsart sehr viel Gutes schuldig: denn um darauf einzugehn gehört große Kenntnis, ja Geist, Witz, Einbildungskraft ist nötig, um auf diese Art die Poesie zur Prosa zu machen. So hat nun auch einer der deutschen Altertumsforscher die Hexen- und Teufelsfahrt des Brockengebirgs, mit der man sich in Deutschland seit undenklichen Zeiten trägt, durch einen historischen Ursprung retten und begründen wollen. Daß nämlich die deutschen Heiden Priester und Altväter, nachdem man sie aus ihren heiligen Hainen vertrieben und das Christentum dem Volke aufgedrungen, sich mit ihren treuen Anhängern auf die wüsten unzugänglichen Gebirge des Harzes, im Frühlings Anfang begeben, um dort, nach alter Weise Gebet und Flamme zu dem gestaltlosen Gott des Himmels und der Erde zu richten. Um nun gegen die ausspürenden bewaffneten Bekehrer sicher zu sein, hätten sie für gut befunden, eine Anzahl der Ihrigen zu vermummen, und hiedurch ihre abergläubischen Widersacher entfernt zu halten, und, beschützt von Teufelsfratzen den reinsten Gottesdienst zu vollenden."

"Ich habe diese Erklärung vor vielen Jahren einmal irgendwo gefunden, ich wüßte aber den Autor nicht anzugeben. Der Einfall gefiel mir, und ich habe diese fabelhafte Geschichte wieder zur poetische Fabel gemacht. . . ."

Note 38: Letter from Zelter to Goethe, December 10–13, 1812 (*MA* 20.1: 306–8 at 307): "Für Ihren Unterricht in Ansehung der ersten Walp[urgisnacht] danke ich bestens. Ich habe die Sache wirklich nach Ihrer Beschreibung, d.h. poetisch genommen und das Historische gibt sich nun von selber. Aus manchen Erfahrungen habe ich mir gemerkt, daß faktische Notizen zuweilen Anklänge veranlassen wodurch eine Art Klarheit und Wahrheit in eine Melodie kommt welche das Verständnis so aufregen daß ein Theil der Arbeit sich selber macht besonders bei mir, der ich äußerer Anregungen so sehr bedarf. . . ."

Note 39: Letter from Goethe to Mendelssohn, September 9, 1831 (*GA* 21: 1004–5): "Du hast mir, mein lieber Sohn, durch deinen ersten römischen Brief viel Freude gemacht, daß ich nun auf deinen zweiten von Luzern mich dankbar zu äußern alle Ursache habe. Ein Zwischenbrief von Mailand, den ich nach Zelterischer Anfrage empfangen haben sollte, ist nicht zu mir gekommen.

". . . Daß du die erste Walpurgisnacht dir so ernstlich zugeeignet hast, freut mich sehr; da niemand, selbst unser trefflicher Zelter, diesem Gedicht nichts abgewinnen können. Es ist im eigentlichen Sinne hoch symbolisch intentioniert. Denn es muß sich in der Weltgeschichte immerfort wiederholden, daß ein Altes, Gegründetes, Geprüftes, Beruhigendes durch auftauchende Neuerungen gedrängt, geschoben, verrückt und, wo nicht vertilgt, doch in den engsten Raum eingepfercht werde. Die Mittelzeit, wo der Haß noch gegenwirken kann und mag, ist hier prägnant genug dargestellt, und ein freudiger unzerstörbarer Enthusiasmus lodert noch einmal in Glanz und Klarheit hinauf. Diesem allen hast du gewiß Leben und Bedeutung verliehen und so möge es denn auch mir zu freudigem Genuß gedeihen. . . ."

Original Texts of Lengthy Translations in Chapter 4:

Note 5: Letter of March 1831 from Mendelssohn to Franz Hauser, quoted from Edouard Hanslick, "Aus dem Leben und der Correspondenz von Franz Hauser," in his *Suite: Aufsätze über Musik und Musiker* (Vienna: K. Prochaka, 1884), 26: "Wissen Sie wohl noch . . . daß ich an Ihrem Clavier einmal eine Stelle aus Goethe's 'Erster Walpurgisnacht' componirte: 'Doch ist es Tag, sobald man mag ein reines Herz dir bringen,' und daß ich Sie nachher sehr damit quälte, indem ich es Ihnen immer wieder vorspielte? Mir baut sich das Ding nun zusammen, und ich werde das ganze Gedicht als eine neue Sorte von Cantate componiren, für Chöre und großes Orchester; es kann bunt genug werden, denn es sind prächtige Elemente darin."

Note 7: Letter of February 22, 1831, from Mendelssohn to his family in Berlin, held in the Bodleian Library, Oxford (MS MDM d. 13, fol. 40f.), quoted from Hellmundt, "Mendelssohns Arbeit", 101. ". . . namentlich aber kann ich gar nicht sagen, wie sehr mir die neuen Sonntagsmusiken gefallen, das ist ein brillanter Einfall, u. ich bitte Dich um Gotteswillen, o Fanny laß es nicht wieder einschlafen, sondern gieb vielmehr Dein[em] reisenden Bruder Auftrag für Euch einiges Neue zu schreiben, der Mann will das gerne thun, denn er freu[t] sich gar zu sehr über Dich u. Deine Idee. . . . Ein Stück dankt d[iesen] Sonntagsmusiken wahrscheinlich seine Entstehung schon; als Du mir nämlich neulich davon schriebst dachte ich, ob [ich] nicht Dir was dazu schicken könnte, u. da tauchte denn ein alter Lieblingsplan wieder auf, dehnte sich aber [so] breit aus, daß ich Emil nichts davon mitgeben kann u. also später nachliefere. Höre und staune [!] Die erste Walpurgisnacht von Goethe habe ich seit Wien halb componirt u. keine Courage sie auf[zu]schreiben, nun hat sich das Ding gestaltet, ist aber eine große Cantate mit ganzem Orchester geworden, [und] kann sich ganz lustig machen, denn im Anfang giebt es Frühlingslieder u. dgl. vollauf, dan[n,] wenn die Wächter mit ihren Gabeln u. Zacken u. Eulen Lärm machen, kommt der Hexenspuk dazu u. [Du] weißt daß ich für den ein besonderes faible habe, dann kommen die opfernden Druiden in Cdur mit Po[saunen] heraus, dann wieder die Wächter, die sich fürchten, wo ich dann einen trippelnden, unheimlichen Chor bringen wi[ll,] u. endlich zum Schluß der volle Opfergesang—meinst Du nicht, das könne eine neue Art von Cantaten w[erden?] Eine Instrumentaleinleitung habe ich umsonst, u. lebendig ist das Ganze genug. Bald denke ich soll es fertig sein."

Note 8: Letter of March 5, 1831, translated from Hellmundt, "Mendelssohns Arbeit," 102: "Währenddessen habe ich also Zeit ruhig in der Fasten hier zu arbeiten und fleißig zu componiren; was mich seit einigen Wochen fast ausschließlich beschäftigt, ist die Musik zu dem Gedicht von Ew. Excellenz, welches die erste Walpurgisnacht heißt; ich will es mit Orchesterbegleitung als eine Art großer Cantate componiren, und der heitre Frühlingsanfang, dann die Hexerey und der Teufelsspuk, u. die feierlichen Opferchöre mitten durch könnten zur schönsten Musik Gelegenheit geben. Ich weiß nicht, ob mirs gelingen wird, aber ich fühle, wie groß die Aufgabe ist, und mit welcher Sammlung und Ehrfurcht ich sie angreifen muß."

Note 10: Letter of April 27, 1831, translated from Hellmundt, "Mendelssohns Arbeit," 102: "Ich muß aber zu meinen Hexen zurück, verzeiht, wenn ich für heut aufhöre. [. . .] Der ganze Brief schwebt eigentlich in Ungewißheit, oder ich schwebe vielmehr darin, ob ich die große Trommel nehmen d[arf] oder nicht: 'Zacken, Gabeln u. wilde Klapperstöcke' treiben mich eigentlich doch zur großen Trommel, ab[er] die Mäßigkeit räth mir ab. Ich bin auch gewiß der einzige der den Bloxberg ohne kleine Flöte componir[t,] aber um die große Trommel thäte es mir leid, u. ehe Fannys Rath ankommt, ist die Walpurgisnacht fertig u. eingepackt, ich fahre schon wieder durchs Land, u. Gott weiß, wovon dann die Rede ist; ich bin überzeugt, Fanny sagte Ja, aber ich bin doch unschlüssig. Großer Lärm muß auf jeden Fall gemacht werden."

Note 13: Letter of July 13, 1831, translated from Hellmundt, "Mendelssohns Arbeit," 103: "Ich habe auch seitdem wieder eine große Musik componirt, die auch vielleicht äußerlich mal wirken kann: 'Die erste Walpurgisnacht' von Goethe; ich fing es an, blos weil es mir gefiel u. mich warm machte, u. an die Aufführung habe ich nicht gedacht. Aber nun da es fertig vor mir liegt, sehe ich daß es zu einem großen Concertstück ser gut paßt und in meinem ersten Abonnementsconcert in Berlin mußt Du den bärtigen Druidenpriester singen, die Chöre ausgeführt von, unter gütiger Mitwirkung des etc. Ich habe Dir den Priester in die Kehle geschrieben, mit Erlaubniß, also mußt Du ihn wieder heraussingen, und wie ich bis jetzt die Erfahrung gemacht habe, daß die Stücke, die ich mit der wenigsten Rücksicht auf die Leute gemacht hatte, gerade den Leuten immer am besten gefielen so glaub ich wird es auch mit diesem Stück gehn. Ich schreibe das blos, damit Du siehst, daß ich auch ans Praktische denke. Freilich immer erst hinterher, . . ."

Note 18: Letter from Lucerne to Goethe, August 28, 1831, translated from Hellmundt, "Mendelssohns Arbeit," 105: "Daß ich die Kühnheit gehabt habe, Ihre 'erste Walpurgisnacht' zu componiren, schrieb ich Ihnen schon von Rom aus; nun habe ich sie in Mailand fertig gemacht; es ist eine Art Cantate für Chor und Orchester geworden, länger und ausgedehnter, als ich zuerste gedacht hatte, weil die Aufgabe sich ausdehnte und größer ward und mir mehr sagte, je länger ich sie mit mir herumtrug. Erlauben Sie mir, Ihnen meinen Dank zu sagen für die himmlische Worte; wenn der alte Druide sein Opfer bringt, und das Ganze feierlich und unermeßlich groß wird, da braucht man gar keine Musik erst dazu zu machen, sie liegt so klar da, es klingt Alles schon, ich habe mir immer schon die Verse vorgesungen, ohne daß ich dran dachte. Wenn ich in München wohin ich morgen abreise, und wo ich mich bis gegen Ende des Septembers aufhalten will, einen guten Chor und die Gelegenheit dazu finde, so nehme ich mir vor, es dort aufzuführen. Das einzige, was ich hoffe ist, daß man es meiner Musik anhören mag, wie tief ich die Schönheit der Worte empfunden habe."

Note 59: Letter to Karl Klingemann, November 18, 1840, translated from Karl Klingemann, [jr.], *Felix Mendelssohn Bartholdys Briefwechsel mit Legationsrat Karl Klingemann in London* (Essen: G. D. Baedecker, 1909), 251: "Zum Konzert für die alten und kranken Musiker hier soll Ende des Monats mein Lobgesang aufgeführt werden; da hab ich mir nun vorgenommen, ihn nicht noch einmal in der unvollkommenen Gestalt zu geben, wie er in Birmingham aufgeführt werden musste, meiner Krankheit wegen; und das gibt mir tüchtig zu tun. . . . Du hast übrigens mit Deinem vortrefflich gefundenen Titel viel zu verantworten; denn nicht allein schick ich das Stück nun als Symphoniekantate in die Welt, sondern ich denke auch stark daran, die erste Walpurgisnacht, welche mir seit langem da liegt, unter dieser Benennung wieder aufzunehmen, fertig zu machen und los zu werden. Sonderbar, dass ich bei der ersten Idee dazu nach Berlin schrieb, ich wolle eine Symphonie mit Chor machen; nachher keine Courage dazu hatte, weil die 3 Sätze zu lang als Einleitung wären, und doch immer das Gefühl behielt, als fehlte etwas bei der blossen Einleitung. Jetzt sollen die Symphoniesätze nach dem alten Plan hinein, und dann das Stuck heraus. Kennst Du es denn? Ich glaube nicht, dass es viel für Aufführungen taugt, und habe es doch so gern."

Note 63: Letter from Mendelssohn to Fanny Hensel, January 13, 1843, translated from Hellmundt, "Mendelssohns Arbeit," 110: ". . . die Geschäfte und Arbeiten (äußerliche) drängen sich auch diesmal wieder sehr, und machen mich recht wüst. Wogegen das ruhige Notenschreiben, in dem kleinen Kämmerchen, das ich mir dazu eingerichtet habe, mein bestes und einziges Trost- und Zerstreuungsmittel ist. Ich hatte, wie ich Dir schon früher schrieb, zum Glück die ganze Walpurgisnacht umgeschrieben, aber blos den 4 stimmigen Chor, weil es in 8 Tagen gesungen werden sollte, und die Proben schon angefangen hatten; nun war noch das ganze Orchester aufzuschreiben, und die Masse kleiner Details, die da hineinkommen mußten, waren das erste u. einzige wie gesagt, was mich wirklich beschäftige, nicht blos scheinbar. Sie ist jetzt längst ferig, und ich glaube, selbst Du, die das Frühere so genau kannte, wie keine Seele außer mir, wirst Dich wundern, wie unglaublich das Ganze nun besser geworden ist. Ich kann jetzt den Gedanken gar nicht leiden, daß irgend jemand es in der ersten Bearbeitung kennt; denn alles was gut darin war, und geblieben ist, bekommt erst seine rechte Bedeutung indem das Mangelhafte und Verfehlte weggefallen und ersetzt ist."

Note 64: Letter of January 17, 1843, from Mendelssohn to Klingemann, translated from Klingemann, *Briefwechsel*, 279: ". . . In den Tagen vor dem 11. hatte ich unternommen, was ich mir schon lange vorgesetzt hatte, meine Walpurgisnacht neu aufzuschreiben, und hatte von der ganzen dicken Partitur die Singstimmen aufgeschrieben und kopieren lassen, hatte schon dran probiert, denn es sollte bei Anwesenheit des Königs gegeben werden. Da wurde ich nach Berlin gerufen, und nach wochenlanger Unterbrechung fing ich nun auf meinem kleinem Arbeitsstübchen . . . die Instrumente dazu zu schreiben."

Note 81: Letter of February 4, 1844, from Mendelssohn to Friedrich Kistner, translated from Elvers, *Verleger*, 326: "Lieber Herr Kistner [paragraph break:] Empfangen Sie den schönsten Dank für die superbe Ausstattung meiner Walpurgisnacht, deren 3 Exemplare ich gestern empfing, und nun gar für das prächtige Pracht-Exemplar, das heut nachfolgte. Das ist wirklich etwas Einziges, wie Sie diese Sachen auszuschmücken verstehen, und wie es deutlich und zierlich und zweckmäßig zugleich ist! Vielen, vielen Dank dafür. Ich bedarf weder von Singstimmen noch vom Clavier-Auszug mehr, als Sie so freundlich waren mir zu schicken, und sollte ich später davon bedürfen, so würde ich mich auf Ihr gütiges Anerbieten berufen und es mir zu Nutz machen. Wenn Hr. Otten in Hamburg und der Musikverein in Zwiebrücken sich um Singstimmen &c. bei Ihnen gemeldet haben sollten, so thun Sie mir wohl den Gefallen die Sendung sobald es thunlich ist zu bewirken. . . ."

Note 88: Becker, "Die erste Walpurgisnacht," 65–66: "Die höchste Idee des Schönen, geoffenbart in einem Meisterwerke der Kunst, läßt sich nur bis auf einen gewissen Punct analysiren, und der Versuch, die heilige *Dreieinigkeit* des Wahren, Schönen und Guten als eine *Dreifaltigkeit* in ihm darzuthun, gehört meist jenen abstracten Speculationen an, welche gar zu leicht ihre praktische Bedeutsamkeit für die Kunst und namentlich für die Musiker verlieren. Dagegen bleibt gewiß, daß, je größer ein Kunstwerk ist, es auch um so größere Bewegungen in unserm künstlerischen Bewußtsein hervorruft; daß, je entschiedener und bedeutungsvoller es uns entgegentritt, wir ihm auch unwillkührlich entschiedenere Auffassung und bedeutungsvolleres Urtheil bieten. . . . Die Wahrheit geht ja stets, sei es früher oder später, siegreich aus allen Kämpfen hervor! Auch Mendelssohn-Bartholdy theilt in dieser Beziehung das Loos aller hervorragenden Geister ihrer Zeit!—

"Wenden wir uns nun nach diesen einleitenden Bemerkungen, die uns gleichwohl ein Wort zu seiner Zeit dünkten, seinem letzt erschienenen Werke, der 'ersten Walpurgisnacht' zu, so wissen wir in der That nicht, zu welcher der bekannten Gattungen der Gesangscompositionen wir diese in Erfindung wie Ausführung großartige Tondichtung zählen sollen. . . . So viel ist gewiß, daß der Name

Oratorium, welchen auch der von diesem Werke begeisterte Hector Berlioz für die Walpurgisnacht offenbar in Ermangelung eines bezeichnenderen vorschlägt, schon deshalb nicht geeignet sei, weil das Oratorium, streng genommen, nur der Kirche angehört, und der Name 'weltliches Oratorium' nur dadurch entschuldigt werden kann, daß man den Begriff Oratorium blos auf die äußere musikalische Form anwendete und das 'weltlich' auf dem gewählten Stoff bezog, der jeder andere, nur kein geistlicher sein durfte. Noch weniger reicht der Name 'Cantate' dafür aus, da in ihr das lyrische, dagegen in vorliegendem Stoffe das epische Element vorherrscht. . . . Obwohl nun vorliegendes Werk das, was wir Musiker unter Ballade verstehen, weit überbietet, so dürfte noch dieser Name der bezeichnendste sein, um so mehr, als das Gedicht denselben bedingt. Bedarf es einer besondern Bezeichnung für den Musik zum Unterschied dieser von den bisher bekannten, so wäre vielleicht 'Concertballade' der entsprechendste."

Note 91: Becker, "Die erste Walpurgisnacht," 72: "So begrüßte denn der hohe Meister mit diesem Werk auf's Neue den deutschen Genius, nachdem er als Componist der 'Antigone' und des 'Sommernachtstraumes' den Dichterheroen Griechenlands und Brianniens einen Lorbeerzweig in ihre unverwelkliche Ruhmes-Krone geflochten.—Freue dich dessen, mein Deutschland, und bedenke, daß es deiner größten Dichter einer war, der das an der Spitze unseres Aufsatzes als Motto stehende Wort sprach, gleich als gälte es einem deiner größten Tondichter, Mendelssohn-Bartholdy!"

Original Texts of Lengthy Translations in Chapter 6:

Note 54: Goethe, *Über Kunst und Altertum* 6, no. 1 (1827) (*GA* 14: 890): ". . . ein Künstler, dem man ein entschiedenes Talent nicht ableugnet, dessen wilde Art jedoch, womit er davon Gebrauch macht, das Ungestüm seiner Konzeptionen, das Getümmel seiner Kompositionen, die Gewaltsamkeit der Stellungen und die Roheit des Kolorits keineswegs billigen will. Deshalb aber ist er eben der Mann, sich in den Faust zu versenken und wahrscheinlich Bilder hervorzubringen, an die niemand hätte denken können."

Note 55: Goethe *Über Kunst und Altertum* 6, no. 2 (1828) (*GA* 14: 953–54): ". . . Herr Delacroix scheint hier in einem wunderlichen Erzeugnis zwischen Himmel und Erde, Möglichem und Unmöglichem, Rohstem und Zartestem, und zwischen welchen Gegensätzen noch weiter Phantasie ihr verwegnes Spiel treiben mag, sich heimatlich gefühlt und wie in dem Seinigen ergangen zu haben. Dadurch wird denn jener Prachtglanz wieder gedämpft, der Geist vom klaren Buchstaben in eine düstere Welt geführt und die uralte Empfindung einer märchenhaften Erzählung wieder aufgeregt. . . ."

Note 77: Adami, "Die erste Walpurgisnacht," 113–14: "Die erste Walpurgisnacht ist ein Werk, das wirklich Epoche in der Kunstwelt machen wird, und unbedenklich *Mendelssohn's* schönste Schöpfung genannt werden kann. Ich mißtraute einigermaßen dem Ausspruche des fantasiereichen und enthusiastischen *Berlioz*, den ich vor einigen Monataen im 'Journal des débats' gelesen hatte; denn die Begeisterung, die den Componisten erhebt und befähigt, steht dem Kunstrichter nur schlecht an und man muß nüchtern sein, wenn mann ein gründliches Urtheil fällen will. Aber hier hat *Berlioz* nicht zu viel gesagt. Ueber die gründlichen musikalischen Kenntnisse, die ausgezeichnete Orchestration, die Auffassungsgabe, die innige Bekanntschaft *Mendelssohns* mit allen Hilfsmitteln der Kunst, herrscht schon lange nur eine Stime in der musikalischen Welt und die auswärtigen Zeitschrften haben nicht gesäumt, seinen Ruf nach Kräften zu verbreiten. Bei uns, die wir an *Mozart* und *Beethoven* gewöhnt sind, hatte er noch im eigentlichen Sinne nicht gezündet; sein größtes Werk, das Oratorium: 'Paulus,' ist, trotz vieler Schönheiten, etwas gedehnt; seine Ouvertüre zum 'Sommernachtstraum' verdankte den Erfolg der vortrefflichen Aufführung in den philharmonischen Concerten und wir hatte Mühe, uns mit seiner strengen, fast puritanischen Manier, welcher der Genius des alten *Sebastian Bach* sichtbar zum Grunde lag, zu befreunden; bei vieler Bewegung in der Begleitung, bei reicher Anwendung der Kunstmittel vermißten wir die breiten melodischen Gedanken, an welchen wir in musikalischen Werken gewöhnt oder verwöhnt sind, und hauptsächlich die hinreißende Gluth, welche besonders *Beethovens* Schöpfungen belebt und ihren Eindruck unwiderstehlich macht. In der "Walpurgisnacht" ist *Mendelssohn* Hand in Hand und gleichen Schrittes mit dem Altvater *Goethe* gegangen und siehe! der Wurf ist ihm gelungen, und es ist eine Schöpfung entstanden, die Wiederhall in der Welt finden wird und muß. Wer aber tief in diese herrliche Dichtung eingedrungen ist, wer sie verstanden hat, sei er auch kein Künstler, hat schon ein Kunstwerk erschaffen, in seinem Innern zwar nur, aber seine Seele fühlt sich erhoben, und schwebt hoch empor über das gewöhnliche Dasein. Man hat Goethe verketzert, weil er das gewöhnliche Kannegießern, das Drängen um Stellen, den Ruf: 'Hebe dich da weg, damit ich mich hinsetze,' nicht leiden mochte. Aber er hat die schönen Verse gedichtet . . ."

Note 79: Adami, "Die erste Walpurgisnacht," 114: ". . . Daß *Goethe* das Licht nicht rauben wollte, ist doch so unverkennbar, und nicht zu bestreiten, und somit zerfallen viele der gegen ihn erhobenen Beschuldigungen in ihr Nichts zurück. Diesen Weltstoff, mit seinen erhaben-ernsten, seinen humoristischen Partien, mit seinem Jammer und seinem Entzücken, hat *Mendelssohn* echt poetisch aufgefaßt, und die musikalische Dichtung trägt ganz das wahre Gepräge einer Meisterarbeit; die schönen Glieder sind nothwendig verbunden, Solostimmen und Chor wechseln effectvoll mit einander ab, die Gedanken sind neu, wirkungsreich, den Worten stets angemessen, es herrscht im Ganzen ein üppiger, reicher Wechsel, Alles tritt gehörig heraus, trotz der reichen, überall klaren Figuren der Instrumente, und das Ganze ist ein Guß, oder vielmehr der schöne Lauf eines breiten Flußes an anmuthigen Ufern vorüber, in das weite, ruhige, von der glänzendsten Sonne bestrahlte Meer, wo der Gedanke wohlthuend ruhen kann beim Anblicke der Unendlichkeit, im Genusse der Wunder der Schöpfung: dieser Stoff sagt der Individualität des Componisten zu, das fühlt man bei jedem Tacte, und seine Arbeit flieht ihm um die Stirne wie eine glänzende Lorbeerkrone. Vielleicht wäre einem anderen Componisten ein anderes Bild zur Ouvertüre beigefallen; den Uebergang des Winters zum Frühlinge in Tönen zu schildern, lag aber in der Individualität *Mendelssohns,* und ist ihm gelungen. Ich will mit ihm darüber nicht streiten. Frisch und erhebend ist der erste Chor mit Tenorsolo, so wie die effectreiche Stretta; characteristisch der Gesang der alten Frau mit dem Weiberchor, erhaben die vom Druiden vorgetragene Melodie; doch noch wirkungsreicher der herrliche Chor: 'Vertheilt euch [wackre Männer] hier!' Der darauf folgende: 'Kommt mit Hacken [*sic*] und mit Gabeln,' ist wahrhaft genial. Welche Abwechslung! welcher Effect! wie geistreich die Instrumentirung, die Vertheilung der Stimmen! Ernst und mit innerem Grimme singt darauf der Druide die Worte: So weit gebracht u. s. w. Die Wächter fliehen und den imposanten Schluß bilden die schon angeführten Verse, der Schlußstein des Ganzen. . Ich wiederhole es, dieses Werk, das keine zu großen Schwierigkeiten bietet, wird überall im hohen Grade gefallen und, wie ich hoffe, auch bald aufgeführt werden. Es erhielt verdiente Anerkennung und am Schlusse großen Beifall. Daß dieser nach den einzelnen Nummern nicht immer laut wurde, liegt wohl in dem Baue der Cantate, die ein Ganzes bildet und keine einzelnen Arien, Duette oder Chöre darbietet, die, mit einem gewöhnlichen Schlusse versehen, dem meistens zerstreuten Publikum zu sagen scheinen: Jetzt bin ich zu Ende, plaudite. Dichtung und Musik sind tief und wollen im Innersten erfaßt werden, das aber nicht immer Sache der Zuhörer bei einem ganz neuen Werke ist."

Note 82: Kreutzer, "Société des Concerts et Société Saint-Cécile (2e article)," 121: "Tel est le sujet très-extraordinaire de l'une des ballades de Gúthe. Est-ce une tradition recueillie? Est-ce une dérision du culte des chrétiens, ce que, dans son scepticisme, Gœthe se permettait volontiers? Je ne sais ; mais ce que je ne puis m'expliquer, c'est la singulière traduction que M. Bélanger a faite de cette ballade. Mendelssohn, en traçant les premiers morceaux de son œuvre, a dû chercher une couleur originale et sévère qui exprimât les sombres profondeurs des forêts séculaires, qui nous peignit ces druides aux traits austères, à la robe blanche et à la ceinture d'or. Devinez . . . des bohémiens. D'un trait de plume, M. Bélanger a fait disparaître les druides et leurs forêts, puis il leur a substitué quelle sort de gens? Quant aux soldats chrétiens, ils deviendront des archers. Des archers, cela ne compromet pas; des archers, il y en a partout. A leur tour, les gardiens des forêts druidiques seront transformés en nécromants et en sorciers. Par ces substitutions tout le caractère de l'œuvre disparaît: en prend au sérieux la *Nuit du sabbat,* qui n'est qu'une plaisanterie, un bon tour joué à des soldats peureux, et en définitive on compromet le nom du grand poëte allemand—Je ne demande pas que le christianisme intervienne dans cette ballade où le burlesque est mêlé au grandiose: mais qu'on nous laisse au moins les druides et qu'on leur cherche d'autres ennemis que des archers sur qui ils puissent exercer leurs sortiléges [*sic*]. Des archers et des bohémiens! j'y reviens. . . ."

Note 83 : Kreutzer, "Société des Concerts et Société Saint-Cécile (2e article)," 121: "C'est l'hiver glace du Nord, alors que les sapins secouent mélancoliquement leur noire chevelure poudrée de neige ; alors que la gelée a surpris et glacé la cascade dans sa chute, qui tout est nuit et silence au fond des forêts, et qu'un pâle soleil verse une faible lumière à travers les nuages chargés de frimas et de grêle. Comment tout cela est-il exprimé par la musique de Mendelssohn? Allez l'entendre. Lorsque l'impression est aussi profonde, il vaut mieux la constater que rechercher les moyens dont le compositeur s'est servi pour la produire."

Note 85 : Kreutzer, "Société des Concerts et Société Saint-Cécile (2e article)," 122: "La veritable scène du sabbat qui vient ensuite est e morceau le plus important après l'ouverture. Choisir les moyens d'effet, distribuer habilement les couleurs, tel est le secret de la musique pittoresque. La mélodie dans des morceaux de cette nature, est impuissant à reproduire la pensée. L'harmonie, le rhythme [*sic*], et surtout le mélange des sonorités, telles sont les ressources offertes au compositeur. Mendelssohn les a habilement employées. Ainsi rien n'est plus saisissant que l'effet *pp.* de la grosse caisse unie aux cymbales qui commence cette grande scène: c'est véritablement une évocation funèbre . . . La lune semble se voiler comme pour un mystère, la forêt solitaire se peuple de fantômes étranges et monstrueux. Avec les violons qui sifflent à l'aigu, descendent des essaims de sorcières à cheval sur le balai classique ; avec le murmure des basses, les sourds mugissement des trombones, les tombeaux s'en trouvent et vomissent leurs pâles hôtes ; avec le cri aigu de la petite flûte, un démon donne le signal de la ronde infernale. La vallée était déserte, elle fourmille maintenant d'êtres sans nom. Aux premiers accords, un hibou, ennuyé de tout ce tapage, s'envole du creux d'un vieux tronc. On entend le bruit sinistre de ses ailes assourdi par la plume épaisse qui les couvre. Comment cet effet a-t-il été obtenu ? Un basson, instrument dont le timbre au médium et mat, presque hideux, exécute sur une même note une série de notes prodigieusement rapides : ce sont les battements accélérés des ailes de notre hibou qui fuit discrètement vers un asile plus tranquille. Telle est l'interprétation que je fais du plus étrange des passages. Je la crois bonne ; peut-être mon voisin en a-t-il fait une autre qu'il croit bonne également ; je regretterais cependant qu'on me prouvait que j'ai tort, car je trouve que ce nouvel acteur joue un rôle aussi imprévu qu'intéressant. . . ."

Note 92: Devrient, *Meine Erinnerungen an Felix Mendelssohn-Bartholdy*, 156: "Vier Concerte gab er im Concertsaale des Schauspielhauses vom November bis Januar, und darin unter anderen seiner Compositionen zum ersten Male: 'Die erste Walpurgisnacht,' woran er hier noch vielfach geändert hatte. Schon hier trat mir der Eindruck, den eine dramatische Aufführung dieser Cantate hervorbringen müßte, lebhaft vor Augen. Als ich Felix davon sagte, erwiderte er nachdenklich: 'Kann sein; versuch's einmal.' Das will ich—antwortete ich—sobald einmal eine Bühne zu meiner Verfügung steht."

Note 106: Zauder, *Ueber Mendelssohn's* Walpurgisnacht, 32: "Von dem am Schluß der Nummer (wie immer) dreimal hinter einander gesungenen 'Kommt' greift das letzte schon in die Nr. 7. gerade wie das letzte 'Kommt' aus Nr. 5. in Nr. 6. hinüber schlug. Ebenso folgt auch hier ein Instrumentalsatz, den ersten Takt mit dem 'Kommt' mitgerechnet 20 Takte zählend, äußerlich, gleich dem obigen, die Einleitung zu der neuen Nummer bildend, innerlich aber viel mehr mit der vorigen zusammenhängend, und mehr aus ihr hinaus, als in die neue hineinleitend, jedesfalls den Uebergang vermittelnd. Sehr richtig scheint es empfunden, daß ein so ausgedehnter und ausgearbeiteter Satz, wie der eben dagewesene, besonderer Theile zur Verbindung mit den Nachbarstücken bedarf. Sehr geistreich ist dieselbe hier bewerkstelligt. Nicht nur daß der in der Orchesterbegleitung der Nr. 6. mehrfach eingetretene 2/4 Takt (während die Singstimmen den 6/8 konsequent festhielten) gegen den Schluß wiederkehrend den 6/8 Takt allmählig verdrängt, indem er den 6. und 5. Takt vom Ende, und dann wieder den vorletzten und letzten einnimmt, worauf dann Nr. 7., *L'istesso Tempo*, in diesem 2/4 Takt beginnt; sondern die Figuren dieses neuen Anfangs kehren aus der zweitvorhergehenden Nr. 5. (und nicht aus Nr. 6.) wieder, so daß nun aus der wilden Nr. 6. ebenso hinaus, wie früher in sie hineingeleitet wurde, wodurch die Besonderheit dieser Scene so recht hervorgehoben, und es dem Zuhörer bemerklich gemacht wird, daß er nun wieder zu dem vorhin verlassenen Wege zurückkehrt. In dem *Diminuendo* der vier letzten Takte dieses Orchester-Uebergangssatzes, in welchem wir alle für die vorherige Scene charakterischen Instrumente (Piccoloflöte, große Trommel und Becken) zum letzten Male gleichsam noch ganz aus der Ferne vernehmen, und während auch der oben bezeichnete in Nr. 6. einführende Paukenwirbel hinausführend sich wieder vernehmen läßt, erbleicht das Bild ganz nach Art der *Dissolving views,* und es entsteht vor uns rasch ein neues, nämlich das Bild des Opferplatzes der Druiden mit dem Allvater von dem Priester und dem Volke gebrachten Opfer, indem plötzlich ein *Andante Maestoso* im 4/4 Takt mit einem starken Eintritt des Orchesters anhebt, welcher sich für uns als eigentlicher Anfang von Nr. 7. gestaltet."

Notes

Preface

1. Program from premiere of revised version of Mendelssohn's *Die erste Walpurgisnacht*, Gewandhaus Orchestra Leipzig, concert of February 2, 1843: "('In den letzten Zeiten des Heidenthums in Deutschland, wurden von den Christen die Opfer der Druiden bei Todesstrafe untersagt. Trotz dem suchten die Druiden und das Volk zu Anfang des Frühlings die Höhen der Berge zu gewinnen, dort ihre Opfer zu bringen, und die christlichen Krieger (gewöhnlich durch deren Furcht vor dem Teufel) einzuschüchtern und zu verjagen. Auf solche Versuche soll sich die Sage von der ersten Walpurgisnacht gründen.')"

Chapter One

Epigraph. William James, *A Pluralistic Universe: Hilbert Lectures at Manchester College on the Present Situation in Philosophy* (New York: Longmans, Green, and Co., 1928), 21.

Epigraph. Stefan Zweig, "Anmerkung zum *Ulysses*," *Die neue Rundschau* 34 (1928): 476–79, quoted from *James Joyce: The Critical Heritage*, ed. and trans. Robert H. Deming (New York: Barnes and Noble, 1970; reprint, London: Routledge: 1977), 2: 444–46 at 444.

1. See chapter 4.
2. See Eyck, *Religion and Politics in German History*, 17–18; further, William Harvey Maehl, *Germany in Western Civilization* (University: University of Alabama Press, 1979), 25–29.
3. The best description of these tribes as they existed prior to Charlemagne and converted under his reign is still Wenskus, "Die deutschen Stämme im Reiche Karls des Grossen."
4. See Patrick J. Geary, *Before France and Germany: The Creation and Transformation of the Merovingian World* (New York: Oxford University Press, 1988), 84–86.
5. See Émile Benveniste, *Le Vocabulaire des institutions indo-européennes* (Paris: Les editions de minuit, 1969), 1: 279–92; further, Augustyn, *Semiotics of Fate*, 26–27.
6. The dark sides of this orientation were that an individual's exclusion from the sib was equivalent to death, and that interpersonal conflicts played out on a collective rather than individual basis: like the Montagues and Capulets, the Germanic tribes exacted vengeance not from specific offending individuals, but from any member of their sib or the sib itself. In return, the sib protected the individual and provided for a peaceful existence that transcended the visible world. See Augustyn, *Semiotics of Fate*, 26–27.
7. The Roman historian Tacitus (56-ca. 120 CE) reported in his *Germania* (ca. 98 CE) that "In general, they [the Germans] judge it not to be in keeping with the majesty of heavenly beings to confine them within walls or to portray them in any human likeness. They consecrate woods and groves and apply the names of gods to that mysterious presence

which they see only with the eye of devotion." See Tacitus, *Agricola and Germany*, 42. For a detailed discussion, see Grimm, *Deutsche Mythologie*, vol. 1, 53–71.
8. Grimm, *Deutsche Mythologie*, vol. 1, 328–62; Chantepie de la Sausaye, *The Religion of the Teutons*, 102–3; Paul Herrmann, *Das altgermanische Priesterwesen* (Jena: Eugen Diedrichs, 1929), 16–21 and 51–65; Jones and Pennick, *Pagan Europe*, 114–15.
9. For summaries of these structures, see especially Grimm, *Deutsche Mythologie*, vol. 1, 81–281, and Jones and Pennick, *Pagan Europe*, 111–37.
10. Wuotan is of course familiar to many readers in a romanticized version based on later Germanic religion from Wagner's *Der Ring des Nibelungen*. For a historical discussion, see Grimm, *Deutsche Mythologie*, vol. 1, 109–37.
11. Ragnarök is early Germanic religion's counterpart to the later Ragnarøkkr ("Twilight of the Gods"), which forms the last music drama in Wagner's *Ring* cycle. The latter represents a Christianized view of the end of the world. See Augustyn, *Semiotics of Fate*, 147–62.
12. For an elegant series of studies of the tribes' views on life and death, see Bauschatz, *The Well and the Tree*; further, Augustyn, *Semiotics of Fate*, esp. 25–146.
13. See chapter 2 (pp. 34–35).
14. See Eyck, *Religion and Politics in German History*, 24–31.
15. The popes named Stephen in this group are sometimes considered Stephen III and IV but because Pope Stephen II's predecessor (elected in 752) died just two days after his election and was not consecrated, he is generally not reckoned in the papal succession.
16. Eyck, *Religion and Politics in German History*, 33–34.
17. After Christ and Moses, Boniface would prove to be the most popular subject of inspiration for oratorios in the nineteenth century; see Sposato, *The Price of Assimilation*, 94. I wish to thank Prof. Sposato for sharing his work with me in advance of its publication.
18. See Winston, *Charlemagne*, 201–6.
19. See Einhard, *The Life of Charlemagne*, 31–32.
20. Ibid., 30–31.
21. Robertson, *A History of the Christian Church*, 3: 80.
22. See C. H. Talbot, *The Anglo-Saxon Missionaries in Germany, Being the Lives of SS. Willibrord, Boniface, Sturm, Leoba, and Lebuin* (New York: Sheed and Ward, 1954), 55–58.
23. See "Yggdrasill," in *Encyclopædia Britannica* from *Encyclopædia Britannica Online*, http://search.eb.com/eb/article-9077958 (accessed December 14, 2006); further, Grimm, *Deutsche Mythologie*, vol. 1, 95–99; and especially Erich Jung, *Germanischer Götter und Helden in christlicher Zeit: Urkunden und Betrachtungen zur deutschen Glaubensgeschichte, Rechtsgeschichte, Kunstgeschichte und allgemeinen Geistesgeschichte* (Munich: J. F. Lehmann, 1939), 118–37.
24. Translated from the official court history known as the Royal Frankish Annals (*Annales regni Francorum*); see Scholz and Rogers, *Carolingian Chronicles*, 51. The best compact English account of the "Saxon Wars" is found in Winston, *Charlemagne*, 78–79, but the wars have developed a voluminous literature in German scholarship. See especially Wenskus, "Die deutschen Stämme im Reiche Karls des Grossen," vol. 1, 178–219; and Brandi, "Karl des Grossen Sachsenkriege," 3–28.
25. See Scholz and Rogers, *Carolingian Chronicles*, 59–61; Chamberlin, *The Emperor Charlemagne*, 132–38; and Kahl, "Karl der Grosse und die Sachsen," 49–130; and Lintzel, "Untersuchungen zur Geschichte der alten Sachsen" (1928 and 1934). Other historians have disputed the number who fell at the Verden massacre, and some have estimated the count to have been as low (!) as about 500. See Bauer, "Die Quellen für das sogenannte Blutbad von Verden," in Lammers, *Die Eingliederung der Sachsen*, 109–50; von Klocke, "Um das Blutbad von Verden und die Schlacht am Süntel 782," in Lammers, *Die Eingliederung der Sachsen*, 151–204; Rundnagel, "Der Tag von Verden," in Lammers, *Die Eingliederung der*

Sachsen, 205–42; and Schmitt, "Das Gericht zu Verden 782," in Lammers, *Die Eingliederung der Sachsen*, 243–60.

26. See Rochholz, *Drei Gaugöttinnen*, 80–81; also accessible through Project Gutenberg, www.gutenberg.org/etext/12012 (accessed October 10, 2005).

27. See Grimm, *Deutsche Mythologie*, vol. 2, 878; and especially W. G. Soldan and Henriette Heppe, *Geschichte der Hexenprozesse*, 3rd ed., ed. Max Bauer (Munich: G. Müller, 1912; rpt. Cologne: Parkland, 1999), vol. 1, 301–6.

28. Rochholz, *Drei Gaugöttinnen*, 80.

29. Ibid., 83–84.

30. The above information is consolidated from a number of nineteenth-century studies concerning Wuotan and the mythical process of his selection of the consort; central to most of these studies is Jacob Grimm, "Ueber den Liebesgott," *Philologische und historische Abhandlungen der Königlichen Akademie der Wissenschaften zu Berlin* 36 (1851): 141–56. More easily accessible today is Rochholz, *Drei Gaugöttinnen*, 86–88.

31. The main difficulty in this issue is that the earliest known life of Walpurgis (by Wolfhard of Herrieden) was undertaken more than a century after her death. For a review of the state of research and a meticulously annotated modern edition with German translation see Bauch, *Quellen*, vols. 1 and 2. See Mengs, *Schrifttum zum Leben.*

32. The third miracle that belongs to most accounts is unrelated to the Walpurgis Night legends. This miracle concerns the abbess's healing of a sick maiden; see Bauch, *Quellen*, vol. 1, 256–61.

33. Surius, *Kurtzer Begriff*, 5–6.

34. Trans. from Bauch, *Quellen*, vol. 1, 255–57.

35. The Brocken's coordinates are 51° 48′ 5″ N, 10° 36′ 53″ E.

36. The literature on the subject of the witch hunts is voluminous. Of particular relevance to this study are Ankarloo, Clark, and Monter, *Period of the Witch Trials*; Bailey, *Battling Demons*; Wolfgang Behringer, *Witchcraft Persecutions in Bavaria*; Droß, *Die erste Walpurgisnacht*; Midelfort, *Witch Hunting in Southwestern Germany*; and Scholz Williams, *Defining Dominion.*

37. See Gynz-Rekowski and Gerig, *Der Brocken*, 34–35.

38. A seventy-five-line poem dating from ca. 1300 written in German but stemming from Poland or Lithuania describes the conjurations of a long series of loathsome supernatural creatures who traveled to the "Brochelsberge" for their Sabbaths. Similarly, a manuscript copy of a treatise on the history of the Saxons written ca. 1456 noted that "old women and matrons, seduced by all manner of devilish deception, believed that they had ridden or flown on stags or other household items up to 'Brockensberg (montes Brockensberg),' where they held councils." See Jacobs, *Der Brocken*, 25, 29.

39. Montague Summers, ed. and trans., *The Malleus Maleficarum of Heinrich Kramer and James Sprenger*, online edition, ed. Wicasta Lovelace and Edo Nyland ([n.p.]: Windhaven Network, 1998–2000), 579. See www.malleusmaleficarum.org/mmtoc.html (accessed August 12, 2006).

40. Jakob Sprenger and Heinrich Institoris [pseud. Heinrich Krämer], *Malleus maleficarum* (Cologne, [ca. 1487]). See Segl, *Der Hexenhammer.*

41. This attribute—or symptom—is implicit already in the treatise's title, for "maleficarum" refers to "female evildoers." See Brauner, and ed. Brown, *Fearless Wives and Frightened Shrews*, 34.

42. Summers, *The Malleus Maleficarum*, 99–118.

43. See Brauner, *Fearless Wives and Frightened Shrews*, 29–49.

44. See Grimm, *Deutsche Mythologie*, vol. 2, 878–86 for a detailed pre-*Malleus* account of reports of the so-called witches' ride (*Hexenfahrt*).

45. Ulrich Molitor, *De Lamiis et phitoricus mulieribus* (Strassburg: Johann Prüss, [1489]). Reprinted many times and translated into a variety of languages, Molitor's treatise was written ca. 1430.
46. In the German-speaking lands these evil meeting places included, along with the Brocken, the Heuberg (near Freiburg im Breisgau), the Staffelberg (near Lichtenfels in northern Bavaria), and the Venusberg (near Bonn); see Jacobs, *Der Brocken*, 31.
47. See Hoffmann, *Der Brocken*, 15.
48. See Droß, *Die erste Walpurgisnacht*, 171; Soldan, Heppe, and Bauer, *Geschichte der Hexenprozesse*, vol. 1, 514.
49. *Blockes-Berges Verrichtung oder ausführlicher geographischer Bericht von den hohen trefflich alt- und berühmten Blockes-Berge: ingleichen von der Hexenfahrt und Zauber-Sabbathe, so auff solchen Berge die Unholden aus gantz Teutschland Jährlich den 1. Maij in Sanct-Walpurgis-Nachte anstellen sollen; Aus vielen Autoribus abgefasset und mit schönen Raritäten angeschmücket sampt zugehörigen Figuren; Nebenst einen Appendice vom Blockes-Berge wie auch des Alten Reinsteins und der Baumans Höle am Hartz* (Leipzig: Johann Scheiben, [1668]). The full title of Schulze's treatise reads, in English: "Blocksberg Performance, or detailed geographic account of the high, excellent, old, and famous Blocksberg; also of the witches' flights and sorcerer's Sabbath, which evil creatures from throughout Germany are supposed to hold every year on the 1st of May, the eve of St. Walpurgis Day; compiled from [the works of] many authorities and adorned with fair rarities and their attendant illustrations, as well as an appendix from the Blocksberg as well as the Old Reinstein [Castle] and the Baumann Cave in the Harz Mountains."
50. Hoffmann, *Der Brocken*, 21.
51. See Scholz Williams, "Confronting the Early Modern Other"; Hoffmann, *Der Brocken*, 21; Cohn, *Europe's Inner Demons*.
52. On Goethe's use of Praetorius's book, see chapter 3. Concerning Heine's, see Henning, "Johannes Praetorius und sein Hexenbuch von 1668," in Praetorius, *Blockes-Berges Verrichtung*, I–XXV and XXII–XXV.
53. [Fischer], *Das Buch vom Aberglauben*, [i].
54. Ibid., 125.
55. Ibid., 125–27. For original German, see appendix A.
56. Ibid., 129. For original German, see appendix A.
57. Honemann, *Die Alterthümer des Harzes*, vol. 1, 11–12. For original German, see appendix A.
58. Friedrich Maurer, "Der Brocken: (Aus einer Sammlung ungedruckter Briefe, über den Harz, und die hessischen Lande)." *Berlinisches Archiv der Zeit und ihres Geschmacks* 2 (1796): 519–44. For original German, see appendix A.
59. Maurer, "Der Brocken," 535–37. For original German, see Appendix A.
60. This is doubtless the same count cited in Honemann's *Alterthümer des Harzes* (see above).
61. Maurer, "Der Brocken," 540: ". . . um der nächtlichen Mummerei, dem Tanze, und den übrigen vielleicht nicht sehr züchtigen Freuden, des ihnen zunächst gelegenen Opferplätzes, beizuwohnen."
62. Maurer, "Der Brocken," 541: "So entstand der in der Folge so mörderische Wahnglaube, daß dieser oder jeder Mann eine Hexe zur Frau habe, die in der Mainacht nach dem Brocken reise, um mit dem Teufel zu tanzen."
63. Maurer, "Der Brocken," 540: "Man darf es übrigens nicht unwahrscheinlich finden, daß die heidniscen Sachsen, einer so guten Religion wie die christlichen, sich so halsstarrig widersetzten. . . . Wer hält nicht fest an der Religion seiner Väter?"
64. See chapter 3, pp. 69–73.
65. The title page of Vulpius's book gives the publisher as "Bachdad, bei Beezelbub," but these are topically appropriate fanciful pseudonyms for Leipzig: Reinick. Vulpius was the

brother of Christiane von Goethe (1765–1816), whom Goethe befriended in 1788 and married in 1806. For a vivid account of the development of their relationship, see Boyle, *Goethe*, esp. vol. 1, 537–39.
66. Vulpius, *Hexenfahrte*, IV–V, VI–VII. "Zwar giebt es . . . Zweifler, welche gänzlich die Würklichkeit froher Nächte auf der kahlen Spitze dies Hügels leugnen . . . allein was gehen uns die Zweifler an, die wir zu gewis überzeugt sind, daß unsre Urältern nicht auf den Kopf gefallen, und getrost annehmen, was sie uns sagten."
67. See Frazer, *The Golden Bough*, vol. 6, 158–69.
68. See Brauner, *Fearless Wives and Frightened Shrews*, 1–27.
69. Frazer, *The Golden Bough*, vol. 6, 159.
70. Ibid., 160.
71. Ibid., 161.
72. Such as running about the fields blowing on tin horns and banging on other metal objects; see Frazer, *Golden Bough*, vol. 6, 159–61.
73. The finest exploration of these complexities of transmission is found in Brauner, *Fearless Wives and Frightened Shrews*, esp. 1–28 and 111–19.

Chapter Two

1. In accordance with its application by sociologist Pierre Bourdieu, I use the term "habitus" to mean the totality of nondiscursive knowledges that are inherited by a given social group—knowledges that are taken for granted and in turn strongly inform or even direct that group's assumptions, beliefs, and behaviors. See Pierre Bourdieu, *Outline of a Theory of Practice* (Cambridge: Cambridge University Press, 1977).
2. See Sheehan, *German History*, 144–206, esp. 145–74 at 144.
3. See especially Rolf Engelsing, *Der Bürger als Leser: Lesergeschichte in Deutschland 1500–1800* (Stuttgart: J. B. Metzler, 1974), esp. 182–215; Jost Schneider, *Sozialgeschichte des Lesens: Zur historischen Entwicklung und sozialen Differenzierung der literarischen Kommunikation in Deutschland* (Berlin: Walter de Gruyter, 2004), 162–70; and Peter Uwe Hohendahl, *Literarische Kultur im Zeitalter des Liberalismus 1830–1870* (Munich: C. H. Beck, 1985); and Sheehan, *German History*, 157.
4. See Sheehan, *German History*, 148–49.
5. Most prominent among the modes of religious transmission discussed in the late eighteenth century were those of "natural religion," which proceeded solely from reason and the study of nature, and "revealed religion," which rested primarily on revelations to humans by means of sacred texts.
6. See Jack Goody, *Islam in Europe* (Cambridge: Polity Press, 2004), 1–24.
7. The reception of Islam in German literature at this time contrasts markedly with that in France and England, where it attracted more attention—either as a more rational variety of religion than Christianity, or (more commonly) as a religion whose founder was an impostor and whose adherents were fanatics; see Israel, *Radical Enlightenment*, 571–73. See also the discussion of Voltaire's *Le Fanatisme, ou Mahomet le prophète* and Goethe's *Mahomet*, below (pp. 48–49).
8. See Hartmut Bobzin, ed., *Der Koran in der Übersetzung von Friedrich Rückert*, 4th ed. (Würzburg: ERGON, 2001); Mommsen, *Goethe und die arabische Welt*, 157–72.
9. In the context of these brief remarks, the unwieldy phrase "Jews and Judaism" is necessary because the alterity discussed here is at turns ethnic, social, or religious; and because the specifically religious Judeophobic sentiments that are the subject of this discussion lump together observant Jews into a fictitiously homogeneous group. German Jews of the

late eighteenth and early nineteenth centuries are conventionally (and more realistically) recognized as comprising two distinct groups that sometimes came into conflict with each other: traditionalists or orthodox Jews, and *Haskalah* or *Maskilim*, who generally favored reform or moderation and supported emancipation. To these should be added the *Taufjuden*, Jews who converted to Christianity (stereotypically not out of religious conviction, but to escape discrimination). See Erspamer, *The Elusiveness of Tolerance*, esp. chap. 3 and 5 (64–97 and 113–50).

10. See Erspamer, *The Elusiveness of Tolerance*; further, David C. Itzkowitz, "The Jews and the Limits of Religious Freedom," in *Freedom and Religion in the Nineteenth Century* (Stanford, Calif.: Stanford University Press, 1997), 150–71 at 151.

11. See Jacob Katz, *From Prejudice to Destruction: Anti-Semitism, 1700–1933* (Cambridge, Mass.: Harvard University Press, 1980).

12. Felix Mendelssohn, of course, was an important casualty of this resurgence, not least of all because of the eloquent/virulent critiques submitted by Richard Wagner ("Über das Judenthum in der Musik," 1850) and Franz Liszt (in *Des Bohémiens et de leur musique en Hongrie*, 1859). See Cooper, "Mendelssohn Received."

13. See Friedrich Schleiermacher, *Letters on the Occasion of the Political Theological Task and the Sendschreiben (Open Letter) of Jewish Heads of Households*, trans. Gilya G. Schmidt, *Schleiermacher Studies and Translations*, vol. 21 (Lewiston: Edwin Mellen Press, 2001), esp. 24–33. So pronounced were the negative repercussions of these letters that one contemporary published a copperplate engraving that showed a short, hunchbacked Schleiermacher walking obsequiously along beside an imperious and buxomy Henriette Herz as Friedrich Schlegel's scandalous play *Lucinde* is performed on stage behind them. Since Schleiermacher was not, in fact, hunchbacked, this portrayed deformity is probably supposed to be an inheritance from Moses Mendelssohn.

14. These issues come to the fore in Schleiermacher's writings in three main documents: his immensely popular (if also controversial) *Ueber die Religion: Reden an die Gebildeten unter ihren Verächtern* (On Religion: Speeches to Its Educated Despisers, written in 1798–99, first published anonymously, and issued in significantly revised subsequent editions in 1806, 1821, and 1831); the *Briefe bei Gelegenheit der politisch-theologischen Aufgabe und des Sendeschreibens jüdäischer Hausväter* (Letters on the Occasion of the Political-Theological Task and the Open Letter of Jewish Householders, published in July 1799); and *Der christliche Glaube* (The Christian Faith, 1822; revised 1830/31).

15. See Pickle, "Schleiermacher on Judaism," and Pleger, *Schleiermachers Philosophie*, esp. 31–37, 104–29.

16. See Mendelssohn's letter of November 18, 1830, to Julius Schubring, in Julius Schubring, [Jr.], ed., *Briefwechsel zwischen Felix Mendelssohn Bartholdy und Julius Schubring, zugleich ein Beitrag zur Geschichte und Theorie des Oratoriums* (Leipzig: Duncker & Humblot, 1892; rpt. Wiesbaden: Martin Sandig, 1973), 13–15 at 15. For a discussion of the influence of Schleiermacher's *Gemeindetheologie* on Mendelssohn, see especially Sposato, *The Price of Assimilation*, 48–49.

17. See Pfister, ed., *Briefwechsel Goethe—Zelter*, xvii.

18. See Hey'l, *Der Briefwechsel zwischen Goethe und Zelter.*

19. See Todd, *Mendelssohn: A Life in Music*, 43–47 at 44, and *Mendelssohn's Musical Education*; and Schmidt-Beste, " 'Alles von ihm gelernt?' "

20. See Wehnert, "Zu Goethes Verhalten gegenüber Mendelssohn," 206.

21. See Mendelssohn's letter of June 6, 1830, to his family, quoted in Sutermeister, ed., *Felix Mendelssohn Bartholdy*, 23–29, esp. 24. Mendelssohn reports that he had planned to stay in Weimar "several days after his last letter," written on May 25, but that when he told

Goethe of this plan the poet convinced his daughter-in-law Ottilie to talk him into staying longer. Mendelssohn finally departed on June 3.

22. The fragment survives in the Bodleian Library, Oxford (shelfmark MS M. Deneke Mendelssohn d. 18, fol. 16–17). See Todd, *Mendelssohn: A Life in Music*, 227.

23. Ernst Wilhelm Theodor Hengstenberg (1802–69), Old Testament scholar and Orientalist, professor of Theology at the University in Berlin. Hengstenberg initially won prominence as an advocate of Unitarian religion but later became a strong opponent of it and of the rationalist sentiments that were increasingly predominant in theological studies of the day. Immortalized in Caput XVIII of Heine's *Atta Troll*, he is best known today for his influential *Christologie des Alten Testaments* (3 vols., Berlin: Ludwig Oehmigke, 1829–35).

24. See Mendelssohn's letters to his family of May 21, May 25, and June 6, 1830, in Sutermeister, *Eine Reise durch Deutschland, Italien und die Schweiz*, 21–29.

25. Letter from Goethe to Zelter, June 3, 1830, printed in *GA* 21: 907–8. For original German, see appendix A.

26. *Die beiden Neffen, oder der Onkel aus Boston*, Singspiel in three acts on a libretto by J. L. Casper, completed on November 6, 1823. See Todd, *Mendelssohn: A Life in Music*, 124–26.

27. Letter from Zelter to Goethe, February 8–10, 1824 (*MA* 20: 785–86). For original German, see appendix A.

28. Letter from Goethe to Zelter, March 8, 1824 (*MA* 20: 787).

29. Letter from Goethe to Zelter, May 21, 1825 and March 28, 1829 (*MA* 20: 844, 1210).

30. *Meeresstille und glückliche Fahrt* was first composed in 1828 and finally published, after substantial revision, as Mendelssohn's Op. 27 in 1835. See Todd, *Mendelssohn: "The Hebrides" and Other Overtures*, esp. 20–26.

31. See Todd, *Mendelssohn: A Life in Music*, 149–53.

32. Taken from the *West-östliches Divan*, both of these poems are actually by Marianne von Willemer, with whom Goethe had an affair in 1837. For a discussion of the relevance of Mendelssohn's use of these poems with (mis-)attribution to Goethe, see Douglass Seaton, "With Words: Mendelssohn's Vocal Songs," 661–700 at 666–68.

33. The choral songs "Im Nebelgeriesel, im tiefen Schnee," ("Zigeunerlied," Op. posth. 120, no. 4; 1820s) and "So lang man nüchtern ist" ("Trinklied," Op. posth. 75, no. 3; 1837), as well as solo songs "Ein Blick von deinen Augen" ("Die Liebende schreibt," Op. posth. 86, no. 3; 1831) and "Ach, wer bringt die schönen Tage" ("Erster Verlust," Op. posth. 99, no. 1; 1841) and the third movement of the A-major ("Italian") Symphony (1830–34), which may be based on the humorous poem *Lilis Park* (see John Michael Cooper, *Mendelssohn's "Italian" Symphony* [Oxford: Oxford University Press, 2003], 183–87).

34. The choral songs "Lasset heut am edlen Ort" (1828) and "Trunken müssen wir alle sein" ("Lob der Trunkenheit"; 1838), and the solo song "Zarter Blumen leicht Gewinde" ("Die Freundin"; 1837), and another solo setting of "Ach, um deine feuchten Schwingen" ("Suleika," ca. 1834–37) (see Wehner and Krummacher, "Mendelssohn, Mendelssohn Bartholdy, col. 1585).

35. See Seaton, "With Words," 667.

36. See especially Sengle, "Die didaktischen und kulturkritischen Elemente im 'West-östlichen Divan'"; further, Mommsen, *Goethe und die arabische Welt*, esp. 264–475.

37. Heinrich Heine, *Ludwig Börne: Eine Denkschrift*, Heinrich Heines sämtliche Werke, ed. Wilhelm Bölsche (Berlin: R. Trenkel, [n.d.]), vol. 6, 138; trans. quoted from Gay, *The Enlightenment*, vol. 1, 451.

38. Expounded in the 1813 essay "Über die verschiedenen Methoden des Übersetzens," Schleiermacher's theory of translation proposed that the goal of the hermeneutic art of

translation was to reproduce meaning faithfully, and that translators have two principal means for attaining this goal: either to bring the original author's world closer to that of the reader or vice versa. The most easily accessible modern edition of Schleiermacher's text is found in H. J. Storig, ed., *Das Problem des Übersetzens* (Darmstadt: Wissenschaftliche Buchgesellschaft, 1973), 38–70; an English translation is available in André Lefevre, ed. *Translating Literature: The German Tradition* (Assen: Van Gorcum, 1977), 67–89. See also Adam Schnitzer, "A History in Translation: Schleiermacher, Plato, and the University of Berlin," *Germanic Review* 72 (2000): 53–71; and T. H. Curran, "Schleiermacher: True Interpreter," in *The Interpretation of Belief: Coleridge, Schleiermacher and Romanticism*, ed. David Jasper (New York: St. Martin's, 1986), 97–103.

39. "Zu brüderlichem Andenken Wielands" (*GA* 15: 1086). For original German, see appendix A. See also Lefevre, *Translating Literature*, 35–39.

40. Most important among these is *Die Geschichte des Agathon* (The Story of Agathon; 1766–77), which is generally acknowledged as the first *Bildungsroman.*

41. See Allan Martin Cress, "The Decline of a Classic: The Critical Reception of Wieland in Nineteenth-Century Germany" (Ph.D. diss., University of Illinois, 1952); further, George Leuca, "Wieland and the Introduction of Shakespeare into Germany," *German Quarterly* 28 (1955): 247–55, esp. 253–55.

42. See Leuca, "Wieland and the Introduction of Shakespeare into Germany," 253.

43. German from *HA* 1: 160; Eng. trans. from Lind, *Johann Wolfgang von Goethe's "Roman Elegies" and "Venetian Epigrams,"* 45.

44. Letter from Mendelssohn to an unidentified doctor, March 22, 1820, trans. in Brown, *A Portrait of Mendelssohn*, 63–64.

45. See Brown, *Portrait*, 65–73.

46. See Kes, *Die Rezeption der Komödien von Plautus und Terenz im 19. Jahrhundert*, 45–49; further, Botstein, "Neoclassicism, Romanticism, and Emancipation, 5–9.

47. Letter from Goethe to Zelter, October 11, 1826 (*GA* 21: 707).

48. See Botstein, "Neoclassicism, Romanticism, and Emancipation," 5–9.

49. Ibid., 7.

50. See Botstein, "The Aesthetics of Assimilation and Affirmation," esp. 32–37; further, Geck, "Religiöse Musik 'im Geist der gebildeten Gesellschaft' "; and Todd, *Mendelssohn: A Life in Music*, passim.

51. See Garratt, "Mendelssohn's Babel."

52. See Sposato, *The Price of Assimilation*, 7–8, 177–80.

53. See Timm, *Ketzer und Dichter.*

54. Letter from Abraham Mendelssohn to Felix, July 8, 1829, quoted in Schneider, *Mendelssohn oder Bartholdy?* 20: ". . . einen christlichen Mendelssohn giebt es so wenig als einen jüdischen Confucius. Heißt du Mendelssohn so bist du eo ipso ein Jude, und das taugt dir nights, schon weil es nicht wahr ist." For a discussion of Mendelssohn's family name see also Sposato, *The Price of Assimilation*, 24–34.

55. See pp. 39–40, earlier.

56. Although Goethe was not the first to conceive this idea and term (they also figured in the agenda of Wieland, who had used the term already in the same sense already in 1813), he was the first to advocate for it programmatically. See Hans-J. Weitz, " 'Weltliteratur' zuerst bei Wieland," *Arcadia: Zeitschrift für vergleichende Literaturwissenschaft* 22 (1987): 206–8; further, Stich, *Goethe and World Literature*; and Saul, "Goethe the Writer and Literary History," 37–40.

57. See Eckermann's accounts of conversations that took place on January 31, and July 15, 1827 (*GA* 24: 229, 262).

58. For a collection of Goethe's writings that trace his ideas on *Weltliteratur*, see *GA* 14: 908–17.

59. Goethe reportedly considered publishing his translations of the Psalms but destroyed them because "the German people would never accept a Jewish hero." His translation of the Song of Songs has survived (see *GA* 15: 323–29).
60. On these issues see especially Berghahn, "Patterns of Childhood."
61. See Ward Jones, "The Library"; further, Crum, *Catalogue*.
62. See Cooper, "'For You See I Am the Eternal Objector . . .' ".
63. See Applegate, "Bach Revival, Public Culture, and National Identity." Michael Marissen has proposed that Mendelssohn made cuts to the *St. Matthew Passion* in order to diminish its anti-Semitic overtones, but Jeffrey Sposato, observing that the work retained pronounced anti-Semitic texts even after Mendelssohn's excisions, has argued that the alterations were made in order to increase its dramatic pace and compress it by eliminating repetitious material. See Michael Marissen, "Religious Aims in Mendelssohn's 1829 Berlin-*Singakademie* Performances of Bach's *St. Matthew Passion*," *Musical Quarterly* 77 (1993): 718–26; Sposato, *The Price of Assimilation*, 41–46.
64. See his letter of August 25, 1829, written in Llanglollen (Wales), which begins: "But please, no national music! May ten thousand devils take all this folkishness" ("Nur keine Nationalmusik! Zehntausend Teufel sollen doch alles Volksthum holen"), trans. from Elvers, *Felix Mendelssohn Bartholdy*, 85. In recent years some scholars (most prominently Thomas Schmidt-Beste and Peter Mercer-Taylor) have argued that the "national" element of the A-minor Symphony is, if anything, more German than Scottish. See Mercer-Taylor, "Mendelssohn's 'Scottish' Symphony"; further, Schmidt-Beste, "Just How 'Scottish' Is the 'Scottish' Symphony?"
65. See Walther Siegmund-Schulze, "Handels Nachwirkung in Deutschland von der Klassik bis zu Friedrich Chrysander," in *Wissenschaftliche Konferenz zu den 25. Händelfestspielen der DDR: Funktion und Wirkung der Musik Georg Friedrich Händels in Vergangenheit und Gegenwart*, ed. Walther Siegmund-Schultze (Halle: Martin-Luther-Universität, 1976), 26–47; Hellmut Federhofer, "Zu Felix Mendelssohns Händel-Interpretation im Urteil der Mit- und Nachwelt," *Musicologica austriatica* 8 (1988): 27–39.
66. See Stolzenberg, *Die Valentinszene und die Walpurgisnach*, vol. 1, 16.
67. *HA* 9: 350–51; for original German, see appendix A.
68. Letter to Johann Caspar Lavater, July 28, 1782 (*GA* 18: 680): "[I]ch (binn) [*sic*] zwar kein Widerkrist, kein Unkrist aber doch ein dezidiierter Nichtkrist . . ." For an exemplary study of Goethe's attitudes toward Christianity see Nisbet, "Religion and Philosophy."
69. Ward Jones, "The Library," 299.
70. See Locke, "Mendelssohn's Collision with the Saint-Simonians."
71. See Botstein, "Mendelssohn and the Jews," 213; Sposato, *The Price of Assimilation*, 179–80.
72. All the translations cited here, plus numerous others of lesser importance, are included in *GA* 15.
73. Voltaire, *Le Fanatisme, ou Mahomet le prophète*, 457.
74. Ibid.
75. Advertisement published in 1816 (*HA* 2: 268).
76. Goethe, "Noten und Abhandlungen zu besserem Verständnis des West-Östlichen Divans" (*HA* 2: 206). "Warum sollte [der Dichter] nicht ehrfurchtsvoll jene heilige Nacht feiern, wo der Koran vollständig dem Propheten von obenher gebracht ward?" See also Mommsen, *Goethe und die arabische Welt*, 157–72.
77. See Mommsen, *Goethe und die arabische Welt*, 218–38. See also Carlson, *Goethe and the Weimar Theatre*, esp. 133–39; and Kilchenmann, "Goethes Übersetzung der Voltairedramen *Mahomet* und *Tancred*."

78. The title page of Goethe's translation describes it as a "tragedy in five acts after Voltaire" (*Trauerspiel in fünf Aufzügen nach Voltaire*; *GA* 15: 166), but Goethe elsewhere referred to it as a "translation" (*Übersetzung*; e.g., *GA* 14: 260, 359, 763, 765).
79. See Hennemann, "Mendelssohn and Byron."
80. On Op. 69 see the Foreword to my edition for Bärenreiter Urtext (Kassel, 2006; BA 8934–8936); further, David Brodbeck, "*Eine kleine Kirchenmusik*: A New Canon, A Revised Cadence, and an Obscure 'Coda' by Mendelssohn," *Journal of Musicology*, 12 (1994): 179–205.
81. See Cooper, "'For You See I Am the Eternal Objector.'"
82. See 2 Kings 12, and 2 Chronicles 24: 1–14. For providing prepublication access to the critical notes for his edition of the *Athalia* music for the *LMA* (ser. 5, vols. 9 and 9a), I am deeply indebted to Armin Koch (Leipzig).
83. On the music for *Antigone* and *Oedipus in Colonos* see Geary, "Ancient Voices"; Flashar, *Inszenierung der Antike*, esp. 60–109, and *Felix Mendelssohn-Bartholdy und die griechische Tragödie*. On the music for *A Midsummer Night's Dream* see especially the introduction to Christian Martin Schmidt's authoritative edition for the *LMA* (ser. 5, vol. 8).
84. See Todd, *Mendelssohn: A Life in Music*, 502–4; further, Armin Koch's introduction to the new critical edition of the *Athalia* music in Series V, Bd. 2 of the *LMA*.
85. Translation by C. H. Cisson, quoted from Racine, *Britannicus, Phaedra, Athaliah*, 209.
86. On the use of the chorales in *Athalia*, with special emphasis on "Ach Gott, vom Himmel sieh darein," see especially Koch, *Choral und Choralhaftes im Werk von Felix Mendelssohn Bartholdy*, 171–83; and Seaton, "Mendelssohn's Dramatic Music," 210–23.
87. For a brilliant reconstruction of this aspect of Mendelssohn's career in the context of Friedrich Wilhelm IV's cultural agenda, see Toews, *Becoming Historical*, 207–78. See also Brodbeck, "A Winter of Discontent"; and Dinglinger, "Mendelssohn: General-Musik-Direktor für kirchliche und geistliche Musik."
88. See Todd, *Mendelssohn: A Life in Music*, 556–57.
89. Mendelssohn, *Jerusalem*, 138–39.

Chapter Three

1. Rose Unterberger, *Die Goethe-Chronik* (Frankfurt am Main: Insel, 2002), 64–65, 95, 102.
2. See Goethe, *Dichtung und Wahrheit* (*HA* 9: 238).
3. One ell equals forty-five inches.
4. Diary entry of December 10, 1777 (*GA* 26: 55): "Früh nach dem Torfhause in tiefem Schnee. 1 Viertel nach 10 aufgebrochen von da auf den Brocken. Schnee eine Elle tief, der aber trug. 1 Viertel nach eins droben. heiterer herrlicher Augenblick, die ganze Welt in Wolcken und Nebel und oben alles heiter. Was ist der Mensch dass du sein gedenckst? Um viere wieder zurück. Beim Förster auf dem Torfhause in Herberge."
5. Letter of December 10, 11, 1777, to Charlotte von Stein (translated from *GA* 18: 383). For original German, see appendix A.
6. Ibid., 384. For original German, see appendix A.
7. See Maisak, *Johann Wolfgang Goethe*, pl. 54 (p. 89).
8. *HA* 1: 50–52: "Und Altar des lieblichsten Danks / Wird ihm des gefürchteten Gipfels / Schneebehangner Scheitel, / Den mit Geisterreigen / Kränzten ahnende Völker."
9. Translated from *HA* 1: 398. For original German, see appendix A.
10. Schöne, *Götterzeichen, Liebeszauber, Satanskult*, 15–52.
11. See chapter 2, pp. 40–41.

12. See Walter Hinck, *Die deutsche Ballade von Bürger bis Brecht: Kritik und Versuch einer Neuorientierung* (Göttingen: Vandenhoeck & Ruprecht, 1968), 19.
13. See Williams, *Goethe's "Faust,"* 25–30; further, Scheibe, "Bemerkungen zur Entstehungsgeschichte des frühen 'Faust.' "
14. Siebel's exclamation beginning, "Wetter und Todt! Grüs mein Liebgen!—Ein Hammelmauspastete mit gestopften dürren Eichenblättern vom Blocksberg . . ." (*GA* 5: 22–23). See Mason, *Goethe's "Faust,"* 200–201.
15. See Williams, *Goethe's "Faust,"* esp. 25–31.
16. See Morris, "Die Walpurgisnacht."
17. Ibid.
18. See Gearey, *Goethe's "Faust,"* 196–97.
19. See Stolzenberg, *Die Valentinszene und die Walpurgisnacht*, vol. 1, 3, 16.
20. *GA* 26: 240. See also Clyde B. Furst, "The Walpurgisnacht in the Chronology of Goethe's *Faust*," *Modern Language Notes* 12 (1897): 166.
21. See Dusella, "Die Chorballade *Die Walpurgisnacht* op. 25," 95–137.
22. Letter from Goethe to Unger, August 5, 1799 (*GA* 19: 380–81).
23. Pfister, ed., *Briefwechsel Goethe—Zelter*, 1–2.
24. Letter from Goethe to Zelter, August 26, 1799 (translated from *GA* 19: 384–85). For original German, see appendix A.
25. Letter from Zelter to Goethe, September 21, 1799 (*MA* 20.1: 8–13 at 13). For original German, see appendix A.
26. See Mason, *Goethe's "Faust,"* 290.
27. See Stolzenberg, *Die Valentinszene und die Walpurgisnacht*, vol. 1, 3.
28. See Ibid., 12.
29. Siegfried Scheibe postulates that the ink and the ductus of Goethe's script in this second textual layer indicate "a slight change in date," but Stolzenberg finds no calligraphic evidence to support that statement. Cf. Siegfried Scheibe, "Zur Entstehungsgeschichte der Walpurgisnacht im Faust I," *Goethe-Studien: Sitzungsberichte der Deutschen Akademie der Wissenschaften zu Berlin, Klasse für Sprachen, Literatur und Kunst* 4 (1965): 19, and Stolzenberg, *Die Valentinsszene und die Walpurgisnacht*, vol. 1, 13.
30. *GA* 19: 424–25.
31. Zelter's setting of "Der Zauberlehrling" (The Sorcerer's Apprentice) was composed in 1799 and published ca. 1802 as part of his *Sammlung kleiner Balladen und Lieder* (Hamburg: J. A. Böhme, [n.d.]).
32. Letter from Zelter to Goethe, December 12, 1802 (trans. from *MA* 20.1: 28–30 at 29). For original German, see appendix A.
33. Goethe, Paralipomena 50 (*GA* 5: 551). See Mason, *Goethe's "Faust,"* 290; Morris, "Die Walpurgisnacht," 82–83; Stolzenberg, *Die Valentinsszene und die Walpurgisnacht*, vol. 1, 19.
34. Mason, *Goethe's "Faust,"* 290.
35. Zelter's beloved stepson committed suicide in November 1812, citing as his reason the fact that Zelter had refused to consent to his plans for marriage and the future. Racked with remorse, Zelter shared this situation with Goethe and asked him for some words of consolation. Goethe penned an extraordinarily sympathetic response—perhaps one of his most touching letters—on December 3, also using the familiar "Du" for the first time (*GA* 19: 681–85). See also Hey'l, *Der Briefwechsel zwischen Goethe und Zelter*, 99–100.
36. Letter from Zelter to Goethe, November 18–21, 1812 (*MA* 20.1: 291–93 at 293): "Was im 6 Buche des Jul. Caesar über das Amt und die Lehre der Druiden gesagt ist, langt nicht aus und ist zu alt für diesen Zweck."
37. Letter from Goethe to Zelter, December 3, 1812 (*MA* 20.1: 301–4 at 303–4). For original German, see appendix A. Goethe's source for this explanation of the Walpurgis

Night may have been the writings by Honemann (1754), Maurer (1796), or Fischer (1799) discussed in chapter 1.

38. Letter from Zelter to Goethe, December 10–13, 1812 (*MA* 20.1: 306–8 at 307). For original German, see appendix A.

39. Letter from Goethe to Mendelssohn, September 9, 1831 (*GA* 21: 1004–5). For original German, see appendix A.

40. Paralipomenon 70 (*GA* 5: 559–60). This summary of Goethe's established plans for *Faust II* was intended for inclusion in his autobiographical *Dichtung und Wahrheit* as an explanation of the planned follow-through on the *Faust* tragedy, but ultimately omitted. See Bohnenkamp, *Die Paralipomena zu Goethes "Faust,"* 389–98.

41. Goethe, diary entries for January 24, and March 16, 1832 (*GA* 26: 587 and 593).

42. See Prandi, "Kindred Spirits."

43. See chapter 1, pp. 20–25.

44. See Prandi, "Kindred Spirits," 138–39.

45. See Lee, "Poetic Intentions and Musical Production," 84.

46. This hint at a monotheistic Saxon religion represents a bit of poetic license on Goethe's part, for all of the Saxon tribes were in fact polytheistic (see chapter 1, pp. 3–4).

47. See Zelter's letter of December 12, 1802, to Goethe, above. Zelter composed six cantatas (most notably, *Johanna Sebus* on a text by Goethe; 1810) between 1792 and 1810, but this number is small when one considers that he was the director of the Berlin Singakademie and in that venue conducted numerous cantatas by various composers.

48. See chapter 2, pp. 40–41.

49. Hector Berlioz, *A Life of Love and Music: The Memoirs of Hector Berlioz 1803–1865*, ed. and trans. David Cairns (London: Folio Society, 1987), 294.

50. See Scheibe, "Bemerkungen zur Entstehungsgeschichte"; Williams, *Goethe's "Faust,"* 32–33.

51. Mammon was the devil of greed and money; Urian, a demon who rules witches and copulates with them.

52. "Ja, den ganzen Berg entlang / Strömt ein wütender Zaubergesang!" (ll. 3954–55).

53. For the relevant Paralipomena, see *GA* 5: 549–57. This material is expertly discussed and reconstructed, in tandem with the other drafts and salient facts of the genesis of the Walpurgisnacht scene, in Schöne, *Götterzeichen, Liebeszauber, Satanskult*, 109–230; and Bohnenkamp, *Die Paralipomena zu Goethes "Faust,"* 83–244. For an English summary see Williams, *Goethe's "Faust,"* 113–14.

54. The term is Goethe's, used in Paralipomena 54–60 (*GA* 5: 552–55).

55. See Fairley, *Goethe's "Faust,"* 66–86; further, Durrani, "The Character and Qualities of Mephistopheles." Schöne has proposed that Goethe deleted the scenes only reluctantly, in an act of self-censorship designed to forestall prudish responses from a public that already regarded him as controversial or (in some sectors) morally and ethically corrupt, and has accordingly reconstructed the Satanic Mass as he believes it was intended; see his *Götterzeichen, Liebeszauber, Satanskult*, 107–216 and 217–29. For all its attractions—and there are many—other commentators have rejected Schöne's arguments on both philological and textual grounds. See Bohnenkamp, *Die Paralipomena zu Goethes "Faust,"* 179; and Lee, "Faust's Harzreise."

56. The "Proktophantasmist" (roughly, the man with a haunted anus) satirizes Friedrich Nicolai (1733–1811), the conservative rationalist philosopher whose 1775 satire of Goethe's *Werther*, titled *Die Freuden des jungen Werther*, earned him the poet's lasting enmity. See Williams, *Goethe's "Faust,"* 112–13.

57. See discussion in chapter 1 (pp. 12–14).

58. *GA* 5: 557–61. See Williams, *Goethe's "Faust,"* 36–37.

59. *GA* 5: 573.

60. See Jantz, *The Form of Faust,* 157–59.
61. “Luftgesänge,” in the seventh issue of *Goethes Neue Schriften* (Berlin: Ungar, 1800), reproduced in *AS1*, was changed to “Lustgesänge” in Goethe’s later editions of the poem.

Chapter Four

1. See Sposato, *The Price of Assimilation,* 78–108. I wish to thank Professor Sposato for providing access to a prepublication version of this book’s discussion of *Paulus* and *Die erste Walpurgisnacht.*
2. The most recent and thorough exploration of this difficult issue is Sposato’s *The Price of Assimilation,* but the debate over the Jewishness of Mendelssohn’s cultural identity seems unlikely to dissipate anytime soon. See, in addition to Sposato’s book, his “Creative Writing”; Botstein, “Mendelssohn and the Jews”; and Steinberg, “Mendelssohn and Judaism.”
3. *Non nobis domine* (Ps. 115; 1830–35); *Wie der Hirsch schreit* (Ps. 42; 1837–38); *Da Israel aus Aegypten zog* (Ps. 114; 1839–40); *Kommt, laßt uns anbeten* (Ps. 95; 1839–42).
4. Most important among these were the *Kirchen-Musiken,* Op. 23 (1830, published in 1832) and the *Drei Motetten,* Op. 39 (1830, published in 1838).
5. Letter of March 1831 from Mendelssohn to Franz Hauser, quoted from Hanslick, “Aus dem Leben und der Correspondenz von Franz Hauser,” 26. For original German, see appendix A.
6. Emil Bendemann (1807–82), brother of the painter Eduard Bendemann.
7. Letter of February 22, 1831, from Mendelssohn to his family in Berlin, held in the Bodleian Library, Oxford (MS MDM d. 13, fol. 40f.). The German text is reprinted in numerous sources with abridgments and other inaccuracies. A reliable transcription is available in Hellmundt, “Mendelssohns Arbeit,” 101. For original German, see appendix A.
8. Letter of March 5, 1831, trans. from Hellmundt, “Mendelssohns Arbeit,” 102. For original German, see appendix A.
9. Letter of March 29, from Rome to the family, trans. from Hellmundt, “Mendelssohns Arbeit,” 102: “. . . Doch fehlt mir nur noch ein Stück Einleitung, wenn mir das einfällt, so ist das Ding zusammen und ich schreibe es in ein Paar Tagen hin; dann lasse ich alle Noten u. das leere Notenpapier dazu hier u. reise nach Neapel u. thue, so Gott will, nichts.”
10. Trans. from Hellmundt, “Mendelssohns Arbeit,” 102. For original German, see appendix A. The 1833 version includes neither bass drum nor piccolo, and the instruments are also absent in the main body autograph score for the 1843 revision. A separate score for those instruments as well as trombones in No. 9 indicates that they were an afterthought to the later version, included as Mendelssohn prepared the revised version for its premiere (see chapter 5, pp. 115–18).
11. Letter of May 10, 1831, to his family, trans. from Hellmundt, “Mendelssohns Arbeit,” 103. “Die Walpurgisnacht ist noch nicht fertig, liebe Fanny, weil sie mir unter den Händen wächst, aber ich schicke sie Dir bald; oder vielleicht auch nicht, denn Du mußt wissen, daß ich mir die besten neuen Sachen in petto behalte, um sie Dir selbst vorzuspielen, wenn ich wiederkomme; wird sie also recht lustig, so behalte ich sie mir vor.”
12. See Hellmundt, “Mendelssohns Arbeit,” 103.
13. Trans. from ibid., 103. For original German, see appendix A.
14. Trans. from ibid., 104. “Nun ist das Ende besser geworden, als ich mir selbst gedacht hatte, das Ungethüm u. der bärtige Druide mit seinen Posaunen die hinter ihm stehen u. tuten machte mir königlichen Spas, u. so brachte ich ein Paar Morgen sehr glücklich zu.”

15. The last page of the autograph score for the 1830–33 version is dated "Milan, July 15, 1831," and Mendelssohn's diary entry for that date likewise confirms the score's completion. The diary entry for July 17, 1831, reads: "*Sunday* the 17th. Work[.] Finished tidying up the Walp[urgisnacht]" ("*Sonntag.* 17 Arb[eit] Walp[urgisnacht] fertig geputzt."). See Hellmundt, "Mendelssohns Arbeit," 104.
16. Carl Thomas Mozart (1784–1858); oldest son of Wolfgang Amadeus and Constanze Mozart. See Hellmundt, "Mendelssohns Arbeit," 104.
17. Letter from Mendelssohn to Eduard Devrient, August 27, 1831 trans. from Hellmundt, "Mendelssohn's Arbeit," 104. The high *F* in question is presumably the one given in m. 29 of No. 9 in the final version, corresponding to the same note located just a few pages from the end of the 1830–33 composing score: ". . . ich wollte, ich könnte einmal einen Abend wirklich bei Dir sein u. Dir meine Walpurgisnacht vorspielen, oder vielmehr Du könntest, sie mir vorsingen; das Ding liegt gut für Dich, doch schreibe mir einmal, ob Du das hohe f nehmen kannst, nicht ausgehalten, sondern nur ein Viertel lang; es kommt am Ende drin vor."
18. Letter from Lucerne to Goethe, August 28, 1831, trans. from Hellmundt, "Mendelssohns Arbeit," 105. For original German, see appendix A.
19. See chapter 3, pp. 59, 61.
20. Letter from Goethe to Mendelssohn, September 9, 1831 (*GA* 21: 1004–5). For the complete text of this letter, see chapter 3; for original German, see appendix A (pp. 62, 224).
21. Letter from Paris to Fanny Hensel, January 21, 1832, and entry of February 4, 1832, in an unpublished diary held in the Staatsbibliothek zu Berlin—Preußischer Kulturbesitz (D-B MA Ms. 143). See Hellmundt, "Mendelssohns Arbeit," 106.
22. Letter of February 13, 1832, trans. from Hellmundt, "Mendelssohns Arbeit," 106–7. "Meine amoll Ouvertüre ist fertig, sie stellt schlechtes Wetter vor. Eine Einleitung, in der es thaut u. Frühling wird, ist auch vor ein Paar Tagen beendigt, u. so habe ich denn die Bogen der Walpurgisnacht gezählt, die 7 Nummern noch ein wenig ausgeputzt, u. dann getrost unter Mailand im July, Paris im Februar hingemalt. Ich denke, es soll Euch gefallen."
23. But see also the remarks on the private performance given in Berlin in October 1832, below.
24. Johann Nepomuk Schelble (1789–1837), singer and conductor renowned as another early advocate of J. S. Bach's *St. Matthew Passion* and as founder and conductor of the Cäcilienverein of Frankfurt am Main.
25. Letter of September 16, 1832, from Mendelssohn to Franz Hauser, trans. from Dinglinger, "Berliner Intermezzo," 108.
26. See Dinglinger, "Berliner Intermezzo," 116–20. The third concert was originally slated and advertised for December 20, 1832, but had to be postponed because of mounting difficulties, including the illness of Eduard Devrient (for whom the role of the druid priest was written).
27. See Mendelssohn's letter of February 22, 1831, to his family, and Moscheles, *Aus Moscheles' Leben*, vol. 1, 252.
28. Posthumously published in 1868 as Mendelssohn's Fifth Symphony, Op. 107.
29. Already enthusiastically received at its premiere in Munich on October 17, 1831, the G-minor Concerto had been published in England as Mendelssohn's Op. 25 already in October 1832; but it remained unpublished in Germany until the late summer of 1833. See Elvers, *Verleger*, 19–29; and Marian Wilson [Kimber], "Felix Mendelssohn's Works for Solo Piano and Orchestra: Sources and Composition" (Ph.D. diss., Florida State University, 1993), 104–83.

30. Like the G-minor Piano Concerto, the *Midsummer Night's Dream* had been performed to considerable acclaim for some time, but was only on the cusp of publication. The parts had been published as Mendelssohn's Op. 21 in England by Cramer, Addison & Beale in July 1832, but they were not published in Germany (by Breitkopf & Härtel in Leipzig) until about two weeks after this concert, in early December 1832. The full score was not published until the spring of 1835. See Todd, *Mendelssohn: The Hebrides and Other Overtures*, esp. 11–20.
31. Originally written for piano solo in September 1831, the *Capriccio brillant* in its orchestral version was newly available in parts (published in early September 1832 by Breitkopf & Härtel [Leipzig] and Mori & Lavenue [London]).
32. This Overture had been performed in an early version in the Mendelssohn household in 1828, but the 1832 concert was its public premiere. It was first published as Mendelssohn's Op. 27 in the spring of 1835 (London: Mori & Lavenue, and Leipzig: Breitkopf & Härtel). See Todd, *Mendelssohn: The Hebrides and Other Overtures*, 20–26.
33. Conceived already in 1829, the *Hebrides* Overture had been performed to great acclaim in London in the summer of 1832. It would be published in Mendelssohn's arrangement for piano duet in October 1833, in parts in October 1834, and in full score in March 1835. See my "'. . . da ich dies Stück gern recht correct erscheinen sähe': Philological And Textual Issues in Mendelssohn's *Hebrides* Overture, Op. 26," *Philomusica Online*, Annata 2003–2004 (http://philomusica.unipv.it/annate/2003-4/intro.html; accessed May 24, 2006).
34. Bach: Harpsichord Concerto in D Minor, BWV 1052; Gluck: excerpts from *Orfeo ed Euridice, Armide*, and *Iphigenie en Aulide*; Mozart: excerpts from *La finta giardiniera*, K. 196; Beethoven: "Grand Piano Sonata in C Major" (probably the "Waldstein" Sonata, Op. 53), Piano Sonata in C-sharp Minor, Op. 27, and Piano Concerto No. 4 in G Major, Op. 58; Weber: insertion aria "Was sag ich? / Fern von ihm," J. 239 for Cherubini's *Lodoiska*, and *Grand duo concertante* in E-flat Major for Clarinet and Piano, J. 204.
35. Translation quoted from Little, "Mendelssohn and the Berlin Singakademie," 77.
36. See Dinglinger, "Berliner Intermezzo," 101–23; further, Großmann-Vendrey, *Felix Mendelssohn Bartholdy und die Musik der Vergangenheit*, 51–52.
37. Rellstab's review of Mendelssohn's concert of November 15, 1832, in *Vossische Zeitung* 71 (November 17, 1832), trans. from Dinglinger, "Berliner Intermezzo," 118.
38. Louis Spohr, *Faust: Romantic Opera in Two Acts*, on a libretto by J. C. Bernard (composed in 1813, premiered in 1816, and published in 1822); Weber, *Der Freischütz: Romantic Opera in 3 Acts*, on a libretto by Friedrich Kind (composed in 1817–21 and premiered and published in 1821).
39. *Königlich privilegirte Berlinsche Zeitung von Staats- und gelehrten Sachen* 10 (January 12, 1833): [6–7]; trans. from Hellmundt, "Mendelssohns Arbeit," 108.
40. Trans. from Hellmundt, "Mendelssohns Arbeit," 109.
41. Devrient, *Meine Erinnerungen an Felix Mendelssohn-Bartholdy*, 156. See also pp. 189–92, below.
42. A double entendre meaning both "the bulk of the public" and "the coarser parts of the public."
43. Letter from Lea Mendelssohn Bartholdy to Ferdinand David, mid-January 1833; trans. from Dinglinger, "Berliner Intermezzo," 121. "Felixens 3 Concerte zum Besten der Orchesterwittwenkasse sind nun vorüber und haben viel Theilnahme und Interesse geweckt. Wenn er und seine Compositionen für le gros de public zu originell sind, so erregt er dafür bei den ihn Goutirenden wahren Enthusiasmus und hat sich neuerdings dadurch eine Masse Anhänger gewonnen."
44. See Hensel's letter of January 17, 1843, later (pp. 90–91).

45. See Klein and Elvers, *Hensel: Tagebücher*, 41. Hensel had also attended the concert in which the *Walpurgisnacht* was performed on January 10, 1833.
46. Klein and Elvers, *Hensel: Tagebücher*, 42.
47. Letter from Hensel to Mendelssohn, ca. February 27–28, 1834, trans. and quoted in Citron, *Letters*, 128, 456.
48. Citron, *Letters*, 192, 503; 198, 507.
49. Letter of April 7, 1834, to Fanny Hensel, trans. from Weissweiler, *Fanny und Felix Mendelssohn*, 160 (original in New York Public Library, no. 186). "Die Walpurgisnacht kann ich Dir jetzt nicht schicken, weil sie in unserm nächsten Concert (am 4ten Mai, in hoffentlich schönem Wetter) wahrscheinlich gemacht wird; ich habe Lust, sie bald in Partitur etc. Herauszugeben, obwohl ich jezt sehe, daß ich sie fast ganz noch einmal abschreiben müßte, weil sie nicht gut instrumentirt ist, das ist mir aber lieb, daß ichs jetzt besser weiß."
50. The concert mentioned in his letter of April 7 was given on May 3, without the *Walpurgisnacht.*
51. See Hensel's list of materials left behind in Berlin that were to be sent to Felix in Leipzig (Weissweiler, *Fanny und Felix Mendelssohn*, 203).
52. This comment is transmitted on the verso of a loose leaf (headed "Gespräche mit Mendelssohn i[n] d[en] Jahren / 1835. 1836. 1837") that appears to have been written on March 15, 1837, and was gathered up with other notes intended for a biographical sketch of Mendelssohn. These notes were first published posthumously in 1848 by Georg Eismann, and reedited (with numerous corrections and a clearer reproduction of the distribution of the content as well as generous explanatory notes) by Heinz-Klaus Metzger and Rainer Riehn in 1980. See *Erinnerungen an Felix Mendelssohn Bartholdy: Nachgelassene Aufzeichnungen von Robert Schumann*, ed. Georg Eismann (Zwickau: Predella-Verlag, 1948), 67; and Schumann, "Aufzeichnungen über Mendelssohn," 108.
53. See Klaus Häfner, "Felix Mendelssohn Bartholdy in seinen Beziehungen zu König Friedrich August II. von Sachsen: Ein Beitrag zur Biographie Mendelssohns," *Mendelssohn-Studien* 7 (1990): 219–68.
54. On Mendelssohn and the founding of the Leipzig Conservatory, see especially Mintz, "Mendelssohn as Performer and Teacher," esp. 115–42; Brown, *A Portrait of Mendelssohn*, 159–80; and Schmidt-Beste, "Lehrer wider Willen?"
55. See Elvers, *Verleger*, 308–9.
56. The *Lobgesang* was written for the Leipzig celebrations commemorating Gutenberg's invention of printing from movable type. See Todd, "On Mendelssohn's Sacred Music," 180–82.
57. On the quandaries of genre and nomenclature associated with the *Lobgesang* see especially Grey, "The Orchestral Music," 427–35.
58. Mendelssohn's reference to "three movements" in the instrumental portion is puzzling, since the published version offers only two. However, his letter of February 13, 1832, refers to three discrete sections—the newly completed "bad weather" section and a previously composed introduction representing the thaw and the arrival of springtime—and a page of sketches for the *Walpurgisnacht* written among rejected pages for Mendelssohn's setting of Psalm 95 (Op. 46) clearly refers to three distinct sections for the instrumental introduction: "No. 1 Allegro con fuoco; No. 2 Largo e mesto; Nr. 3 Ravvivente" (Staatsbibliothek zu Berlin—Preußischer Kulturbesitz, Mus. ms. autogr. F. Mendelssohn Bartholdy 19, p. 68). See fig. 5.4, p. 117.
59. Letter to Karl Klingemann, November 18, 1840, trans. from Klingemann [jr.], *Briefwechsel*, 251. For original German, see appendix A.
60. Letter to Lea Mendelssohn Bartholdy, November 28, 1842; printed in Paul and Carl Mendelssohn-Bartholdy, *Briefe aus den Jahren 1833 bis 1847*, 350–52: ". . . die

Walpurgisnacht möchte ich gern auch nun endlich zu einer Sinfonie-Cantate machen, wozu sie ursprünglich bestimmt u. aus Mangel an Courage nicht geworden war; . . ."

61. See Hellmundt, "Mendelssohns Arbeit," 78.

62. Letter to Rebecka Dirichlet (Mendelssohn's younger sister), December 11, 1842, held in the New York Public Library. Excerpts from this letter have been printed in numerous collections (including *Briefe 1833–47*) with the addressee erroneously identified as Lea Mendelssohn Bartholdy: "Am $21^{\underline{ten}}$ [*sic*] oder $22^{\underline{sten}}$ geben wir hier ein Concert für den König [. . .] im $2^{\underline{ten}}$ Theil soll dann meine Walpurgisnacht wieder auferstehen; freilich in einem etwas anderm [*sic*] Habite, als dem vorigen, das allzuwarm mit Posaunen gefüttert, und für die Singstimmen etwas schabig war; aber dafür habe ich auch müssen die ganze Partitur von a bis z noch einmal schreiben, 2 neue Stücke einsetzen, der übrigen Schneiderarbeit nicht zu gedenken."

63. Letter from Mendelssohn to Fanny Hensel, January 13, 1843, trans. from Hellmundt, "Mendelssohns Arbeit," 110. For original German, see appendix A.

64. Letter of January 17, 1843, from Mendelssohn to Klingemann, trans. from Klingemann, *Briefwechsel*, 279. For original German, see appendix A.

65. Letter from Hensel to Mendelssohn, January 17, 1843, trans. with minor emendations from Citron, *Letters*, 314. For the original German, see Citron, *Letters*, 587, and Hellmundt, "Mendelssohns Arbeit," 111.

66. "('In den letzten Zeiten des Heidenthums in Deutschland, wurden von den Christen die Opfer der Druiden bei Todesstrafe untersagt. Trotz dem suchten die Druiden und das Volk zu Anfang des Frühlings die Höhen der Berge zu gewinnen, dort ihre Opfer zu bringen, und die christlichen Krieger (gewöhnlich durch deren Furcht vor dem Teufel) einzuschüchtern und zu verjagen. Auf solche Versuche soll sich die Sage von der ersten Walpurgisnacht gründen.')" For access to a surviving exemplar of this program (shelfmark Deneke 356) I wish to thank Peter Ward Jones, head of the Music Section of the Bodleian Library, Oxford.

67. For a new, thoroughly annotated critical edition of the German translation published in November 1843 by Mendelssohn's friend Johann Christian Lobe, see *Hector Berlioz in Deutschland: Texte und Dokumente zur deutschen Berlioz-Rezeption (1829–1843)*, ed. Gunther Braam and Arnold Jacobshagen (Göttingen: Hainholz, 2002), 239–327, esp. 268–77.

68. I had not then heard his ravishing *Midsummer Night's Dream*. [Berlioz's addition to the *Memoirs*].

69. See Berlioz, *Memoirs of Hector Berlioz*, 294.

70. Letter to Fanny Hensel, February 11, 1843 (Staatsbibliothek zu Berlin—Preußischer Kulturbesitz, Depos. Berlin 15); for the original German, see Hellmundt, "Mendelssohns Arbeit," 111.

71. "Z" (Oswald Lorenz), *NZfM* 18 (1843): 67–68: "ein außerordentlich schönes Ding, eine Cantata, oder Ballade will er's lieber nennen. Ich habe lange nicht so etwas gesundes und frisches gehört, was einem so das herz erfreute."

72. See Hiller, *Briefe und Erinnerungen*, 180: "Die Walpurgisnacht habe ich von A bis Z neu umgeschrieben—es ist geradezu ein anderes Stück geworden und ein hundert Mal besseres. Ob ich sie aber stechen lasse, darüber bin ich noch im Zweifel."

73. See Hoshino, "Ein neu entdecktes Mendelssohn-Autograph." I wish to thank Professor Hoshino for her assistance in gaining access to this previously unknown source, which is immensely valuable for understanding the 1843–44 revisions to the *Walpurgisnacht*. (The source is discussed in greater detail in chapter 5.)

74. See Faye Ferguson, "Unknown Correspondence," 198–200.

75. See Hoshino, "Ein neu entdecktes Mendelssohn-Autograph," 155–59.

76. Mendelssohn wrote to Kistner on November 21, asking him to return the manuscript of the piano-vocal score so that he could finish proofreading that edition. See Elvers, *Verleger,* 324.
77. The important issue of Mendelssohn's interactions with French publishers remains unconsidered in the scholarly literature; his contacts with Benacci & Peschier were initiated in 1842 and lasted for the rest of his life. See Cécile Reynaud, "Mendelssohn and His French Publishers," in *Mendelssohn and the Long Nineteenth Century,* ed. Jacqueline Waeber and Nicole Grimes (Aldershot-Ashgate, [2007]).
78. See Mendelssohn's letter of January 18, 1844, to Kistner, in Ferguson, "Unknown Correspondence," 200–202; further, Elvers, *Verleger,* 325–26.
79. See Elvers, *Verleger,* 326 n. 3.
80. Of these exemplars, at least the presentation copy of the piano-vocal score and one set of the voice parts survive in the Music Section of the Bodleian Library, Oxford (shelfmarks Deneke 101 and Deneke 99, respectively); the former contains a correction in red chalk on p. 44 in Mendelssohn's hand. See Ward Jones, *Catalogue,* 105, 107.
81. Letter of February 4, 1844, from Mendelssohn to Friedrich Kistner, trans. from Elvers, *Verleger,* 326. For original German, see appendix A.
82. See Elvers, *Verleger,* 327.
83. Kistner advertised his new releases in the Leipzig *Allgemeine Musikalische Zeitung* for April 24, 1844.
84. In Dresden since 1843, Becker (1811–59) was the translator of a German edition of Berlioz's *Voyage musical* (in which the French composer enthused about the *Walpurgisnacht*; see note 68 above). He later achieved renown in his own right as author of a *Männergesang-Schule* (Leipzig, ca. 1845) and composer of an opera titled *Die Entstürmung von Belgrad* (The Evacuation of Belgrad, 1848).
85. For further discussion of this review, which has been overlooked in all the literature on the *Walpurgisnacht* to date, see chapter 6.
86. See discussion in chapter 2, pp. 48–49.
87. [Julius Becker], "Die erste Walpurgisnacht," *NZfM* 20, no. 17 (February 26, 1844): 65–66.
88. Becker, "Die erste Walpurgisnacht," 65–66. For original German, see appendix A.
89. Ibid., 66.
90. Ibid., 71: ". . .dennoch waltet in ihr jener heilige Geist der Ordnung, der, wie Novalis sich ausdrücken würde: 'durch seinen klar gewobenen Flor das Chaos hindurchschimmern läßt.' "
91. Ibid., 72. For original German, see appendix A.

Chapter Five

1. See John Michael Cooper, "Mendelssohn's Two *Infelice* Arias: Problems of Sources and Musical Identity," in *The Mendelssohns: Their Music in History,* ed. Cooper and Julie D. Prandi (Oxford: Oxford University Press, 2002), 43–97 at 82–97.
2. See his letters for Fanny Hensel and Ferdinand Hiller of January 13, and March 3, 1843, quoted in chapter 4.
3. This strophe is written for four-part male chorus in the first version but mixed chorus in four parts in the final version.
4. See pp. 90–91, above. Goethe, of course, specified that this strophe was for male voice ("Einer aus dem Volk").
5. See Melhorn, "Mendelssohn's *Die erste Walpurgisnacht,*" 123–35.

6. See Seaton, "The Romantic Mendelssohn," esp. 406–10.
7. See chapter 4, pp. 89, 91 and 94–96.
8. See Seaton, "A Study of a Collection of Mendelssohn's Sketches," 120–27.
9. See chapter 4, p. 83.
10. See Elvers, *Verleger*, 291–92.
11. For an explanation of this dating along with a facsimile and diplomatic transcription see Todd, "Of Sea Gulls and Counterpoint."
12. See Hoshino, "Ein neu entdecktes Mendelssohn-Autograph."
13. *Hans Schneider, Tutzing: Katalog* 225 (Tutzing: Hans Schneider, 1978), No. 125; further, Hellmundt, "Mendelssohns Arbeit," 79.
14. See chapter 3, pp. 65–67.
15. See Mendelssohn's letter of January 13, 1843, to Fanny Hensel, quoted in chapter 4.
16. See table 5.1 and the discussion of "Structural Revisions," below.
17. Seaton, "The Romantic Mendelssohn"; Hoshino, "Ein neu-entdecktes Mendelssohn-Autograph"; Hellmundt, "Mendelssohns Arbeit"; Krause, "Mendelssohns dramatische Kantate *Die erste Walpurgisnacht*."
18. See Mendelssohn's letters of November 18, 1840, and November 28, 1842, to Karl Klingemann and Lea Mendelssohn Bartholdy, quoted in chapter 4.
19. The sketches for stanzas 1–5 are on pp. 67–68 of Sk3 and the sketch for stanza 12 is on pp. 85–86.
20. The term "continuity draft" (also commonly employed in Beethoven scholarship) refers to sketch-like materials written in two, three, or four staves, with the essential vocal and instrumental parts provided. Unlike sketches, whose primary function was to capture essential melodic and harmonic ideas at a local level, continuity drafts evidently were used to work out the form over extended stretches of music. See Seaton, "A Study," 105–19.
21. Sk3 pp. 79–82.
22. Sk3 pp. 73–74.
23. Sk3 pp. 75–76 (staff 8).
24. Sk3 pp. 83–85.
25. See Mendelssohn's letter of December 11, 1842, to Rebecka Dirichlet, quoted in chapter 4. As shown in table 5.1, stanzas 10 and 11 are grouped together as No. 8 in the 1842–44 revision of the *Walpurgisnacht*.
26. See his letter of November 3, 1844, to Kistner, partially quoted in Elvers, *Verleger*, 330.
27. See Ward Jones, *Catalogue*, vol. III, 105–6 (items 372 and 373).
28. Ibid., 105 (item 371).
29. The first source-critical edition of the revised version of *Die erste Walpurgisnacht* is to be published by Bärenreiter Urtext (Kassel) in 2008.
30. See his letter of March 5, 1831, to Goethe, quoted in chapter 4.
31. See Mendelssohn's letters of July 13 and 14, 1831, quoted in chapter 4.
32. This reading may be reconstructed by moving directly from p. 117 to p. 129 (formerly pasted under p. 122/127 but now visible due to the removal of the paste-over) of AS2.
33. Pp. 138–39 of the *Gesamtausgabe* edition.
34. See David Brodbeck, "Brahms' Mendelssohn," *Brahms Studies* 2 (1998): 209–31.
35. Used in connection with Celtic pagans, the term "druid" specifically denotes a member of the priesthood, but Goethe's 1812 explanation of "Die erste Walpurgisnacht" makes clear that it refers to the Saxon pagans and the Brocken, not the Celts. Goethe's and Mendelssohn's "druids" are thus not all priests.
36. See Melhorn, "Mendelssohn's *Die erste Walpurgisnacht*," 102–3.
37. AS2 p. 115/122.
38. Cf. *A-R* II: 423–26 and mm. 33–36 of No. 7 in Op. 60.

39. See the Critical Notes to *A-R*.
40. See his letter of December 11, 1842, to Rebecka Dirichlet, quoted in chapter 4.
41. See Melhorn, "Mendelssohn's *Die erste Walpurgisnacht*," 101–2.
42. See Mendelssohn's letter of July 14, 1831, quoted in chapter 4.
43. Mendelssohn later employed the same concept in the introduction to *Elijah*, in which the orchestral opening is actually folded into the time of the textual drama.
44. As already established, the final version of the thematic substance of stanzas 5, 9, and 10 would not be composed for another decade.
45. See Dahlhaus, "'Hoch symbolisch intentioniert'"; Seaton, "The Romantic Mendelssohn," 406–10; further, Melhorn, "Mendelssohn's *Die erste Walpurgisnacht*," 101–7. For an illuminating discussion of the aesthetic implications of Mendelssohn's efforts to create cyclical unity by exploring thematic affinities, applied to the Second Piano Trio (Op. 66), see Schmidt-Beste, *Die ästhetischen Grundlagen*, esp. 301–27.
46. See *A-R* Appendix II. 3 for a reconstructed textual history of this passage.
47. See pp. 61 and 91 in chapter 4, above.
48. Hauser, "'In rührend feierlichen Tönen.'"
49. Seaton, "The Romantic Mendelssohn."
50. Steinberg, "Mendelssohn and Judaism," 37; Metzger, "Noch einmal," 95; Botstein, "The Aesthetics of Assimilation and Affirmation," 22.
51. Prandi, "Kindred Spirits"; Lee, "Poetic Intentions and Musical Production."
52. Toews, *Becoming Historical*, 269.
53. See Sposato, *The Price of Assimilation*, 108–13.

Chapter Six

1. On the possible programmatic relationship of *Walpurgisnachtstraum* and *Faust I* generally to the Scherzo of the Octet, see Todd, *Mendelssohn: A Life in Music*, 149–53. Mendelssohn's first setting of the 1799 ballad is available through A-R Editions (Madison, Wisc: forthcoming in 2007).
2. See chapter 2, pp. 35–53.
3. See, for example, Karl August Varnhagen von Ense's 1834 text advocating for the founding of a Goethe-Gesellschaft in Weimar and his 1836 memorandum to Metternich on the "Junges Deutschland" movement, quoted in Mandelkow, *Goethe in Deutschland*, 74–75.
4. Letter of February 27, 1794, from Friedrich Schlegel to August Wilhelm Schlegel, quoted in Mandelkow, *Goethe in Deutschland*, 77.
5. Trans. from Heine, "Französische Maler," in *Heinrich Heine: Sämtliche Schriften, Band 5: Schriften 1831–1837*, ed. Karl Pörnbacher (Munich: Carl Hanser, 1976), 72. See also Mende, "Zu Heinrich Heines Goethe-Bild"; Ulrich Pongs,"Der göttliche Romantiker: Zu Heines Goethe-Bild," *Zeitschrift für Germanistik* 9 (1988): 199–203; Gerhard Söhn, "Heinrich Heines Goethe-Bild," *Goethe-Jahrbuch* 106 (1989): 169–80; Hinck, "Der 'große Jupiter'"; Jost Hermand, "A View from Below"; and Mandelkow, *Goethe in Deutschland*, 101–9.
6. See Charles Edward Horsley, "Reminiscences of Mendelssohn by His English Pupil," excerpted in Todd, *Mendelssohn and His World*, 248.
7. For a summary of these two writings (especially Liszt's, which has attracted little modern attention despite its influence in its day), see Cooper, "Mendelssohn Received," 237–43. On Wagner's "Über das Judenthum" see especially Botstein, "The Aesthetics of Assimilation and Affirmation," 9–16, and "Wagner as Mendelssohn."

8. See especially Marian Wilson Kimber, "The Composer as Other: Gender and Race in the Biography of Felix Mendelssohn," in *The Mendelssohns: Their Music in History*, ed. John Michael Cooper and Julie D. Prandi (Oxford: Oxford University Press, 2002), 335–51; Mintz, "1848, Anti-Semitism and the Mendelssohn Reception,"; and Cooper, "Knowing Mendelssohn."
9. See especially Mandelkow, "Wandlungen des *Faust*-Bildes in Deutschland"; Krummacher, "Aussichten im Rückblick"; Saul, "Goethe the Writer and Literary History"; Hoffmeister, "Reception in Germany and Abroad"; Brown, *Portrait of Mendelssohn*; and Cooper, "Knowing Mendelssohn."
10. Mandelkow's important collection of contemporary reviews, for example, transmits only one reference to the 1799 ballad. This notice, a lengthy review of the first four volumes of *Goethe's Werke* (Tübingen: Cotta, 1806), appeared in Friedrich Schlegel's *Heidelbergische Jahrbücher der Literatur* 5 (1808): 143–84. Schlegel groups "Die erste Walpurgisnacht" with "Der Wanderer und die Pächterin," "Die Braut von Korinth," and "Der Gott und der Bajadere" among the best of what he deems "Romanzen," but adds that "only the all too prosaic explanation of the familiar folk superstition could hardly be appropriate for any poetry, no matter how accomplished" (die "Walpurgisnacht", wo nur die allzu prosaische Erklärung des bekannten Volksaberglaubens wohl durch keine, auch noch so dichterische Behandlung der Poesie angeeignet werden konnte). See Mandelkow, *Goethe im Urteil seiner Kritiker*, 240.
11. For a summary, see Hoffmeister, "Reception in Germany and Abroad"; further, Mandelkow, *Goethe in Deutschland*; and Boyle, "Introduction: Goethe and England."
12. Friedrich Schelling, *Philosophie der Kunst* (Darmstadt: Wissenschaftliche Buchgesellschaft, 1966), 82, 90, quoted and trans. from Mandelkow, "Wandlungen des *Faust*-Bildes in Deutschland," 240. Published in 1859, Schelling's remarks were given in lectures at the universities in Jena and Würzburg between 1802 and 1804.
13. See Braun, *Goethe im Urtheile seiner Zeitgenossen*, vol. 3, 217–23.
14. Ibid., 221: "So hoch poetisch alles seyn mag, so hat es uns doch in sittlicher Hinsicht höchlich misfallen."
15. Quoted from Baldensperger, *Goethe en France*, 127.
16. See *GA* 5: 620–27.
17. Goethe, *Faust: Tragédie*, trans. Louis, compte de Sainte-Aulaire, Chefs-d'oeuvre du théâtre allemand, no. 1 (Paris: Ladvocat, 1823); Goethe, *Faust: Tragédie*, trans. Philipp Albert Stapfer (Paris: A. Sautelet, 1825). For a discussion of these two translations, see Baldensperger, *Goethe en France*, 127.
18. See Besser, *Germaine de Staël Revisited*, 93–107.
19. See Guthke, "Destination Goethe," 112.
20. Quoted from de Staël-Holstein, *Germany*, vol. 1, 361. The French for this passage is "On ne sauroit alle au-delà en fait de hardiesse de pensée"; see de Staël, *De l'Allemagne*, vol. 3, 71.
21. De Staël-Holstein, *Germany*, vol. 1, 380–81; de Staël, *De l'Allemagne*, vol. 3, 112.
22. De Staël-Holstein, *Germany*, vol. 1, 361–62; de Staël, *De l'Allemagne*, vol. 3, 71–73, 74: "Le diable est le héros de cette pièce . . . le méchant par excellence, auprès duquel tous les méchants . . . ne sont que des novices . . . un diable civilisé . . . il a de la gaucherie sans timidité, du dédain sans fierté . . ."
23. De Staël, *De l'Allemagne*, vol. 3, 74–75: "Le caractère de Méphistophélès suppose une inépuisable connoissance de la société, de la nature et du merveilleux . . ."
24. De Staël-Holstein, *Germany*, vol. 1, 363; de Staël, *De l'Allemagne*, vol. 1, 75: "C'est le cochemar de l'esprit, que cette pièce de Faust, mais un cochemar qui double sa force. On y trouve la révélation diabolique de l'incrédulité, de celle qui s'applique à tout ce qu'il peut y avoir de bon dans ce monde . . ."

25. De Staël-Holstein, *Germany*, vol. 1, 229–30, 232; de Staël, *De l'Allemagne*, vol. 2 (1932): 184–86, 191.
26. De Staël-Holstein, *Germany*, vol. 1, 233; de Staël, *De l'Allemagne*, 2: 193: "au people comme aux homes éclairés."
27. De Staël-Holstein, *Germany*, vol. 1, 233; de Staël, *De l'Allemagne*, vol. 2, 193: "et d'ailleurs, quoique le christianisme combatte toutes les craintes non fondées, les superstitions populaires ont toujours une analogie avec la religion dominante."
28. For a perceptive overview of de Staël's critique of *Faust I* and of contemporary responses to *Germany*, see Proescholdt-Obermann, *Goethe and His British Critics*, 122–34.
29. See Simpson, "*The Authority of Culture*," 186–89.
30. See Hauhart, *The Reception of Goethe's "Faust" in England*, esp. 1–17.
31. *The Critical Review* 47 (1779): 477; quoted from Simpson, "*The Authority of Culture*," 187.
32. The classic study on the English Jacobins is E. P. Thompson, *The Making of the English Working Class* (New York: Pantheon, 1963).
33. Hauhart, *The Reception of Goethe's "Faust" in England*, 63–69.
34. Quoted from Simpson, "*The Authority of Culture*," 189.
35. Robert Southey referred to a "Satanic school" of Romanticism in *A Vision of Judgement* (London: Longman, Hurst, Rees, Orme, and Brown, 1821); see Hoffmeister, "Reception in Germany and Abroad," 242–43.
36. See Hauhart, *The Reception of Goethe's "Faust" in England*, 26. Proescholdt-Obermann attributes this review to William Taylor; see *Goethe and His British Critics*, 110.
37. [William Taylor], review of *Faust: Der Tragödie erster Teil, The Monthly Review* 62 (1810): 491–95 at 491; quoted from Hauhart, *The Reception of Goethe's "Faust" in England*, 25.
38. The *Cumulative Index to the London Magazine* attributes this article to the historian, moralist, and poet George Crowley (1780–1860); see Proescholdt-Obermann, *Goethe and His British Critics*, 138.
39. "Goethe and His Faustus," *London Magazine* 2, no. 8 (August 1820): 141, 135.
40. "Goethe and His Faustus," 139–40.
41. See especially Rosemary Ashton, "Carlyle," in her *The German Idea: Four English Writers and the Reception of German Thought, 1800–1860* (Cambridge: Cambridge University Press, 1980), 76–91; further, Hauhart, *The Reception of Goethe's "Faust" in England*, 52–62.
42. Thomas Carlyle, "Art. II—Faustus," 329, 330.
43. Ibid., 330.
44. See Lemmer, *Moritz Retzsch*, [ii–iii].
45. As Meredith Lee has pointed out, "Gegend von Schierke und Elend" is an example of Goethe's well-known thematic/symbolic use of names. In this instance it serves the literal function of situating Faust and Mephistopheles near those two villages, located about two hours away from the summit. Schierke was located in an area that was historically known as the "Sterbetal" (valley of death), and "Elend," in the root sense and its figurative derivatives, connotes Faust's state of spiritual exile and need. See Lee, "Faust's Harzreise," 83–87.
46. See chapter 3, pp. 70–74.
47. See Shelley's letter of April 10, 1822, to John Gisborne, quoted in Jones, *The Letters of Percy Bysshe Shelley*, vol. 2, 407.
48. Letter of Eckermann, February 3, 1829, quoted in Lemmer, *Moritz Retzsch*, [iv].
49. Lemmer, *Moritz Retzsch*, [v].
50. Soane, *Extracts from Göthe's Tragedy of Faustus.*
51. *The European Magazine and London Review* 80 (1821): 362, quoted in Hauhart, *The Reception of Goethe's "Faust" in England*, 39.

52. Goethe, *Faust: Vingt-six Gravures.*
53. Goethe, *Faust: Tragédie de M. de Goethe, traduit en français par M. Albert Stapfer.* Delacroix later recalled that he was not directly familiar with Goethe's play at the time of his exposure to Retzsch's drawings, and that his ideas on the subject had also been based on an opera on the subject he had seen during his trip to London in 1825. The opera in question, *Faustus,* was composed by Henry Bishop, Thomas Cooke, and Horn, on a libretto by D. Terry, adapted from Soane's translation. See Eugène Delacroix, letter of June 16, 1825, to J. B. Pierret and letter of March 1, 1862, to Philippe Burty, in *Eugène Delacroix: Selected Letters,* trans. Jean Stewart (Boston: MFA Publications, 1970), 124–25, 574; further, Lochnan, "Les Lithographies de Delacroix pour *Faust.*"
54. *Über Kunst und Altertum* 6, no. 1 (1827) (*GA* 14: 890). For original German, see appendix A.
55. *Über Kunst und Altertum* 6, no. 2 (1828) (*GA* 14: 953–54). For original German, see appendix A.
56. Goethe, *Faust: Tragédie de Goëthe* [*sic*]. According to Eckermann, Goethe on January 3, 1830, said that he "no longer liked reading *Faust* [I] in German, but in [Nerval's] French translation everything had the effect of being completely fresh, new, and witty" (trans. from Johann Peter Eckermann, *Gespräche mit Goethe in den letzten Jahren seines Lebens* [*GA* 24: 383]). Nerval's translation would also serve as the basis for Berlioz's *Huit scènes de Faust* and (after that original opus 1 was withdrawn) parts of his "scène dramatique" *La Damnation de Faust.*
57. For a meticulous account of the creation and dating of Shelley's "Walpurgisnacht" translation, see Crook and Webb, *The "Faust" Draft Notebook,* lviii–lxii.
58. See Phelps, "Goethe's *Faust* and the Young Shelley."
59. Letter of January 12, 1822, from Shelley to John Gisborne, quoted in Jones, *The Letters of Percy Bysshe Shelley,* vol. 2, 376.
60. Letter from Shelley to Gisborne, April 10, 1822, quoted in Jones, *The Letters of Percy Bysshe Shelley,* vol. 2, 407.
61. See Crook and Webb, *The "Faust" Draft Notebook,* lxi.
62. See Percy Bysshe Shelley, "Scenes from Goethe's Faust," in Shelley, *The Works of Percy Bysshe Shelley,* vol. 4, 304.
63. The text as given below is quoted from Murray, *The Bodleian Shelley Manuscripts,* 110–13. The draft manuscript reveals a different translation (likewise incomplete) of ll. 4136–43; see Crook and Webb, *The "Faust" Draft Notebook,* 224–26. The edition in Forman, *The Works of Percy Bysshe Shelley* (vol. 4, 305) gives l. 4132 as "She with the apples you desired" and omits the last two quatrains altogether.
64. See Hauhart, *The Reception of Goethe's "Faust" in England,* 63–69; further, Proescholdt-Obermann, *Goethe and His British Critics,* 120.
65. Quoted from Hauhart, *The Reception of Goethe's "Faust" in England,* 103.
66. Henkel, "The 'Salvation' of Faust," 92.
67. See chapter 4, pp. 91–96.
68. *The Musical Examiner* 19 (March 11, 1843): 138.
69. *Revue et gazette musicale de Paris* 10, no. 10 (March 5, 1843): 88.
70. For example, the *Musical World* (London) 18, no. 11 (March 16, 1843): 104. There, an anonymous correspondent reports that "the best judges" considered the *Walpurgisnacht* "to be the boldest and most finished production of [Mendelssohn's] pen" and continues: "The overture, a duet, a quartet, a quintet, and the finale, were encored over and over again; and the whole performance was received with an enthusiasm approaching delirium."
71. See Foster, *History of the Philharmonic Society of London,* 183, 188.

72. The "morning contemporary" has as yet not been identified, although other parts of this article quote extensively from the *Morning Post.*
73. This is Bartholomew's counterpart for l. 57 ("durch die engen Felsenstrecken") [JMC].
74. The *Musical World* (London) 19, no. 28 (July 11, 1844): 231–32.
75. The *Musical Examiner* 89, no. 13 (July 13, 1844): 674–75.
76. Adami, "Die erste Walpurgisnacht."
77. Ibid., 113–14. For original German, see appendix A.
78. See chapters 3 and 4, pp. 62 and 92–94.
79. Adami, "Die erste Walpurgisnacht," 114. For original German, see appendix A.
80. A vocal score and set of parts preserving Bélanger's translation survive in the Bibliothèque Nationale de France (Bibliothèque du Conservatoire, D.17598 and D.16854). My thanks to Cathérine Massip for assistance in locating and gaining access to these parts.
81. Kreutzer, "Société des Concerts."
82. Ibid., 121. For original French, see appendix A.
83. Ibid. For original French, see appendix A.
84. Perhaps mm. 18–22 of No. 6 [JMC].
85. Kreutzer, "Société des Concerts," 122. For original French, see appendix A.
86. Ibid., 122: "Ce serait à désespérer et à rentrer dans les cartons la ballade de Mendelssohn, si l'on ne connaissait le public du Conservatoire, public très-difficile et très-ombrageux par dignité et par fausse science, mais très-commode au fond, lorsqu'on lui a prouvé qu'il peut approuver une œuvre sans compromettre l'équité et l'infaillibilité de ses jugements."
87. "Pariser Briefe," *Rheinische Musik-Zeitung für Kunstfreunde und Künstler* 3, no. 43 (April 23, 1853): 1169–71 at 1171: "In den kritischen Blättern hatte sich besonders Leon Kreutzer Mühe gegeben, dem Werk gerecht zu werden . . . —er hatte auch die Dummheiten des Uebersetzers denuncirt, ohne freilich selbst die eigentliche Idee Göthe's gefasst zu haben." Of course, Kreutzer evidently believed that the "swarms of horse-mounted sorcerers" and opening graves were real rather than a ruse—and thus misunderstood the poem in this more literal sense, as well.
88. An exemplar survives in the Bodleian Library, Oxford (shelfmark Harding Mus. A. 1815).
89. "Mendelssohn's 'Walpurgis Night,' " *Dwight's Journal of Music* 21, no. 5 (May 3, 1862): 38.
90. See Grove, "Mendelssohn"; Hermann Kretzschmar, *Führer durch den Concertsaal, II. Abtheilung, 2. Theil: Oratorien und weltliche Chorwerke* (Leipzig: A. G. Liebeskind, 1890), 332–37; Siegfried Ochs, *Der deutsche Gesangverein für gemischten Chor,* vol. 4, 84–102.
91. See Cooper "Knowing Mendelssohn," esp. 35–46, and "Mendelssohn Received."
92. Devrient, *Meine Erinnerungen an Felix Mendelssohn-Bartholdy,* 156. For original German, see appendix A.
93. See Killian, *Beiträge zur Geschichte des Karlsruher Hoftheaters,* esp. 75–115.
94. Pohl, "Auf der Bühne."
95. Ibid., 167.
96. Ibid.
97. Ibid., 166: "Das ist ja der große Vorzug des Oratoriums und der Cantate, daß Beide *der Phantasie des Hörers überlassen, das Scenische sich auszumalen und somit das real nicht Darstellbare in der Idee zu ergänzen.* . . . Alle musikalische und dichterische Mittel können hier, ohne an Raum und Zeit gebunden zu sein, nach Belieben in einander greifen."
98. Ibid., 165, 167.

99. After referring in the main body of the text to "the part of the overture that presents the bad weather of April" (das schlechte Aprilwetter), Pohl (166) adds a footnote that reads: "Is this not that distinctively *program music* on a broader scale than any of the 'Romantics' have yet achieved? To our knowledge no Romantic yet has based an entire overture on 'bad weather.'" ("Ist das nicht so ausgeprägte *Programm-Musik*, wie sie die 'Romantiker' kaum in breiterer Entfaltung jemals durchgeführt haben? Unseres Wissens hat noch kein Romantiker aus 'schlechtem Wetter' eine ganze Ouvertüre gemacht").
100. Haydn, *Die Jahreszeiten* (The Seasons), H XXI: 3, on a libretto by Gottfried van Swieten, 1799–1801 (JMC).
101. Zauder, *Ueber Mendelssohn's* Walpurgisnacht, 12–13.
102. Ibid., 12.
103. Appold, "Landschaften in Mendelssohns Briefen, Zeichnungen und Musik" 54–59.
104. See discussion in chapters 3 and 5, pp. 64–65 and 133–36.
105. Most generally, Pohl considers the "intermezzo" of the Christian sentinels' stanzas gratuitous to the meaning of the poem, but in terms of the significance of the action, the poetic structure, and Goethe's essential drawing of parallels between paganism and Christianity that stanza pair is clearly essential. More specifically, Pohl suggests that the Christian guards have posted sentinels in such a fashion that they hope to prevent the pagans from gaining access to the summit, and that the pagans' ruse enables them to penetrate the Christian lines and thus attain the peaks. What actually happens, however, is that the Christians, posted on their ramparts, witness the ruse from afar (see chapter 3, pp. 63–68).
106. Zauder, *Ueber Mendelssohn's* Walpurgisnacht, 32. For original German, see appendix A.
107. See chapters 3 and 5, pp. 64 and 133–35.
108. A simple optical device that uses slides to project magnified images onto another surface, in use since the late seventeenth century.
109. See Grey, "*Tableaux vivants.*" Todd, "On the Visual in Mendelssohn's Music"; and Appold, "Landschaften in Mendelssohns Briefen, Zeichnungen und Musik."
110. Pohl, "Goethe–Mendelssohn's 'Erste Walpurgisnacht' auf der Bühne," 166.

Chapter Seven

1. *Memoirs of Hector Berlioz from 1803 to 1865 Comprising His Travels in Germany, Italy, Russia, and England*, trans. Ernest Newman (New York: Alfred A. Knopf, 1932), 243.
2. For a summary, with well-chosen quotations and critical commentary, of Wagner's remarks on Mendelssohn as conductor and particularly his tempo choices, see Brown, *A Portrait of Mendelssohn*, 251–54.
3. See Brown, *Classical and Romantic Performing Practice*, 290–96, 303–12.
4. See Reichwald, "Mendelssohn's Tempo Indications." I wish to thank Professor Reichwald for sharing his work with me before its publication.
5. See Cooper "Mendelssohn and Berlioz."
6. See Reichwald, "Mendelssohn's Tempo Indications"; further, Todd, *Mendelssohn: "The Hebrides" and Other Overtures*, 11–20.
7. See Todd, *Mendelssohn: A Life in Music* (Oxford: Oxford University Press, 2003), 328.
8. Letter of November 29, 1839, from Mendelssohn to Breitkopf & Härtel, printed in Elvers, *Verleger*, 98.
9. Thus Andreas Moser described Mendelssohn's influence on Joachim in his *Joseph Joachim: Ein Lebensbild* (Berlin: Behr's Verlag, 1898), trans. Lilla Durham as *Joseph Joachim: A Biography* (London: P. Welby, 1901). The excerpt is quoted from Brown, *A Portrait of Mendelssohn*, 307–8.

10. See Brown, *Classical and Romantic Performing Practice*, esp. 375–411.
11. See pp. 116–18 in chapter 5.
12. For example, the recording by Nikolaus Harnoncourt with the Chamber Orchestra of Europe and the Arnold Schoenberg Choir (Teldec D. 101736) runs to 33′17″; the one by Christoph von Dohnányi with the Vienna Philharmonic and the Chorus of the Vienna Singverein (London 418 882-2) is 33′33″. Kurt Masur's well-known recording with the Gewandhaus Orchestra and the Rundfunkchor Leipzig (Berlin Classics BC 2057-2) comes the closest to the "authentic" duration, with a total time of 31′19″.
13. See Melhorn, "Mendelssohn's *Die erste Walpurgisnacht*," 170; Ochs, *Der deutsche Gesangverein für gemischten Chor*, vol. 4, 87–88.
14. Philip Radcliffe, *Mendelssohn*, rev. ed., ed. Peter Ward Jones (Oxford: Oxford University Press, 2000), 96.
15. See Cooper " 'For You See I Am the Eternal Objector.' "
16. See Léon Kreutzer, "Société des concerts," 121–22; and "Pariser Briefe," *Rheinische Musik-Zeitung für Kunst-Freunde und Künstler* 3, no. 43 (April 23, 1853): 1171.
17. See Ward Jones, "Mendelssohn and His English Publishers," 250. In his letter of July 11, 1843, Buxton referred to Mendelssohn's earlier reference to the poem, and three days later he reported that he had found it and asked the composer to send the score "as soon as [he] please[d]" (Bodleian Library, Oxford, GB 18:17 and 19).
18. Bodleian Library, Oxford, GB 18: 67, p. 3.
19. Ibid.
20. See Mendelssohn's letter of July 17, 1843, to Friedrich Kistner, quoted in Ferguson, "Unknown Correspondence," 200.
21. Buxton wrote to Mendelssohn on December 20, 1843, that "through a second hand I now hear that Novello has said he would publish the work if you had not sold it to any English house . . ." (Bodleian Library, Oxford, GB 18: 255, p. 1).
22. Letter of December 20, 1843, from Buxton to Mendelssohn (Bodleian Library, Oxford, GB 18: 67, p. 1).
23. Letter of December 20, 1843, from Buxton to Mendelssohn (Bodleian Library, Oxford, GB 18: 255, pp. 1–2).
24. Bodleian Library, Oxford, GB 19: 7.
25. See Ferguson, "Unknown Correspondence," 200.
26. Letter of January 4, 1844, from Mendelssohn to Kistner, quoted in Ferguson, "Unknown Correspondence," 200. Buxton expressed his hope that the English text be included also in the German edition on January 19—too late in this scramble toward publication.
27. Letter of March 16, 1844, from Bartholomew to Mendelssohn (Bodleian Library, Oxford, GB 19: 157).
28. See chapter 6, pp. 182–84.
29. The Celts' religious alterity, of course, antedated the spread of Christianity, since they were the religious foe of Roman civilization from about the second century BCE to the first century CE, and in that context had their beliefs into Imperial Roman civilization. See Jones and Pennick, *A History of Pagan Europe*, 79–110.
30. See Dougass Seaton, "With Words: Mendelssohn's Vocal Songs," in *The Mendelssohn Companion*, ed. Douglass Seaton (Westport, Conn.: Greenwood, 2001), esp. 661–64; and John Michael Cooper, "Of Red Roofs and Hunting Horns: Mendelssohn's Song Aesthetic, with an Unpublished Cycle (1830)," *Journal of Musicological Research*, 21 (2002): 277–317.
31. Page 109/116 of the autograph full score for the version of 1830–33 (source AS1 in chapter 5) designates this Chorus of the Christian Watchmen as "Chor der [christlichen] Wächter. (Kleinerer Chor.)"; that is, "Chorus of the [Christian] Watchmen. (Smaller Choir.)."

32. See Koury, *Orchestral Performance Practices in the Nineteenth Century*, 175–238; further, Colin Lawson and Robin Stowell, *The Historical Performance of Music: An Introduction* (Cambridge: Cambridge University Press, 1999), 93–98.
33. See di Grazia, "Rejected Traditions," esp. 198–205.
34. See Botstein, "The Aesthetics of Assimilation and Affirmation," and "Neoclassicism, Romanticism, and Emancipation," 1–23, and especially "Wagner as Mendelssohn."
35. Botstein, "Wagner as Mendelssohn," 258.
36. For example, in *Dichtung und Wahrheit*: ". . . Man wiederholte so oft in jenen toleranten Zeiten, jeder Mensch habe seine eigne Religion, seine eigne Art der Gottesverehrung. . . ." (*HA* 10: 22).
37. Letter to Johann Caspar Lavater, July 29, 1782 (*GA* 18: 680): ". . . [I]ch (bin) [*sic*] zwar kein Widerkrist, kein Unkrist aber doch ein dezidierter Nichtkrist . . ."
38. See Schaub, "Of Believers and Barbarians."

Selected Bibliography

Organization:
I. Manuscript Sources; II. Printed Music; III. Other Printed Sources.

I. Manuscript Sources

Biblioteka Jagiellońska, Krakow, Mus. ms. autogr. F. Mendelssohn Bartholdy 37. Mendelssohn Bartholdy, Felix. *Die erste Walpurgisnacht,* autograph full score. [Version of 1830–33.]

Bibliothèque Nationale de France Paris (Bibliothèque du Conservatoire), Ms. 207. Mendelssohn Bartholdy, Felix. *Die erste Walpurgisnacht,* autograph full-score fragment. [Version of 1830–33.]

Bodleian Library, Oxford, MS M. Deneke Mendelssohn c. 22, fol. 6r. Mendelssohn Bartholdy, Felix. *Die erste Walpurgisnacht,* sketch for stanza 10 of Goethe's poem. [Version of 1843–44.]

Bodleian Library, Oxford. Mus. M. Deneke Mendelssohn c. 47. Mendelssohn Bartholdy, Felix. *Die erste Walpurgisnacht,* sketch for stanza 6. [Version of 1830–33.]

Museum of Educational Heritage at Tamagawa University, Tokyo, Collection of Gaspar Cassadó. Mendelssohn Bartholdy, Felix. *Die erste Walpurgisnacht: Ballade von Goethe,* autograph piano-vocal score. Facsimile edition, ed. Hiromi Hoshino. Tokyo: Yushodo Press, 2005. [Version of 1843–44.]

Musikbibliothek der Stadt Leipzig, PM 143. Mendelssohn Bartholdy, Felix. *Die erste Walpurgisnacht.* [Version of 1843–44.]

Pierpont Morgan Library, New York, Morgan Collection. Mendelssohn Bartholdy, Felix. *Die erste Walpurgisnacht,* album-leaf containing portion of stanza 9 of Goethe's poem, dated Frankfurt April 18, 1845. [Version of 1843–44.]

Staatsbibliothek zu Berlin–Preußischer Kulturbesitz. Mendelssohn-Archiv, MA Ms. 143. Mendelssohn Bartholdy, Felix. [*Tagebuch 1831/1832, mit Eintragungen von Fanny Hensel.*]

———. Mus. ms. autogr. F. Mendelssohn Bartholdy 18, pp. 39–42. Mendelssohn Bartholdy, Felix. *Die erste Walpurgisnacht,* sketches for the instrumental introduction and an incomplete page of score for nine measures of stanza 6. [Version of 1830–33.]

———. Mus. ms. autogr. F. Mendelssohn Bartholdy 19, pp. 67–68, 71–77, 79–86. Mendelssohn Bartholdy, Felix. *Die erste Walpurgisnacht,* sketches for various portions. [Version of 1843–44.]

Staatsbibliothek zu Berlin–Preußischer Kulturbesitz. Mus. ms. autogr. F. Mendelssohn Bartholdy 56, no. 3. Mendelssohn Bartholdy, Felix. *Die erste*

Walpurgisnacht, autograph full-score fragment from setting of stanza 8 of Goethe's poem. [Version of 1843–44.]

———. Mus. ms. autogr. F. Mendelssohn Bartholdy 49, no. 2. Mendelssohn Bartholdy, Felix. *Die erste Walpurgisnacht*, autograph arrangement of Introduction for piano duet. [Version of 1830–33.]

Yale University Music Library, New Haven (Conn.), SC Ma21 / M522 / Er87. Mendelssohn Bartholdy, Felix. *Die erste Walpurgisnacht*, autograph tenor part for setting of stanzas 1–6. [Version of 1830–33.]

II. Printed Music

Mendelssohn Bartholdy, Felix. *Die erste Walpurgisnacht. Ballade für Chor und Orchester. Gedichtet von Goethe, componirt von Felix Mendelssohn-Bartholdy. Op. 60. Clavierauszug.* Leipzig: Fr. Kistner [1844].

———. *Die erste Walpurgisnacht. Ballade für Chor und Orchester. Gedichtet von Goethe, componirt von Felix Mendelssohn-Bartholdy. Op. 60. Partitur.* Leipzig: Fr. Kistner [1844].

———. *Die erste Walpurgisnacht: First Complete Version, 1832–33*, ed. John Michael Cooper. Madison, Wisc.: A-R Editions [2007].

———. *The First Walpurgisnight. (Die erste Walpurgisnacht). A Poem by Goethe. Translated from the German by W. Bartholomew Esqur. and Set to Music by Felix Mendelssohn Bartholdy. Op. 60.* [Piano-vocal score.] London: J. J. Ewer & Co. [1844].

———. *Incidental Music to Racine's Athalia*, ed. Armin Koch. Leipziger Augsaber der Werke von Felix Mendelssohn Bartholdy, ed. Christian Martin Schmidt, Series 5, Vol. 9. Leipzig: Breitkopf & Härtel [2006].

———. *Orchesterstimmen zur Walpurgisnacht. Ballade von Goethe, Musik von Felix Mendelssohn-Bartholdy. Op. 60.* Leipzig: Fr. Kistner [1844].

———. *Singstimmen zur Walpurgisnacht. Ballade von Goethe, Musik von Felix Mendelssohn-Bartholdy. Op. 60.* Leipzig: Fr. Kistner [1844].

III. Other Printed Sources

Adami, H. "Die erste Walpurgisnacht von Felix Mendelssohn-Bartholdy. (Aufgeführt in Wien im 4. Concert spirituel.)" *Signale für die musikalische Welt* 2 (1844): 113–15.

Ankarloo, Bengt; Stuart Clark; and William Monter. *The Period of the Witch Trials.* Philadelphia: University of Pennsylvania Press, 2002.

Applegate, Celia. "Bach Revival, Public Culture, and National Identity: The *St. Matthew Passion* in 1829." In *A User's Guide to German Cultural Studies*, ed. Scott Denham, Irene Kacandes, and Jonathan Petropoulos, 139–62. Ann Arbor: University of Michigan Press, 1997.

Appold, Juliette Laurence. "Landschaften in Mendelssohns Briefen, Zeichnungen und Musik." Ph.D. diss., Philipps-Universität Marburg, 2006.

Augustyn, Prisca. *The Semiotics of Fate, Death, and the Soul in Germanic Culture.* Berkeley Insights in Linguistics and Semiotics, Vol. 50. New York: Peter Lang, 2002.

Bailey, Michael D. *Battling Demons: Witchcraft, Heresy, and Reform in the Late Middle Ages.* University Park: Pennsylvania State University Press, 2003.

Baldensperger, Fernand. *Goethe en France: Étude de litterature comparée.* Paris: Librarie Hachette, 1904.

Bauch, Andreas. *Quellen zur Geschichte der Diözese Eichstätt, Bd. I: Biographien der Gründungszeit,* 2d ed. Regensburg: Verlag Friedrich Pustet, 1984.

———. *Quellen zur Geschichte der Diözese Eichstätt, Bd. II: Ein bayerisches Mirakelbuch aus der Karolingerzeit: Die Monheimer Walpurgis-Wunder des Priesters Wolfhard.* Regensburg: Verlag Friedrich Pustet, 1979.

Bauschatz, Paul C. *The Well and the Tree: World and Time in Early Germanic Culture.* Amherst: University of Massachusetts Press, 1982.

Behringer, Wolfgang. *Witchcraft Persecutions in Bavaria: Popular Magic, Religious Zealotry and Reason of State in Early Modern Europe,* trans. J. C. Grayson and David Lederer. Cambridge: Cambridge University Press, 1997.

Berghahn, Klaus L. "Patterns of Childhood: Goethe and the Jews." In *Goethe in German-Jewish Culture,* ed. Berghahn and Jost Hermand, 3–15. Rochester, NY: Camden House, 2001.

Berlioz, Hector. *The Memoirs of Hector Berlioz, Member of the French Institute, including his Travels in Italy, Germany, Russia, and England, 1803–1865,* ed. and trans. David Cairns. Corrected edition. New York: W. W. Norton, 1975.

Besser, Gretchen Rous. *Germaine de Staël, Revisited.* Twayne's World Authors Series, no. 849. New York: Twayne, 1994.

Bohnenkamp, Anne. *". . . das Hauptgeschäft nicht außer Augen lassend": Die Paralipomena zu Goethe's "Faust."* Frankfurt am Main: Insel, 1994.

Botstein, Leon. "The Aesthetics of Assimilation and Affirmation: Reconstructing the Career of Felix Mendelssohn." In *Mendelssohn and His World,* ed. R. Larry Todd, 5–42. Princeton, NJ: Princeton University Press, 1991.

———. "Mendelssohn and the Jews." *Musical Quarterly* 82 (1998): 210–19.

———. "Neoclassicism, Romanticism, and Emancipation: The Origins of Felix Mendelssohn's Aesthetic Outlook." In *The Mendelssohn Companion,* ed. Douglass Seaton, 1–27. Westport, Conn.: Greenwood, 2001.

———. "Wagner as Mendelssohn: Reversing Habits and Reclaiming Meaning in the Performance of Mendelssohn's Music for Orchestra and Chorus." In *The Cambridge Companion to Mendelssohn,* ed. Peter Mercer-Taylor, 251–68. Cambridge: Cambridge University Press, 2004.

Boyle, Nicholas. *Goethe: The Poet and the Age.* Vol. 1, *The Poetry of Desire (1749–1790).* Oxford: Clarendon, 1991.

———. "Introduction: Goethe and England; England and Goethe." In *Goethe and the English-Speaking World: Essays from the Cambridge Symposium for His 250th Birthday,* ed. Boyle and John Guthrie, 1–17. Rochester, NY: Camden House, 2002.

Brandi, Karl. "Karl des Grossen Sachsenkriege." In *Die Eingliederung der Sachsen in das Frankenreich,* ed. Walther Lammers, 3–28. Wege der Forschung, 185. Darmstadt: Wissenschaftliche Buchgesellschaft, 1970.

Braun, Julius W. *Goethe im Urtheile seiner Zeitgenossen. Zeitungskritiken, Berichte, Notizen, Goethe und seine Werke betreffend. Bd. 3, 1802–1812.* Berlin: F. Luckhardt, 1885.

Brauner, Sigrid, and Robert H. Brown. *Fearless Wives and Frightened Shrews: The Construction of the Witch in Early Modern Germany.* Amherst: University of Massachusetts Press, 1995.

Brodbeck, David. "A Winter of Discontent: Mendelssohn and the *Berliner Domchor.*" In *Mendelssohn Studies,* ed. R. Larry Todd, 1–32. Cambridge: Cambridge University Press, 1992.

Brown, Clive. *Classical and Romantic Performing Practice, 1750–1900.* Oxford: Oxford University Press, 1999.

———. *A Portrait of Mendelssohn.* New Haven, Conn.: Yale University Press, 2003.

Carlson, Marvin. *Goethe and the Weimar Theatre.* Ithaca, NY: Cornell University Press, 1978.

Carlyle, Thomas "Art. II—Faustus: From the German of Goethe." *New Edinburgh Review* 3 (1822): 316–34.

Chamberlin, Russell. *The Emperor Charlemagne.* Stroud, Glouchestershire: Sutton Publishing, 2004.

Chantepie de la Sausaye, P. D. *The Religion of the Teutons,* trans. Bert J. Vos. Boston: Ginn & Co., 1902. Reprint, Portland, Maine: Longwood, 1977.

Citron, Marcia J., ed. and trans. *The Letters of Fanny Hensel to Felix Mendelssohn.* [Stuyvesant, N. J.]: Pendragon, 1987.

Cohn, Norman. *Europe's Inner Demons: An Enquiry Inspired by the Great Witch-Hunt.* New York: Basic Books, 1975.

Cooper, John Michael. " 'For You See I Am the Eternal Objector . . .': On Performing Mendelssohn's Music in Translation." In *Mendelssohn Performance Studies,* ed. Siegwart Reichwald. Bloomington: Indiana University Press, [2007].

———. "Knowing Mendelssohn: A Challenge from the Primary Sources." *Notes* 61 (2004): 35–95.

———. "Mendelssohn and Berlioz: Selective Affinities." In *Changing Identities-Hector Berlioz in the Age of Romanticism,* ed. Frank Heidlberger. Denton: University of North Texas Press [forthcoming].

———. "Mendelssohn Received." In *The Cambridge Companion to Mendelssohn,* ed. Peter Mercer-Taylor, 233–50. Cambridge: Cambridge University Press, 2004.

Crook, Nora, and Timothy Webb, eds. *The Bodleian Shelley Manuscripts, Volume XIX: The "Faust" Draft Notebook. A Facsimile of Bodleian MS. Shelley adds. e. 18.* New York: Garland, 1997.

[Crowley, George.] "Goethe and His Faustus." *London Magazine* 2, no. 8 (August, 1820): 125–45.

Crum, Margaret. *Catalogue of the Mendelssohn Papers in the Bodleian Library, Oxford.* Vol. II, *Music and Papers.* Musikbibliographische Arbeiten, ed. Rudolf Elvers, Bd. 8. Tutzing: Hans Schneider, 1983.

Dahlhaus, Carl. " 'Hoch symbolisch intentioniert': Zu Mendelssohns *Erster Walpurgisnacht.*" *Österreichische Musikzeitschrift* 36 (1981): 295–97.

de Staël, Mme [Germaine]. *De l'Allemagne: Nouvelle Édition publiée d'après les manuscrits et les éditions originales.* 5 vols., ed. Jean de Pange. Paris: Librairie Hachette, 1959.

de Staël-Holstein, Madame [Germaine]. The Baroness. *Germany,* ed. O. W. Wight. Boston: Houghton, Mifflin and Co., 1887.

Devrient, Eduard. *Meine Erinnerungen an Felix Mendelssohn-Bartholdy und seine Briefe an mich.* Leipzig: J. J. Weber, 1869.

di Grazia, Donna M. "Rejected Traditions: Ensemble Placement in Nineteenth-Century Paris." *Nineteenth-Century Music* 22 (1998): 190–209.

Dinglinger, Wolfgang. "Felix Mendelssohn Bartholdys Berliner Intermezzo." *Mendelssohn-Studien* 13 (2003): 101–23.

Dinglinger, Wolfgang. "Mendelssohn: General-Musik-Direktor für kirchliche und geistliche Musik." In *Felix Mendelssohn Bartholdy: Kongreß-Bericht Berlin 1994*, ed. Christian Martin Schmidt, 23–36. Wiesbaden: Breitkopf & Härtel, 1997.

Droß, Annemarie. *Die erste Walpurgisnacht: Hexenverfolgung in Deutschland.* Reinbek bei Hamburg: Rowohlt, 1985.

Durrani, Osman. "The Character and Qualities of Mephistopheles." In *A Companion to Goethe's "Faust," Parts I and II*, ed. Paul Bishop, 85–86. Rochester, NY: Camden House, 2001.

Dusella, Reinhold. "Die Chorballade *Die Walpurgisnacht* op. 25 und die Kantate *Die Hochzeit der Thetis* op. 120a als mögliche Gattungsbindeglieder von Solo-Ballade und Oratorium, nebst Anmerkungen zum Begriff '*balladisches Oratorium*' bei Philipp Spitta." In *Karl Loewe, 1796–1869: Bericht über die wissenschaftliche Konferenz anlässlich seines 200. Geburtstages vom 26. bis 28. September 1996 im Händel-Haus Halle*, ed. Konstanze Musketa and Götz Traxdorf, 95–137. Halle: Händel-Haus, 1997.

Einhard. *The Life of Charlemagne*, trans. Samuel Epes Turner. Ann Arbor: University of Michigan Press, 1966. (Originally written ca. 840.)

Elvers, Rudolf, ed. *Felix Mendelssohn Bartholdy: Briefe an deutsche Verleger.* Veröffentlichungen der Historischen Kommission zu Berlin beim Friedrich-Meinecke-Institut der Freien Universität Berlin. Berlin: Walter de Gruyter, 1968.

Erspamer, Peter R. *The Elusiveness of Tolerance: The "Jewish Question" from Lessing to the Napoleonic Wars.* University of North Carolina Studies in the Germanic Languages and Literatures, 117. Chapel Hill: University of North Carolina Press, 1997.

Eyck, Frank. *Religion and Politics in German History: From the Beginnings to the French Revolution.* New York: St. Martin's Press, 1998.

Fairley, Barker. *Goethe's "Faust": Six Essays.* Oxford: Clarendon, 1953.

Ferguson, Faye. "Unknown Correspondence from Felix Mendelssohn Bartholdy to his Leipzig Publisher Friedrich Kistner." In *Festschrift Wolfgang Rehm zum 60. Geburtstag*, ed. Dietrich Berke and Harald Heckmann, 197–206. Kassel: Bärenreiter, 1989.

[Fischer, Heinrich Ludwig]. *Das Buch vom Aberglauben*, 2d ed. Leipzig: Schwickert, 1791.

Flashar, Hellmut. *Felix Mendelssohn-Bartholdy und die griechische Tragödie: Bühnenmusik im Kontext von Politik, Kultur und Bildung.* Leipzig: Verlag der Sächsischen Akademie der Wissenschaften zu Leipzig, 2001.

———. *Inszenierung der Antike: Das griechische Drama auf der Bühne der Neuzeit, 1585–1990.* Munich: C. H. Beck, 1991.

Foster, Myles Birket. *History of the Philharmonic Society of London, 1813–1912.* London: John Lane, 1913.

Frazer, James George. *The Golden Bough: A Study in Magic and Religion*, 3d ed. London: Macmillan, 1955.

Garratt, James. "Mendelssohn's Babel: Romanticism and the Poetics of Translation." *Music and Letters* 80 (1999): 23–49.

Gay, Peter. *The Enlightenment: An Interpretation.* Vol. 1, *The Rise of Modern Paganism.* New York: Alfred A. Knopf, 1966.

Geary, Jason Duane. "Ancient Voices: Mendelssohn's Incidental Music to Sophocles's *Antigone* and *Oedipus at Colonos.*" Ph.D. diss., Yale University, 2004.

Gearey, John. *Goethe's "Faust": The Making of Part I.* New Haven, Conn.: Yale University Press, 1981.

Geck, Martin. "Religiöse Musik 'im Geist der gebildeten Gesellschaft': Mendelssohn und sein *Elias.*" In *Von Beethoven bis Mahler: Leben und Werk der grossen Komponisten des 19. Jahrunderts,* 256–79. Reinbek bei Hamburg: Rowohlt-Taschenbuch Verlag, 2000.

Goethe, Johann Wolfgang. *Faust: Tragédie de Goëthe* [sic], *nouvelle traduction complète en prose et en vers,* trans. Gérard de Nerval. Paris: Dondey-Dupré père et fils, 1828.

———. *Faust: Tragédie de M. de Goethe, traduit en français par M. Albert Stapfer, ornée d'un portrait de l'auteur, et de dix-sept dessins composées d'après les principales scènes de l'ouvrage et exécutés sur pierre par M. Eugène Delacroix.* Paris: Ch[les]. Motte, 1828.

———. *Faust: Vingt-six Gravures d'Après les dessins de Retzsch, avec une analyse du drame de Goëthe* [sic], *par Mme Elise Voïart* (Paris: Audot [1828]).

———. *Johann Wolfgang Goethe: Gedenkausgabe der Werke, Briefe und Gespräche, 28. August 1949,* ed. Ernst Beutler. Bd. 1, *Sämtliche Gedichte, erster Teil: Ausgabe letzter Hand,* ed. Emil Staiger. Zurich: Artemis, 1950. ["Die erste Walpurgisnacht," pp. 146–49.]

———. *Johann Wolfgang Goethe: Gedenkausgabe der Werke, Briefe und Gespräche, 28. August 1949,* ed. Ernst Beutler. Bd. 14, *Schriften zur Literatur,* ed. Fritz Strich. Zurich: Artemis, 1950.

———. *Johann Wolfgang Goethe: Gedenkausgabe der Werke, Briefe und Gespräche, 28. August 1949,* ed. Ernst Beutler. Bd. 18, *Briefe der Jahre 1764–1786.* Zurich: Artemis, 1951.

———. *Johann Wolfgang Goethe: Gedenkausgabe der Werke, Briefe und Gespräche, 28. August 1949,* ed. Ernst Beutler. Bd. 19, *Briefe der Jahre 1786–1814.* Zurich: Artemis, 1951.

Goethe, Johann Wolfgang. *Johann Wolfgang Goethe: Gedenkausgabe der Werke, Briefe und Gespräche, 28. August 1949,* ed. Ernst Beutler. Bd. 20, *Briefe der Jahre 1814–1832.* Zurich: Artemis, 1951.

Goethe, Johann Wolfgang von. *Johann Wolfgang von Goethe: Hamburger Ausgabe in 14 Bänden,* ed. Erich Trunz et al. Bd. 3, *Dramatische Dichtungen.* Neubearbeitung. Munich: C. H. Beck, 1981. [*Faust: Der Tragödie erster Teil; Faust: Der Tragödie zweiter Teil; Urfaust*]

———. *Johann Wolfgang von Goethe: Hamburger Ausgabe in 14 Bänden,* ed. Erich Trunz et al., Bd. 9. Neubearbeitung. Munich: C. H. Beck, 1981. *Aus meinem Leben: Dichtung und Wahrheit.*

———. *Johann Wolfgang von Goethe: Hamburger Ausgabe in 14 Bänden,* ed. Erich Trunz et al. Bd. 12, *Schriften zur Kunst und Literatur.* Neubearbeitung. Munich: C. H. Beck, 1981. [*Maximen und Reflexionen*]

Grey, Thomas S. "*Tableaux vivants*: Landscape, History Painting, and the Visual Imagination in Mendelssohn's Orchestral Music." *Nineteenth-Century Music* 21 (1997): 38–76.

Grey, Thomas. "The Orchestral Music." In *The Mendelssohn Companion,* ed. Douglass Seaton, 395–550. Westport, Conn.: Greenwood Press, 2001.

Grimm, Jacob. *Deutsche Mythologie,* 4th ed. 3 vols. Berlin, 1875; rpt. Darmstadt: Wissenschaftliche Buchgesellschaft, 1965.

Großmann-Vendrey, Susannah. *Felix Mendelssohn Bartholdy und die Musik der Vergangenheit.* Studien zur Musikgeschichte des 19. Jahrhunderts, Bd. 17. Regensburg: Gustav Bosse Verlag, 1969.

Grove, George. "Mendelssohn." Article in *Grove's Dictionary of Music and Musicians,* ed. Grove, 2: 253–310. London: Macmillan, 1880.

Guthke, Karl S. "Destination Goethe: Traveling Englishmen in Weimar." In *Goethe and the English-Speaking World: Essays from the Cambridge Symposium for His 250th Anniversary*, ed. Nicholas Boyle and John Guthrie, 111–42. Rochester, NY: Camden House, 2002.

Gynz-Rekowski, Georg von, and Uwe Gerig *Der Brocken: Historie–Heimat–Humor.* Königstein am Taunus: Ruth Gerig, 1991.

Hanslick, Edouard. "Aus dem Leben und der Correspondenz von Franz Hauser." In *Suite: Aufsätze über Musik und Musiker*, 1–37. Vienna: K. Prochaka, 1884.

Hauhart, William Frederic. *The Reception of Goethe's "Faust" in England in the First Half of the Nineteenth Century.* New York: Columbia University Press, 1909.

Hauser, Richard "'In rührend feierlichen Tönen': Mendelssohns Kantate *Die erste Walpurgisnacht*, mit einem Exkurs: Goethes unvertonbarer Allvater." In *Felix Mendelssohn Bartholdy*, ed. Heinz-Klaus Metzger and Rainer Riehn. Musik-Konzepte, vols. 14/15, 75–92. Munich: edition text + kritik, 1980.

Heine, Heinrich. "Französische Maler." In *Heinrich Heine: Sämtliche Schriften.* Bd. 5, *Schriften 1831–1837*, ed. Karl Pörnbacher, 70–81. Munich: Carl Hanser, 1976.

———. *Ludwig Börne: Eine Denkschrift.* Ed. Wilhelm Bölsche. Heinrich Heines Sämtliche Werke, vol. 6, 129–235. Berlin-R. Trenkel, [n.d.].

Hellmundt, Christoph. "Mendelssohns Arbeit an seiner Kantate *Die erste Walpurgisnacht*: Zu einer bisher wenig beachteten Quelle." In *Felix Mendelssohn Bartholdy: Kongreß-Bericht Berlin 1994*, ed. Christian Martin Schmidt, 76–112. Wiesbaden: Breitkopf & Härtel, 1997.

Henkel, Arthur. "The 'Salvation' of Faust—by Goethe." In *Faust through Four Centuries: Retrospect and Analysis / Vierhundert Jahre Faust: Rückblick und Analyse*, ed. Peter Boerner and Sidney Johnson, 91–98. Tübingen: Max Niemeyer, 1989.

Hennemann, Monika. "Mendelssohn and Byron: Two Songs Almost Without Words," *Mendelssohn-Studien* 10 (1997): 131–56.

Henning, Hans. "Johannes Praetorius und sein Hexenbuch von 1668." In Johannes Praetorius [pseud. Hans Schulze], *Blockes-Berges Verrichtung oder ausführlicher geographischer Bericht von den hohen trefflich alt- und berühmten Blockes-Berge: ingleichen von der Hexenfahrt und Zauber-Sabbathe [. . .]*, 1–25. Rpt. Leipzig: Edition Leipzig, 1968.

Hermand, Jost. "A View from Below: H. Heine's Relationship to Johann Wolfgang von Goethe." In *Goethe in German-Jewish Culture*, ed. Klaus L. Bergman and Hermand, 44–62. Rochester, NY: Camden House, 2001.

Hey'l, Bettina. *Der Briefwechsel zwischen Goethe und Zelter: Lebenskunst und literarischer Projekt.* Untersuchungen zur deutschen Literaturgeschichte, Bd. 81. Tübingen: Max Niemeyer, 1996.

Hiller, Ferdinand. *Felix Mendelssohn-Bartholdy: Briefe und Erinnerungen.* Cologne: DuMont-Schauberg, 1874.

Hinck, Walther. "Der 'große Jupiter'? Zum Wandel in Heinrich Heines Goethe-Bild." *Goethe-Jahrbuch* 117 (2000): 165–79.

Hoffmann, Hans. *Der Brocken: Mythos und Geschichte.* Bad Harzburg: Verlag der Buchhandlung Hoffmann, 1996.

Hoffmeister, Gerhart. "Reception in Germany and Abroad." In *The Cambridge Companion to Goethe*, ed. Lesley Sharpe, 232–55. Cambridge: Cambridge University Press, 2002.

Honemann, Rudolf Leopold. *Die Alterthüme des Harzes: Aus Zeugnissen bewährter Schriftsteller gröstentheils* [sic] *aber aus ungedruckten Urkunden zusammen getragen.* Clausthal: Johann Heinrich Wendeborn, 1754.

Hoshino, Hiromi. "Ein neu entdecktes Mendelssohn-Autograph in Japan: Der Klavierauszug 'Die erste Walpurgisnacht' op. 60." *Die Musikforschung* 57 (2002): 151–59.

Israel, Jonathan I. *Radical Enlightenment: Philosophy and the Making of Modernity 1650–1750.* Oxford: Oxford University Press, 2001.

Jacobs, Eduard. *Der Brocken: Geschichte und Sage.* Halle: Pfeffer, 1879.

Jantz, Harold. *The Form of Faust: The Work of Art and Its Intrinsic Structures.* Baltimore, Md.: Johns Hopkins University Press, 1978.

Jones, Frederick L., ed. *The Letters of Percy Bysshe Shelley.* 2 vols. Oxford: Clarendon, 1964.

Jones, Prudence, and Nigel Pennick. *A History of Pagan Europe.* London: Routledge, 1995.

Kahl, Hans-Dietrich "Karl der Grosse und die Sachsen: Stufen und Motive einer historischen 'Eskalation'." In *Politik, Gesellschaft, Geschichtsschreibung: Giessener Festgabe für Frantisek Graus zum 60. Geburtstag,* ed. Herbert Ludat and Rainer Christoph Schwinges, 49–130. Cologne: Böhlau, 1982.

Kes, Barbara. *Die Rezeption der Komödien von Plautus und Terenz im 19. Jahrhundert: Theorie, Bearbeitung, Bühne.* Amsterdam: Grüner, 1988.

Kilchenmann, Ruth J. "Goethes Übersetzung der Voltairedramen *Mahomet* und *Tancred.*" *Comparative Literature* 14 (1962): 332–40.

Killian, Eugen. *Beiträge zur Geschichte des Karlsruher Hoftheaters unter Eduard Devrient: Statistik des Repertoirs, nebst einem Auszug aus Eduard Devrients handschriftlichen Aufzeichnungen.* Karlsruhe: G. Braunscher Buchhandlung, 1893.

Klein, Hans-Günter, and Rudolf Elvers, eds. *Fanny Hensel: Tagebücher.* Wiesbaden: Breitkopf & Härtel, 2002.

Klingemann, [jr.], Karl, ed. *Felix Mendelssohn Bartholdys Briefwechsel mit Legationsrat Karl Klingemann in London.* Essen: G. D. Baedecker, 1909.

Klocke, Friedrich von. "Um das Blutbad von Verden und die Schlacht am Süntel 782." In *Die Eingliederung der Sachsen in das Frankenreich,* ed. Walther Lammers, 151–204. Wege der Forschung, Bd. 185. Darmstadt: Wissenschaftliche Buchgesellschaft, 1970.

Koch, Armin. *Choral und Choralhaftes im Werk von Felix Mendelssohn Bartholdy.* Abhandlungen zur Musikgeschichte, Bd. 12. Göttingen: Vandenhoeck & Ruprecht, 2003.

Koury, Daniel J. *Orchestral Performance Practices in the Nineteenth Century: Size, Proportions, and Seating.* Studies in Musicology, No. 85. Ann Arbor, Mich.: UMI Research Press, 1986.

Krause, Peter. "Mendelssohns dramatische Kantate *Die erste Walpurgisnacht*: Ergänzende Bemerkungen zur Werkgeschichte auf der Grundlage von Untersuchungen des Leipziger Autographs der Letztfassung." In *Musik + Dramaturgie: 15 Studien Fritz Hennenberg zum 65. Geburtstag,* ed. Beate Hiltner-Hennenberg, 101–21. Frankfurt am Main: Peter Lang, 1997.

Kreutzer, Léon. "Société des Concerts et Société Saint-Cécile (2e article)." *Revue et gazette musicale de Paris* 20, no. 14 (April 3, 1853): 121–23.

Krummacher, Friedhelm. "Aussichten im Rückblick: Felix Mendelssohn in der neueren Forschung." In *Felix Mendelssohn Bartholdy: Kongreß-Bericht Berlin 1994,* ed. Christian Martin Schmidt, 279–96. Wiesbaden: Breitkopf & Härtel, 1997.

Lammers, Walther, ed. *Die Eingliederung der Sachsen in das Frankenreich.* Wege der Forschung, Bd. 185. Darmstadt: Wissenschaftliche Buchgesellschaft, 1970.

"Last Philharmonic Concert." *Musical Examiner* 89, no. 13 (July 13, 1844): 673–75.

Lee, Meredith. "Faust's Harzreise." In *Interpreting Goethe's "Faust" Today,* ed. Jane K. Brown, Lee, and Thomas P. Saine, 81–93. Columbia, SC: Camden House, 1994.

———. "Poetic Intentions and Musical Production: 'Die erste Walpurgisnacht.'" *Goethe Yearbook* 12 (2004): 81–91.

"Leipsic, February 26." *Musical World* (London) 18, no. 11 (March 16, 1843): 104.

Lemmer, Klaus J. *Moritz Retzsch: Illustrationen zu Goethes Faust.* Berlin: Rembrandt, 1980.

Lind, L. R. *Johann Wolfgang von Goethe's "Roman Elegies" and "Venetian Epigrams": A Bilingual Text.* Lawrence: University of Kansas Press, 1974.

Lintzel, Martin. "Untersuchungen zur Geschichte der alten Sachsen." *Sachsen und Anhalt: Jahrbuch der Historischen Kommission für die Provinz Sachsen und für Anhalt* 4 (1928): 1–28.

———. "Untersuchungen zur Geschichte der alten Sachsen." *Sachsen und Anhalt: Jahrbuch der Historischen Kommission für die Provinz Sachsen und für Anhalt* 10 (1934): 30–70.

Little, Wm. A. "Mendelssohn and the Berlin Singakademie: The Composer at the Crossroads." In *Mendelssohn and His World,* ed. R. Larry Todd, 65–85. Princeton, NJ: Princeton University Press, 1991.

Lochnan, Katharine A. "Les Lithographies de Delacroix pour *Faust* et le théâtre anglais des années 1820."*Nouvelles de l'estampe* 80, no. 7 (July 1986): 6–13.

Locke, Ralph P. "Mendelssohn's Collision with the Saint-Simonians." In *Mendelssohn and Schumann: Essays on Their Music and Its Context,* ed. Jon W. Finson and R. Larry Todd, 109–22. Durham, NC: Duke University Press, 1984.

[Lorenz, Oswald]. "Die erste Walpurgisnacht." *Neue Zeitschrift für Musik* 20, no. 17 (February 26, 1844): 65–66; 20, no. 18 (February 29, 1844): 70–71.

Maisak, Petra. *Johann Wolfgang Goethe: Zeichnungen.* Stuttgart: Philipp Reclam Jun., 1996.

Mandelkow, Karl Robert. *Goethe in Deutschland: Rezeptionsgeschichte eines Klassikers.* Band I, *1773–1918.* Munich: C. H. Beck, 1980.

———. "Wandlungen des *Faust*-Bildes in Deutschland." In *Interpreting Goethe's "Faust" Today,* ed. Jane K. Brown, Meredith Lee, and Thomas P. Saine, 239–51. Columbia, SC: Camden House, 1994.

Manning, Eugene W. "The First *Paralipomenon* of Goethe's *Faust,* When Written?" *Publications of the Modern Language Association of America* 14 (1899): supplement, v–viii.

Mason, Eudo C. *Goethe's "Faust": Its Genesis and Purport.* Berkeley: University of California Press, 1967.

[Maurer, Friedrich]. "Der Brocken: (Aus einer Sammlung ungedruckter Briefe, über den Harz, und die hessischen Lande)." *Berlinsches Archiv der Zeit und ihres Geschmacks* 2 (1796): 519–44.

Melhorn, Catherine Rose. "Mendelssohn's *Die erste Walpurgisnacht.*" D.M.A. diss., University of Illinois at Urbana-Champaign, 1983.

Mende, Fritz. "Zu Heinrich Heines Goethe-Bild." *Etudes germaniques* 23 (1968): 212–31.

Mendelssohn, Moses. *Jerusalem; or on Religious Power and Judaism*, trans. Allan Arkush, with introduction and commentary by Alexander Altmann. Hanover, NH: Brandeis University Press, 1983.

"Mendelssohn's First Walpurgis Night." *Musical World* (London) 18, no. 28 (July 11, 1844): 231–32.

"Mendelssohn's 'Walpurgis Night.'" *Dwight's Journal of Music* 21, no. 5 (May 3, 1862): 38.

Mendelssohn Bartholdy, Felix. *See* Elvers, Citron, Sutermeister, Weissweiler.

Mendelssohn-Bartholdy, Paul, and Carl Mendelssohn-Bartholdy, eds. *Briefe aus den Jahren 1833 bis 1847 von Felix Mendelssohn Bartholdy*. Leipzig: Hermann Mendelssohn, 1863.

Mengs, Maria. *Schrifttum zum Leben und zur Verehrung der Eichstätter Diözesanheiligen Willibald, Runibald, Walburga, Wuna, Richard und Sola*. Kirchengeschictliche Quellen und Studien, no. 13. Eos: St. Ottilien, 1987.

Mercer-Taylor, Peter. "Mendelssohn's 'Scottish' Symphony and the Music of German Memory." *Nineteenth-Century Music* 19 (1995): 68–82.

Metzger, Heinz-Klaus. "Noch einmal: *Die erste Walpurgisnacht*, Versuch einer anderen Allegorese." In *Felix Mendelssohn Bartholdy*, ed. Metzger and Rainer Riehn, 93–96. Musik-Konzepte, vols. 14/15. Munich: edition text + kritik, 1980.

Midelfort, H. C. Erik. *Witch Hunting in Southwestern Germany, 1562–1684: The Social and Intellectual Foundations*. Stanford: Stanford University Press, 1972.

Mintz, Donald. "1848, Anti-Semitism and the Mendelssohn Reception." In *Mendelssohn Studies*, ed. R. Larry Todd, 126–48. Cambridge: Cambridge University Press, 1992.

———. "Mendelssohn as Performer and Teacher." In *The Mendelssohn Companion*, ed. Douglass Seaton, 87–142. Westport, Conn.: Greenwood, 2001.

Mommsen, Katharina. *Goethe und die arabische Welt*, 2d ed. Frankfurt am Main: Insel, 1989.

Morris, Max. "Die Walpurgisnacht." In *Goethe-Studien*, Vol. 1, 54–96. 2d ed. Berlin: Conrad Skopnik, 1902.

Moscheles, Charlotte. *Aus Moscheles' Leben: Nach Briefen und Tagebüchern*. 2 vols. Leipzig: Duncker & Humblot, 1872–73.

Murray, E. B., ed. *The Bodleian Shelley Manuscripts, Volume XXI: Miscellaneous Poetry, Prose and Translations from Bodleian Shelley adds. C. 4, etc.* New York: Garland, 1995.

Nisbet, H. B. "Religion and Philosophy." In *The Cambridge Companion to Goethe*, ed. Lesley Sharpe, 219–31. Cambridge: Cambridge University Press, 2002.

Ochs, Siegfried. *Der deutsche Gesangverein für gemischten Chor, 4. Teil: Über die Aufführungspraxis bei Berlioz, Liszt, Mendelssohn, Hugo Wolf, Max Reger*. Max Hesses Handbücher, Bd. 81, 1st Auflage. Berlin-Schöneberg: Max Hesses Verlag, 1928.

"Pariser Briefe." *Rheinische Musik-Zeitung für Kunstfreunde und Künstler* 3, no. 43 (April 23, 1853): 1169–71.

Pfister, Werner, ed. *Briefwechsel Goethe–Zelter: Eine Auswahl*. Zurich: Artemis, 1987.

Phelps, Leland R. "Goethe's *Faust* and the Young Shelley." In *Wege der Worte: Festschrift für Wolfgang Fleischhauer, anlässlich seines 65. Geburtstags und des 40. Jahres seines Wirkens als Professor der deutschen Philologie an der Ohio State University*, ed. Wolfgang Fleischhauer and Donald C. Riechel, 304–12. Cologne: Böhlau, 1978.

Pickle, Joseph W. "Schleiermacher on Judaism." *Journal of Religion* 60 (1980): 115–37.

Pleger, Wolfgang H. *Schleiermachers Philosophie.* Berlin: Walter de Gruyter, 1988.

Pohl, Richard. "Goethe–Mendelssohn's 'Erste Walpurgisnacht' auf der Bühne." *Neue Zeitschrift für Musik* 26, no. 20 (May 16, 1862): 165–67.

Praetorius, Johannes [pseud. Hans Schulze]. *Blockes-Berges Verrichtung oder ausführlicher geographischer Bericht von den hohen trefflich alt- und berühmten Blockes-Berge: ingleichen von der Hexenfahrt und Zauber-Sabbathe, so auff solchen Berge die Unholden aus gantz Teutschland Jährlich den 1. Maij in Sanct-Walpurgis-Nachte anstellen sollen; Aus vielen Autoribus abgefasset und mit schönen Raritäten angeschmücket sampt zugehörigen Figuren; Nebenst einen Appendice vom Blockes-Berge wie auch des Alten Reinsteins und der Baumans Höle am Hartz.* Leipzig: Johann Scheiben, [1668]. Reprint, with Afterword by Hans Henning. Leipzig: Edition Leipzig, 1968.

Prandi, Julie D. "Kindred Spirits: Mendelssohn and Goethe, *Die erste Walpurgisnacht.*" In *The Mendelssohns: Their Music in History,* ed. John Michael Cooper and Prandi, 135–46. Oxford: Oxford University Press, 2002.

Proescholdt-Obermann, Catherine Waltraud. *Goethe and His British Critics: The Reception of Goethe's Works in British Periodicals, 1779–1855.* Frankfurt am Main: Peter Lang, 1992.

Racine, Jean. *Britannicus, Phaedra, Athaliah,* ed. C. H. Cisson. Oxford: Oxford University Press, 1987.

Reichwald, Siegwart. "Mendelssohn's Tempo Indications." In *Mendelssohn Performance Studies.* Bloomington: Indiana University Press, [2007].

Robertson, James C. *A History of the Christian Church: From the Apostolic Age to the Reformation, A.D. 64–1517.* 8 vols. London: John Murray, 1874–75.

Rochholz, E. L. *Drei Gaugöttinnen: Walburg, Verena und Gertrud als deutsche Kirchenheilige.* Leipzig: Friedrich Fleischer, 1870.

Rundnagel, Erwin. "Der Tag von Verden." In *Die Eingliederung der Sachsen in das Frankenreich,* ed. Walther Lammers, 205–42. Wege der Forschung, Bd. 185. Darmstadt: Wissenschaftliche Buchgesellschaft, 1970.

Saul, Nicholas. "Goethe the Writer and Literary History." In *The Cambridge Companion to Goethe,* ed. Lesley Sharpe, 23–41. Cambridge: Cambridge University Press, 2002.

Schaub, Diana. "Of Believers and Barbarians: Montesquieu's Enlightened Toleration." In *Early Modern Skepticism and the Origins of Toleration,* ed. Alan Levine, 225–47. Lanham, Md.: Lexington Books, 1999.

Scheibe, Siegfried. "Bemerkungen zur Entstehungsgeschichte des frühen 'Faust.'" *Goethe* 32 (1970): 61–71.

Schmidt-Beste, Thomas. "'Alles von ihm gelernt?' Die Briefe von Carl Friedrich Zelter an Felix Mendelssohn Bartholdy." *Mendelssohn-Studien* 10 (1997): 25–56.

———. *Die ästhetischen Grundlagen der Instrumentalmusik Felix Mendelssohn Bartholdys.* Stuttgart: M und P Verlag für Wissenschaft und Forschung, 1966.

———. "Just How 'Scottish' Is the 'Scottish' Symphony?" In *The Mendelssohns: Their Music in History,* ed. John Michael Cooper and Julie D. Prandi, 147–65. Oxford: Oxford University Press, 2002.

———. "Lehrer wider Willen?–Felix Mendelssohn als Pädagoge." In *Dem Stolz und der Zierde unserer Stadt: Felix Mendelssohn Bartholdy und Leipzig,* ed. Wilhelm Seidel, 149–61. Leipzig: Edition Peters, 2004.

Schmitt, Wilhelm. "Das Gericht zu Verden 782." In *Die Eingliederung der Sachsen in das Frankenreich,* ed. Walther Lammers, 243–60. Wege der Forschung, Bd. 185. Darmstadt: Wissenschaftliche Buchgesellschaft, 1970.

Schneider, Max F. *Mendelssohn oder Bartholdy? Zur Geschichte eines Familiennamens.* Basel: Internationale Felix-Mendelssohn-Gesellschaft, 1962.

Scholz, Bernhard Walter, and Barbara Rogers, ed. and trans. *Carolingian Chronicles: Royal Frankish Annals and Nithard's "Histories."* Ann Arbor: University of Michigan Press, 1972.

Scholz Williams, Gerhild. "Confronting the Early Modern Other: Johannes Praetorius (1630–1680) on Wonders and Violence." In *Imaginationen des Anderen im 16. und 17. Jahrhundert,* ed. Ina Schabert and Michaela Boenke, 99–123. Wolfenbütteler Forschungen, no. 97. Wiesbaden: Harrassowitz, 2002.

———. *Defining Dominion: The Discourses of Magic and Witchcraft in Early Modern France and Germany.* Ann Arbor: University of Michigan Press, 1995.

———. *Götterzeichen, Liebeszauber, Satanskult: Neue Einblicke in alte Goethetexte.* Munich: C. H. Beck, 1982.

Schumann, Robert. "Aufzeichnungen über Mendelssohn, mit Anmerkungen von Heinz-Klaus Metzger and Rainer Riehn." In *Felix Mendelssohn Bartholdy,* ed. Heinz-Klaus Metzger and Rainer Riehn, 97–122. Musik-Konzepte, vols. 14/15. Munich: edition text + kritik, 1980.

———. *Erinnerungen an Felix Mendelssohn Bartholdy: Nachgelassene Aufzeichnungen,* ed. Georg Eismann. Zwickau: Predella-Verlag, 1948.

Seaton, Stuart Douglass. "Mendelssohn's Dramatic Music." In *The Mendelssohn Companion,* ed. Seaton, 143–243. Westport, Conn.: Greenwood, 2001.

———. "The Romantic Mendelssohn: The Composition of *Die erste Walpurgisnacht.*" *Musical Quarterly* 68 (1982): 398–410.

———. "With Words: Mendelssohn's Vocal Songs." *The Mendelssohn Companion,* ed. Douglass Seaton, 661–700. Westport, CT-Greenwood, 2001.

———. "A Study of a Collection of Mendelssohn's Sketches and Other Autograph Material: Deutsche Staatsbibliothek Berlin *Mus. Ms. autogr. 19.*" Ph.D. diss., Columbia University, 1977.

Segl, Peter, ed., *Der Hexenhammer: Entstehung und Umfeld des "Malleus maleficarum" von 1487.* Bayreuther Historische Kolloquien, Bd. 2. Cologne: Böhlau, 1988.

Sengle, Friedrich. "Die didaktischen und kulturkritischen Elemente im 'West-östlichen Divan.'" In *Neues zu Goethe: Essays und Vorträge,* 173–93. Stuttgart: J. B. Metzlersche Verlagsbuchhandlung, 1989.

Sheehan, James. *German History, 1770–1866.* Oxford: Clarendon, 1989.

Shelley, Percy Bysshe. "Scenes from Goethe's Faust." In *The Works of Percy Bysshe Shelley in Verse and Prose,* ed. Harry Buxton Forman. Vol. 4, *Poetry IV,* 284–309. London: Reeves and Turner, 1880.

Simpson, James. "*The Authority of Culture:* Some Reflections on the Reception of a Classic." In *Goethe and the English-Speaking World: Essays from the Cambridge Symposium for His 250th Birthday,* ed. Nicholas Boyle and John Guthrie, 185–98. Rochester, NY: Camden House, 2002.

Soane, George. *Extracts from Göthe's Tragedy of Faustus, Explanatory of the Plates by Retsch* [sic] *Intended to Illustrate that Work.* London: J. H. Bohte, 1820.

Sposato, Jeffrey S. "Creative Writing: The [Self-] Identification of Mendelssohn as Jew." *Musical Quarterly* 82 (1998): 190–209.

———. *The Price of Assimilation: Felix Mendelssohn and the Nineteenth-Century Anti-Semitic Tradition.* Oxford: Oxford University Press, 2006.

Steinberg, Michael P. "Mendelssohn and Judaism." In *The Cambridge Companion to Mendelssohn*, ed. Peter Mercer-Taylor, 26–41. Cambridge: Cambridge University Press, 2004.

Stich, Fritz. *Goethe and World Literature*, trans. by C. A. M. Sym. London: Routledge, 1949.

Stolzenberg, Ingeborg. *Die Valentinszene und die Walpurgisnacht aus Faust I: Faksimile der Handschriften Ms. germ. qu. 475 und 527 der Staatsbibliothek Preußischer Kulturbesitz in Berlin.* 3 vols. Hagen: Linnepe, [1975].

Surius, Laurentius [pseud. Lorenz Haim]. *Kurtzer Begriff, oder, Innhalt dess Lebens der h. wunderthätigen königlichen Closter-Jungfrauen und Abbtissin Walburgis dess Hoch-Stüffts-Aychstätt.* Aichstätt [i.e., Eichstätt]: Francisco Strauß, 1700.

Sutermeister, Peter, ed. *Felix Mendelssohn Bartholdy, Eine Reise durch Deutschland, Italien und die Schweiz: Briefe, Tagebuchblätter, Skizzen, mit einem Lebensbild.* Tübingen: Heliopolis, 1979.

Tacitus. *Agricola and Germany*, trans. Anthony Birley. Oxford: Oxford University Press, 1999.

Timm, Eitel. *Ketzer und Dichter: Lessing, Goethe, Thomas Mann und die Postmoderne in der Tradition des Häresiegedankens.* Beiträge zur neueren Literaturgeschichte, Folge 3, Bd. 88. Heidelberg: Carl Winter, 1989.

Todd, R. Larry. *Mendelssohn: A Life in Music.* Oxford: Oxford University Press, 2003.

——— *Mendelssohn: The Hebrides and Other Overtures.* Cambridge: Cambridge University Press, 1992.

———, ed. *Mendelssohn and His World.* Princeton, NJ: Princeton University Press, 1991.

———, ed. *Mendelssohn Studies.* Cambridge: Cambridge University Press, 1992.

———. *Mendelssohn's Musical Education: A Study and Edition of His Exercises in Composition, Oxford, Bodleian MS Margaret Deneke Mendelssohn C. 43.* Cambridge: Cambridge University Press, 1983.

———. "Of Sea Gulls and Counterpoint: The Early Versions of Mendelssohn's Hebrides Overture." *Nineteenth-Century Music* 2 (1979): 197–213.

———. "On Mendelssohn's Sacred Music, Real and Imaginary." In *The Cambridge Companion to Mendelssohn*, ed. Peter Mercer-Taylor, 167–88. Cambridge: Cambridge University Press, 2004.

———. "On the Visual in Mendelssohn's Music." In *Cari Amici: Festschrift 25 Jahre Carus Verlag*, ed. Barbara Mohn and Hans Ryschawy, 115–24. Stuttgart: Carus, 1997.

Toews, John Edward. *Becoming Historical: Cultural Reformation and Public Memory in Early Nineteenth-Century Berlin.* Cambridge: Cambridge University Press, 2004.

Voltaire, François Marie Arouet de. *Œuvres complètes de Voltaire.* Vol. 1, *Vie de Voltaire—Theatre.* Paris: Firmin-Didot, 1876. (*Le Fanatisme, ou Mahomet le prophète*, pp. 438–57.)

Vulpius, Christian August. *Hexenfahrten und Teufelskünsten, aus dem geheimen Archiv der Walpurgis Nächte auf dem Blocksberg.* "Bachdad, bei Beezelbub" [i.e., Leipzig: Reinick], 1797.

Ward Jones, Peter. *Catalogue of the Mendelssohn Papers in the Bodleian Library, Oxford*, Vol. III, *Printed Music and Books.* Musikbibliographische Arbeiten, Bd. 9. Tutzing: Hans Schneider, 1989.

———. "The Library of Felix Mendelssohn Bartholdy." In *Festschrift Rudolf Elvers zum 60. Geburtstag*, Ernst Herttrich and Hans Schneider, 289–328. Tutzing: Hans Schneider, 1985.

Ward Jones, Peter. "Mendelssohn and His English Publishers." In *Mendelssohn Studies,* ed. R. Larry Todd, 240–55. Cambridge: Cambridge University Press, 1992.

Wehner, Ralf, and Friedhelm Krummacher. "Mendelssohn, Mendelssohn Bartholdy, 3. Felix (Jacob Ludwig)." Article in *Die Musik in Geschichte und Gegenwart,* 2d ed., ed. Ludwig Finscher, Personenteil, vol. 10, cols. 1542–642. Kassel: Bärenreiter, 2003.

Wehnert, Martin. "Zu Goethes Verhalten gegenüber Mendelssohn." In *Dem Stolz und der Zierde unserer Stadt: Felix Mendelssohn Bartholdy und Leipzig,* ed. Wilhelm Seidl, 205–19. Leipzig—Musik und Stadt: Studien und Dokumente, Bd. 1. Leipzig: Edition Peters, 2004.

Weissweiler, Eva, ed. *Fanny und Felix Mendelssohn, "Die Musik will gar nicht rutschen ohne Dich": Briefwechsel 1821 bis 1846.* Berlin: Propyläen, 1997.

Wenskus, Reinhard. "Die deutschen Stämme im Reiche Karls des Grossen." In *Karl der Grosse: Lebenswerk und Nachleben,* ed. Helmut Beumann. Vol. 1, *Persönlichkeit und Geschichte,* 178–219. Düsseldorf: L. Schwann, 1965.

Williams, John R. *Goethe's "Faust."* London: Allen & Unwin, 1987.

Winston, Richard. *Charlemagne: From the Hammer to the Cross.* New York: Vintage Books, 1960.

Wilson Kimber, Marian. "The Composer as Other: Gender and Race in the Biography of Felix Mendelssohn." In *The Mendelssohns: Their Music in History,* ed. John Michael Cooper and Julie D. Prandi, 335–51. Oxford: Oxford University Press, 2002.

Zauder, Friedrich. *Ueber Mendelssohn's* Walpurgisnacht. Königsberg: Wilhelm Koch, 1862.

Index of Works by Goethe and Mendelssohn

I. Works by Goethe

(See also under "individual poems," "periodicals and series," and "translations," below.)

II. Works by Mendelssohn

(See also under "choral songs," "psalm settings," and "solo songs," below.)

General Index

Eastman Studies in Music

The Poetic Debussy: A Collection of His Song Texts and Selected Letters (Revised Second Edition)
Edited by Margaret G. Cobb

Concert Music, Rock, and Jazz since 1945: Essays and Analytical Studies
Edited by Elizabeth West Marvin and Richard Hermann

Music and the Occult: French Musical Philosophies, 1750–1950
Joscelyn Godwin

"Wanderjahre of a Revolutionist" and Other Essays on American Music
Arthur Farwell, edited by Thomas Stoner

French Organ Music from the Revolution to Franck and Widor
Edited by Lawrence Archbold and William J. Peterson

Musical Creativity in Twentieth-Century China: Abing, His Music, and Its Changing Meanings (includes CD)
Jonathan P. J. Stock

Elliott Carter: Collected Essays and Lectures, 1937–1995
Edited by Jonathan W. Bernard

Music Theory in Concept and Practice
Edited by James M. Baker, David W. Beach, and Jonathan W. Bernard

Music and Musicians in the Escorial Liturgy under the Habsburgs, 1563–1700
Michael J. Noone

Analyzing Wagner's Operas: Alfred Lorenz and German Nationalist Ideology
Stephen McClatchie

The Gardano Music Printing Firms, 1569–1611
Richard J. Agee

"The Broadway Sound": The Autobiography and Selected Essays of Robert Russell Bennett
Edited by George J. Ferencz

Theories of Fugue from the Age of Josquin to the Age of Bach
Paul Mark Walker

The Chansons of Orlando di Lasso and Their Protestant Listeners: Music, Piety, and Print in Sixteenth-Century France
Richard Freedman

Berlioz's Semi-Operas: Roméo et Juliette *and* La damnation de Faust
Daniel Albright

The Gamelan Digul and the Prison-Camp Musician Who Built It: An Australian Link with the Indonesian Revolution (includes CD)
Margaret J. Kartomi

"The Music of American Folk Song" and Selected Other Writings on American Folk Music
Ruth Crawford Seeger, edited by Larry Polansky and Judith Tick

Portrait of Percy Grainger
Edited by Malcolm Gillies and David Pear

Berlioz: Past, Present, Future
Edited by Peter Bloom

The Musical Madhouse
(Les Grotesques de la musique)
Hector Berlioz
Translated and edited by Alastair Bruce Introduction by Hugh Macdonald

The Music of Luigi Dallapiccola
Raymond Fearn

Music's Modern Muse: A Life of Winnaretta Singer, Princesse de Polignac
Sylvia Kahan

The Sea on Fire: Jean Barraqué
Paul Griffiths

"Claude Debussy As I Knew Him" and Other Writings of Arthur Hartmann
Edited by Samuel Hsu, Sidney Grolnic, and Mark Peters
Foreword by David Grayson

Schumann's Piano Cycles and the Novels of Jean Paul
Erika Reiman

Bach and the Pedal Clavichord: An Organist's Guide
Joel Speerstra

Historical Musicology: Sources, Methods, Interpretations
Edited by Stephen A. Crist and Roberta Montemorra Marvin

The Pleasure of Modernist Music: Listening, Meaning, Intention, Ideology
Edited by Arved Ashby

Debussy's Letters to Inghelbrecht: The Story of a Musical Friendship
Annotated by Margaret G. Cobb

Explaining Tonality: Schenkerian Theory and Beyond
Matthew Brown

The Substance of Things Heard: Writings about Music
Paul Griffiths

Musical Encounters at the 1889 Paris World's Fair
Annegret Fauser

Aspects of Unity in J. S. Bach's Partitas and Suites: An Analytical Study
David W. Beach

Letters I Never Mailed: Clues to a Life
Alec Wilder
Annotated by David Demsey
Foreword by Marian McPartland

Wagner and Wagnerism in Nineteenth-Century Sweden, Finland, and the Baltic Provinces: Reception, Enthusiasm, Cult
Hannu Salmi

Bach's Changing World: Voices in the Community
Edited by Carol K. Baron

CageTalk: Dialogues with and about John Cage
Edited by Peter Dickinson

European Music and Musicians in New York City, 1840–1900
Edited by John Graziano

Schubert in the European Imagination, Volume 1: The Romantic and Victorian Eras
Scott Messing

Opera and Ideology in Prague: Polemics and Practice at the National Theater, 1900–1938
Brian S. Locke

Ruth Crawford Seeger's Worlds Innovation and Tradition in Twentieth-Century American Music
Edited by Ray Allen and Ellie M. Hisama

Schubert in the European Imagination, Volume 2: Fin-de-Siècle Vienna
Scott Messing

Mendelssohn, Goethe, and the Walpurgis Night: The Heathen Muse in European Culture, 1700–1850
John Michael Cooper

This paperback edition of *Mendelssohn, Goethe, and the Walpurgis Night* addresses tolerance and acceptance in the face of cultural, political, and religious strife. Its point of departure is the Walpurgis Night. The Night, also known as Beltane or May Eve, was supposedly an annual witches' Sabbath that centered around the Brocken, the highest peak of the Harz Mountains.

After exploring how a notoriously pagan celebration came to be named after the Christian missionary St. Walpurgis (ca. 710–79), John Michael Cooper discusses the Night's treatments in several closely interwoven works by Goethe and Mendelssohn. His book situates those works in their immediate personal and professional contexts, as well as among treatments by a wide array of other artists, philosophers, and political thinkers, including Voltaire, Lessing, Shelley, Heine, Delacroix, and Berlioz.

In an age of decisive political and religious conflict, Walpurgis Night became a heathen muse: a source of spiritual inspiration that was neither specifically Christian, nor Jewish, nor Muslim. And Mendelssohn's and Goethe's engagements with it offer new insights into its role in European cultural history, as well as into issues of political, religious, and social identity—and the relations between cultural groups—in today's world.

John Michael Cooper is professor of music at Southwestern University and author of *Mendelssohn's "Italian" Symphony* (Oxford University Press).

"A fascinating study of the genesis, musical structure, and reception of this neglected great work of the choral literature. Cooper spreads out a colorful panorama of the Witches' Sabbath as a cultural idea and artistic motif. He argues brilliantly across the divide of music and literature that Goethe and Mendelssohn were animated by a common ethical and aesthetic sense."

—Julie Prandi, professor of German, Illinois Wesleyan University

"A highly entertaining and authoritative account of the Walpurgis Night tradition in European culture, and of Mendelssohn's cantata, which Berlioz praised for the 'perfection' of its interweaving of voices and instruments. The author blends skillfully history, criticism, musical analysis, and source studies to shed new light on Mendelssohn's perhaps most provocative, and unjustifiably neglected, work."

—R. Larry Todd, Arts & Sciences Professor of Music, Duke University, and author of *Mendelssohn: A Life in Music*

www.ingramcontent.com/pod-product-compliance
Lightning Source LLC
Chambersburg PA
CBHW060241100726
47907CB00003B/724
9781580463683